The Tsimshian and Their Neighbors
of the North Pacific Coast

The Tsimshian
and Their Neighbors
of the
North Pacific Coast

Edited by Jay Miller
and Carol M. Eastman

University of Washington Press
SEATTLE AND LONDON

Library of Congress Cataloging-in-Publication Data
The Tsimshian and their neighbors of the North Pacific Coast.

1. Tsimshian Indians—Addresses, essays, lectures.
2. Indians of North America—Northwest coast of North
America—Addresses, essays, lectures. 3. Garfield, Viola
Edmundson, 1899–   . I. Garfield, Viola Edmundson,
1899–1983. II. Miller, Jay, 1947–   . III. Eastman,
Carol M., 1941–   .
E99.T8T75 1984   306'.08997   83-23364
ISBN 0-295-96126-0

This volume is dedicated to

Viola Edmundson Garfield

December 5, 1899–November 25, 1983

in appreciation for her inspiration to her colleagues
and students, and in recognition of her contributions
to Northwest Coast anthropology

Contents

APPENDIX

Kin Term Abbreviations

Anthropologists have developed a series of abbreviations that are used to describe the kinship terms and systems of relationships that occur among all human societies, sometimes in bewildering complexity. Some of these are used in articles in this book.

p	parent(s)
F, Fa	father(s)
M, Mo	mother(s)
B, Br	brother(s)
Z, Si	sister(s)
S, So	son(s)
D, Dau	daughter(s)
C, Ch	child(ren)
G, Gr	great, grand
Cz	cousin(s) [X and //]*
H, Hu	husband(s)
W, Wi	wife(wives)
=, --	marriage relationship
¦	descent relationship
△	male, man
○	female, woman
♂	male speaker(speaking)
♀	female speaker(speaking)

*Cross cousins(XCz) are children of siblings of the same sex[FBC, MZC], while parallel cousins(//Cz) are children of siblings of opposite sex[FZC, MBC].

Introduction

Academic anthropology was a young field when Viola Garfield entered Columbia University in 1932 to be trained by the great ethnographer Franz Boas. As one of a small but prominent group of Northwest scholars in the first half of the twentieth century, she was a pioneering force in the development of anthropology in the Northwest, devoting much of her teaching career to introducing undergraduates to the wonders of the region. An authority on the Tsimshian, with interests that ranged widely over their social structure, economy, folklore, and art, she is perhaps best known for her classic monograph *Tsimshian Clan and Society* (1939).

In the 1930s she started collecting an impressive volume of documentation on totem poles. Many of her photographs show poles now long since decomposed. The twenty-five binders containing these photographs that reside in the University of Washington library are a resource of great value for Canadian, European, and American scholars (see Seaburg 1982). Countless students have built upon her ethnographic base to amplify and improve our understanding of native peoples of the Northwest Coast. The present gathering of papers by her former students and colleagues, echoing in its title her 1951 study "The Tsimshian and Their Neighbors," is a tribute to her role in the dynamic tradition of Americanist scholarship that she did so much to nurture.

Over thirty years ago, Garfield pointed out problems which continue to be important in Northwest studies: "we lack much comparative data on the relationships between the Tsimshian and their neighbors. There is also little historical depth to our data. Some of these gaps can be filled by comparative analytical studies of the Tsimshian with other tribes of Northwest America, using existing literary sources. Other problems will only be solved in the future by systematic field work" (1951:4). The essays in this volume do much to fill important gaps such as these in our understanding of the region.

The book is divided into two parts. Part I is devoted to the Tsimshian themselves because they were Garfield's primary focus of study. Part II is concerned with neighbors of the Tsimshian. We include a map prepared for Garfield's ethnography (1951), showing the relation of the Tsimshian to their immediate neighbors (map 1). In 1972, Wayne Suttles authored a map (map 2) of the native languages

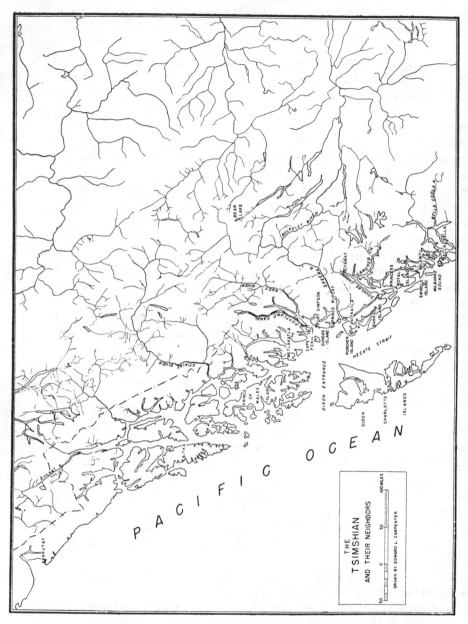

Map 1. From *The Tsimshian Indians and Their Arts* (Garfield and Wingert, 1966)

of the Northwest, an unusual and particularly appropriate representation showing the entire region as seen from the Pacific Ocean.

Map 2 has the advantage of reflecting the strong cultural emphasis on the sea throughout the area. Every detail of the sea and shore was named, and every resource utilized, with the emphasis on fishing and the bounty of shellfish, seaweeds, and marine mammals. Of all resources, salmon, faithfully returning year after year in fluctuating runs, was the focus of the economic and religious life. Away from the beaches, the land was a bramble of thorns, berries, and luxuriant bushes under a canopy of tall cedars. These trees were basic to the technology since the long straight-grained wood was efficiently worked into planks for houses and shelters, bentwood boxes for cooking and storage, canoes for travel and work, and totem poles for publicly displaying important figures from legends owned by specific households.

The fine arts were particularly well developed, with the Tsimshian the acknowledged masters of the formline style. Throughout the coast, men worked for the most part in wood, stone, and copper, while women worked with basketry and textiles. The northern or matrilineal formline style, expressing timeless concerns with inherited crests fundamental to these societies, is one of the great artistic accomplishments of the world.

A crest derives from inherited legends and sagas owned by a household and its members by right of birth. A crest is an art form: a carving, painting, design, song, dance, place, or dramatic event mentioned in such mythic sagas. The most important crests belonged to the most prominent houses and provided the means for claiming membership and differential rank within the nobility. Most Northwest societies recognized three classes: nobility, commoners, and slaves. The slaves were mostly war captives and a few poor people unable to compensate for an insult or indiscretion. Slavery conferred a stigma so the descendants of slaves themselves belonged to that class.

Certain recurrent themes commonly appear in the ethnographies of these societies. All groups had fish as their staple food, sharing a fondness for candlefish (eulachon) oil and other grease as a condiment. During summer, men generally fished and hunted while women gathered berries, wild plants, and vegetables. Winter was the time of the ceremonials and active participation in religion. During spring and summer economic activities, people moved widely among campsites strategically located for fishing and foraging. Later in the fall, games and contests were held in special locations, before

Map 2. From "Native languages of the north Pacific coast of North America"

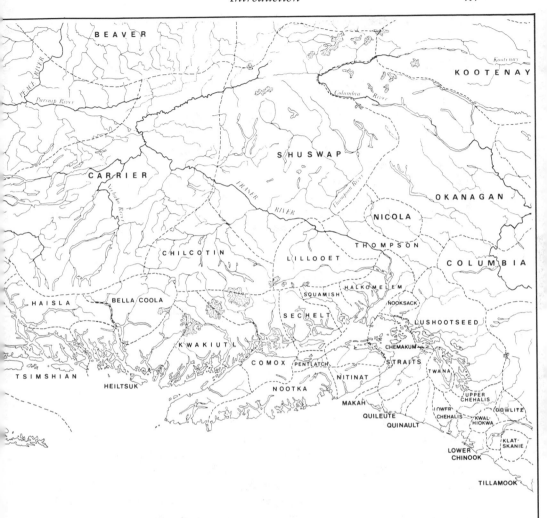

Native Languages of the North Pacific Coast of North America

0 50 100 150 200
km

[map] (Wayne Suttles, 1978)

people gathered again in the permanent winter towns for ceremonials.

The different peoples of the regions have, however, maintained distinctive systems of social organization. In the north the Haida, Tlingit, and Tsimshian trace descent through the mother, and reside with men from their matriline after childhood. While the Haida and Tlingit have two explicit moieties (divisions into halves) named Raven and Eagle-Wolf, the Tsimshian previously were described as having four phratries or crest groups, which we now realize are semi-moieties equivalent to the moieties of other tribes, but with an even more elaborate and complex system of crests. Further south, the Wakashans, represented here by the Nootka, or Westcoast, people, and the Salishans, exemplified by the Twana and Klallam, have an ambilateral system, tracing descent through the mother or the father for different purposes.

Because the first part of the book deals with the Tsimshian, we will summarize some important aspects of their society.

Viola Garfield broke new ground with her work on Tsimshian social organization. Hers was the first fieldwork and observation of the system in operation. Boas had based his discussions of kinship and clans on mythological texts, appropriate to some extent since the Tsimshian believe that everything, or the most important things—names, crests, resource area ownership—are derived from mythology.

Since the work of Boas and Garfield, with their Tsimshian colleagues Henry Tate and William Beynon, many of the authors in this volume have contributed to our improved understanding of the Tsimshian. Among the most significant refinements has been the recognition of a consistent patterning by fours. Thus, unlike other northwestern tribes, the Tsimshian had four classes: royalty, nobility, commoner, and slave. There were also four languages: Nishka and Gitksan in the interior, and Coast and Southern along the lower Skeena River and offshore as far south as modern Klemtu on Swindle Island.

The four matriclans (the semi-moiety crest groups of Gispudwada, Ganhada, Eagle, and Wolf), studied so carefully by Garfield, are now recognized as the result of many towns coming together at trading posts like Fort Simpson or missionary settlements like that of William Duncan at Metlakatla. Kitkatla, Gitka'ata (Hartley Bay), and Klemtu—towns which remained in their aboriginal territories—each functions in terms of moieties, with the Gispudwada Killerwhales identified as owners of the village.

Despite these amplifications, the basis of the system remains as Garfield recognized it, the "house" defined as a building, residential household, and repository for art works manifesting the crests. An equally fundamental distinction between crests (*ptɛx*) and powers (*naxnox*), reflected in public and private art, is only now being explored. Our hope is that Tsimshian research is on the brink of an exciting new synthesis based on topographic symbolism, with this volume as one of its major bridges.

According to the mythology, the Tsimshian world consists of a flat disk that we know as the earth, supported by a pole resting on the chest of Smoke Hole, a supernatural being lying inside a gigantic house below the earth. When he dies the world will end. At the corners of the world live the four winds, with the ocean and various island abodes of supernaturals intervening.

During the Myth Age, many people lived at Temlaxam (Prairie Town) on the upper Skeena River near modern Hazelton in Gitksan territory. Stories about life in this village are the source for the Grizzly Bear crests of the Gispudwada. In the ocean were fish, sea mammals, and supernaturals, the most famous of which was "Chief of the Undersea" living at Ngwinaks in the Moore Islands and the source of Killerwhale crests of the Gispudwada. No other crest has such a rich and varied tradition among the Tsimshian, suggesting both a priority and an antiquity for it.

The killerwhales were divided into the same four crests as were humans, with membership identifiable from the dorsal fin. Those of the Wolf crest had a long, thin fin similar to the tail of a wolf; the Eagles had a white line down the middle of the fin; the Raven Ganhada had a short stubby fin like a beak; and the Gispudwada had a round hole in the center of the fin. Each species of salmon had a village near the edge of the world. In the spring, scouts were sent to the Nass and Skeena rivers to find out when their "salmon" were running. These "salmon" were cottonwood leaves floating in the water. Each species left at the appropriate time to spawn in the rivers based on the information of the scouts.

Before they relocated to Fort Simpson, there were nine Coast Tsimshian towns along the lower Skeena, each distinguished by a local feature, and three towns to the south on inlets or islands. During the summer economic season, each winter village dispersed into camps for fishing, hunting, and collecting seaweed, berries, and shellfish. Ownership of these camps and resources was vested in hereditary names carrying this privilege with them.

The Gitksan maintain their earlier seven towns, but many people have moved into Hazelton and other modern cities to earn money. Their upper Skeena territory overlaps that of the Athapaskan-speaking Carrier towns of Hagwilget (Tsik) and Moricetown. These are the last vestiges of upriver Athapaskans who acculturated to coastal styles and became the Gitksan. The Niska have moved closer to the mouth of the Nass River in historic times, congregating around Anglican missions at Kincolith, New Aiyansh, Greenville, and the Salvation Army settlement of Canyon City.

All of these groups trace clanship and household membership through the mother, but a woman moved to the home of her husband upon marriage so children were not raised in their own household. In the case of nephews due to inherit a name or position from their mother's brother, they moved into his household after puberty to begin training for their responsibilities. In all, Tsimshian matrilineality diversified loyalties and allegiances throughout the area.

Trade, missionaries, and settlement have altered traditional Tsimshian society. The devotion of William Duncan converted the Tsimshian to Christianity (initially Anglican before other shepherds introduced Methodism and the United Church of Canada), giving everything a Christian context: feasts, crests, and even shamanism where the power now comes from God.

Stephen McNeary's chapter on Tsimshian mythology leads off this section. Dealing with "image and illusion," McNeary seeks to "discover the sense in which traditions identify animals as human, and the significance of this identity." Mythological animals are believed to have human shapes in their own precincts, as witnessed by people who married or lived with animals in the sagas. After discussing the concept of souls, shape-shifting, and willful illusion, he concludes that the belief represents a philosophical acceptance of Nature in its many guises.

Marjorie Halpin examines the rules underlying the ownership and display of crests, which provide the visual splendor of the potlatch. She finds Tsimshian totemic classification to be "the most complex on the Northwest Coast," and proceeds to explain how basic elements in the art reveal the rankings and elaborations in the system. Her structural model of the Tsimshian crest system should lead to other comparative studies, particularly ones developing her work on process during historical changes in the system.

Among the nobility, Tsimshian traditionally expressed a preference for the marriage of a boy with his mother's brother's daughter (MBD), matrilateral cross-cousin marriage. In practice, however, marriage held a wide variety of choices, expressing different strategies for prestige and inheritance. According to John Dunn, the choice between a matrilateral and a patrilateral cross-cousin (FZD) marriage distributes wealth to different "grandchildren." The matrilateral preference produces an equitable distribution to all relatives, while the patrilateral option is more daring and produces a greater distribution to people outside the circle of kin, providing prestige throughout the community.

Relating marriage patterns to the potlatch, Daniel Vaughan uses ethnographic materials on the Tsimshian by Garfield and others to critique the important analysis in *Feasting with Mine Enemy* (1971), by Rosman and Rubel, who argue for a close structural relationship between marriage alliances and potlatching.

In a chapter on the kinship terms used by the Gitksan, Alice Kasakoff examines actual usage of "kinship terminology to express changing relationships between the individual and various corporate groups, many of which reflect basic political processes in the society."

George MacDonald looks at the relation between people and wealth, as symbolized in art and mythology. He uses many photographs of painted housefronts, some appearing here for the first time, and woven blankets to derive basic features, such as the pentagonal form, that express concepts of wealth and integration. Other art forms such as copper shields and storage boxes are also structurally related as further aspects of the wealth complex.

In the final chapter, Jay Miller turns to Tsimshian religion, making use of original notes by Viola Garfield and William Beynon to trace changes that have occurred since the era when shamans (*swansk*) were the spiritual leaders. Another account from Beynon treats the Carrier prophet Bini, who brought a nativistic revival to the Tsimshian and other people on the north coast. Miller ends with the tragic story of a woman caught between her obligation to inherit a shamanic power and her new faith in the Christian God.

The essays in Part II deal with neighbors, near and far, sharing Northwest Pacific Coast patterns: the Haida, island neighbors and former foes of the Tsimshian, the Westcoast–Nootka of Friendly Cove on Vancouver Island, and the Klallam and Twana of the Olympic Peninsula in Washington State. General information on these tribes is provided below.

The Haida consist of the Masset and Skidegate divisions on the Queen Charlotte Archipelago, and the Kaigani, five or six towns of emigrants from the northern Charlotte Islands, who settled around Prince of Wales Island in southeastern Alaska, former Tlingit territory. Kasaan was the largest as well as the most northerly Kaigani settlement, with subsistence patterns of fishing, hunting, and gathering shellfish and plants duplicating those on the Charlottes, except that the Alaskan Haida relied more heavily on hunting land animals.

The Haida language is considered a linguistic isolate, unrelated to any other language and unclassified within any linguistic stock. Recent research indicates the Kaigani dialect at Hydaburg is distinct from both the Masset and Skidegate dialects to the south. Despite the cultural homogeneity of the North Pacific Coast on many levels, social organization and languages appear to maintain rigid intertribal distinctions. The lack of mutual intelligibility among Tlingit, Haida, Tsimshian, Kwakwala (Kwakiutl), Nootkan, Salishan, Athapaskan, and others, except for a polyglot elite of nobles, apparently contributed to the maintenance of certain cultural distinctions as well.

Margaret Blackman makes use of notes and photographs by Garfield to describe Kasaan before it was abandoned in 1904. Using her own notes and measurements, these visual documents enable her to analyze recent Alaskan culture history and to illustrate changes in architectural style, totem pole innovations, new burial practices, and shifting village settlement. Today, only vestiges of Kasaan remain, an archaeological site with few indications of what we see in the photographs.

The Masset community of northern Haida is the focus of the chapter by Mary Lee Stearns, dealing with the rules and types of succession to high office. There was a preferred rule for automatic matrilineal succession, from brother to brother of the same mother within a generation, or from mother's brother to sister's son across generations. In rare cases, flexible criteria of appointment are applied, stressing personal ability confirmed by council or by competitive potlatching. Brief case studies of particular chiefs show how limited in scope individual initiative and competition was in the political process of succession. Stearns concludes that, for all of its notoriety, the competitive potlatch has been overdrawn, since it was actually concerned with rivalry within a status and maintaining boundaries rather than with usurpation of office. The political process of succession among the Haida, and elsewhere in the Northwest, was an aspect of routine social existence, not disruptive antagonisms between individuals.

Again, dealing with the Haida, Carol Eastman provides the only strictly linguistic treatment in the volume, based on Kaigani data gathered in the 1970s. She specifies the forms of negation used in various grammatical constructions, showing what effects these have in sentences and how the process interacts with other important inherent features of the Haida sentence. After a fifty-year pause in linguistic work in the region, researchers are again analyzing Northwest languages, discovering that surviving languages have undergone change at a more rapid rate than reported from other parts of the world. Eastman discusses this type of change as "linguistic erosion."

On Vancouver Island, south of the Haida, are about twenty separate named groupings of Westcoast-Nootkans, famous throughout the continent for their active pursuit of whales. Their kinship and social structure share a number of features with their Kwakiutl neighbors, who also speak a language of the Wakashan stock. The Nootka-Westcoast, Nitinat, and Makah (of Washington State) are organized by patrikindreds, with titled names ranked according to seniority in the male line of succession. Often, the northern Nootka formed confederacies, each sharing a common summer camp. Typically, each took the name of the highest ranked tribe, which also supplied the nominal head chief. The chief had considerable economic responsibility but little formal authority; he played an important spiritual role in the life of the community, and monopolized economic specialties such as hunting sea animals, harpooning whales, and owning esoteric gear. Chiefs' aides were younger brothers of lesser ranking aristocrats, acting as orators, heralds, war leaders, and retainers. Some positions were relatively open; commoners might become warriors, and both women and slaves could become shamans.

Using nineteenth-century sources on the Nootka, Joyce Wike examines the controversial question of cannibalism. Many ethnographic accounts from the early Northwest claim that human flesh was ingested only ceremonially by people imbued with ceremonial powers. This interpretation contrasts sharply, however, with sensational eyewitness accounts by early explorers reporting tales of horror. As Wike shows, such "horrors" relate to a native belief that severed limbs could poison strangers, enemies, and unwelcome visitors. Ceremonial cannibalism, such as the Hamatsa ritual, can therefore be traced back to the sixteenth century, contrary to the opinion of Boas that it began in the nineteenth century.

The Salishans are the last distinct tribes treated in this volume. The Coast Salish live along protected saltwater in southern British

Columbia and Washington State, and extend inland along rivers rising into the coast ranges. Combining fishing, hunting, and gathering, people occupied permanent winter villages at good fishing locations, moving in summer and fall to camps near seasonal resources. Saltwater people depended more on fishing, while upriver groups did more hunting. These various geographical specialties were exchanged across tribal divisions. The winter town was the basis of the Salishan polity, functioning in an intertribal network of trade, marriage alliances, potlatching, and visiting to redistribute people and resources over a large area and to reduce occasional conflicts.

The Klallam of the Strait of Juan de Fuca reported by Langness founded Jamestown as "a conscious, rational attempt on the part of a group of American Indians to alleviate tensions and dissatisfactions stemming from culture contact." He pays particular attention to the psychological motivations of two leaders instigating the reform movement.

Using linguistic categories from the Twana of Hood Canal on the Olympic Peninsula, Elmendorf looks at the domain of supernatural power, finding that while the language made no distinction between *spirit* and *power*, conceptualizations and behavior did. He concludes that if one wishes to discover and describe distinctions that are not unambiguously maintained in a vocabulary, it is necessary to make inferences not only from labels but also from behavioral and other contexts.

The final chapter in Part II, by Pamela Amoss, deals with the ambiguous position of the dog in Northwest cultures. She uses ethnographic reports to speculate on the symbolic function of the domestic dog, sometimes considered human and sometimes animal. The dog is an anomaly, having characteristics of two domains usually quite distinct. This intermediate position made the dog a source both of power and of danger, emphasized in myth and ritual, where the eating of dogs is equated with cannibalism.

The essays in this volume serve to remind us again of the ethnographic richness of the Northwest Coast, within on-going traditions or stored in archives. These studies of technology, language, personality, ethnohistory, culture change, and symbolism testify to the continuing stimulation provided by the pioneering work of Viola Garfield and other scholars of her stature.

PART I
The Tsimshian

Image and Illusion in Tsimshian Mythology

STEPHEN A. MCNEARY

~~~~~~

> For Mercy has a human heart,
> Pity a human face,
> And Love, the human form divine,
> And Peace, the human dress.
>
> —William Blake, "The Divine Image"

Animals are also in some sense human, according to many native traditions of North America and northeastern Asia. In the American Northwest, animals, birds, and fish are said to have villages deep in the forest or under the sea where they appear in human form and live, work, and converse in a human way. The myths of the Northwest Coast in particular tell how animals, sky beings, underwater monsters, and a variety of other creatures and personages live in houses of wooden planks where they receive guests, give feasts, and perform songs and dances which human visitors may later adopt as part of their individual, clan, or secret society heritage.

This essay is concerned with one Northwest Coast group: the Tsimshian-speaking peoples who live on the Nass and Skeena rivers and the adjacent coast of British Columbia. My purpose is to discover the sense in which traditions depict animals as human and the significance of this identity for the Tsimshian. This inquiry will also lead to a concept of perception—namely, that the appearance of physical reality depends on the point of view of the perceiver—a concept I believe is implicit in at least some Tsimshian tales.

Most of the ideas presented here come from my own fieldwork on the Nass,* but the documentation is drawn largely from the work of Franz Boas and Henry Tate, who collected Nass and Coast Tsimshian myths between 1888 and 1914. I am using these materials to

---

*The fieldwork on which this chapter is based was supported by the National Museum of Man, Ottawa.

3

test my hypotheses mainly because my own notes on myth and religion are not extensive enough for adequate crosschecking, but also because I wanted to test the impressions which I had gotten in 1972–74 against the myths collected in the earlier period. By restricting this study to the extensive body of recorded Tsimshian mythology, we will be able to state some conclusions without too many confusing qualifications and ethnographic cross references. It should be noted, however, that many of the tales discussed here are found in similar form among the Tlingit and Haida, and certainly some of the basic underlying themes are even more widely distributed throughout the American Northwest.

I will try to extract a philosophy from a heterogeneous collection of tales. There is no single doctrine of animal-human relations which encompasses all the varied incidents in the texts. Nevertheless, there must be a pattern of some sort to Tsimshian beliefs. By analyzing the concepts that seem to underlie various incidents, even if we find logical contradictions, we will be better able to understand the basic configuration. Only then can we compare Tsimshian ideas with our own and with those of other people.

We are all familiar with animals who talk and act like people. We sometimes dress these creatures in coats and shoes and grant them four-fingered hands (Mickey Mouse), or we picture them simply as bipedal animals (Krazy Kat), or we make do with any other whimsical compromise that pleases our fancy (such as the Oysters and Walrus in "The Walrus and the Carpenter"). Such images of imaginary animal-people have a long history in our culture through our heritage of European folktales and nursery rhymes. Of course, in oral or unillustrated versions it is not necessary to be precise about the character's form. We are simply told what the animals said and did without any explanation of how it can be that a donkey can play a clarinet. This ambiguity adds to the delight and mystery of the tales.

A number of Tsimshian tales contain similar humanized animals. Most of them are in stories set in an era of mythology before the historic clans came into being. This is the time of Txamsem, the Trickster-Transformer who stole the sun and fire from their ungenerous keepers, and who arranged such things as the tides and the timing of the eulachon run for the greater convenience of human beings. Txamsem is constantly hungry, and his ravenousness and trickery are the subjects of many humorous episodes. He often encounters human beings, but these people are never identified as members of any specific ethnic group or clan. Stories that concern animals only, and stories of beings such as the Four Winds, also seem to be set in this era.

Let us briefly mention a few of the animal-people from these tales. When Txamsem tries to trick Crab into a "game" so that he can kill and eat him, the Crab says, "Oh, no!" and grabs Txamsem with a claw, pulling him under the sea (Boas 1916:70). Txamsem is more successful in his encounter with Gull, whom he challenges to a gambling game (Boas 1902:27–28). The animal tale in which Grizzly Bear bullies Porcupine opens with Grizzly Bear much annoyed because it is raining and his fur is wet. When he sees porcupine, he asks him to join him for a meal, and builds a fire (Boas 1912:237). In another story, the Wolves invite the Deer to a feast. The Wolves laugh heartily, but the Deer are reluctant to laugh. When at last the Deer do laugh, the Wolves see that they have no teeth; then they attack them and eat them (Boas 1902:83–85). These and similar incidents invite us to picture creatures that combine animal form with human activities such as talking, gambling, building fires, and giving feasts.

The richest tale for representations of this sort is the story of Txamsem's war on the South Wind. Various fishes join Txamsem in his war canoe. The Cockle brags that he will kick the South Wind down the beach, but fails. Txamsem breaks his shell and eats him. Then Red Cod uses his firedrill to start a blaze in South Wind's house and takes cedar bark from under his blanket to produce smoke. Halibut lies down at the door so that as South Wind emerges, coughing and sneezing, he steps on the slippery fish (Boas 1916:79–81). Boas warns us, however, that this tale and another with a similar setting (which describes the meeting of all animals) are influenced by published Kwakiutl texts (Boas 1916:79, 106).

More common in Tsimshian mythology than the talking animal is the convention of simply introducing animals (or other creatures) as "people." Their animal identity or particular animal characteristics usually come into play later in the story. In the Txamsem tales, an actual transformation is sometimes described, sometimes not. Among the stories that are ambiguous on this point, the one about Txamsem and the Deer is typical. Txamsem meets a "man and his wife" in a house. We learn that the man is the Deer, whom Txamsem subsequently tricks, kills, and eats. Returning to the house, he tells Deer's wife that the wolves killed her husband. According to the story, she "shook her little tail and ran away from him" (Boas 1916:88–90). It is not clear whether the wife changes into deer form, or if this "person" was a deer all along.

In the story of Txamsem and Little Pitch, however, a clear transformation does take place. Txamsem is entertained at the house of Little Pitch and his wife, who are described as a man and a "very pretty young woman." Later, while out fishing for halibut, Txamsem tricks Little Pitch into staying out in the sun too long. Little Pitch crawls under a mat to hide from the sun, but finally weakens and dies, changing into a puddle of melted pitch in the bottom of the canoe. When Txamsem (as usual, adding insult to injury) tries to return to the house to get supper from his victim's wife, he finds only a small spruce tree with a drop of pitch on one side. Returning to the canoe full of halibut, Txamsem finds in its place a spruce log with roots (Boas 1916:86–87).

As mentioned above, the animal tales and stories of Txamsem seem to occur at a time (or in a context) that is vaguely "more remote" than the world of quasi-historical persons and ancestors of the present kin groups. Even though there are no origin tales for the clans and lineages, these social groups do not seem to have existed in the days of Txamsem and of such events as the feast of the Wolves and Deer, since specific ancestors are never mentioned in these stories. Parallel to this separation of "mythical" contexts from those of "historical" ancestors is a different emphasis in the treatment of animals.

In the quasi-historical tales there is usually a distinction between ordinary dumb animals and animals that have assumed fully human form. It is true that a few instances can be found of talking animals, such as the series of increasingly powerful creatures that seek to marry Gauo's granddaughter (Boas 1912:199–209; 1974:469). Also, in a number of cases, the exact form of the animal-person remains ambiguous, just as it is in many of the Txamsem stories. Such incidents are rare, however, and these stories often depict ordinary animals as nontalking, noncultural beings. In the presence of "real" people, the animals seem to have retreated. They show their human characteristics mainly at their villages, which are remote and inaccessible to men.

On those extraordinary occasions when people meet animals who do reveal their hidden side, they usually appear to be essentially human, though there may be some clues to their animal identity. A girl who is visited at night by a young man finds he has skin "as smooth as glass." In reality, he is a Snail (Boas 1916:161–62). When a man brings his two Wolf wives back to his village, they seem to have human form, but always bear twins (multiple births being an animal trait) and are able to smell out and capture game (Boas 1916:321–22). Often when a person is taken to an animal village he does not even realize that these "people" are not ordinary people, and part of the plot of the story is his discovery that he is really among the Bears, Wolves, or other animals. Almost invariably it is the Mouse Woman who, in exchange for a humble offering of wool or fat, tells the man who his hosts are and advises him how to behave. (Since the mouse is a forest creature that also frequents the houses of men, Mouse Woman is an ideal go-between.)

If changes from animal to human form are possible, how do these transformations take place? The most graphic method is to don or shed an animal skin. The skin is often referred to as a "blanket" or robe. In Tsimshian tales, this trick is commonly employed by protagonists who wish to assume an animal guise temporarily. Txamsem, who is primarily human in form, dons a raven skin to fly (Boas 1916:60). In another version, Sucking Intestines (who is later reborn as Txamsem) puts on a woodpecker skin to reach Heaven. He then seduces the Sun's daughter by donning a duck skin; when she takes him into bed, he removes the skin (Boas 1974:453–55). Txamsem also dresses in a deer skin: once to steal fire and once to deceive some villagers (Boas 1916:63, 82). Another hero, named Tsak, tries on bird skins to fly over a tall mountain, but fails (Boas 1902:126–27). In the tale of the boy who was fed by eagles, the young man skins a sea gull and puts on the skin to fly to the Nass River. But his disguise is not perfect: "One of the people, looking after the gull, saw his feet and called, 'Look, the gull has human feet'" (Boas 1974:501–2).

In all these examples, skins are donned by humans (or heroes) for temporary convenience. In a few stories, animals are shown to be "human" under their skins. This kind of transformation occurs in the story of the Mountain Goats' revenge. At the end of the tale, the kind man who survives the destruction of his cruel village mates is helped to descend the mountain by the Goat whom he has befriended. The Goat appears as a human youth. First, the youth puts on his goatskin himself and demonstrates the technique of leaping from ledge to ledge; then he removes the skin and lends it to the man, who is thus enabled to get down safely (Boas 1916:134). In another story a man, who himself uses a sparrow blanket to fly, reaches the house of Chief Hummingbird. The chief puts on his hummingbird blanket in order to accompany the protagonist on his journey (Boas 1916:311–12). Related to the idea of putting on a skin to take animal form is an incident in the story of a woman who was abducted by the Killerwhales. When her husband comes to their undersea village to rescue her, he is told that the Killerwhales are making a wooden dorsal fin for her, presumably to complete her conversion to killerwhale form (Boas 1912:173–81).

Skins are also mentioned in a story about a princess who marries a Bear. When the princess is about to return to her people, the Bear says: "They shall put my skin by the side of the fire to dry it; and when you hear a creaking noise, you shall know that I feel chilly and shall add fuel to the fire" (Boas 1916:283). These examples suggest that skins may be seen as the "form souls" of animals (cf. Goldman 1975:124–25). While the animal has an undifferentiated human form underneath its "garment" of skin, the pelt embodies the characteristics that mark the creature's particular species.

But putting on or removing a skin is not the only way that transformations are depicted in Tsimshian mythology. It is equally common for a transformation to be described as an instantaneous change of shape. Again, this power is attributed to mythic heroes. Txamsem, for example, assumes the shape of a woman to deceive some hunters (Boas 1916:75). It is said of Asdiwal that he "transformed himself into a bird" (Boas 1974:478)—here, a direct change of shape is a simple alternative to the conventional device of donning a bird skin.

Animals may transform themselves at will into human form (but not into the forms of other animals). In one tale of the ancestors, a girl is visited at night by a young man, even though her parents guard her bed carefully. The young man always leaves before daybreak. Curious about the identity of her lover, she stays awake one night to watch him leave: "and when the young man arose, he was transformed into a mouse, which went through the knot-hole above her bed" (Boas 1916:233). In another story, some hunters kill a frog by burning it in their campfire. The next day a beautiful young woman accosts the men, but when they stop their canoe she vanishes and a frog is seen hopping away. This is the mother of the murdered frog (Boas 1916:261–62).

Whether the mechanism of transformation is by taking off a skin or by a magical and instantaneous change of shape, the implication is that an animal can physically change to human form and back again. These narrative conventions are not fully in accord with the ritual obligations that people have to the game and fish they catch. These rites imply that the human forms of animals are inner forms— souls or essences—which may exist separately from the physical body that is taken by the hunter or fisherman, even though they retain a close connection to it. If the mortal remains are not treated properly, the human form of the animal, which has returned to its hidden village, will suffer. In the story of the Mountain Goats' revenge, the narrator gives some insight into this connection: "It is said that when a hunter burned the bones and [unused] meat, then the animals would recover from their sickness; but as long as the bones lay scattered on the ground, then the animals' sickness would grow worse and worse, and they could not be cured" (Boas 1916:135). In another tale, Porcupine advises people to eat porcupine meat before winter and to throw the bones into the fire, "so that my people may not have any sickness in winter" (Boas 1916:110). Although this is no longer the practice today, older informants recall that animal bones should be burned and should be "talked" to as they are stirred about in the flames.

There are similar rules for fish. One story tells of a woman who had kept a dried spring salmon stored in a box for two years. This caused the chief of the Spring Salmon village, whose body it was, to have palsy. When the woman's son took the dried salmon out of the box, unfolded it, and ate a little, the chief felt better. To cure the chief completely, the salmon had to be eaten entirely. Therefore, dried salmon must not be kept more than one season (Boas 1916:194–95, 198). It is also necessary to drink fresh water after eating any kind of fish, "that the salmon or other kinds of fishes may be revived again, and so go home again gladly" (Boas 1916:195). The salmon apparently agree to be caught if they feel that they will be treated properly (Boas 1916:200).

This is one kind of reciprocity between the human and animal worlds. In exchange for the meat of an animal's body, human beings agree to treat the remains properly, ensuring the well-being of the animal's hidden form. But people also enter into more intimate relationships with animals, as we have already seen. They may visit the animal villages, and even have animal lovers, wives, or husbands. In doing so, people may actually make the transition to the hidden world of animals. The stories make it clear that a visit to an animal village, or to the abode of any supernatural, is no ordinary adventure. It is an experience that entails crossing to the "other side," to a different reality. This "otherness" may be marked by a difference in perceived time: the visitor seems to spend only two or three days in the house of the supernatural, but when he returns to the human world he finds that an equal number of years have passed.

After a prolonged stay in an animal village, the visitor may begin to become part of the animal world. This is seen as another kind of physical transformation, this time from human to animal form, which takes place gradually over a period of time. An example is the case of a man abducted by a Black Bear. He returned to his own village after two years: "When he arrived, all the people were afraid of him, because he looked like a bear. One man, however, caught him and carried him to the house. He was unable to speak and did not want to eat boiled meat. Then the people rubbed him with medicine, until finally he resumed his human form" (Boas 1916:297).

It is not possible to recover the person if the transformation has gone too far. A woman who was shamed by her husband's rebukes went to live in a lake. She had Beaver children, and was herself transformed into a Beaver. Her brothers pleaded with her to return, and finally drained the lake. They found her on the bottom: "Her body was all covered with fur, but her face was still the same. She could not speak. Her fingernails were like animal claws, and her leather apron had become a beaver tail. She was glad to see her brothers. She died right there, because she was on dry ground" (Boas 1916:139–41).

There are also a few tales in which animals cross over from their own world to the human one. In one of these stories, a man brings his Grizzly Bear wife back to his home village. The Bear remains in animal form. The picture of a grown female grizzly living in an ordinary village as a man's wife is obviously a ludicrous one, and the humorous possibilities are fully exploited. These animals are notoriously temperamental, and one could easily imagine this story being told with not-too-veiled reference to someone in the audience. The Bear's behavior soon leads to quarrels and violence, and she finally stalks back to her forest home (Boas 1902:200–210).

In the story of a prince who marries Wolf sisters and brings them home, the animal wives make a better adjustment to the human village. These are the Wolves mentioned earlier who apparently adopt human form but display the wolflike characteristics of multiple births and hunting by smell. Most of the children of these Wolf women also remain in the village, although two return to the Wolves (Boas 1916:321–22). These tales, then, reverse the more common theme of people being carried off to the animal world.

It is natural to imagine the possibility of a more complete symmetry between the animal and human worlds, and some of the stories do actually explore this idea. The tale of a princess who is abducted by Bears is a good example. The princess and some friends are on their way home from a berrying expedition when her carrying strap tears, spilling her basket of berries on the ground. This happens repeatedly and at last she sends her friends on. Two young men appear, help her with her berries, and lead her to a village which (as the Mouse Woman tells her) is the village of Bears. She marries there. She notices that sometimes a villager disappears for several days, and finally returns with a downcast air. If it is a man, his absence is explained by saying, "His fishing-line is broken." But if it is a woman, they say, "Her carrying strap tore." In reality (from the human point of view) what has happened is that the Bear has been killed by a hunter (Boas 1916:278–80). Thus an explicit parallel is drawn between the princess's captivity in the village of the Bears and the involuntary sojourn of a Bear in the village of a successful hunter. This double perspective calls to mind the love of double meanings and visual puns that is characteristic of Northwest Coast art. In both visual and oral arts there seems to be a pleasure in showing that what appears to be one thing may, from another point of view, be part of something quite different.

We have come, by a circuitous route, to one more way of thinking about animal-human transformations: that is, that the transformations do not involve physical change at all, but are matters of perception. This concept was suggested to me by a Nass River man who was telling another story of a marriage between an ancestress and a Bear. The Bear appeared to her as a man, and took her back into the forest. She stayed with the Bear for some time, learning the use of various berries, but did not know her husband's real identity. She had some suspicions, and once or twice she even asked him, "Are you a bear?" But he would not answer. Even as she returned home, "Her eye saw the man as human." As she began the final stretch of path down to the human village, leaving her husband behind in the forest, she turned to look at him once more. Only then did she see a black bear, walking away. What I understood this to mean was that it was not the Bear who changed, but the way the woman's "eye" saw. When she entered the Bear world, she perceived the Bear as a person like herself. When she left it, she saw a bear.

Several stories, in fact, play upon this idea of complementary realities, with truth in the eye of the beholder. When Asdiwal visited the Sea Lions (whom he saw as people) they appealed to him to cure an "epidemic." Many of the Sea Lion people were ill and "nobody knew the cause." Only Asdiwal could see the arrows which human hunters had shot into their bodies. Asdiwal battled over the sick as though he were a shaman, but he actually cured them simply by pulling out the arrows (Boas 1912:131; 1974:479). Thus just as ordinary shamans are able to see beyond human reality because they have experienced the supernatural world, so Asdiwal, coming from the human side, can see the arrows that are invisible to the Sea Lions.

The theme of varying perceptions of reality is highly elaborated in the story of the young prince who is adopted by the chief of the Spring Salmon. In this tale we are told that the spring "leaves" of cottonwood that fall in the river are called "salmon" by the Spring Salmon people. This is why they leave their ocean village and move to the rivers in the spring, just as humans leave *their* villages and move to salmon camps (Boas 1916:195–96). What appears to us to be spring salmon jumping in the river is really the Salmon people standing up in their canoes to stretch their bodies (Boas 1916:202). The prince, being admitted to the Spring Salmon village, sees them as people. Yet they are at the same time fish, for when he follows Mouse Woman's advice and goes behind the Salmon village to club down a "beautiful fat youth," the child becomes a fat spring salmon for him to eat. He forgets to burn one of the salmon ribs and when he returns to the house finds the same child, complaining of a pain in his side (Boas 1916:195–96).

It would be easy to push this idea of complementary realities just a bit further and imagine that everything that can be said about people's relationships with animals can also be said about animals' relationships with people. I do not believe that the Tsimshian would carry speculation this far. The storytellers enjoy playing with symmetry, paradoxes, and double meanings, but there remains a basic asymmetry between the human world and that of animals. Animals are animals *and* people, but "real" people are just people.

Another important feature of this asymmetry is that people's perception of the "other" world is largely subject to the whims of the animals (and supernaturals) themselves. When a person wishes to initiate a relationship with an animal or supernatural being, as in a vision quest where the seeker desires a gift of supernatural power, the "other" always has final control. The seeker fasts, bathes, and abstains from sex to make himself pure. He may isolate himself in the forest and undergo hardships. If he is fortunate, he may coax the animal or supernatural to appear—but always of its own free will, out of "pity."

Likewise in mythology, all cases of animal transformation to human form (or the admission of humans to the animal world) seem to be willed by the animal. This is especially clear in the many tales in which animals initiate a relationship (whether for marriage or other purposes) by appearing to people in human form. Sometimes the end of a relationship is also indicated by a change of form, as when the woman who is returning to her own village finally sees her forest husband as a bear. A transformation also signals the end of the relationship when the daughter of the supernatural Chief Peace flees from her unfaithful husband. Repentant, he pursues her, but he is powerless to grasp her, "because she had become like unto a cloud" (Boas 1916:213).

Some of the most dramatic tales of manipulated perceptions are those in which people encounter Land Otters. The Land Otters want to entice people to join them, which is felt to be a horrible fate. Otters are associated with madness. Nass informants said that it is dangerous to think about a spouse or lover when one is alone in the forest because a Land Otter is then capable of appearing as the object of one's desire. A story was told of a man who was thinking of his wife while walking alone in the woods. He thought he saw her, but realized he was mistaken when he noticed that the apparition had short fingers and patches of fur behind the ears. He fired his gun at the creature, though he had to look away as he did so, so much did it resemble his wife. The creature did indeed prove to be a Land Otter once it lay dead on the ground. Similar incidents are recorded in Boas (1916:166–72, 345–46). Although the Land Otter is unique in its particular power of mimicry, these tales do provide a good illustration of the more general power of supernatural beings to manipulate perceptions over which the human subject has little control.

To summarize, we have discovered at least four ways of thinking about the relationships between animals and their hidden, humanoid forms. One way, which accords well with the ritual treatment of game, is to imagine that animals have separate souls which are different from, but linked to, their physical bodies. In the mythology, however, we more commonly find that animals change (or appear to change) from one form to another, whether through skin changes, changes in shape, or changes in the frame of reference of the viewer. Seen as a philosophical system, these various mechanisms are obviously contradictory; but the criteria by which they must be judged are not only logical or philosophical but also narrative. While these stories may be "good to think" it is equally essential that they be "good to tell." The narrator holds his audiences through suspense, wonder, or humor more than through the intellectual content of his story. Various methods of transformation are suited to various incidents of plot, and consistency is of secondary concern. Thus we find, in the same oral repertoire, the Salmon People who, stretching in their canoes, appear to us to be fish jumping in the water; the Mountain Goat who lends his skin to his human friend so that he may descend the precipice; and the young man who magically shrinks to his Mouse form to sneak out of his lover's bedroom.

Yet all these stories—from the most "philosophical" explanation of the ritual obligations of man to animal, to the most inconsequential tale of Beaver and Porcupine—agree on one central point: animals and people, on some level, share a similar nature. I do not want to imply that the average Tsimshian lives in a mystic world where animals might at any moment change their form. They know animal behavior intimately, and some have claimed to understand the speech of birds, wolves, or killerwhales; but clearly for the most part it is a workaday world. Only shamans can contact the spirit realm at will; for most people such an experience is a possibility rarely, if ever, realized. Yet the concept of the human nature of animals is there, backed up not only by myth and daily ritual, but also by tales of shamans, Land Otter Men, and other strange phenomena. This insistence that animals are more like us than they appear to be has, I think, an important psychological function.

All hunting and fishing societies seem to have some way of expressing their relationship to the creatures on which they depend for food, and some way of trying to insure the abundance of these creatures. Arctic Eskimos, for example, might pray to Sedna, who controls the sea mammals, while some Algonkians believe that each species has its Keeper to whom humans can appeal. Curiously, there are hints of the latter belief in two Tsimshian myths. When Txamsem tricks the Eulachon Chief into releasing the run ahead of schedule, the phrasing seems to indicate that the Chief is not a fish himself, but a Keeper of the fish (Boas 1902:28–30). Again, when Txamsen marries Bright-Cloud Woman, his wife is depicted as a being who can control the salmon, which are her "tribe" (Boas 1916:76–79). But this is an unusual motif for the Tsimshian. In every other case, people set up a direct relationship with the animals themselves.

For such a relationship, there must be some common ground, for it is not at all clear that a man and a fish have much to say to each other. For the Tsimshian this problem was solved by the assertion that animals are not alien beings. They are, in fact, "people." Because animals are people, they understand reciprocity in the same way that people do. The Salmon or the Mountain Goats can appreciate our fulfillment of our ritual obligations to them because it affects the health of their human forms. The Killerwhales welcome offerings of tobacco and paint because, being people, they have use for these things. Being people, animals may even choose human beings as partners in the reciprocal relationship of husband and wife. The Tsimshian do not assert that people are descended from animals or have any genealogical relationship to them. Rather, the significance of the marriage theme is to show that the real nature of animals is so like our own as to allow the intimate reciprocity of sex. It is within the context of the humanity of animals that the qualities mentioned by Blake can also permeate the relationship between man and nature.

The Structure of Tsimshian Totemism*

MARJORIE HALPIN

Had we been given the privilege of attending a mid-nineteenth-century Tsimshian potlatch, we would have seen a visual spectacle of great splendor, a magnificent panoply of human faces juxtaposed with animal headdresses, of human bodies enveloped in animal skins and robes bearing animal representations. The firelight would have lit up great carvings of strange animal forms in human postures. Had we understood the language, we would have heard long and formal speeches in which men told of their ancestors' encounters with talking wolves and of the marriages of their ancestresses with bears and frogs. These events would have been presented as primal happenings constituting the very identities of the speakers and their relatives. At first, visually and intellectually stunned by this conjunction of the human and animal realms, which we keep so separate in our own lives, we would have soon begun to see some order in the myriad forms of birds and mammals and frogs before us. We would have noticed that the animal representations tended to cluster, like with like. We would have noted that the men who made the speeches wore the more elaborate headdresses, richly decorated with shining abalone. We would have noticed that younger men and women were being presented to the assembly, with special attention being called to the animal representations they were wearing. We would have begun to realize that some kind of *system* utilizing the natural world was being displayed.

That system is the topic of this essay. Most anthropologists writing about the potlatch have dealt with the forms and consequences

*The primary data used in this study were lists and other information about several hundred Tsimshian crests extracted from the field notes of Marius Barbeau and William Beynon (1915–57), his Tsimshian collaborator, which have been preserved in the Centre for the Study of Canadian Folklore, National Museum of Man, Ottawa. These notes were augmented by museum documentation for some 1,600 Tsimshian objects in the National Museum of Man, the Royal Ontario Museum, the British Columbia Provincial Museum, the Field Museum, and the Museum of the American Indian.

of social actions involved in it. This essay examines the rules underlying the system of crests, or totemic classification, which accounted for the visual splendor of the potlatch. Now for the most part lying unknown and unused on museum shelves, crest representations were once objects of profound meaning and importance to the people who made and used them. We have tended to reduce those meanings—to simplify that system.

The Tsimshian system of totemic classification proved upon analysis to be both more subtle and more extensive than previously suspected. It appears to be the most complex system on the Northwest Coast. The rules governing the social locations of crest elements and combinations of elements in totemic representations (art) discovered in the course of the study constitute at least a gross matrix within which undocumented museum pieces can be provisionally assigned on the basis of corresponding formal elements. Here on the Northwest Coast, where the totem pole will always be with us, it seems worthwhile to attempt to elaborate the meaning of the term "totemism."

THE USE OF CRESTS

Each Tsimshian was born a member of a named "house" or corporate matrilineage, which owned hunting, fishing, and gathering territories as well as numerous noncorporeal privileges: myths, ceremonial rights, songs, names, and crests. Each house belonged to one of four major nonlocalized, exogamic groups or clans (usually called phratries in the literature), which was associated with or identified by certain crest animals. Houses were ranked and divided into chiefly and commoner "classes." Within the clans, subclans consisting of houses owning the same or similar myths and crests can be identified. Some of these subclans were named, some were not. Several hundred crests owned by houses of Tsimshian-speaking peoples from all three divisions—Coast Tsimshian, Niska, Gitksan—were collected between 1915 and the late 1920s by Marius Barbeau and William Beynon (these are listed in Appendix II of Halpin 1973). A precise number of these crests cannot be calculated since the lists are obviously incomplete and crests that appear to be the same sometimes show up under different names.

Tsimshian crests are a series of named entities or objects, usually referring to animals, which were owned by social groups who were privileged to represent them according to certain rules on totem poles, house fronts, ceremonial headdresses and robes, and certain other

objects of material culture. Crests were jealously guarded possessions. They were a legacy from myth time, acquired by the ancestors, and held in perpetuity by their lineal descendants. To display
the crest of another house without having secured the right to do
so was a challenge to the integrity and very identity of that house.
Crests were sometimes captured in war and displayed by the victors
as humiliating reminders of defeat until purchased back by their
owners. Some were not repurchased and show up in crest lists as
possessions of alien houses (and were so identified by informants).
Crests were also taken in compensation for murder. Sometimes crests
were lent, usually to clan relatives, as a gesture of generosity and
solidarity. On rare occasions, they were given away. When they had
been forcibly seized, crests were no longer displayed by their original owners; when they were lent voluntarily, the original owners continued to display them. Crests were never sold or transferred
in marriage by the Tsimshian: such actions would have been in
violation of their very meaning. The ownership of common crests
implied kinship—membership in the same clan or subclan. Clan
kinship was extended on the basis of crest correspondences to the
Haida, Tlingit, Bella Bella, and neighboring Athapaskans.

Although crests were the property of the house, they were vested
in its highest-ranking names, and under the control of its chief or
headman. The house was perpetuated through its names, which
were assumed or occupied by successive generations of matrilineally related men and women. Becoming Tsimshian—in the sense of
becoming a fully adult, responsible member of the community—
was to assume these names publicly in a sequence of increasing
importance and responsibility (see Duff 1959:40; Garfield 1939:224–
26; Boas 1916:510–13). The chief or headman of the house was the
man, and rarely the woman, who had assumed its most important
name.

Names were assumed at potlatches. A person who attempted to
take a name without giving or participating in a potlatch was subject
to ridicule. At the potlatch, the name was assumed in context or
association with crests owned by the house. The person assuming
the name was usually also invested with the right to wear or display
crests of the same general degree of importance as his or her new
name. In the case of succession to the name of a deceased chief,
the new incumbent erected a memorial totem pole which displayed
important crests of the house. Crests were also transferred by a chief
to his successor during his lifetime, in which case he was publicly
affirming his successor.

Crests (other than those serving as primary clan symbols, to be defined below) were linked with houses by myths (*adaox*), which were also owned. The relationship between the myth and the crest was a necessary one. This was recognized immediately by Barbeau and became one of the basic themes in his publications. In his review of Boas's *Tsimshian Mythology* (1916), written during his first field season, Barbeau (1917:560) described this relationship more succinctly than he ever did later: "A crest without a myth to explain its origin and its connection with the owner was an impossibility; and such a myth was the patrimony of a clan or a family."

In a manifest functional sense, the telling of a myth at a potlatch asserted one's right to claim and display the crests associated with it. There were at least three necessary features involved in such an assertion:

1. The action was ritually "framed" in a potlatch context.

2. The action included some formal presentation of the crest or crests being validated. These were represented on a new totem pole which was being raised, painted on the front of a new dwelling which was being dedicated, worn on the person of someone who was receiving a name, or dramatically presented in a staged performance. Such a performance was sometimes the occasion for a potlatch. That is, the formal reason for giving a potlatch was to display a crest in a dramatic and memorable (and therefore prestigious) fashion. This was likely to have been the case when a crest had been challenged, or the potlatch itself constituted a challenge to the declared owner of a crest. More typically, the reason for giving a potlatch was to commemorate a dead chief, assume a new name, or raise a totem pole (all three of which were usually involved in a chief's mortuary potlatch), and crest display was included as part of the series of actions performed to achieve the more inclusive end.

3. It was the telling of the associated myth that transformed a crest display into an assertion of crest ownership. The myth included two features which linked the claim of the owner with the ancestors: it described the events, usually involving a journey, when the crest or the crest animal was encountered, and it in some way indicated the relationship of the teller of the myth to an ancestor involved in that encounter.

The crest assertion of ownership was validated by the assembled guest-witnesses. A formal speech by a guest acknowledging the mythteller's right to the myth or the congruence of the told version with some previously heard and acknowledged version of the same myth (or, perhaps, with some native myth model) may or may not have been necessary. Such a formal acknowledgement was included in each of the crest validation scenes at a series of Kitsegukla (a Gitksan village) potlatches recorded by William Beynon (1945), but it also seems possible that the acceptance of gifts distributed by the mythteller might constitute sufficient acknowledgment on the part of the guests.

In a dispute over a crest at the Kitsegukla potlatches, the house opposing another house's right to display a particular crest on its new totem pole sang the following song (Beynon 1945):

> I gaze up to the sky
> I gaze up to the sky
> Where I see my uncle
> Who never lies about his myth.

At the potlatch following the pole raising, the chief explained his right to the crest in question by reciting his myth and the details of the crest's acquisition, and the visiting chiefs made speeches confirming his claim. The opposing house was forced to accept the situation.

Not only was crest display and validation an integral part of the potlatch, but crest emblems were not worn in everyday social interaction. Sapir (1915:6) reports that "one cannot even pay a neighbour a visit and wear a garment decorated with a minor crest without justifying the use of such regalia by the expenditure of property at the house visited." Barbeau's Tsimshian informants were quite specific that crest-bearing costume items were worn at potlatches.

These facts tend to confirm that totemic representations—the display of crests—can be considered the visual dimension of the potlatch: the visual celebration and confirmation of the social order. The power of these visual statements was such that they were not to be made during the course of ordinary day-to-day life. They were statements to be made only in front of witnesses who could attest to their propriety.

CREST-BEARING OBJECTS

This crest/potlatch association is supported by rules about which kinds of objects could bear crest representations. These rules were an unexpected bonus in the Barbeau and Beynon field notes. A general assumption in Northwest Coast ethnology has been that a crest can be represented on any kind of artifact and, conversely, that any artifact decorated with a representation of an animal is therefore to be classified as "crest art." This understanding must now be modified—for the Tsimshian at least—for there is a distinction to be made between representations of crests and other representations of animals (including some of the same animals used as crest animals in the totemic context). The distinction depends on the kind of artifact involved.

When listing crests and their owners, Tsimshian informants almost invariably mentioned the kinds of artifacts on which the crests could, and more rarely could not, be represented. When the crest lists were examined for the categories of material culture that were specified for crests, it was obvious that they were directly related to the potlatch. The categories most often specified, and clearly most important for crest representations, were (1) architectural features: totem poles, including house entrance poles, house posts, house front paintings, beams, rafters, and ceremonial entrances; (2) costume features: robes and headdresses; and (3) less often, feast dishes and ladles. In other words, the most important objects for crest representations were those worn on the person in the potlatch, used in the feast, and represented on the house, which was where potlatches occurred. The focus or climax of these crest expressions were the person and dwelling of the chief, who was the embodiment of his group's power and prestige.

Artifacts that were not mentioned as crest-bearing objects included masks, halibut hooks, spoons, boxes, coppers,[1] rattles, dance aprons, Chilcat blankets,[2] and so forth. Animal representations on these other categories of objects were not crests, but expressed other, primarily "power" aspects of Tsimshian cosmology. Thus the raven of the raven rattle was a power form, while the raven on a totem pole or headdress was a social statement. The rattle, correspondingly, could be used by persons in all four clans; the headdress or totem pole could be used only by those in the one clan entitled to claim the raven as a crest.

1. One copper was included in the crest lists, but as a crest itself; there was no indication that another crest was represented on it. Coppers did, of course, change ownership, a process essentially antithetical to the crest concept among the Tsimshian.

2. Typical Chilcat blankets, that is. Two atypical Chilcats were included in the lists, and there is evidence that both depicted realistic forms: one a bear and two killerwhales and the other a school of ten killerwhales (see Halpin 1973:217–18).

So-Called Totemism

Totemism as an analytical concept and a "primitive" mode of consciousness has engaged the attention of outstanding thinkers for a
century (see Lévi-Strauss 1963; Burridge 1973:176–87). According to
Burridge (1973:185), the relationship between totem and "totemite"
(his word) might be variously "kinship with, descent from, inheritance of, identity through, fate or destiny determined by, particular
kinds of awareness achieved through, place in the cosmos given
by," and so on. Attempts to confine such phenomenologically varied relationships in a single formulation have consistently floun-
dered, to the extent that many anthropologists have rejected the
idea of totemism as having any conceivable utility at all. But the
word dies hard, and Lévi-Strauss (1963:16) has resurrected it as "so-
called totemism." As such, it no longer encompasses the range of
relationships listed by Burridge, but has become a system of "ethno-
logic" (ibid.:31), or only one manifestation of a manner of thought
utilizing elements of nature: "As I showed in an earlier book and
am continuing to establish here, so-called totemism is in fact only
a particular case of the general problem of classification and one of
many examples of the part which specific terms often play in the
working out of a social classification" (Lévi-Strauss 1966:62).

The key concept in Lévi-Strauss's formulation is that "the differences between animals, which man can extract from nature and
transfer to culture . . ., are adopted as emblems by groups of men
in order to do away with their own resemblances" (1966:107). "The
passage from a concrete to a formal definition of totemism," he says
(1963:10), "actually goes back to Boas." He is referring to *Tsimshian
Mythology* (1916:519), in which Boas states that totemism is the application of a rule of homology between a *system* of denotation and
a *social system* which is being denoted, and that "the homology of
distinguishing marks of social divisions of a tribe is proof that they
are due to a classificatory tendency" of the human mind. Boas
(ibid.:517) believed that the use of natural species as the basis for a
totemic system of denotation was arbitrary, and that to consider it
otherwise was to take on the entirely different problem of "the relationship of man to nature, which is obviously quite distinct from
that of the characterization of kinship groups." On the contrary,
according to Lévi-Strauss, there are necessary logical relations between the system of denotation and the system that is denoted: "The
animal world and plant life are utilized not merely because they are

there, but because they suggest a mode of thought" (1963:13).

This mode of thought is based on the operation of what Lévi-Strauss calls the "species notion" or the "totemic operator." Plant and animal species are admirably suited as logical vehicles because of their "intermediate position as logically equidistant from the extreme forms of classification: categorical and singular" (Lévi-Strauss 1966:149). Being thus a "medial classifier," the species concept can widen its referent upward in the direction of associated elements (e.g., sky/earth) and categories (e.g., high/low), or contract it downward, in the direction of proper names (Tsmishian cross-clan naming, in which a child was given a name that referred to a very specific action or attribute of his father's clan animal, is an excellent example). It thus allows a basic twofold movement between "the unity of a multiplicity [and] the diversity of a unity" (ibid.:136). The species concept suggests logical movement or connection between the concrete and individual on the one hand and the abstract and categorical on the other.

Social classification by differences between species and species as medial classifiers can be diagrammed as horizontal and vertical axes in a general totemic model, as presented in Table 1. The horizontal axis is composed of units (species) and intervals (discontinuities) in nature which are borrowed to characterize units (social groups) and intervals (differences) among humans. The vertical axis is composed of logical operations performed on the species unit which correspond to distinctions within the social unit. In the next section, this generalized totemic model will be applied to Tsimshian crests.

TABLE 1

GENERALIZED HORIZONTAL AND VERTICAL AXES IN TOTEMIC
CLASSIFICATION

		Species (descent group)			
		grizzly^{+2}	wolf^{+2}	raven^{+2}	eagle^{+2}
Social distinction (rank)	/	grizzly^{+1}	wolf^{+1}	raven^{+1}	eagle^{+1}
	/	GRIZZLY	WOLF	RAVEN	EAGLE
	Logical operations	grizzly^{-1}	wolf^{-1}	raven^{-1}	eagle^{-1}
	/	grizzly^{-2}	wolf^{-2}	raven^{-2}	eagle^{-2}

NOTE: Each term has a corresponding social referent.

THE STRUCTURE OF TSIMSHIAN TOTEMISM

The most significant structural feature of the Tsimshian crest system, and one that distinguishes it from other northern Northwest Coast totemic systems, was its ability to differentiate along the vertical axis, resulting in the generation of a number of crests from a single crest animal. This was based on a fundamental difference in conceptualizing crests between the Tsimshian and their neighbors (see the comparative lists in Boas 1916:520–21). Among the Haida and Tlingit, for example, it was the crest animal—grizzly, killerwhale, raven, eagle, and so forth—which was owned, and its various representations or manifestations were apparently matters of individual and artistic preference. Among the Tsimshian, on the other hand, specific manifestations of the animal were owned as crests. Thus the Haida had a single Raven crest, while the Tsimshian had over a dozen: Raven, Supernatural Raven, Raven of the Sky, Raven of Copper, All Abalone Raven, Split Raven, Raven on Top of Raven, Raven Eating Salmon Liver, Chief Raven, Raven Hanging by One Claw, Prince Raven, White Raven, Raven with Starfish in Its Beak, Raven's Nest, Raven Sitting Quietly, Soaring Raven, Raven of the Water. Such specific crests will be called *particularized* crests to distinguish them from *generalized* crests (i.e., the animal species itself).

If crests were visual expressions of social organization, there should be some significant structural difference between Tsimshian and Haida/Tlingit social organizations underlying their different kinds of crest systems. The pertinent difference was in group ranking: the Tsimshian ranked houses, subclans, and clans in definite serial order (see Halpin 1973, Appendix I, for ranked lists), whereas according to Rosman and Rubel (1971:47), "among the Haida and Tlingit rank order of groups is hardly present." The Haida considered families as being of high or low rank, and there were families known as those that "stood first" in a village (Swanton 1905:70). Similarly, among the Tlingit "certain clans were regarded as 'high' whereas others were generally regarded as low caste for varying reasons," although "there was no sharp distinction between commoners and nobles" (Olson 1967:47). In every Tlingit village the highest chief of the "leading clan" was considered a sort of "town chief" (ibid.:49), and there was also a town chief or "town mother" among the Haida. There were, however, no ranking systems equivalent to that of the Tsimshian among either people.

Correspondingly, the Haida and Tlingit crest systems were single axis systems—they expressed only descent group membership along the horizontal totemic axis (although some crests were exclusively owned and considered prerogatives of especially high rank)—while the Tsimshian crest system was a double axis system, expressing both descent group membership along the horizontal axis and rank along the vertical axis (as will be demonstrated below). The Tsimshian system, thus having a greater symbolic "load," needed a greater number of contrastive units to express it.

The Horizontal Axis

Along the first or horizontal axis of the Tsimshian system, and in the Haida and Tlingit systems, are the units and intervals representing descent groups: the discontinuities between grizzly, wolf, eagle, raven, and so on. For it is the differences between natural species that totemic systems utilize in order to symbolize social differences: "the homology [totemic systems] evoked is not between social groups and natural species but between the differences which manifest themselves on the level of groups on the one hand and on that of species on the other. They are thus based on the postulate of a homology between *two systems of differences,* one of which occurs in nature and the other in culture" (Lévi-Strauss 1966:115, his emphasis). In other words, the Eagle (Laxskik) clan differs from the Wolf (Laxkibu) clan just as the eagle differs from the wolf. There was no sense of identification or "relationship of substance" (ibid.:135) between the animal species and human group; people did not think of themselves as eaglelike or wolflike. If they did, argues Lévi-Strauss (ibid.:117), exogamy, by which links between groups were maintained, would be difficult: "the more each group tries to define itself by the image which it draws from a natural model, the more difficult will it become for it to maintain its links with other social groups and, in particular, to exchange its sisters and daughters with them."

Each Tsimshian clan was associated with and identified by two main or *primary* crest animals, as shown in Table 2 (the clan names are those of the Coast Tsimshian). These eight animals were the main building blocks in the Tsimshian crest system. As such, they shared several attributes that set them apart from other categories of crests: (1) they were the principal clan identification symbols and, with rare exceptions, could be displayed by all members of a clan; (2) they were each the source of multiple particularized crests, far more than any other animals in the system; and (3) they could be displayed in their generalized form by clan members without a validating myth; indeed, there do not seem to be myths accounting for the origins of the primary animals as generalized crests. Validating

TABLE 2
PRIMARY CREST ANIMALS BY CLAN

	Laxkibu	Gispudwada	Ganhada	Laxskik
Primary animals	wolf	grizzly	raven	eagle
	bear	killerwhale	frog	beaver

myths were, however, reported, and obviously were required to display particularized crests.

In most of these characteristics, the primary animals differed markedly from all other categories of crests, and I have hypothesized that these eight were the original crest animals of the Tsimshian, and probably of the Tlingit and Haida as well. This hypothesis, in part, follows a suggestion of Sapir (1966:44) that crests can be stratified by frequency of occurrence: "the older the crest, the greater number of times it is found in the various clans; on the other hand, a crest found in only one clan may be suspected to be of recent origin." Boas (1916:528) supports this view: "Among the Tsimshian the most highly specialized crests . . . may be considered as of recent origin."

All other animals used as crests might be called *secondary* animals. Except for a series of eight among the Coast Tsimshian, they were all claimed by houses and subclans rather than having clan-wide distribution. These Coast Tsimshian exceptions, which were also found in limited distribution among the other two divisions of Tsimshian-speaking peoples, are shown in Table 3. These eight secondary animals were said by Barbeau and Beynon's informants specifically to have been used by all (crane, mosquito, grouse, owl, halibut) or many (starfish, sculpin, octopus) houses in a clan, and seem to have functioned as minor clan symbols. Two of them, the octopus and sculpin, were also sources of multiple particularized crests, and

TABLE 3
SECONDARY CREST ANIMALS BY CLAN

	Laxkibu	Gispudwada	Ganhada	Laxskik
Secondary animal	crane	grouse	sculpin	halibut
	owl	mosquito	starfish	octopus

resemble primary animals in this respect. It is also probable that general forms of these secondary animals could be displayed without validating myths. All other secondary animal crests were claimed by houses or subclans only and required validating myths to be displayed. In most cases, they were reported in one form only.

Plants form a very small category of crests, of limited distribution. Even among the Gitksan, whose clan name Gisgast translates as "people of the Fireweed" (corresponding to the Coast Tsimshian Gispudwada clan), a Fireweed crest was claimed by only two houses. The most important plant crests were a series of seaweed crests which were claimed by houses of the Coast Tsimshian Gispudwada. Seaweed crests were not claimed by houses in any other clan or division.

In the strictest sense, these natural species were the "images drawn from nature" that constituted the horizontal axis of Tsimshian totemism. They are what Boas (1916:517) calls totemism in its "most marked" form. He instructs us, however, not to separate these from totemism in its "weaker" form, which consists of crests derived from objects other than natural species. For the Tsimshian, I have categorized these into four groups: natural phenomena, artifacts, humans, and monsters.

Natural phenomena crests were a relatively small category. Most of them were celestial phenomena: Moon, Sun, Stars, Big Dipper, Rain, Clouds, Snow, Rainbow, Mirage, Thunder, Hole in the Sky, Light, and Red Sky of Morning. There were also water crests, Whirlpool and Riptide, and varieties of fire. One of the most interesting aspects of the natural phenomena crests is that many of them were said to be represented by forms of humans or the human face.

Artifacts claimed as crests were mainly the same kinds of artifacts on which other crests were represented: items of costume and personal decoration, some weapons, house parts, house types, house names, and a scattering of ladles and feast dishes. An important artifact claimed by houses in three clans was the woven spruce root hat topped with woven disks or rings—the *lanemgeit*. Its crest aspect was the number of disks the owner was permitted to claim, which varied from three to nineteen according to the lists. The greater the number of disks, the more prestigious the crest. In the literature, such disks have been said to reflect the number of potlatches the wearer had given, but there is no confirmation of this in the Tsimshian case. The number of disks was part of the crest, an inherited privilege.

Human and monster crests, which seem to violate the very basis of totemic classification, will be described at the conclusion of this chapter.

The Vertical Axis

The second or vertical axis of the Tsimshian crest system added another dimension by means of which discriminations in rank could be expressed. It did this by applying a group of *operators* which transformed the general crest animal into a series of particularized forms. The operators are attributes that I extracted from the names and descriptions of particularized crests as given by Barbeau's informants.

Below are three pairs of crest names in which the animals differ by the modifiers "Prince," "Real," and "Of the Sky":

łkwelksem medik	Prince of Grizzlies
łkwelksem haots	Prince of Cormorants
semnexł	Real Killerwhale
semganao	Real Frog
gagum laxha	Raven of the Sky
medigem laxha	Grizzly of the Sky

The operators are particularizing attributes contained in or signified by the crest names. Each operator seems to have a corresponding visual representation. In most cases, the operator is in fact contained in the name, as in *Standing* Bear, *Split* Person, *White* Marten, Grizzly *of the Sea* (i.e., with fin). In other cases, however, the logic connecting the name and the operator is more obscure.

In Table 4, five operators (abalone, split, young, human faces, white) have been combined with the eight primary crest animals in order to produce twenty of the particularized crests reported by Barbeau's informants. Although the relationship between the operators abalone, young, and human faces and the crest names is not obvious, they were found to be consistently associated in descriptions of the crests bearing these names as given by informants (see Halpin 1973, Appendix II). Such arrangements or "classification events" may be seen as paradigms, defined as "multidimensional forms of arrangement organized by class intersection" (Conklin 1969:107). Perfect paradigms (i.e., those in which all of the spaces representing

TABLE 4
PARTICULARIZED CRESTS

Operator	Primary Crest Animals							
	Wolf	Bear	Grizzly	Killerwhale	Frog	Raven	Eagle	Beaver
abalone	Prince of Wolves	Prince of Bears	Prince of Grizzlies	Prince of Killerwhales		Prince of Ravens	Prince of Eagles	Prince of Beavers
split		Split Bear		Split Killerwhale			Split Eagle	
young		Without Knowledge			Children of Chief Frog			
human faces			Supernatural Grizzly		Supernatural Frog	Supernatural Raven		Supernatural Beaver
white	White Wolf	White Bear	White Grizzly			White Raven		

possible combinations of components are filled) are rare in folk taxonomies.

Isolation of the operators permits the identification of the same
animal-and-attribute relationships in material culture. A headdress
of a grizzly with a dorsal fin can be interpreted with reasonable cer-
tainty as the crest named Grizzly of the Sea, owned by the Gispudwada clan, and so forth. Although there are still problems and
interpretations remaining to be resolved in working out such correspondences, the crest lists are available as primary data upon which
refined iconographic interpretations can be based. As far as we know,
the lists themselves can no longer be substantially improved. However, as more crest representations in museums are identified and
brought into this framework, we should be able to analyze, rather
than merely identify, the relationships between the semantic and
visual systems.

It has been asserted that the action of operators upon crest animals produced a vertical axis of particularized crests which reflected
rank distinctions. This can be substantiated by means of rules given
by informants, as well as by showing that certain operators were
consistently associated with higher ranked houses in the actual crest
lists themselves.

Tsimshian informants described different rules to be observed in
crest use by the chiefly (or "royal") houses and by other houses.
For example, the Coast Tsimshian commoner house of Watidaax had
the right to "use the grizzly in the same manner as other Gispudwada of this class": (1) as a house front painting representing the
whole animal, painted in red and black, (2) as a wooden headdress
representing the head of the bear only, (3) on a totem pole, and (4)
painted on a skin robe. Similarly, the killerwhale could be displayed
as follows: (1) painted in black outline with red details on a skin
robe, (2) as a house front painting, and (3) on a totem pole. On the
other hand, when the killerwhale was claimed by "one of the royal
family, it is under a different name—'so and so' killerwhale—and
then it is represented in a different manner." A Gitksan informant
reported that "the individual crests were restricted to the head chiefs."
Two other rules consistently reported by Coast Tsimshian informants were that only the chiefly houses could decorate crest representations with abalone and wear the actual head or complete skin,
including the head, of crest animals (i.e., impersonate the animal);
other houses were permitted only to wear wooden representations
of the animal's head, without abalone, and animal skins, minus heads,
as robes. Interestingly enough, it was only those of high rank who

could become the actual "image drawn from nature," which was the totem animal itself.[3]

The general rule, then, was that only chiefly or high-ranking houses could own particularized crests. Most of the specific representational rules given above (e.g., representation with or without abalone, etc.) can be derived from this general one. When the actual distribution of particularized crests was checked in the crest lists, however, this rule was not confirmed, although there was a very strong tendency for particularized crests to cluster in the higher ranks. It may be that the rule is essentially a function of the relationship between rank and wealth. Since it was necessary, in order to validate a particularized crest, to have both an inherited right to it and the wealth needed to stage a potlatch, or at least to participate in a relative's potlatch, the opportunities for low-ranking houses to claim particularized crests were restricted. It is also possible that the general rule given by informants pertained to the precontact period, before new wealth from the fur trade gave low-ranking houses the wealth to potlatch.

Although all particularized crests tended to cluster in the higher ranks, some were found there more often than others. For example, crests named Prince of (Animal Species), produced by the application of the operator abalone to crest animals, were consistently associated with first-ranking position in a group. Twenty-six houses claiming these crests were distributed by rank as shown in Table 5 (see Halpin 1973, Appendices I and II, for particulars): In five of the ten cases in which the Prince of (Animal Species) crest was claimed by a house other than the first-ranking house, modifying circumstances were reported by informants. In the case of the Prince of Eagles claimed by a second-ranking house, the crest representation was said to have been in red appliqué and no abalone was mentioned. Similarly, the Prince of Wolves crests claimed by houses ranking eighth and third were said to have "no pearl decoration." In each of these cases, then, an essential feature of the Prince of (Animal Species) crest—abalone—was missing. The Prince of Ravens claimed by a house ranking fourth was taken as a compensation for murder, hence was claimed by force rather than social and hereditary right. The Prince of Beavers was claimed by a Niska subclan which ranked fourth, but the name of this subclan translates as "on the beaver," and it was not considered to be of the "real" Laxskik (Eagle) clan. If it were to be considered a separate Beaver

3. Quotations in this paragraph are from the Barbeau and Beynon field notes.

TABLE 5
CRESTS DISTRIBUTED BY RANK

Crest	First Rank Houses	Other Ranks
Prince of Eagles	I, I	II
Prince of Wolves	I	VIII, III
Prince of Grizzlies	I, I, I, I	XV
Prince of Bears	I, I	II
Prince of Killerwhales	I, I, I, I	II
Prince of Ravens	I, I	II, IV
Prince of Beavers		subclan IV
Prince of Cormorants	I	
Prince of Martens		V

clan in its own right, its highest-ranking house could be considered a first-ranking house.

Of the other houses claiming Prince of (Animal Species) crests, houses ranking second claimed three and a house ranking third claimed one. The only two instances, then, of a Prince of (Animal Species) crest being claimed by low-ranking houses for which there were no extenuating circumstances recorded were the Prince of Grizzlies crest claimed by a house ranked fifteenth and the Prince of Martens crest claimed by a house ranked fifth. These are the only such cases out of the twenty-six recorded instances of this type of crest and are considered atypical.

Other widespread crests consistently claimed by houses of high rank (I to IV) were those formed by the addition of the operator white to crest animals, as in White Raven, White Bear, White Owl, White Marten, and so forth. It was therefore no surprise to discover a particular kind of chief's hat that seems to have no specific crest associations, but which combines the two prestigious operators abalone and white. An example of this kind of hat is in the British Columbia Provincial Museum (Catalogue Number 1531). It is a cap of ermine skin (mounted on a cloth base) with rectangular pieces of abalone sewn on it. It was collected by C. F. Newcombe on the Nass River in 1913 and called simply "chief's cap." It is at this point, with a chiefly symbol having no crest associations but utilizing prestigious crest operators, that we can clearly see Tsimshian ceremonial headdresses shifting from the horizontal axis to the vertical axis expressing rank.

HUMAN AND MONSTER CRESTS

The crests so far described are clearly totemic both in form and function, conforming to the general totemic model derived from Lévi-Strauss's so-called totemism. We turn now to two categories of crests, human and monster, which not only do not conform to the totemic model but move in the opposite direction. Although my explanation for these crests is provisional, I believe that defining them as problematical forms, especially in relation to totemic crests, is useful and I hope it will direct further attention to them.

The first baffling category of crests is the one deriving from the human, forms of which were claimed by houses in all four clans in all three divisions of the Tsimshian. At least three identical human crests were claimed by houses in different clans: the Two-Headed Man by the Laxkibu, Laxskik, and Gispudwada; the Whole Being by the Laxskik and Ganhada; and the Robe of Scalps by the Laxkibu and Ganhada. This, of course, runs counter to the basic principle of totemic systems: differences or discontinuities between *natural species* are used to characterize differences between *human groups*. Use of the human in crests, and in crests claimed by all four clans, obviously invalidated such crests from functioning as totemic classifiers. Furthermore, since human crests were claimed by houses of all ranks, they could not have functioned as symbols of rank. They were so widely distributed throughout the Tsimshian crest system that they could have been some kind of pan-Tsimshian symbol.

The beginning of an explanation for the widespread distribution of human crests was suggested to me by the crest representations on Gitksan totem poles (see plates in Barbeau 1929). Many of these poles display both human and animal figures. If we exclude for the moment the crest aspect of the human representations, and regard them only as the generalized humans they are to the eye—human representations characterized by a bland and almost boring sameness (in contrast to masks, which exhibit great variability)—they can then only be distinguished by their relationship to different sets of animal figures. In other words, the humans on the poles have little or no difference or distinction in the absence of the totemic animals with which they are associated. Similarly, according to the totemic principle, the sameness of human beings in society is differentiated by the association of people with different animal species. Before attempting further discussion of this visual dimension, it is necessary to present the other category of problematical crests, the monsters.

An unexpectedly large number of crests fall into this category, which I have called monsters because they are composite animal and animal/human forms not found in nature. They were most often described as bird-like creatures, often with recurved beaks, which were subject to transformation into other forms, such as sea monsters and humanlike creatures. Significantly, Tsimshian informants had difficulty in providing English glosses for the native names for these crests, resorting to such terms as "extinct," "hawklike," or "like an eagle, but not an eagle," indicative of the lack of natural prototypes for these forms. Some examples of monster crests are the *gibelk*, which was said to be a large monster with a head like an eagle and a large fin protruding from its back; also said to have wings and human forms around its face and on its back; also said to be related to the Supernatural Mosquito; also said to resemble a human being. The *xskemsem* was said to be a bird like an eagle but with a more recurved beak; also said to be an extinct bird like an eagle; also said not to be a hawk.[4] The *tsagaxło* ("hooked nose" or "glass nose") was said to be a bird with a recurved beak, with characteristics of a thunderbird; also said to be a human with a long, hooked, recurved nose; also said to be a human with a large belly and a sharp or glasslike nose. The *laxom* ("on top") was said to be a supernatural bird with a long, straight beak; also a human with a long nose; also a human with a recurved beak. The *hagwelox* was described as a sea monster, usually a killerwhale, but also having aspects of grizzly; its fin was a dangerous snag; another *hagwelox* was said to be a large box full of humans, with a fin, which swam as though alive. The *winil* ("large eyes") was described as a bird with a long recurved beak. Most of these crests were claimed by houses in more than one clan. (The information in this paragraph comes from crest lists in the Barbeau and Beynon field notes; see Halpin 1973:157–160.)

Why monsters? There were still many unused animals in the natural environment of the Tsimshian with which they might have extended the horizontal axis of the crest system. Instead, they actually blurred the distinctions between animals already used in the system by tranferring attributes between them. Some kind of reverse process was taking place, one that created crests of a new order. Crests

---

4. No hawk crest was reported in the crest lists, despite the widespread assumption that birds with recurved beaks are hawks.

that contained echoes of animals already used, but in a bewildering complex of parts and transformations: one bird becomes another, birds become humans, humans have beaks, killerwhales are also grizzlies.

The deeper we penetrate the secrets of Northwest Coast thought, the more we find transformation as its essence. The ever-shifting of life substance between forms. It is so clear in the art. Edmund Carpenter (1975:9) says it well (see also Goldman 1975):

> When depicting . . . reality, Northwest Coast artists often showed two beings simultaneously occupying a single space by sharing various parts. Such visual puns did more than express complexity: they depicted transformation. Before one's eyes, Bear became Wolf, and then Bear again. The image didn't change, of course. What changed was the observer's organization of its parts. But the effect was one of transformation.

The visual experience of transformative gestalts at our nineteenth-century Tsimshian potlatch must have been especially powerful when a person wearing a crest headdress raised and lowered his or her head, becoming successively human/animal/human/animal.

Monster crests, I will hypothesize, are human and animal forms merged into even more concentrated and powerful images which are embodiments of the transformative act itself. They were, as we have already seen, elusive and ambiguous forms in the minds of Barbeau's informants, with unnatural concatenations of parts and attributes, both animal and human. As ever-shifting forms, they force the mind to focus on something other than the forms themselves— that is, on the transformations between them. No longer imprisoned in fixed natural forms, they are supernatural forces, more energy than substance. They are power itself, some of them personified, as George MacDonald argues (elsewhere in this volume) from mythological evidence, as capricious Chiefs of Wealth.

Tsimshian Grandchildren

Redistributive Mechanisms in Personal Property Inheritance

John Asher Dunn

~~~~~~

This paper is dedicated to the proposition that the attitudinal, the connotative, is central to anthropological inquiry, and to the proposition that the current positivist-etic trend in American cognitive anthropology lacks balance. More importantly, it is dedicated with gratitude, respect, and affection to Viola Garfield, whose published work and personal knowledge comprise a rich storehouse of the Tsimshian sentiment. Finally, it is dedicated to all those Tsimshian people who have worked with anthropologists; they have made grandchildren of us all.

I

Writers on Tsimshian society have always said that the Tsimshian peoples are divided into four exogamous matrilineal totemic groups, called "phratries" or "clans" by anthropologists and "tribes" or [bupʰtʃéx] by Tsimshian people. Until recently, available field data from the Tsimshian were collected either in Ottawa (Sapir 1915; 1920) or in one of the post-contact Tsimshian villages, namely Port Simpson (Boas 1911; 1912; 1916; Garfield 1939) or Metlakatla (Beynon 1941). The traditional anthropological characterization of Tsimshian society as quadripartite is certainly accurate based on these data. But recent fieldwork (Adams 1973; Dunn and Dunn 1972) indicates that the aboriginal villages of both the Gitksan and the Coast Tsimshian were quadripartite in quite a different sense. This older societal arrangement still exists, or is at least remembered, in the precontact villages of Kitkatla and Hartley Bay and in the Gitksan villages.

In most of these towns only two of the four phratries or tribes are present. This is very nearly true in reality and absolutely true ideally, that is, in the thinking of the people involved. Garfield is aware of this fact (1951:19), as was Boas (1895:50). The combination of phratries in a particular village is, furthermore, not random but structurally restricted. In Kitkatla most people are either Killerwhale or Raven; in Hartley Bay most are Killerwhale or Eagle. Only Wolf and Raven were present in Kitwancool in the latter part of the nineteenth century (Boas 1895:50). In the Gitksan villages most people are either Frog or one of the following: Eagle, Wolf, or Fireweed (Adams 1973:23). It is not conceivable that a coast village would be comprised of Killerwhale and Wolf or of Raven and Eagle. The limitations on phratry combinations begin to make sense when they are related to the Haida and Tlingit moiety systems. In interethnic marriages a Haida Raven could not marry a Tsimshian who was either Killerwhale or Wolf; a Haida Eagle could not marry Tsimshian Ravens or Eagles; a Tlingit Raven could marry neither Tsimshian Ravens nor Eagles, and so on (Boas 1916:521–22; Garfield 1939:230–31). In Hartley Bay it is said that "Wolf goes with Killerwhale" and that the two should not marry. Tsimshian society at the village level was dual and was comprised of one subphratry or submoiety from each of two divisions (see Fig. 1), and, furthermore, it is evident that these divisions were interethnic or panethnic on the North Pacific Coast. Boas found an indication of this in his comparative analysis of crest distributions (1916:521) and Garfield confirmed it by direct inquiry (1939:231). William Beynon hints at this dual Tsimshian system in his unpublished materials (1953), while John Adams has found most direct and explicit evidence for it: in Kitwanga with Eagle, Wolf, and Frog houses present, both Wolf and Eagle must marry Frog, i.e., Eagle and Wolf "form a single Crest" (1973:23). Adams' data contradict the usual association of Fireweed with Killerwhale (Garfield 1951:19); one would expect that Wolf could not marry Fireweed (see Fig. 1) and that Wolf and Fireweed would form the single crest. Barbeau found that in Kispiox, Fireweed could not

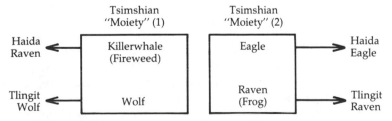

Fig. 1. North Coast interethnic moiety "brothers" (from Garfield 1939:230; 1951:19)

marry Wolf or vice-versa but both must marry Frog (1929:155); Adams, however, could not confirm this apparently lapsed Kispiox moiety arrangement (1973:23). All four submoiety totems are present in Port Simpson and in Metlakatla because these post-contact villages are amalgamations of people from many older villages (Beynon 1941; Dorsey 1897; Duff 1965:18–19; Dunn 1970:10–13; Garfield 1939:175–77). It is evidently in these later towns that the quadripartite exogamy developed.

In the aboriginal villages, however, the quadripartite system was not defined solely in terms of exogamy but was derived by the paradigmatic intersection of submoiety membership with house membership. *This* quadripartite system was, furthermore, egocentric or relative, rather than sociocentric or absolute. The moiety appearance of the precontact village is relevant only to this egocentric paradigm. It tends to disappear when one begins to look at intersubjectively defined groups. Coast Tsimshian people conceive of village society in terms of their own house [wa·pʰ], inside versus outside, and in terms of their own totemic division [pʰtʃɛx], own side versus other side (see Fig. 2). One recognizes "others" as either (1) my own side (tribe) of my house, (2) the other side of my house, (3) my tribe of another house, or (4) the unrelated.

Adams describes a similar situation for the Gitksan (1973:21–50). Each of the four categories, including and especially the fourth— the unrelated—will consist of persons one considers kinsmen (see Fig. 3). The first division—my own side of my house—will consist of my matrilineal kin group defined in terms of its own crest, privileges, and, formerly, the house (building) occupied by its adult male members. The second division—the other side of my house—includes the wives of the male members of the first division and their children. The third division includes distant matrilineal relatives whose male membership formerly occupied other houses. The fourth division—the unrelated or other side-outside—will include the speaker's adult sons, if the speaker is male, and other kinsmen as discussed in part II of this paper.

Three of these four divisions, namely those which include one's own house or tribe in their description, i.e., (1) my own tribe of my house, (3) my tribe of another house, and (2) children of my house, are sociocentric categories in an egocentric domain. Thus the precontact quadripartite village system is egocentric in character while at the same time utilizing sociocentric concepts. It is in some sense a compromise between or synthesis of two imperfect systems: on the one hand, a dual egocentric classification (my side-other side)

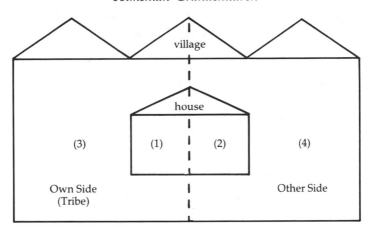

Fig. 2. Egocentric quadripartite division of a precontact town

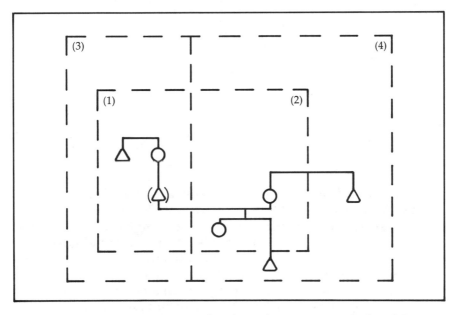

Fig. 3. Village division membership of some important kinsfolk

which characterizes a man's adult sons as "unrelated," and on the other hand a tripartite sociocentric organization (tribe-house-children of the house), which fails to characterize spouses at all (see Fig. 4).

As a male child I will live in my father's house and will be con-

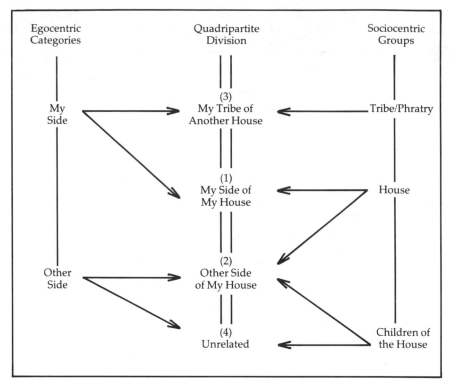

Fig. 4. Synthesis of egocentric and sociocentric categories

sidered a child of his house and a member of the other side of his house. As a man I would have in the past lived in my maternal uncle's home, the focal point of my house, and my father would have still considered me a child of his house but would have been unable to call me "other side" of his house and unwilling to call me "other side-outside," i.e., unrelated. I cannot be a stranger to him, yet as an adult I would have no longer been a part of his house and never was a part of his tribe. A woman, unmarried, married, or widowed, could have been both child of her father's house and still a member of the other side of his house. It is only when a woman was currently married to someone other than her paternal cross cousin that she lived away from her father and acquired the status of child of her father's house without local designation. The details of house membership and residence rules are thoroughly described in Garfield (1939).

The ambiguity surrounding children of the house seems to be related to the fact that the egocentric categories of the sociocentrically
compromised village division system are in themselves compro-
mises between kin defined categories and locally defined groups (see
Fig. 5). The house has two sides. My side of my house consisted
not only of my matrilineal kinsfolk living with the household head
but also of matrilineally connected children living away in the houses
of their fathers and of matrilineally connected women married out.
The other side of one's house encompassed only non-clansfolk actually living in the home (for an adult male speaker) or only the
non-clansfolk living in one's maternal uncle's home (for a woman
or a child speaker).

Egocentric categories are by their nature kinship defined. Yet the
Tsimshian expressions "my side" and "other side" imply location.
The division "my side of my house," bristling with local designa-
tors, was nevertheless a category encompassing dispersed kinsmen
with but a localized core: the personnel of the home of the house
chief. On the other hand the "other side of my house" was a local
group, including women, possibly unrelated among themselves before their marriages into the same house, and the children of these
unrelated women, children all of the same house, who, as far as
their fathers were concerned, fell into a kind of limbo when they

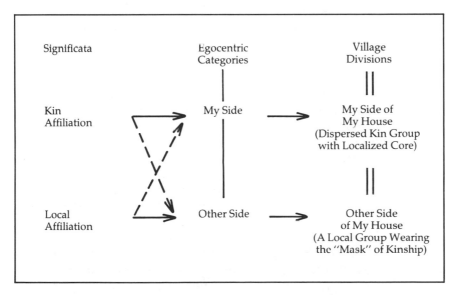

Fig. 5. Synthesis of egocentric categories

left his home. The only thing that made them a kin group was the place where they were born. The actual local arrangements as described here rarely exist at present, but the local aspect of division definitions is still valid in the minds of those who remember. In summary, if the quadripartite village division is an egocentric system resulting from the interplay of egocentric and sociocentric primitive terms, the egocentric primitive terms are themselves the result of an even more profound interplay between kin and locale.

II

How does this egocentric village division, derived from a series of accommodations, locale/kin, individual/society, relate to that other egocentric classification, the kin terminological system? The answer to this question as well as to the question, "What *is* the kinship terminology?" are a crucial part of appreciating what a Tsimshian grandchild is. Boas was the first to collect anything that remotely resembled a complete terminology (1916), but it was Theresa Durlach who very meticulously extracted this terminology from Boas' mythology texts and from other less complete sources (1928). The Boas/Durlach terminology, of course, does not contain a complete set of kin-type denotata, but only the translations from the texts. Sapir collected the first complete set of denotata (1920), but for the cognate Nass River terms rather than for Tsimshian proper. In 1968, L. Dunn and I collected the linguistic terms and what we believe to be a complete set of denotata, using real and abstract genealogies, from three informants, all from Kitkatla, all female, and all more than sixty years of age (Dunn and Dunn 1972). Data were collected independently from each, and their responses were remarkably consistent. The terminological data are compared in Table 1. See also Kasakoff's essay in this volume.

It is important for the development of the subsequent parts of this paper to call attention to certain aspects of the kinship system. First, the term "grandfather" can connote "ancestor." In none of the data sources do the terms for grandparents denote parallel cousins of any generation, nor is there any term in any data source to refer to parallel cousins in any ascending generation. Second the term "grandchild" is a singular and remarkable discrepancy in the denotata given by my respondents and by Sapir's: the Kitkatla call certain parallel cousins of descending generations "grandchildren," but the Nass do not. Note that in the other terms there is a close correspondence between the Nass River and the Kitkatla denotations. These cousin grandchildren, whom the Kitkatla respondents distinguished as a group by excluding them from the denotation of the semantically endocentric expression "own grandchildren," include FBSC(C) and MZCC; there is no term denoting their reciprocals, i.e., for $(\{^M_F\})$FFB$\{^S_D\}$ and $\{^M_F\}$MZ$\{^S_D\}$. "Grandfather" thus *connotes* not only "ancestor" but also the reciprocal of "cousin grandchild," or, the "cousin grandfather." The Kitkatla expression for ancestor, "father of our grandfather," now takes on new, rich and unexpected significance, specifically, $(\{^M_F\})$FFB and $\{^M_F\}$MZH. Note that FB and MZH are denotata of [ʼag^{W}ɪnəg^{w}át^h] (*distant father*) and that FFB is a denotatum of [ʼyéʼɛ] (*grandfather*). Finally FBSC(C) and MZCC must be seen as standing somewhere between being denotata and connotata of "grandchild." This elaborate connotational system, or symbolic use of grandparent-grandchild terms, plays a central role in the inheritance of personal property, the subject of this paper.

Before I discuss the inheritance system in detail, I still must show the relationship between the egocentric quadripartite village structure and the kinship terminology. Table 2 shows all the possible village division memberships that denotata of kin terms can have, assuming any marriage possibility except for parallel cousin marriage.

In any attempt at a componential analysis of Tsimshian kin terms, the use of etic kin attributes of the culture of anthropology (for example, sex of relative, generation) is doomed to failure. Any formal semantic analysis of this system that is limited to operations on genealogically derived denotata will be equally disappointing and even a waste of time. The structural properties of the Tsimshian terminological system responsible for this state of affairs are present in both Sapir's data and the Kitkatla data and are discussed in detail in Dunn and Dunn (1972). Briefly, there are several sets of kin terms none of which can be given a unique componential definition based on genealogical features. At the same time there are sequences of equivalence-reduction-expansion rules which must operate in some sets of terms but improperly collapse and confuse other sets. The only solution for someone committed to ignoring connotation is to conclude that Tsimshian kinship terms do not comprise a solitary semantic domain. Then the problem becomes how to characterize the cognitively real category "my kinspeople" [wɪlwʊlá·ysgu].

The use of features derived from the egocentric quadripartite village division system in any attempt at a componential analysis of [wɪlwʊlá·ysgu], although also ultimately unsuccessful, nevertheless divides the category into useful subcategories. Put in another way,

TABLE 1
Tsimshian Kin Terms

Dunn/Dunn	Boas/Durlach	Sapir/Nass
1. [ʔyéʔɛ] FF, MF, FFB, MFB	[yấ'ⁱᵒ] FF, MF, MMB	[nyeˈ'] FF, MF, FFB MFB, MMB, FMB FFF, FMF, MFF, MMF
1.1 ancestor: "father of our grandfather"	ancestor	
2. [ncʃíʔiʔcˀ] FM, MM	[(n)ʤzdēˀⁱᵒdz] FM, MM	[ŋʦˈseˈˈe'ˈs] FM, MM, MMM, MFM, FMM, FFM
2.1 [ʔagʷuncʃíʔiʔc>] FMZ, FFZ, MFZ, MMZ		
3. [ₕʧʷgeu] F, FB	[(nE)gwấ'ⁱᵒp] F	[pcⁱ·ᶜₘgeu] F, FB, MZH
3.1 [ₕʧʷgeugʋc] FB, MZH		
4. [nəbⁱpₕ] MB, FZH	[(nE)bⁱˀⁱᵒp] MB	[dʒədeu] MB
5. [nc·] M, MZ, MBW, FBW	[(na)lấ(n-ôx)] M, MZ	[nω·ˈ'] M, MZ 5.1 [ẋcuꭓᵖ] FRW

5.2	[*nəkʰtʃä·*] FZ	[*ínE)ktä·*] FZ	[*nɔxdä·'*] MBW, FZ
6.	[*wekʸⁱʰ*] ♂B, ♂FBS, ♂MZS	[*waik·*], [*waȧk·*] ♂B	[*wag*] ♂B, ♂FBS, ♂MZS, ♀MZS
7.	[*ƚᵞⁱmktʰⁱ*] ♂Z, ♂FBD, ♂MZD ♀B, ♀FBS, ♀MZS	[*ƚᵉmkdäʔ*] ♂Z, ♀B	[*ƚ̣umxtl'*] ♂Ẑ, ♂FBD, ♂MZD ♀B, ♀FBS, ♀MZS
8.	[*ƚgá·wkʰ*] ♀Z, ♀FBD, ♀MZD, ♂MZD	[*ƚga'uk*] ♀Z	[*ƚgiʼgw*] ♀Z, ♀FBD, ♀MZD, ♂MZD
9.	[*ƚgʷⁱtʰaʔɔ·*] FZC, MBC FZSW, FZDH	[*ƚgu)txaä*] FZC, MBC	[*kwvtxaʔω·'*] FZC, MBC
9.1	[*ʔagʷⁱʔɔ́ʔɔ*] FZCC, MBCC		
10.	[*ƚquƚkʰ*] C, BC, HBC, HZC, WZC, WBC	[*ƚgǘⁱᵒᴺk(s)*] C	[*ƚo·'ᵘᵞgw*] C, ♂BC, ♀ZC, HBC ♂BWC, WZC, ♀ZHC
11.	[*ƚⁱkʰʔtʼa·yn*] CC, FBSC FMSCC, MZCC	[*ƚukta'en*] CC	[*hoxdä·ʔkʼen*] CC, CCC
11.1	[*ʔagʷⁱƚⁱkʰtʃáʔyn*] (Hartley Bay and Metlakatla) CCC	[*agwi-ƚukta'en*] CCC, descendant	

TABLE 1 (*continued*)
TSIMSHIAN KIN TERMS

Dunn/Dunn	Boas/Durlach	Sapir/Nass
11.2 [*ʔúʔlis*] (Kitkatla) CCC, MZCCC, great grandparent	[*ōˀoˀlis*] great grandparent, great grandson	[*oˑˀˀls*] great grandparent
12. [*ʔnɑks*] H, W	[*nɑks*] H, W	[*näˀk̯c*] H, W
13. [*ɬems*] WM, WF, HM, HF, SW, DH, MZSW, MZDH	[*ɬɑms*] WM, WF, HM, HF SW, HD	[*ɬämc*] WF, HF, WM, HM, SW, DH, WFB, HFB, WMB, HMB
13.1 [*ʔɑgʷiɬems*] CSW, CDH		
14. [*ɬgʷiȝús*] ♀BW, HZ, ♀FBSW	[*ɬgu-)dzus*] ♀BW, HZ	[*kʷvdjiˑˀc*] ♀BW, HZ
15. [*ɬukʃɔˑtʰks*] ♂BW, ♂FBSW, ZH WB, WZ, HB, FBDH	[*ɬgu)kɬátks*] ♂BW, WZ	[*k̯ˀωˑtˀks*] ♂BW, ♀ZH, WZ, HB

TABLE 2
VILLAGE DIVISION ALLOCATION OF KINSFOLK

	Village Divisions			
	(1) own side own house	(2) other side own house	(3) own tribe another house	(4) other side out- side
Kin Designation				
1. [ʔyéʔɛ]	+	+	+	+
2. [ncʕíʔiʔc˃]	+	+	−	+
2.1 [ʔagʷʊncʕíʔiʔc˃]	+	+	+	+
3. [nəgʷátʰ]	−	−	−	+
3.1 [ʔagʷʊnəgʷátʰ]	−	−	−	+
4. [nəbípʰ]	+	+	+	+
5. [nɔ·]	+	+	+	+
5.2 [nəkʰtʕá·]	−	+	−	+
6. [wɛkʸʰ] ♂ego	+	−	+	+
7. [ɬṃkʰtʰí]	+	+	+	+
8. [ɬgá·wkʰ] ♀ego	+	+	+	+
♂ego	+	−	−	−
9. [ɬgʷɨtʰaʔɔ·]	+	+	+	+
9.1 [ʔagʷɔ́ʔɔʔ]	+	+	+	+
10. [ɬguɬkʰ]	+	+	+	+
10.1 [ɬgʷɨslískʰ]	+	+	−	−
11. [ɬikʰtʕáʔyn]	+	+	+	+
11.2 [ʔúʔlis]	+	+	+	+
12. [ʔnɑks] ♀ego	−	−	−	+
♂ego	−	+	−	−
13. [ɬɛms]	+	+	+	+
13.1 [ʔagʷiɬɛ́ms]	+	+	+	+
14. [ɬgʷɨʒús] ♀ego	+	+	+	+
15. [ɬukʕɔ́·tʰks]	+	+	+	+

it is possible that the cognitive organization of Tsimshian society includes, but is not confined to, a tree arrangement of classes of people, which is created by the intersection of village division features and kinship term features (see Fig. 6).

Class 1 as identified in figure 6 is large and includes all but six (for female ego) or eight (for male ego) of the kin terms. Although

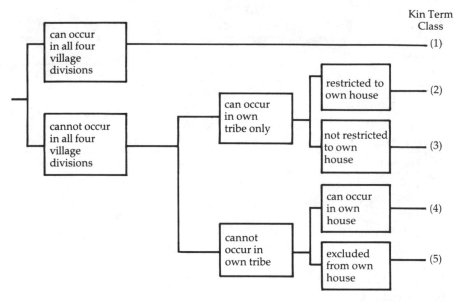

Fig. 6. Toward a componential analysis of own kinspeople

much more data need to be collected to confirm it, a pattern seems to be emerging demonstrating that class 1 relatives, who can appear in any of the four village divisions, have, relatively speaking, more precisely delimited connotative value; the other four classes of relatives, with more restricted denotative value, have richer connotative structure. In other words there is an inverse relationship between denotative and connotative complexity.

Class 5—those relatives who are excluded from ego's own house and tribe—consists of males who have taken (or, who typically take) as wives women from ego's own side of ego's own house (see Table 3). Class 4—those excluded from ego's tribe but not from his house—consists of females who have been given (or, who are typically given) as wives to ego's own house and of women *owed* to ego's house by virtue of the gift of ego's mother to ego's father, i.e., the father's sister. Class 3—tribal relatives not limited to one's own house—includes only those women one calls "grandmother," women who may be viewed as given away (locale frame) yet kept (tribe/house frame). Class 2 relatives are house-mates, where for female ego "house" can mean locale, kin group, or *both* (see Table 4). Classes 2 through 5 show a progressive enrichment or ambiguity of role connotation, from the simple "woman-taker" of class 5 to the complex "house-mate" of class 2. See Table 5.

TABLE 3
[WɪLWɪLÁ·YSGU] CLASSES

Class	♀ ego	♂ ego	Role(s)
(1)	[ʾyéʾɛ], [ɬikʰtˤáʾyn], . . . etc.		---
(2)	[ɬgʷislískʰ]	[ɬgʷislískʰ], [wékʸʰ], [ɬgá·wkʰ]	house mates
(3)	[ṇcˤiʾíˤcˀ]		given/kept women
(4)	[nəkʰtʃá·]	[nəkʰtʃá·] [ʾnáks]	received/ receivable women
(5)	[nəgʷátʰ] [ʾagʷɪnəgʷátʰ] [ʾnáks]	[nəgʷátʰ] [ʾagʷɪnəgʷátʰ]	wife takers

TABLE 4
CONNOTATIVE AMBIGUITY/RICHNESS OF CLASS 2 RELATIVES

meaning of "house"	♀ ego	♂ ego			
locale	BC	BC	B	FBS	MZS
			↕		⋮
kin-group	ZC	ZC	B	MZD	MZS

The paradoxical character of Tsimshian society is now apparent. Kin terms restricted as to village quarter are yet undifferentiated as to role. Grandmother is both given and withheld. Niece is both received and not received. Kinsfolk who cannot be defined in terms of village quarter have more narrowly defined roles. Grandfather is giver; grandchild is receiver.

III

The roles of grandfather and grandchild were succinctly described in the following statement quoted in translation from one of my Kitkatla respondents (Brown 1968):

I'm going to tell you what I heard when I was a little girl. I saw some of the traditions of the old people, of our ancestors, of our grandfathers, of our uncles. In the old days when the mother's brother died, then the sister's son stood up and talked about the belongings of his uncle. He took all the property of his uncle. Our grandfathers and uncles did not argue about wills. They followed their own laws and customs. Their sisters' children and their grandchildren could talk about their possessions.

"Talk about" in this context is a euphemism for "take one's share of." The relationship of this kind of inheritance to the distribution of a dead chief's property as described by Garfield (1939:235–47) is unclear to me.

Upon investigating specific past family situations I noticed that lineal grandchildren did not have a share in the inheritance. Upon asking about this I was told, "The own grandchildren don't get anything; it comes back to them in the next generation" (Vickers 1971). There seems to be, then, a cognitively real discrimination of "own grandchildren" as opposed to grandchildren in general. Furthermore, "own grandchildren," that is, lineal descendants, are marked for exclusion in the inheritance system. This is true in Kitkatla but not in Hartley Bay where the grandchild category is undivided and all share in an inheritance. Although I am not aware of any such Kitkatla lexical category, for the sake of convenience I will refer to "grandchildren" other than "own grandchildren" as "inheritor

TABLE 5
DIMENSIONS OF AMBIGUITY IN THE ASSIGNMENT OF ROLES TO KIN TERM CLASSES

(5)	(4)	(3)	(2)
---	received/receivable	given/kept	given/kept; received/receivable
---	---	tribe/locale	tribe/locale
---	---	---	male/female (relative)
---	---	---	male/female (ego)

grandchildren." Kitkatla inheritor grandchildren are MZCC, FBSC, FBSCC. If matrilateral cross-cousin marriage were the norm, then a man's own grandchildren would in fact become the inheritor grandchildren of his nephew, that is property would come back to them in the "next generation" (see Fig. 7).

This indirect evidence for an apparent preference for matrilateral marriage is in my opinion more substantial than the fact that the Tsimshian myths (Boas 1916), many of which were collected from the Nisga and Gitksan, and versions of which are found among many of the neighboring peoples, show a predilection for matrilateral marriage. Hartley Bay respondents agree among themselves that formerly a designated nephew-heir was obligated to take his uncle's widow as wife and that brother and sister might obligate their children to a matrilateral marriage if the brother were concerned for the welfare of his daughter. Garfield says that the stated ideal marriage was between cross-cousins, either first or second, and the one example she mentions from her data is of a patrilateral second cross-cousin marriage (1939:232). The traditional desirability of second cross-cousin marriage is more recently confirmed in Hartley Bay statements. The assertion from my Kitkatla respondent concerning the possibility of a delayed inheritance by own grandchildren might be interpreted simply as knowledge of the consequences of matrilateral marriage; there is no indication that matrilateral marriage will give one's children any but a situation specific inheritance advantage. In

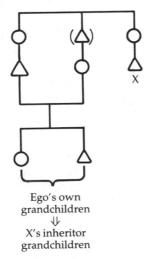

Ego's own
grandchildren
⇓
X's inheritor
grandchildren

Fig. 7. Delayed inheritance by own grandchildren

fact only a *patrilateral* union will result in what might be considered the ideal situation: an own grandchild as nephew's nephew (see Fig. 8). In light of this possibility, my respondent's remarks about delayed inheritance must be interpreted more broadly and not simply with reference to matrilateral marriage. (See Rosman and Rubel 1971 and Kasakoff 1974 for a fuller treatment of marriage among the Tsimshian.)

There is one example from the Kitkatla family histories during the early part of the twentieth century in which a patrilateral second cousin marriage was proposed by the boy's mother but rejected by the girl's father, not because it was not the preferred pattern, but because the boy's mother had mistakenly decided that the marriage would assure her own grandchildren of a share in her own father's estate, an estate then in the control of her cousin, the girl's father. Much of the factional difficulty plaguing Kitkatla in 1968 could be traced to this and similar misunderstandings and to the conflict between this inheritance system and the first attempts some years ago to use personal wills.

But no matter how families may contrive marriage, the purpose of grandchild inheritance is incompatible with any attempt to retain property exclusively in any kin group. On the contrary, the purpose of grandchild inheritance is the redistribution of wealth throughout the quadripartite village division. This must be the case since any combination of cross-cousin or non-lateral marriages will result in the presence of inheritor grandchildren in each of the four village divisions.

If a rule of matrilateral cross-cousin marriage is strictly and uni-

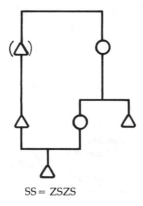

SS = ZSZS

Fig. 8. Delayed inheritance by own grandchildren

formly followed, and if only two totemic exogamous groups (tribes) are present, then the inheritor grandchildren will fall into the village divisions in the following manner: MZDS and MZDD will be in the grandfather's own side of his own house, FBSSS and FBSSD will be in the grandfather's own tribe but from another house, MZSD and FBSD (who are the same person) will, along with FBSDD, be in the other side of the grandfather's house first as children of the house and then as spouses in the house, MZSS and FBSS (who are the same person) will, along with FBSDS, be in the other side of the grandfather's house as children, and as adults they will be strangers, i.e., "other side, outside." As figure 9 indicates MZSD and FBSD would be the same person; likewise, MZSS would equal FBSS. In effect each of the four village divisions would contain one quarter of the adult inheritor grandchildren.

A consistently applied rule of patrilateral marriage in a moiety village would, according to figure 10, place one quarter of the adult inheritor grandchildren in the grandfather's own side of his own house, one quarter in the other houses of his tribe, and one half in the other side of his house as children and in the unrelated village

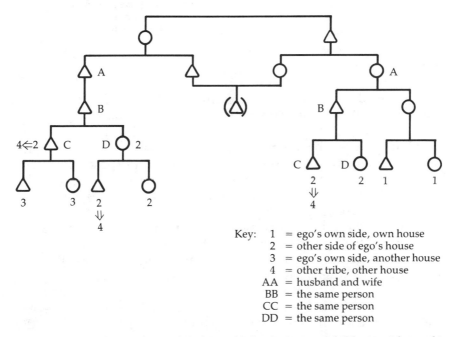

Key: 1 = ego's own side, own house
2 = other side of ego's house
3 = ego's own side, another house
4 = other tribe, other house
AA = husband and wife
BB = the same person
CC = the same person
DD = the same person

Fig. 9. Village division membership of inheritor grandchildren with a rule of matrilateral marriage

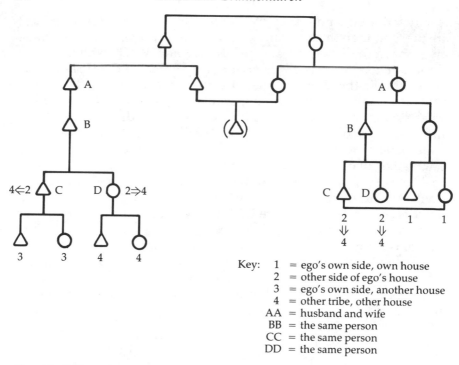

Key: 1 = ego's own side, own house
      2 = other side of ego's house
      3 = ego's own side, another house
      4 = other tribe, other house
     AA = husband and wife
     BB = the same person
     CC = the same person
     DD = the same person

Fig. 10. Village division membership of inheritor grandchildren with a rule of patrilateral marriage

division as adults. A possible economic motivation for matrilateral marriage finally becomes apparent: it will result in maximum retention of personal possessions within the house, and it will result in an absolutely equitable distribution of possessions to the four village divisions. Since it must now be clear that the purpose of the inheritance mechanism is to build the prestige of the deceased, to make him connotative grandfather and thus ancestor of all four parts of the village, a double motive for patrilateral marriage also becomes apparent: it will result in a greater distribution to the village quarter totally unrelated by tribe or house to the deceased and will thus in the logic of the potlatch accord him even greater prestige. Finally, this last quarter (unrelated, outside) contains the children of his own house.

The genius of the Tsimshian sentiment finally begins to reveal itself. The classes of inheritor grandchildren defined by village division membership are mirror images of the classes of kin terms defined by village division exclusion. Kin term class 2 from figure

6 (kinsmen restricted to ego's own house) are "housemates" and relatives of third degree or closer. At the same time they for the most part can be housemates in a locale sense or in the sense of tribe but not both at the same time (see Table 4). Related to them are the inheritor grandchildren that fall into village division (1) from figure 2, i.e., MZDS and MZDD; they are also housemates with the difference that, being fourth-degree relatives, they are, nevertheless, housemates in the sense of both tribe and locale. Closer relatives are not housemates in the fullest sense of the word, but more distant relatives are housemates fully. Kin term class 3 (grandmothers) includes women given away (locale sense) by ego's house, yet kept (tribe sense). By contrast inheritor grandchildren in the other side of ego's house, i.e., MZSD, FBSD, FBSDD of village division 2, are women kept (locale sense) in ego's house, yet lost (tribe sense). Kin term class 3 and the inheritor grandchildren in village division 2 are connotative reciprocals and mirror-image opposites. Kin term class 4 (aunt and wife) includes women received into the other side of the house and "owed" to the house; inheritor grandchildren of own tribe, another house, i.e., FBSSS and FBSSD in village division 3, are persons neither received nor owed, not in a tribal sense or in a local sense. Kin term class 5 consists of wife takers, F, FB, MZH, and H; inheritor grandchildren in other tribe and other house, i.e., MZSS, FBSS, and FBSDS in village division 4, are "given-away-men," sons of the house who have left the protection of their fathers for the protection of their uncles. Table 6 summarizes these connotative reciprocal relationships between village division exclusion classes and village division defined categories of inheritor grandchildren.

IV

The naming of collateral grandchildren as inheritors of personal property is not inheritance at all if inheritance is a mechanism for identifying or maintaining the corporate property holding group. At one and the same time it is a redistributive mechanism and a ceremonial-symbolic act which calls attention to the alliance myth (see Lévi-Strauss 1969; Mauss 1954).

First, it is a redistributive, anti-inheritance mechanism involving property of economic value. It is a kind of inheritance tax levied against the inheritance of clan privileges, which are a kind of socioritual property. It involves a distribution of property to kin and nonkin in both sides of the village and both within and without the house. It is a custom more related to potlatch than to inheritance,

TABLE 6
SOME CONNOTATIVE RECIPROCALS

Kin Term Class	Inheritor Grandchild Class
(2) housemates close relatives not housemates in fullest sense	housemates (1) distant relatives housemates in fullest sense
(3) grandmothers lost to ego← (locale) →kept by ego kept by ego← (tribe) →lost to ego	granddaughters (2)
(4) aunt/wife received by ego owed to ego	FBSSS, FBSSD (3) neither received nor owed
(5) father/husband wife-takers	grandsons (4) given-away-men

and one must wonder if it was not used as an alternative to potlatch in a time when the potlatch was suppressed. It is an occasion for the family of the deceased to turn their uncle's property of economic value into property of prestige value more suitable to his new status, a dead man; this prestige value validates his new status as ancestor-grandfather of the four parts of society. It places the whole village in a dependent grandchild relationship to the dead man and to his house. It elevates the dead man's father's house to a distant and remote position of prestige and respect. Since the father's house members play important roles in the life-cycle rites (Garfield 1939:215, 220–23, 235–47), this house must be seen as parental to or the establisher of one's own house. Thus consequent to the inheritance-distribution it becomes "father of the new grandfather," and, deprived of any inheritance from that house, it nevertheless gains much in prestige. The [dé·wl], or funeral payment, made to the father's family is considered compensation for expenses incurred and *not* payment for services rendered.

Second, it is a ceremonial-symbolic act. It is a symbol of alliance in that it causes the daughters of the house, strangers in blood, to remember that they have been given and received into the protection of the deceased. It is a symbol of the alliance myth in that it causes given-away men, house sons who have become strangers, unaffiliated in lineage or locale, to remember the basic social debt, according to the principle of reciprocity, that their own lineages and houses owe to the lineage and house of the deceased, the house where they were once children and have become grandchildren. Finally, it is a symbol of the alliance myth in that it silhouettes the quadripartite society created by the exchange-studded intersection of hearth and totem.

Tsimshian Potlatch and Society

Examining a Structural Analysis

J. DANIEL VAUGHAN

~~~~~~

Rosman and Rubel's *Feasting with Mine Enemy* (1971) is intended as a contribution to the understanding of the potlatch and social organization on the Northwest Coast. In that work, the authors look at the potlatch and social organization in six Northwest Coast cultures in light of theories of marriage alliance and exchange developed by Lévi-Strauss. It is the purpose of this chapter to critique the analysis of Rosman and Rubel insofar as it treats Tsimshian data. Specifically, I will address myself to the way Rosman and Rubel used the ethnographic data to test their analysis. Much of this data comes from the work of Viola Garfield (e.g., 1939, 1951).

My aim is to point out certain problems in using descriptive data to support formal characterizations such as the model proposed by Rosman and Rubel. I should stress that my argument is not intended to be an empirical stand against structuralism, at least not structuralism in the Lévi-Straussian sense. But I will deal with how Rosman and Rubel have presented data in support of a structural model.

Following the theories of Marcel Mauss and Claude Lévi-Strauss, Rosman and Rubel perceive the unity of all societies to rest on certain principles of human interaction. One of the more important involves the notion of exchange and reciprocity between people or groups. The exchange of goods, services, and commodities between groups has long been recognized as an important aspect of the overall social organization of any society. Among certain kinds of societies it has been shown that intermarriage between groups is comparable to exchange of commodities between groups (see Lévi-Strauss 1969). This idea might be easier to grasp if marriage was itself viewed as a form of exchange. Lévi-Strauss discusses it as the exchange of spouses, usually women, between groups.

Two groups that systematically intermarry and exchange women over time can be said to have a marriage-alliance relationship with each other. Thus societies are composed of groups establishing, maintaining, and sometimes changing marriage-alliance relationships among themselves. When the composition of these groups is determined by a system of unilineal descent, the kinship terminology frequently is interwoven in such a way that anthropologists characterize the groups of this society as practicing "cross-cousin" or classificatory cross-cousin marriage. It is not the case that all societies made up of unilineal descent groups practice cross-cousin marriage, but neither is it altogether an uncommon occurrence. For those that do, schematic relationships between groups intermarrying can be diagrammed according to the particular form of cross-cousin marriage practiced.

There are basically three forms of cross-cousin marriage recognized by anthropologists: matrilateral, when a man marries a woman in the category of mother's brother's daughter (MBD); patrilateral, when a man marries a woman in the category of father's sister's daughter (FZD); and bilateral cross-cousin marriage, when a man marries a woman who is either a matrilateral or a patrilateral cross-cousin. Each of these marriage types, if consistently practiced, generates a different form of exchange and alliance relationship between groups. Models of each can be diagrammed.

Rosman and Rubel propose a model of matrilateral cross-cousin marriage for the Tsimshian on the basis of an expressed preference for this type of marriage reported both by Boas (1916:440) and Garfield (1939:231–32).

According to this model proposed by Rosman and Rubel, a male is married to a female who stands related to him as MBD. It is also the case that the males from any particular descent group (take B for example) marry women from just one other descent group (C). The females of group B consistently marry their father's sister's sons (FZS), who are always from group A. Rosman and Rubel propose this model as characteristic of Tsimshian social organization, and they liken it to the Jingpaw Kachin *mayu-dama* (wife-giver/wife-taker) marriage system as it has been described by Edmund Leach (1971). The men of group B are viewed as the wife-takers to group C and wife-givers to Group A. Although not every marriage must conform to the preference, at least one marriage must be forged in every generation to maintain the alliance.

Rosman and Rubel are intent on validating this model empirically, yet they offer marriage data as only a secondary means of doing so. They reason that if exchange, as it takes place in the Tsimshian potlatch, could be viewed as conforming to the pattern of wife-exchange in the marriage model, then a structural relationship between marriage and potlatch would be demonstrated. This would be the case if they could show that when group B gives a potlatch they would host group A and give them wealth. From the point of view of any one group, wealth and women would move via exchange in the same direction. Therefore, group B would be recipients of feasts and wealth at those potlatches hosted by group C. Rosman and Rubel (1971:5) claim that if this were found to be the case, then it would constitute a verification of the Tsimshian marriage alliance structure they propose. Marriage and potlatch-wealth transfers are regarded by Rosman and Rubel as similar mechanisms of exchange between descent groups serving to link them into alliance relationships functioning to give cohesion to all of Tsimshian society. It should be pointed out that this model is a nonreciprocal one. Exchange of women and goods flow in only one direction in exchange for services, causing the alliance relationships to be asymmetrical. This view conflicts with that expounded by Homer Barnett (1938), who believes that the notion of symmetrical reciprocity is a vital feature of the potlatch everywhere on the Northwest Coast.

Tsimshian society shares many features with neighboring Tlingit, Haida, and Haisla society. These include matrilineal descent and inheritance with a general norm of avunculocal residence. Postcontact Tsimshian society was divided into four matrilineal exogamous phratries. The English names for these groups refer to the major crests used by each; Raven, Eagle, Wolf, and Killerwhale. Phratries are dispersed so that there are segments of each in every Tsimshian village. Within Tsimshian villages, the members of these localized phratry segments normally share a strong sense of commonality, often considering themselves to be of common descent. The Tsimshian say that the different phratry groups within a village make up the "sides" of the village. The sides of a village are further segmented into house groups, which for our purposes may be called lineages. Lineage members are those persons who can claim matrilineal descent from a common grandmother, or who, by some formal procedure, have been adopted into lineage membership and thus share a common store of crests, privileges, and prerogatives.

Women reside with their husbands after marriage. Children spend their early years in the household of their parents. A daughter will live with her parents until she marries, at which time she goes to live with her husband. Sons commonly leave their father's household between the ages of eight and fourteen to live with their mother's brother. This practice of avunculocal residence often results in a core of matrilineally related males, sometimes three generations in depth, residing together. These males symbolically represent the lineage. Along with these males live their spouses and young children.

The Tsimshian consider every individual to be a member of a village. A person is a member of his or her lineage's village yet does not necessarily reside in that village. For example, a father's house may be in a different village from his child's. By Tsimshian reckoning, everyone by matrilineal account can identify membership with a lineage, a side of a village, and that village. For the purpose of the discussion here, the important group for analysis is the lineage, for it is at this level that Rosman and Rubel see groups allied in marriage.

The principal marriage rule observed among the Tsimshian is phratry exogamy. Rank and wealth are also important in spouse selection. According to Garfield: "Marrying beneath one's position has always been deplorable in Tsimshian eyes. In general those who belonged to the chiefs' families should marry only those of the same rank, and wealthy lineages formed alliances with those of equal wealth" (1939:232).

As suggested in this passage, such considerations could indeed lead to important alliance relationships. Both Garfield and Boas record examples of marriage arrangements whereby lineage heads had married each other's sisters (Garfield 1939:278–79; Boas 1916:510). Lineage alliances based on this pattern of marriage would certainly be compatible with Tsimshian social organization and marriage rules, but they would not result in the asymmetrical pattern proposed by Rosman and Rubel. It was on the basis of the matrilateral cross-cousin marriage preference referred to by Boas and Garfield that Rosman and Rubel proposed the model in Figure 1. However, no actual examples of this form of marriage are offered by either Boas or Garfield.

There is another Tsimshian marriage preference that Garfield apparently felt was important enough to discuss in some detail: "The marriage of persons whose grand-parents were brother and sister, either own or clan, was also considered a very desirable type of union. . . . One woman is married to a man whose maternal grandfather belonged to the the same lineage as herself. Her husband's grandfather and her maternal grandmother were brother and sister" (1939:232).

Rosman and Rubel (1971:19, 20) refer to this statement by Garfield

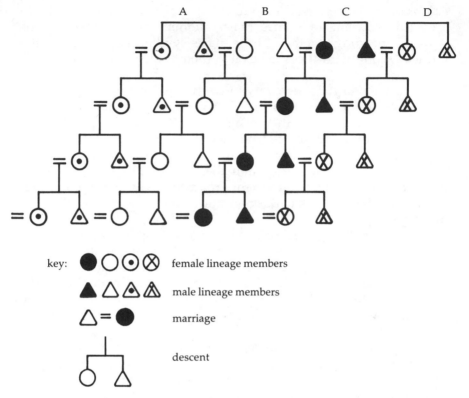

Fig. 1. Mother's brother's daughter marriage pattern (after Rosman and Rubel 1971)

as evidence of a transgenerational version of the MBD preference. They claim that the example offered by Garfield testifies to the practice of MBD marriage (for they believed this to be an example of it), and to the fact that lineages are allied by MBD marriages generation after generation.

I contend that Rosman and Rubel's interpretation of this preference is too narrow. When one considers the bilateral nature of Tsimshian kinship terminology, then the marriage of persons whose grandparents were brother and sister, either own or lineage (i.e., phratry), encompasses a range of women far greater than a man's mother's brother's daughter. Indeed, Garfield's example identified as a MBD marriage by Rosman and Rubel does not conform to Rosman and Rubel's model. Garfield states that the woman is married to a man whose maternal grandfather was a brother of her maternal grandmother. This combination cannot be made to match the pattern of MBD marriage in Figure 1. Tracing the collateral direction of the marriage reveals that it is in a patrilateral, not matrilateral, direction with reference to the male's matrilineage.

Patrilateral cross-cousin marriage is not mentioned by either Boas or Garfield, but Drucker (1950:212) notes that it as an acceptable Tsimshian form. Kasakoff (1974), writing on Gitksan marriages, states that "cousin" marriage was expressed as a major preference, meaning cross-cousins in the bilateral sense. Tsimshian kinship terminology is bilateral, so that MBD and FZD are designated by the same term. The reason any of this is important to our discussion is that these features stand in marked contrast to the *mayu-dama* system of the Kachin, to whom Rosman and Rubel liken the Tsimshian. Leach states that the Kachin express strong disapproval of FZD marriage (1971). Brother-sister exchange would also be an inappropriate form of marriage for a Kachin, but this is not inappropriate to the Tsimshian. I think that it is important to understand that although Rosman and Rubel characterize the Tsimshian as having a *mayu-dama* type of structure, they exhibit a number of patterns not at all typical of the Kachin system as described by Leach.

One final point should be made concerning Tsimshian marriages. It should not be assumed that because a particular form of marriage is expressed as a preference there is any correlation with actual behavior. Consider the following statement by Garfield: "A man should marry his mother's brother's daughter; a woman her father's sister's son. While cross-cousin marriage is an expressed social ideal it is very probable that such marriages did not constitute a majority of all marriages. In the genealogies obtained a very small number have been cousin marriages, even with relationships further removed than first cousins. Three first cousin marriages are known in Port Simpson now" (1939:231–32).

Elsewhere Garfield (1951:23) states, "If a survey of marriages of living persons is indicative, it suggests that in former times only a small percentage of marriages conformed to the ideal." Rosman and Rubel refer to these passages as accounts in which the MBD preference is documented, yet do not mention that Garfield's findings were that such marriages were rare. Kasakoff (1974:148–49) reports that although the Gitksan express a preference for marriage with cross-cousins, only one instance of a first cousin marriage could be found in genealogies involving 750 marriages dating back to 1850. Even classificatory cousin marriages she found to be rare.

Although Rosman and Rubel's goal may have been to describe an

underlying structure, their means of verifying the model they propose is to show that the exchange that takes place in the potlatch
is in accordance with the exchange they propose takes place in the
marriage structure.

Tsimshian potlatches are usually associated with specific social occasions. The most important potlatches revolve around a memorial
for a deceased chief, the erection of his grave post, and the assumption of his chiefly names and position by his matrilineal suc-
cessor(s). These events may occur as part of one potlatch or may
involve a series of separate potlatches over time. Other events that
may take place during a potlatch include the dedication of a newly
built house, the initiation of individuals into secret societies, and
the piercing of the ears, nose, and lips of young nobles for the wearing of jewelry. The changing of names is also a common feature
during potlatch proceedings. Any of these events involves the performance of some service by invited guests, and it is the Tsimshian
view that for any ceremonial service rendered, compensation must
be given. These services are never performed by members of one's
own phratry. Marius Barbeau (1954:109) describes the Tsimshian attitude about this as follows: "Just as incest is abhorrent, so is the
notion of a clan member being helped by his own kin in functions
obtaining to childbirth, naming initiation, marriage, raising in the
ranks, raising a totem pole, and at burial."

For any individual, the main link to a phratry other than one's
own is through one's father. It is along this social structural line that
the services and phratry interactions of the potlatch take place. The
tie between an individual and his father's lineage is a close and af-
fectionate one. From birth, formal duties are performed by parent
lineages and a relationship is begun between the child's and the
father's lineages which play a significant part in many of life's important events.

When a child is named, the father or maternal uncle gives a feast
and the father's brother announces the child's name (Garfield
1939:194, 215, 222, 324). Whenever a person takes a new name, it
is the father's people who proclaim it in a potlatch (Boas 1916:512).
It is the father's people who perform the service of publicly perfo-
rating the ears, nose, and lips and also provide the jewelry to be
worn in these perforations. Members of the father's lineage carve
the masks and other paraphernalia used in the dancing society performances, and they also act as attendants for the dancers. At death,
the father's lineage takes care of the mortuary services, and it is
responsible for the preparation and raising of the totem pole in honor

of the deceased (Boas 1916:512, 534; Garfield 1939:209, 215, 235–47, 325). It supplies the materials for the building of a new house. It later dedicates the house and tells the history and emphasizes the greatness of the lineage and those attached to it. The father's people give the recitation of lineage myths, privileges, and crests at potlatches (Garfield 1939:215).

For all these services and more, the participating members of the father's lineage are compensated. The compensation usually takes place with the distribution of potlatch goods by the host group (i.e., father's children's lineage), during which other guests are given goods for "witnessing" the proceedings (Garfield 1939:248–56).

Rosman and Rubel feel that the potlatch relationship that exists between one's own and one's father's lineage can be viewed as an expression of the alliance relationship brought about by MBD marriage. They show this by correlating the role of the father's lineage in the alliance model (as wife-takers) with the role of the father's lineage in the potlatch: "This relationship between father's lineage and son's lineage finds its greatest expression in the potlatch. Ego's lineage gives women to father's lineage but in addition it gives goods to father's lineage which are conceived of as an exchange for the services performed by the father's lineage at various ceremonies" (Rosman and Rubel 1971:32).

Rosman and Rubel analyze the events of a particular potlatch described by Garfield. This was the potlatch given by a certain Niəs-gane·'s, a Raven of the village of Gınado'iks. The potlatch was multipurpose. The reasons given for it were: (1) to signify the termination of the period of mourning for the death of Niəs-gane·'s's predecessor, the former Niəs-gane·'s; (2) the assumption and validation of ancestoral names by Niəs-gane·'s and other lineage relatives; (3) a performance of a supernatural power ceremony (*t'si·k-hala'it*) for three children of one of Niəs-gane·'s's sisters; the children each received a "spirit" (*naxnɔx*) and name-title to accompany it; and (4) an initiation (*hala'it*) for two girls, daughters of two of Niəs·gane·'s's sisters—one into the Dancer society, the other into the Dog Eaters (Garfield 1939:195, 206, 298–300).

All the people mentioned were, of course, members of Niəs-gane·'s's matrilineage; all were Ravens from Gınado'iks. Garfield discusses the performance of services by the father or father's kin. There are four fathers involved: La·'is, Wolf phratry of the village Gılutsa'u, the father of Niəs-gane·'s; the father of the *naxnɔx* performers (name not given), who was a Wolf from Gıspaxlɔ·'ts; and the last two, Niəs-maɬa and Ǧaphaitk, both of the Wolf phratry from

TABLE 1
PRINCIPALS OF *NIəS-GANE·'S* POTLATCH

Gʋnadóiks Ravens	Wolf fathers	fathers' villages
Niəs-gane·'s	La·'is	Gʋlutsa'u
Naxnɔx initiates (3 children)	name not given	Gɪspaxlɔ·'ts
Dog Eater initiates (2 girls)	Niəs-maƚa Ģaphaitk	Gʋnado'iks

Gʋnado'iks, the fathers of the two girls initiated into the dancing societies.

Thus all the fathers of the hosts involved were members of the Wolf phratry. Rosman and Rubel analyze this situation as follows (1971:26): "In this case, the Raven lineage of the host stands as wife-giver to the Wolf lineage, which is the father's lineage. . . . The father's lineage for Ego and for the initiates, his sister's children (succeeding generation of Ego's lineage) *is the same,* reiterating our points about the transgenerational alliance between lineages through marriage. . . . At any given potlatch only two of the three units which form the *mayu-dama* structure are interacting. Nowhere in the ethnographic account of Nisgane or his potlatch does Garfield indicate awareness of the structural significance of this paternal interaction between Ego's lineage and his father's lineage" (emphasis added).

With the analysis of this one potlatch, Rosman and Rubel claim to demonstrate the validity of their alliance model. Their analysis implies, however, that the fathers listed above are all members of one and the same Wolf lineage, and this condition is central to their analysis. But these fathers came from three different villages. From what has been said above regarding Tsimshian social organization, we may assume that since the fathers represent the Wolf side of three different villages, they represent three (and possibly more) different lineages. Niəs-gane·'s's sisters were married to men who, as far as we know, were members of Wolf lineages unaffiliated with the lineage of La·'is (their father). There is no evidence that these women were given as wives to men of La·'is's lineage.

Moreover, Garfield is fully aware of the role that the members of a host's father's lineage play in the potlatch. Had Rosman and Rubel examined the other potlatches described by Garfield as well, a case might have been made that the structural rules of the Tsimshian potlatch operate independently of supposed marriage patterns. The lineage relationship in a potlatch context can just as easily be interpreted as a relationship of filiation between a child and his father's lineage as a marriage alliance relationship between two lineages. Garfield's account of the funeral potlatch for Niəs-we·xs will serve as an example (Garfield 1939:246–47). The purpose of this occasion was to hold a "last feast" and funeral for Niəs-we·xs, who was a Blackfish (Killerwhale) chief from Gınado'iks, and for the succession to his name and position by his maternal nephew. In Garfield's own words: "Niəs-we·xs, Blackfish chief of the Gınado'iks, died in Port Simpson about 1925. His sister's son had been selected to succeed him. . . . The paternal lineage of Niəs-we·xs was of the house of Niəs-hʊt, the Raven chief of the Gıtsaxɫa'ɫ, so he was called upon to perform the death services" (1939:246).

Up to this point, it can be seen that a Raven lineage from Gıtsaxɫa'ɫ stands as the father's lineage of Niəs-we·xs. According to the marriage alliance model, the paternal lineage of Niəs-we·xs's nephew should be the same as Niəs-we·xs's paternal lineage. Garfield continues as follows: "Cigars were passed and smoked, a ceremony taking the place of the more usual last feast with the dead. . . . When the smoking was over, the nephew was announced and called to come forward. The spokesman asked if he were ready to accept the responsibility of the chieftainship, to which he answered that he was. He was then led to the coffin by a *Wolf clansman, a brother of his father*" (1939:246–47; emphasis added).

In this potlatch, although the paternal lineage of the deceased belonged to the Raven phratry, the paternal lineage of his successor (nephew) was of the Wolf phratry. Both Ravens and Wolves were invited as guests to the potlatch given by these Blackfish of Gınado'iks and both groups received goods in the potlatch distribution for the services they performed.

This example indicates that the rule that one hosts one's father's lineage at a potlatch may operate outside the framework of the MBD marriage alliance. An analysis of the paternal lineage interactions with ego's lineage would not demonstrate that marriage patterns of a certain type exist. The marriages of most of the women of this particular Blackfish lineage would bear little relevance to the structural situation that existed in this potlatch, since the rule is to host one's father's lineage and not a wife-taking lineage per se. Other than the fact that Niəs-we·xs's mother was once married to a Raven from Gıtsaxɫa'ɫ and his sister was once married to a member of the

Wolf phratry, we do not know, nor is it important to know, the lineages of other Blackfish women's husbands.

Furthermore, the exchange relationship between the lineages does not focus on a man and his "in-laws" but rather on a man and his child. The exchange relationship between the lineages in the potlatch is not instigated by a marriage but rather begins only after the birth of a child to a married couple. The services performed by members of the paternal lineage for a child are viewed by them as part of their paternal duties, and rights. This relationship that children have with their paternal lineages lasts a lifetime whether there are marriages linking the lineages or not. It is with death and the performance of final services by members of one's father's lineage that the paternal lineage relationship comes to an end.

Both marriage and the potlatch are important aspects of Tsimshian culture, and the people like to maintain close ties between intermarried lineages. Still, actual cousin marriages are rare despite an "ideal" preference for marriage to mother's brother's daughter.

Rosman and Rubel's attempt to validate a *mayu-dama* type of marriage model for the Tsimshian by pointing to the potlatch role of the host's father's lineage is a test of tempting simplicity. From their presentation it would seem that potlatching one's father's lineage is not only in complete agreement with the marriage model, but is a direct expression of it. Actually, Rosman and Rubel have fallen short of accounting for the facts. A close scrutiny of the available data does not support the assertion of a necessary structural relationship between potlatch and marriage.

Similar findings have been arrived at in critiques on the structural analysis of marriage and potlatching among Tsimshian neighbors (Vaughan 1975a, 1975b) and also of the structural analysis of Tsimshian myth (Thomas et al. 1976). The problems found with structural analysis in each of these critiques focus on the lack of rigor in accounting for data used, and on failure to take into consideration *all* relevant data. Much of the latter appears to be left unconsidered simply because of conflicts with the structural analysis at hand.

While the application of a model of kinship group alliance offers an interesting perspective on Tsimshian potlatching, the concept of filiation which is important among all Northwest Coast cultures, gives a more reasonable explanation of the structural features of the potlatch institution.

Gitksan Kin Term Usage

ALICE BEE KASAKOFF

In recent years linguists have become dissatisfied with their traditional concentration on the "literal sense of isolated sentences" (Gumperz 1975:xv). Realizing that the same message can have different meanings depending on the verbal, nonverbal, and social context in which it occurs, they have come to shift their studies from literal meaning to the way in which language is used (see Bauman and Sherzer 1974; Sanches and Blount 1975). Thus, Hymes (1974:436–73) has distinguished between the referential and the stylistic functions of language and considers them at least of equal importance. Reference is concerned with the designative role of language, its "literal sense," the naming of things talked about, while style has to do with characterizing or qualifying what has been said or "modifying things talked about and saying how what is to be said about them is to be taken" (Hymes 1974:437).

Traditionally, anthropologists have made frequent use of the analogy between language and culture in the study of kinship terms, and thus in no other anthropological concern did the study of referential meaning go as far. But perhaps because of this very thoroughness, it is in this realm that the limitations of a concern with referential meaning alone have become most apparent. As a result, the recognition that kinship terms can be manipulated for political purposes pervades most recent ethnographies (see, for example, Chagnon 1977:54–81). Studies have been made of alternative (Lave, Stepick, and Sailer 1977; Tyler 1972) and nonreferential usage of kinship terms in other cultures (Fox 1971). Moreover, controversies about the nature of kinship in other cultures and the universality of certain conceptions of kinship have arisen (Needham 1971:4; and Scheffler and Lounsbury 1971) which require attention to alternative usages and nonreferential meaning for their solution.

Do all cultures encode concepts of blood kinship into their referential usage of kinship terms? Or are there some societies in which kin terms refer to groups within which no distinctions between close and distant kin are made? Is "kinship," then, a matter of blood or of politics? Little information is available to answer these questions, because the answers depend on details of the usage of kinship terms that are not usually collected, analyzed, or published by anthropologists.

This chapter brings together my observations on kin term usage among the Gitksan. The Appendix describes the terms in detail, giving both the basic referential terms, defined as they are normally used, and several other terms that are used by the Gitksan in discussing kinship, including prefixes, suffixes, and terms for types of relatives not in the basic set. The chapter itself highlights some of the more important kinds of nonreferential usage. When I did my fieldwork, I was concerned with the referential meanings of terms and did not pay much attention to the other usages; they had not yet assumed the theoretical importance they now have in anthropology. But I did obtain enough information on these other usages to be able to make a number of observations. I hope that, given the paucity of such accounts for any society, my observations of nonreferential usage among the Gitksan will be useful in describing the variety of ways kinship terms can be used in a single society. Moreover, the recognition of such multiple usages may be important in resolving some of the controversies that have developed recently about the nature of Northwest Coast marriage systems. Kinship systems that belong to radically different structural types on the basis of referential meaning are in fact quite similar when usage is considered.

The reader should know that I do not speak Gitksan myself. These observations were gathered in the course of fieldwork in which I interviewed people intensively in English about the referential meanings of Gitksan kinship terms using the standard genealogical method.[1] Often, however, other types of usage were discussed and

1. The fieldwork on which this paper is based was conducted between 1965 and 1967 and supplemented by later interviews and correspondence. It was supported by an NIMA Pre-doctoral Fellowship, No. 4-F01-MA-21, 971-04 (CUAN). The Canadian Center for Folk Culture Studies and the Ethnology Division at the Museum of Man, National Museums of Canada, and the Smithsonian Institution Urgent Anthropology Program have supported my work in archives and further analysis of the data. I would also like to thank Sarah Hindle, Sarah Marshall, and Wallace Morgan for their help in gathering the information on which this chapter is based. I am grateful to John Dunn for his comments on the paper and his help with the comparison of Gitksan and Kitkatla; to Bruce Rigsby and Lonnie Hindle for sharing their notes about Gitksan kinship; to Carol Eastman for her helpful suggestions; and most of all to John W. Adams, who struggled with me over successive drafts, and who

terms that referred to concepts of kinship that were not part of the basic set of reference terms described. My most salient examples of nonliteral usage, however, come from English conversations with Gitksan about other Gitksan. In some of these, the terms for relatives coincided with proper Gitksan usage, though not proper English usage (as when "grandfather" is used to refer to the individual's mother's mother's brother). At other times—and these were the most interesting moments—English terms corresponded neither to literal English usage nor to literal Gitksan usage. Often I would ponder for days why it was, for example, that a female was said to be someone's "father." When I asked about these instances, I obtained a great deal of information on the nonliteral usage of kinship terms, more than I had thought possible for a non-Gitksan speaker to gather. The fact that my findings are similar to those of persons more fluent in the language than I was (see Rigsby's examples in the Appendix, for example), as well as similar to the nonliteral usage others have recorded (Durlach 1928; Sapir 1920), confirms that I am describing regular features of the ways in which Gitksan kinship terms are used. Of course, it would be important for a person fluent in Gitksan to record Gitksan conversations about kinship, but I am confident that what I am about to describe is not incorrect and, more than that, that it describes major features of Gitksan kin term usage.

Both the consistency of my findings with what Boas and Sapir described over fifty years ago and the fact that Gitksan fits so nicely into the classic Iroquois type of kinship terminology indicates that the kinship system has not changed greatly over the years. However, my data come only from people between forty and sixty years of age.[2] And I provide a conservative view of the system because I have given as full a set of terms as possible: if some people said particular relatives were not called by a kinship term but others said they were, I included the term as supplied. The majority of missing terms were for people outside one's own house, particularly affines such as niece's husband and nephew's wife, and so forth. That traditional terms are still used within the house shows that even informants who did not supply the entire set still make use of some traditional concepts. Relationships within the house are conceived of according to the traditional categories; and in some villages and

---

was a partner in the fieldwork and without whom the work would not have been carried to completion.

2. Four informants provided most of the data. This age group was chosen in order to get a traditional view of the kinship system.

age groups the entire system is intact. Many of the missing terms seemed to reflect the difficulty informants had bridging the gap between English and Gitksan rather than basic changes in the kinship terminology itself over the past fifty years.

Hindle and Rigsby (1973:58) note important alternative usages indicating that some speakers are tending to use an English model. They report that some people use *nibib* for both the paternal and maternal uncle and *nixtaa* for either aunt. Some people also use the English distinction between sibling and cousin in speaking Gitksan rather than employing the cross-parallel distinction basic to the traditional system. That my informants did not provide those usages is further evidence that they were on the conservative end of the acculturative scale.

THE GITKSAN AMONG THE TSIMSHIAN: TERMINOLOGIES COMPARED

The Gitksan share with the other Tsimshian groups an Iroquois type of kinship teminology. The Gitksan would receive a perfect score of 10, on the scale Buchler and Selby have devised (1968: 219–47), to measure the degree to which a kinship terminology approximates the Iroquois type. The similarity between the Gitksan terms and the system described by Durlach for the Coast and Nass River Tsimshian (Durlach 1928) is evidence that the Gitksan share the referential meaning of basic kinship concepts with the other Tsimshian groups. The differences between what she reported and my description are all relatively minor: the Gitksan have a choice of terms for three relatives, while the Coast and Nass River people do not. They use only *stik'eekw* for sister, *galan* for brother-in-law, and *nigwood* for father's brother, while among the Gitksan these alternate with *lgiikw*, *wilaiskxw*, and *galan* respectively. Among the Gitksan the difference between *wilaiskxw* and *galan* for brother-in-law and *galan* and *nigwood* for father's brother is that the former have a connotation of greater respect than the latter. Thus these differences do not reflect basic conceptual differences between the Gitksan and other Tsimshian groups.

The system of kin terminology used in Kitkatla (Dunn and Dunn 1972), however, differs in more important ways from the systems Durlach, Sapir, and I have described (Table 1 summarizes the differences between Kitkatla and Gitksan). The Gitksan make more use—and more consistent use—of the sex of the speaker than the Kitkatla do. Most of the other differences depend on the distinction the Kitkatla make between direct and collateral matrilineal kin—a distinction the Gitksan do not make in normal referential usage. The Kitkatla use the *agwii*-prefix to distinguish female siblings of the grandmother from the real grandmother, for example, while among the Gitksan all women of the grandmother's house and generation are referred to by a single term. Usually, however, the Kitkatla mark the distinction between direct and collateral kin by merging the collateral kin with the next descending generation. This results in the "grandchild" usage Dunn discusses in this volume, in which mother's sister's children's children are "grandchildren," even though they are members of the first descending generation from ego. In keeping with this, the children of these grandchildren are "greatgrandchildren" and, again using generation to express collateral distance, the spouses of mother's sister's children are referred to by terms which otherwise are used only for spouses of members of the first descending or ascending generations. The Gitksan, on the other hand, have only one term (*galan*) that applies to members of different generations, and this term is clearly unusual.

Dunn and Dunn (1972) have concluded that a formal analysis of the referential meaning of Kitkatla kin terms requires that they be split into three sets, each of which uses different principles of classification. Since virtually all the terms in the second and third sets have denotations that differ from those of cognate terms in the other descriptions of Tsimshian kin terms, either because of generational displacement or inconsistent use of sex of speaker, I suspect that the set of rules sufficient to explain the first set would also account for Gitksan referential usage as well as the systems Sapir (1920) and Durlach (1928) described. Thus all the Tsimshian systems described so far are similar except for these Kitkatla terms. At least two of the deviant Kitkatla terms are members of two of the three sets Dunn and Dunn postulate. They are used in two senses: as kinship terms and as what Dunn and Dunn call "kin status terms." It is tempting, then, to view this kin status system as a Kitkatla variation of the pan-Tsimshian kinship ideology. The ideas that this kin status system expresses are consistent with those that the Gitksan express in their nonreferential usages described later.

REFERENTIAL AND STYLISTIC USAGE

The referential meaning of Coast and Nass River Tsimshian kinship terms has been described so thoroughly before (Dunn and

TABLE 1

COMPARISON OF GITKSAN AND KITKATLA KIN TERMS

Gitksan(G)	Kitkatla(K)	Features
gutxao'o	*tgʷitʰa'ɔ·yu*	Kitkatla includes FZW and FZDH as "cross-cousins"; Gitksan uses *naks gutxao'o* "spouse of cousin," a compound form.
nɔx/nixtaa *nixtaa*	*nɔ·yu/nʌktá·yu* *nʌktá·yu*	K includes FBW with "mother"; G includes her with FZ in "aunt."
ndziits *agwii ndziits*	*ņčʔičʋ* *'agʷiņčʔičʋ*	In K the distinction is between GP and their siblings; in G it is between GP and their GGP.
o'l	*'úlisʋ*	In G this term is a synonym for *agwii ndziits*, but is used within the same phratry as the speaker. In K it is used for GGP and GGC, also for MZSCC and MZDCC.
agwii guxdagin *agwii thuthu o'l*	*'úlisʋ*	same as above
niye'e	*ỳέ'ɛsʋ*	G includes FMB and MMB; K does not.
tguutxw *gʷislis*	*tgútgu* *tgislĭsgu*	HZC (and probably WBC) are *gʷislis* in G but *tgutgu* in K. Sex of speaker determines the meaning of these terms in G, but not in K

TABLE 1 (*continued*)

Gitksan(G)	Kitkatla(K)	Features
guxdagintw	*łiktá'ynu*	In G restricted to second ascending generation. In K includes some in first descending generation: FBSS, FBSD, MZSS, MZSD, etc. G does not use it to trace relationship to FBCC.
giodxs *gwidziis* *gałan*	*łukɔ́·tksu* *łgʷisúsu*	All G terms depend on sex of speaker; K terms only sporadically do. G does not use these terms for FBSW, FBDH.
łems	*łémsu*	In G restricted to adjacent generation, thus not used as in K for MZSW, MZDH; G would use *giodxs* for these relatives instead.
no term	*'agʷi'ɔ́'ɔsu*	G does not have a kin term for C of cross-cousins (X-Cz); K does.
no term	*'agʷiłemsu*	G does not have a kin term for spouse of a GC; K does.

Dunn 1972; Durlach 1928; Sapir 1920) and the terminologies are so similar to that of the Gitksan that another description is hardly necessary. Dunn and Dunn (1972) have raised the issue of the different senses in which kin terms can be used for the Tsimshian, but the two senses they discussed were both referential. My discussion focuses on the important nonreferential meanings kin terms carry and covers a broader range. In the process, I describe what could be called kinship metalanguage—that is, how the Gitksan express how what is said about kinship is to be taken.

These usages form a counterpoint to the basic set of kin terms because they denote groups of people that either combine or cut across groups denoted separately in the basic set. They call attention to features people have in common even though they are referred to by different kinship terms. Speaking in this way is a form of marking: it calls attention to similarities people have that the Gitksan generally do not make note of. There is a need for these usages because the basic set of kin terms, used literally, does not allow important ideas about kinship to be expressed.

That important Tsimshian kinship concepts are *not* expressed in the referential usage of kinship terms is evident in Garfield's study of Tsimshian social organization (1939), which includes an excellent description of the exchanges between a person (and his descent group) and his father's relatives. These exchanges, beginning at birth and ending at death, are at the basis of the potlatching system, yet a term denoting "father's relatives" does not exist, nor is there a reciprocal term for "children." Although the Gitksan do have a term for father's relatives (*wilxsitxwitxw*), it is not part of the basic set of kinship terms and its referents are not isomorphic with any of those terms or even with a combination of them.[3]

A further example is the words used to denote siblings. Since these terms are used for children of men in the same house,[4] as well as

---

3. The term for father refers only to a male in the real father's generation and house, even though men in other generations may be important in exchanges with the father's house. Females in the house are called *nixtaa*, "aunt," but this term is also used for the wife of the mother's brother, who is not involved in the kind of exchange Garfield describes. The word "child" when used by males does refer to children of the men in the house in the same generation. Again, however, as these men die, persons of the same age will treat each other as "children" for the purposes of these exchanges (though calling each other "cousin"). Moreover, when used by female speakers, the same term refers to members of their own house. I have not been able to find a Coast Tsimshian equivalent for the Gitksan *wilxsitxwitxw*.

4. The term "house" as used here refers to a corporate group, not a dwelling. In the past members of the same house did not always live in the large community houses that were common. Nowadays these structures have disappeared and peo-

children of women in the same house, they are also not isomorphic with any of the important groups in the exchange system. At each potlatch or feast those present are divided into hosts and guests; those not in the host phratry are guests. The host has "siblings," therefore, not only in his own phratry but in the guest phratries as well, as long as the men of one's father's house and generation have married women in different phratries, which is almost always the case. The "siblings" in one's own house help one in the duties of host at the feast while those in the other phratries do not. The only time these other siblings act together at a feast is when they contribute a special payment upon the death of persons in their father's house, but this payment is clearly separate in feast protocol from payments made by the host phratry, and the persons one calls siblings never act as a unit at a feast for ego. Thus there is no feast role corresponding to the kinship terms referring to siblings.

The basic set of kinship terms and the set of roles in the feasting system are two different templates that are placed by Gitksan upon their society. They do not often coincide—hence the need for broader use of kinship terms, general concepts, prefixes, and suffixes. These often refer to the intersection of the two sets of concepts, and represent an accommodation of the basic set of kinship terms, as it is used normally, to the demands of the exchange system. Thus the concept *wilxsitxwitxw* refers to the group of people in the father's house involved in exchanges, while persons called by sibling terms who are not in one's phratry can be distinguished from those who are by calling them siblings, *lixs giat*, meaning "of a different sort."

BOUNDARIES AND DEGREES OF KINSHIP

Among the most important ideas expressed by the Gitksan kinship terminology are notions of closeness and distance. These are shown by how the terms are used—that is, to whom they are applied and on what occasions—rather than by the structure of the terminology itself. Tsimshian do not classify everyone in the society as a relative of some sort and are therefore not obliged to marry a relative; they distinguish between relatives and nonrelatives. Normally they marry only nonrelatives—that is, persons not called by

---

ple live in nuclear family dwellings, but this group is still the building block of the society. It is not a descent group, since it usually consists of at least two lineages between which relationships cannot be traced.

kinship terms in strict referential usage (Kasakoff 1974). Each marriage initiates a cycle in which kinship relations are created and extinguished. The boundary line between the group of people called by kinship terms and those who are not is as important, if not more important, for the understanding of Gitksan society than the distinctions between different types of kin within the group to whom kinship terms are applied.

The boundaries of the normal referential use of the terms are determined strictly by the houses, the basic corporate groups of Gitksan society. Adams (1973) has provided ample evidence for the competition that exists among the lineages within a house for the highest status, particularly when houses are large. Repeated questioning showed that members of feuding sides of the same house normally *do* use kinship terms for each other; an individual also uses kinship terms for the feuding sides of his father's house. Members of houses that have split apart, however, do not use kinship terms for each other in ordinary circumstances. Thus the kinship terms are applied by house and refer either to an entire generation in a house or to the children, grandchildren, and spouses of those in one's own house.

The Gitksan also have a concept of blood kin, expressed in the phrase *lip wil ʔiiɬeʔe,* which crosscuts the categories expressed in the kinship terms themselves. The blood kin are one's own lineage, one's father's lineage, and one's father's brother's children—persons who have a grandparent in common, since lineages are traced only to the grandparents. Since a house consists of at least two lineages, this concept divides the house into blood kin and those I will call pseudo kin (persons who belong to other lineages than those to which one is related by descent). There is no term for this latter group. Each house contains small groups of kin who refuse to acknowledge common descent. They are, therefore, not descent groups.

Thus in its normal usage, Gitksan terminology is not in the strict sense a "kinship" terminology at all. Rather it is used to define a pseudo-kinship group, because it expresses relationships between individuals who are descended from members of the same corporate groups, male or female. For example, the children of men in the same house are descended from the same corporate group and generation; and although they are themselves in different corporate groups, they use sibling terms for each other.

One of the ways to slight those who are pseudo kin but not blood kin is to use affine terms instead of kinship terms for them if there is an affinal as well as a pseudo-kinship relationship. This is done particularly between feuding sides of the same house. Thus the blood kin are implicitly singled out in kin-term usage, in addition to the concept of *lip wil?iiɬe?e*, because they are the only ones who are always called by kinship terms.

The referential and nonreferential meanings taken together can express both blood relatedness (Scheffler and Lounsbury 1971) and social classification based on other criteria (Needham 1971). Does the notion of blood relatedness take precedence over house membership? Sapir (1920:271) collected a term that denoted a subset of relatives he translated as "self-relative, relative *par excellence*," that appears to have the same denotations as the Gitksan *lip wil?iiɬe?e*. This is strong evidence that the primary reference of the concept of kinship is to blood relationships, at least on the Nass. If one takes the shorter form as closer to the primary meaning, as is common in discussions of marking (Greenberg 1966:25–28), then the phrase for "blood relative" would definitely be shorter than the circumlocution that might be necessary to specify pseudo kin; this would make blood relatedness primary among the Gitksan too. However, more investigation into how the concept of pseudo kin is expressed is needed. Yet it deserves repeating that although this may be the primary meaning of the terms, they are most frequently applied to an entire social category, including both blood and pseudo kin. To restrict them to blood relatives would probably be considered an insult.

THE CYCLE OF GENERATIONS

When asking about the status of relationships that originated in the past through marriage, I often received the answer, "They would call me x [kinship term] if they knew me." I was told that the present generation, even the holders of one's mother's father's or one's father's father's name, are completely different from the people who originally made the marriage in one's grandparent's generation. These people may or may not remember ego. Thus the linguistic connections of *wilaisxw* (brother-in-law for the Gitksan; "relative" on the Coast) with "to know" (Boas 1911:399; Dunn and Dunn 1972:241; Durlach 1928:134) are not metaphorical or accidental. The relationships established by marriage require active recognition to continue. In the case of these "grandfathers," that is all that they require, since although there are feast obligations and services a father's house must provide for its children, these do not carry over to their grandchildren. Relationships such as this "fade away," as the Gitksan say, in the third generation. In his grammar of Coast Tsimshian,

Boas notes the rarity of what he calls the indicative form of the verb (1911:404), "every sentence that does not express the speaker's own immediate experience" (Boas 1911:399) is expressed in the subjunctive. Thus it is not surprising that the Gitksan distinguish relationships established before a speaker's observation from those to which he is an eyewitness.

"Fading away" is implicit in the type of kinship terminology in which kin and affinal relationships are not perpetual but created anew in each generation, as Lévi-Strauss has pointed out in his remarks on the Crow-Omaha systems (1969). In the first generation, a person moves from being unrelated to a particular house to being an affine. After he has children, his generation then becomes related as fathers and fathers' sisters to his child; for a woman, the next generation is made up of the children of men in the houses related affinally to the previous generation. The third generation, the oldest, is the grandfathers and grandmothers of the children of the marriage. In the fourth generation there is no relationship (see Table 2). It is important to note that these are not relationships between two houses per se; they are relationships between an individual and the houses to which he is linked by his own marriage, and his father's and children's marriages. Thus all individuals in a particular generation of a House share one group of brothers-in-law, the men who married persons in their own generation of their house; but each person also has brothers-in-law unique to him, the men in his spouse's house and generation.

The first step in this cycle is the marriage of a man and a woman. The members of her house and generation call him *wilaisxw* (brother-in-law)—that is, recognize or *know* him as a relative—and he calls them that in return. The native etymology of *wilaisxw* is "to become in a family." The same was also said of the term *giodxs* (sibling-in-law of opposite sex). This is said to be a "big word" and denotes "respect" because it means the person is part of your family. Thus even in the generation before the person becomes a "father," the in-law is not really an affine—in the sense that Dumont describes perpetual affinity (1957)—but is made part of the "family." The important distinction is thus not between kin and affines but between two types of kin: (1) *wilaisxw* or father's people (in the next generation these become grandfather's people), those who "know," that is, recognize and support the individual, and (2) persons in one's *wilnadał*, that is matrilineal relatives.

The second step in the cycle is fatherhood, which continues until the "child" dies. If the father dies first, his heir takes on his role.

TABLE 2
THE CYCLE OF GENERATIONS

Generation/Steps	Own House	Father's House and Kin Terms	
First/O	a woman	affine spouse brother-in-law	*naks* *giodxs* *gaɫan* etc.
Second/"one step away"	siblings, children of the woman	father child cousin	*nigwood* *lguuɫxw* *gutxao'o*
Third/"two steps away"	children of sisters, *'nastik'eekut* (limits of genealogical memory)	grandparents grandchildren	*niye'e ndziitz* *guxdagin*
Fourth/"three steps away"	Kin terms used, but pseudo kin	No terms, not recognized as kin	

lip wil ʔiiɫeʔe (bracketing the kin terms of the first three generations)

At the death of the child the relationship between the father's house and the descendants of his children begins to "fade away," and the only people left are the *guxdagin* (grandchildren). Whether the *guxdagin* are recognized as such by the younger generations of their mother's father's and father's father's houses depends on whether the members of the present generation, who now hold the names, know them. In practice this occurs if a more recent marriage has been made or if the *guxdagin* live in the village to which the grandfather's house belongs. Some tangible ties must exist. This is the "third generation." By the time the fourth generation comes on the scene the tie has "faded away." The distinction between a Dravidian cousin terminology and an Iroquois cousin terminology, which depends on what children of cross-cousins are called, is meaningless for the Gitksan, since in referential usage these children are not considered kin (see also Durlach 1928).

Within the other group of kin—the wilnadał (matrilineal group)—the same cycle occurs. People in the third generation in relation to each other within the house are in the same position as the *guxdagin* outside the house. Their status depends on recognition of a common grandparent. In the next generation, one finds that people "don't know" how they are related.

Fading away may be bridged by reincarnation, which links an individual to the fourth generation. A woman's grandparents are reincarnated in her children. The structure of formal groups—houses and phratries—and the application of kinship terms within the whole house prevent the relationships in the house and phratry from fading away to nothing in the fourth generation (as relationships begun as affines and leading to fatherhood do), but that they do fade away is evidenced by the vague knowledge people have of relationships beyond those of their grandparents within their house. The importance of the members of the father's group as "recognizers" or "knowers" also applies to intra-house affairs, because it is the job of a father's group to know the real descent of the children within the matrilineage and to mention it in disputes about succession.

Relationships between children of men in the same house also begin to fade away in the next generation. Children of men in the same generation and house share "grandparents" in their father's house and are in the third generation. The change in their relationship in the fourth generation is expressed in marriage rules: children of men in the same generation of a house cannot marry each other, but their grandchildren can.

The Gitksan describe these cycles in terms of "steps" when speaking English. (I did not collect a Gitksan term for step, although I suspect that one exists.) Relatives can be either one step away or two steps away; when someone is three steps away, he or she is no longer a relative. Relationships one step away are those formed by a marriage in the previous generation—the *gutxao'o* and children of men in the same generation of a house. Their children are two steps away.

Thus the cycle of generations is three generations long—ego's generation, the generation consecutive to it, and a third generation (grandparents or grandchildren). Each person is a member of a five-generation span made up of ego's generation in the middle and two three-generation cycles, one from grandparent to grandson begun by his grandparents and one from himself to his grandchildren. The fact that the cycle does not go on after three generations is evidenced by the lack of terms for affines of grandchildren. One does not use affine terms for the spouses of siblings, *lixs giat* (or, people who call each other by sibling terms because their fathers are in the same house and generation). They are not considered relatives, and there are no kinship terms for their children. Similarly one does not use affine terms for spouses of *gutxao'o* (cross-cousins), and their children are not considered to be related (except in the sense of *guxdagin* used for positional succession (which will be discussed below). In an Iroquois kinship terminology the boundaries of the system can be traced by the use of affine terms as much as they can by the use of kin terms. (The Gitksan principles of steps and their distinction between blood kin and other kin serve to express many of the distinctions between direct and collateral relatives that the Kitkatla make by moving collateral relatives one generation away.)

The similarity between the Gitksan and the Chinese systems (Lévi-Strauss 1969:311) is striking. It seems that systems organized on a "circular" pattern, in which degrees are important, share certain characteristics: (1) the need to define a boundary between relatives and nonrelatives, which the Chinese set at the fifth ascending generation and the Gitksan at the third; (2) a symmetry that stretches the system equally in all directions—that is, five up, five down, and five collateral lines for the Chinese, three for the Gitksan; and (3) some idea of reincarnation, or identification of the present generation with the generation that is no longer considered to be related.

By the very existence of separate affine terms and the cycle they initiate, the descent groups do *not* have a perpetual affinal relation to each other according to the ideology of the referential system (*pace* Ackerman 1975, Cove 1976, Rosman and Rubel 1971). Nor do they in fact (see Kasakoff 1974). Garfield (1939:232) could also find only a few marriages between cousins: "In the genealogies obtained a very small number have been cousin marriages, even with relationships further removed than first cousins." This does not, of course, preclude some houses from having such alliances, but these should not be taken as a basic attribute of the system (Vaughan 1975a).

MORE DISTANT RELATIONSHIPS

There are terms for the fourth generation (great-grandparent or great-grandchild) in the cycle, and this lengthens the double cycle out to seven. One is reciprocal (*o'l*), the others are not (the *agwii-* forms), but I have rarely heard these terms used to refer to distant relationships except within the house, and this seems to be their only function. (One informant said *o'l* could only be used within one's house, but another disagreed.) The effect of these terms is probably to deny kinship by expressing the minimum relationship that can exist by descent within a house.

Lesser relationships exist within a house—those of adoption or hearsay. Thus the use of *o'l* and *agwii-* terms simply means that so and so is a bona fide house member and was not adopted. I was told by one informant that *agwii-* and *o'l* are used only for people who have died. Someone who is alive is called "grandfather" or "grandmother." Thus these terms would only be used to trace remembered relationships, again consistent with the Tsimshian distinction between immediate experience and hearsay expressed grammatically.

An interesting usage that bridges the fourth generation of the cycle is to call one's child by grandchild terms. This indicates reincarnation. Unfortunately, I did not collect systematic information on how long this continues in the child's life or whether anyone other than the parent does this. It is interesting in this regard, that *o'l* ("great-grandparent" or "great-grandchild") is reciprocal in contrast to the grandparent and grandchild terms. Perhaps *o'l* refers to someone who is a reincarnation of his great-grandparent and thus is simultaneously a great-grandchild and a great-grandparent. Certainly if the term refers to a remembered relationship in contrast to one that a person is familiar with at first hand, the *o'l* must have died. Since dead persons are reincarnated shortly after death (Adams 1973:31) *o'l* may refer to reincarnated ancestors.

Relationships of adoption are expressed by the prefix *anxs-*. This term is also used for those linked in the *agwii-* generation or beyond;

therefore, the prefix equates a relationship formed by dead ancestors with an adoption relationship. Both are established by hearsay (from the point of view of persons who are alive) rather than by blood. Thus the *anxs-* prefix stands for the distinction between blood relatives in the kin group and distant relatives within it. The *agwii-* term is on the borderline between the two. An *agwii-* relative is closer than an *anxs-* relative, but more distant than actual "grandfathers."

FORMAL USAGE

A Gitksan has pseudo kin in houses other than those in which he or his close kin are members. These are singled out in the use of kinship terminology in connection with feasting and the formal obligations it entails. This formal usage marks out a much larger group of "relatives" than the ordinary use of kinship terms. If someone wants to call a person by a kinship term, he can find an appropriate one by fitting that person in according to whether he or she belongs to his own phratry, his father's phratry, or his spouse's or siblings' spouse's phratry. The chances are that everyone will have one of those relatives in each of the Gitksan phratries, and thus he can call any other Gitksan by kinship terms. That such broad usage of kinship terms is not normal is indicated by jokes people make about certain individuals who call everyone by kinship terms. This is definitely not the proper thing to do. One of the implications of this behavior is that the individual does not really know his history; the use of kinship terms is supposed to denote some definite relationship, whether of services in the present or in the past—such as the fact that the two houses were once the same. People who do not use the terms according to this information, some of which may be esoteric, are thought of as foolish.

Here are examples of situations in which kinship terms may be applied to persons in Houses that are not directly related to ego. If a person has traveled to another village for a feast, his host may use kinship terms for him to show he is not a real stranger but has "relatives" there. Or in a speech at a feast all guests might be called "fathers." Or someone may have adopted "fathers" or people in other phratries who do things that *wilxsitxwitxw* usually do; they will call them by kinship terms even though there is no real relationship and such people may be distributed among several houses. Sibling terms will be used between members of houses in the same phratry which are *gapgapxw* to each other (more closely connected than they are to other houses in the phratry). These usually contribute more heavily to each other's feasts than members of other houses (see Adams 1973).

Through this formal usage, the Gitksan system comes to resemble a Dravidian system in which everyone in the society is called by kinship terms and in which one always marries a "cross-cousin." In fact the only relative in one's own generation one can marry is someone called "cross-cousin" (*gutxao'o*), but when informants say that they marry their "cross-cousin," this is always a reference to either pseudo kin or formal usage, it is never a reference to a blood relative. One should not be misled by such statements into considering that the Gitksan actually have a Dravidian system.[5]

The formal use of kinship terms widens the group of political allies in other houses and villages. And the shifting boundary formed by various kinds of metaphorical and formal usage is of great interest to the Gitksan compared with the settled question of who is or is not a relative in normal usage.

POSITIONAL SUCCESSION

Yet another way the Gitksan can use kinship terms to express concepts that are not part of their strict referential meaning is the result of positional succession. Terms that refer to descendants of members of another house in previous generations can be used in their normal way or can refer to the inheritance of names. Since names pass from one generation to another within the house, the result is a Crow type of situation in which members of different generations in the same house are called by the same kinship terms. For example, informants say that there is no word for the children of *gutxao'o* (cross-cousin); but they also refer to this relationship as *guxdagin* (grandchild). Similarly, one can speak of marrying one's grandfather and simply mean a member of one's mother's father's house in one's own generation. Or one can say that a given individual in one's own generation is one's "grandfather," simply because he has the name of one's mother's father or father's father. This usage occurs only when one wants to call attention to the relationship, such as on formal occasions connected with feasting, or when telling a stranger about it. Ordinarily persons related in this

---

5. Hindle and Rigsby (1973) use the word "formal" in a different sense from the way I use it here. They provide two terms for father, one of which they call formal. Their distinction is like that between "father" and "dad" in English. In my terms, father when used formally would refer to more individuals than it would in informal usage.

way refer to and address each other by name, rather than by kinship terms.

The term *nigwood* (father) is used in similar fashion. It can be used for "father's heir" when it replaces the cousin terms which would ordinarily apply between a person and a member of his father's house and his own generation. For example, one woman called her father *nigwood* and his blood brothers and distant relatives in his generation (in the other lineages in the house) *galan*. However, she calls the person who inherited her father's name *nigwood* even though he is not a blood relative and her father's brothers are. This person has now appointed an heir whom she in turn calls *nigwood* even though he is the age of *gutxao'o*. She called the present holder of her father's name *gutxao'o* before calling him *nigwood*. Such usage may also overrride the application of the terms by sex. One woman, who is the last in her house and generation, told us that a man of the same age calls her "dad"; in contrast to the grandchild/grandparent terms, this usage for the father's heir replaces the ordinary usage of kinship terms between the two individuals and is not just used on formal occasions.

GITKSAN USAGE AND KINSHIP TYPOLOGY

Linguists have pointed out that what is done by lexical means in some languages is done by grammatical means in others, and have concluded that a general theory of language cannot be confined to either. Hymes (1974:438) has made a similar point about reference and style, arguing that to obtain an adequate idea of linguistic universals both must be considered; universals are more numerous than they seem from referential usage alone. The same is true of kinship concepts. Morgan's basic types were devised from referential usage (1870), but if it is possible to express the concepts that underlie all of them through nonreferential usage, as I have shown for the Gitksan, many ideas about kinship must be more widespread than they appear to be.

Scheffler and Lounsbury (1971) argue that some notion of blood relatedness underlies even the most classificatory of kinship terminologies. Their argument, however, was based only on referential usage and may force some kinship terminologies into a mold that is foreign to them. A better case could have been made based on the entire set of kinship usages. Certainly on the Coast the Northern tribes that have kinship terminologies organized on a lineal basis have other ways of expressing degree of relationship.

Concepts of the Crow-Omaha type may also be more widespread than they seem from referential usage alone. On the Coast the succession of an heir to the name and social identity of his predecessor might make it necessary to transfer the kin terms applied to the predecessor to his heir even in societies where this is not a regular feature of the terminology, as it is among the Haida and Tlingit. This is not to say, however, that the concepts that underlie *all* of Morgan's types are equally common. Do the Southern societies on the Northwest Coast, which have an Hawaiian type of terminology that groups all relatives in each generation together regardless of lineage, express lineality and the cross-parallel distinction in nonreferential usage? This question certainly deserves further research.

There appear to be universal principles underlying kinship usage reflecting the universal dimensions of social relationships. In all of the societies in which kinship usage has been described, for example, there are respect gradients in which the more inclusive form is the more respectful, and to include persons in a category that is ordinarily limited to a small group of relatives is also an indication of respect. Similarly, all societies seem to make a distinction between formal and informal usage based on the social occasions in which interaction occurs: the more public and the larger the group of "witnesses," to use a Coast concept, the more formal the occasion. Also it would seem that a universal mode of insult is to disown a person as a relative and not use kinship terms for that person.

But once the entire set of kinship usages is described, there is still the issue of giving priority to one among them. Can we safely say that any usage is "primary" or "more important" than any other and thus use the relative importance of various usages as a basis for assigning societies to different structural types? Which is more important, the unmarked ideas, those coded into the referential meanings of the set of basic kinship terms and accepted more or less unconsciously by speakers, or the marked ideas, the counterpoint expressed in nonliteral usage and the more general terms? These, when they crosscut the basic categories, often contradict them.

The referential meanings form a base line, to which the others are modifications, and thus seem to be psychologically more available than the other meanings. They also appear to represent the most efficient solution. Thus I have argued that the cycle of generations expressed in a kinship terminology that has separate affine terms is more reflective of the marriage system in which perpetual alliances between groups do not exist than are the usages that refer to all the members of the society by kinship terms and thus could express such alliances. If, in fact, there were perpetual alliances, it would be wasteful to have an entire set of terms, the affine terms, that were redundant. They would gradually drop out of use. This does not, however, mean that some Houses might not have alliances with other houses for short periods of time, or that chiefly groups might not be so linked. But the referential usage reflects widespread characteristics, not these special alliances.

But since the ways of organizing kinship terms are mutually exclusive, it is impossible to use more than one in a system of referential meaning for a particular set of relatives even though it might be important to express several contradictory principles pertaining to kinship in a single society. Thus the referential meaning system should not be the sole basis for typologies of societies. The differences between kinship philosophies are matters of when, how often, and under what circumstances particular ideas are expressed.

On the Coast, for example, the social organization of the tribes is similar *despite* major differences in kinship terminologies. Kroeber (1934) shows that this is also true of California tribes, and Murdock (1949:195) provides a table showing it to be true of all but two of the fourteen culture areas of the New World. The similarities within these culture areas must be expressed in the nonreferential ways kin terms are used. Thus it may well be that Kroeber's stress on psychological and historical factors rather than social ones as determinants of kinship terminologies is correct, but only for the referential system of meanings. The importance of historical factors on the Coast is shown by the fact that language family boundaries coincide with differences in referential kinship terminologies. The other systems of meaning, however, would be free to follow the vicissitudes of social life more closely. A comparison of the full range of usage in Kitkatla with that of the Gitksan, two societies at opposite ends of the Tsimshian territory and the status gradient, might demonstrate a correlation between features of social organization and kinship usage that would be manifested in intracultural variation.

CONCLUSIONS

I have just added yet another description of Tsimshian kinship terminology to the literature. But because of the neglect of nonreferential usage, basic issues still remain to be solved. The questions go beyond the confines of the Northwest Coast area, although the description of a full range of kinship usage in every Coast society would be extremely valuable for discovering the true extent of cultural differences in the area. They address problems of significance to anthropology as a whole: the nature of kinship universals and how cultures should be compared.

Although as a system of denotative meaning the Gitksan terms form an Iroquois type of system, this is only a baseline to which various other usages form an important counterpoint. These "extensions" cannot be made along blood lines, since the Gitksan do not remember relationships between people beyond the grandparents. Their forgetting, however, makes it possible for them to use the terms to express a variety of other relationships. Thus they are able to use the kinship terminology to express changing relationships between an individual and various corporate groups, many of which reflect basic political processes in the society.

Many of these "extensions," if carried out on a large scale, would result in the Gitksan having another kind of system entirely. For example, the Gitksan approach a Dravidian type of system in some of their formal usages; they approach a Crow type of system in their use of terms related to succession to names. Their idea of blood kin and steps is very close to our own idea of kinship. Instead of embodying a limited set of concepts which are the core of a single kinship philosophy, their terminology—considered from the way it is *used*—expresses most of the ideas of kinship known to man.

Gitksan Kinship Terms

Note: Bruce Rigsby, who did fieldwork in the area, has generously allowed me to see his field notes; terms or usages that he collected and I did not are noted. I also added the items from Hindle and Rigsby's dictionary (1973) that I did not collect. These are designated HR followed by page numbers.

Native Terms	Use	Definition and Remarks

I. TERMS OF REFERENCE IN NORMAL REFERENTIAL USAGE

A. Kin

1) *Own Generation:*

stik'eekw	sister (woman speaker) fa bro da (woman sp) mo sis da (woman sp)	sibling of same sex (woman sp) used by woman for other woman in the same generation in the same house used by women for female children of men in the same generation as their father in their father's house used reciprocally "my other half"

Iguwii *Igiiwigi* *Igiikw* *xIgiikw* *Igigwii*	same as *stik'eekw*	same as *stik'eekw*

gimxdii	brother (woman sp)
	sister (man sp)
	fa bro da (man sp)
	mo sis da (man sp)
	fa bro son
	  (woman sp)
	mo sis son
	  (woman sp)
		sibling of opposite sex
		used by both sexes for people of opposite sex and in their own generation whose mother is in their own house or whose father is in their father's house and generation
		used reciprocally

waik	brother (man sp) fa bro son (man sp) mo sis son (man sp)	sibling of same sex (man sp) used by men for men in the same generation in their house and for men in the same generation whose fathers were in their father's house and generation used reciprocally
gutxao'o	cross-cousin	child of a man in one's own house and first ascending generation; member of father's house in own generation child of a *nixtaa* or a *nibib* used reciprocally used regardless of sex of speaker or of designee

2) *First Ascending Generation:*

naa'a	mother mother's sister	informal usage compared with *nox* (HR:57–8)
nox	mother mother's sister fa bro wife	women of ascending generation in own house; used by man or woman reciprocal is *lgulxm giet* (*hanaq*) (woman sp) "anyone your mother calls sister (in your own house) you call mother" formal usage compared with *naa'a* (HR:57–8)
nixtaa	father's sister mo bro wife	women married to a man in ascending generation of one's own house; all women in father's house in father's generation used only for the one person married to the uncle, and not extended to her house reciprocal is *gwislis* (woman sp)

galan	foster father father's brother (also see affine terms)	men in father's house and father's generation denotes a more distant relation than *nigwood* reciprocal is *łgulxm giet* (*hanaq*) (man sp) used for foster father if he is a relative of the father
baap	father	informal usage compared with *nigwood* (HR:57)
nigwood	father father's brother father's heir (i.e., person who took his name)	men of ascending generation in father's house closer than *galan* used for men in own generation if they took father's name (this may be only a formal usage; informally or if the person is the same age or younger than ego, he will continue to be called *gutxao'o*) reciprocal is *łgulxm giet* (*hanaq*) (man sp)
nibib	mother's brother	men of ascending generation in own house used by men or women reciprocal is *gwislis* (man sp)

3) *Second Ascending Generation:*

ndziits	grandmother mother's mother (mo fa sister?) father's mother (fa fa sister?)	used by both sexes for any older woman in their house, or in houses related by marriage one or two generations back. Not used for such relation- ships established by people other than the real mo's mo and fa's mo and fa's fa; can be used for any older woman in own phratry reciprocal is *huxda- gin* (woman sp)
niye'e	grandfather father's father father's mo bro mother's father mother's mo bro	used by both sexes for any older woman in the house or in houses related by marriage reciprocal is *huxda- gin* (man sp) can be used for any older man in own phratry

4) *Third Ascending Generation:*

agwii niye'e	great grandfather	reciprocal is *agwii huxdagin* or *agwii ɫguɫxm giet (hanaq)*
agwii ndziits	great grandmother	
o'l	great grandmother or grandfather (see third de- scending genera- tion)	used reciprocally; must be used in- side phratry

5)   *First Descending Generation:*

ɬguuɬxw *ɬguu*	child	own child or child of same sex person in the same generation in one's house reciprocal is *nigwood, gaɬan* for men; reciprocal is *nox* for women
ɬgii'ii	child sister's child (woman sp) brother's child (man sp) husb bro child (woman sp) (wife sis child?)	
gwislis	nephew or niece sis son (man sp) sis da (man sp) bro son (woman sp) bro da (woman sp) husb sis children (woman sp)	child of person of opposite sex and same generation in one's own house

6)   *Second Descending Generation:*

guxdagintw *huxwdaak'in*	grandchild	children of female *gwislis* used by men and women child of a member of house in first descending generation, child's child of a member of house in same generation reciprocal is *ndjiits* and *niye'e*

7) *Third Descending Generation:*

agwii guxdagin	great-grandchild	can be used inside or outside of house—e.g., a man's child's child
agwii łhułhu	great-grandchild	reciprocal is *agwii ndjiits, agwii niye'e*
o'l	great-grandchild (see third ascending generation)	*o'l* must be used inside phratry

B. **Affines**

1) *Own Generation:*

giodxs	bro in law (woman sp) husband's brother (woman sp) sister's husband (woman sp)	cross-sex term: man married to woman in own generation in house (woman sp) woman married to man in own generation in own house (man sp)
	sis in law (man sp) brother's wife (man sp) wife's sister (man sp)	used reciprocally
gwidziis	sis in law (woman sp) husband's sister (woman sp) brother's wife (woman sp)	used only between a woman and the men in her husband's house and generation, for the women husband calls sister used reciprocally

gałan *alaxantxw* *ha'axlantxw* (plural)	sis husband (man sp) wife's bro (man sp) (bro wifc bro?)	used for any man married to a woman in own generation in house or to any man in that generation in wife's house used reciprocally between men only in own generation
	(fa sis husb?) mo sis husband foster father fa bro (see Kin terms)	when used for first ascending generation the term is not reciprocal; then the reciprocal is *łgułxm giet*
wilaisxw or *wi-laiskxw*	wife's bro (man sp) sis husband (man sp)	same as *gałan* in own generation
naks	husband wife	used reciprocally; used just for the one person

2) First Ascending Generation:

gałan	see above	
łems	son in law, da in law, fa in law, mo in law, husb or wife mo bro and mo bro wife husb or wife's mo sis (and her husb) sis child husb or wife	used between adjacent generations; used reciprocally a person married into the house is *łems* to the entire ascending generation in the house, but only that one person is called *łems*—not his or her brothers and sisters see usage in *Downfall of Temlaham* (Barbeau 1928) in which wife's mo bro = *łems*

3) *First Descending Generation:*

lems   (see above)

C. Absent Terms

There are no terms for the following relationships:

daughter's husband's parents   use *nox* (first name of daughter's husband)

son's wife's parents

husband of cross-cousin   use *naks guxao'o*

wife of cross-cousin

children of male cross-cousin

children of female cross-cousin   use *lgiis* (name of cousin). These persons are referred to collectively as *guxdagin*, but it is not in use all the time as a kin term. One informant said *guxdagin* would only be used if the person were in one's own phratry. Durlach (1928) reports no terms for these relatives.

grandchild's husband and wife

niece's daughter's husband

mother's mother's brother's wife

husband's grandniece and nephew

mother's *wilxsitxwitxw*
father's *wilxsitxwitxw*
uncle's son's child   Here again these would be collectively called "grandfathers" or "grandmothers," but this is not a regular kinship term since it would be used only rarely and then just to denote a previous marriage.

wife's brother's wife

D. **Evidence for the terms exists but is slight:**

fa sis husb = *gaɫan*

> comes from an informant's statement that the husband of a *nixtaa* is either *gaɫan* or *nibib*. Two other informants reported that there was no term for father's sister's husband.

wife sis child = *ɫgii'ii*

> seems to be required from reciprocal usage.
> No informant gave the term.

husb or wife mo sis husb = *ɫems*

> argued from analogy with the fact that husband and wife's mother's brother *and his wife* are called *ɫems*. No evidence from informants.

II. OTHER AND COMPOUND FORMS

A. **Prefixes**

1) *cuwingidm-*   younger

cuwingidm-wekt	younger brother (man sp)	(Rigsby MS:69)
dzawingida-	youngest	
dzawingida-ɫgigwii	youngest sister (woman sp)	

2) *'enxs-*
'anxs-
enis-

step relative

> compound of prefix 163 (Boas 1911: 335) and prefix 166 (Boas 1911: 336) meaning lit. "the one who is like"
> means a relationship that is either too far back for the blood connection to be known to the speaker—

		i.e., people in another lineage in his house, or a relationship by adoption
'anxsɫgim-ditcwl	distant parallel cousin; adopted sis (person who helps one at feasts, relationships established in adult life)	(Rigsby MS:97)
'enuxs nig-wood	foster fa, used if fa is not a blood rel—i.e., for man mo married after the fa of the child. If child is taken in by a rel of his real fa, the foster fa is called *gaɫan*.	
'enis naxw	step mother	
'enisɫuɫxum giet	step son	
-hanaq	step daughter	

3) *agwii-*   "on the outside"

agwii ndziits	great-grandmother	
agwii niye'e	great-grandfather	
agwii guxdagin	great-grandchild	
agwii gutxao'o	child of a cousin (invented form by one informant)	
agwii nigwood	"doesn't make sense except possibly as step father"	(response to my invention)
agwii wil-nada'ɫii	next or different generation	
agwii ganni-yeetxw	plural distributive of grandparent	(Rigsby MS:67)

4) *anu-*   on my own side, in
                                 the sense of own
                                 crest used by one
                                 informant as op-
                                 posite of *agwii*

    anugo'o'ii   "on my own side"

    anu wilnada'Ʉii   my family, includ-
                                 ing mo, mo bro,
                                 bro, sis, mo mo
                                 or mo sis chil-
                                 dren, "anyone in
                                 family line"

    anu nigwood   people with the
                                 same crest as
                                 father

5) *lip-*   "my own"

    lip Ʉgii'ii   my own children
                                 (in sense of blood
                                 children)

    lip gapgapxwi   my own relatives—
                                 i.e., not sister's
                                 children

B. **Suffixes**

1) *-lixs giat*   "of a different sort"

    -lixs giedii   used to distinguish
                                 "siblings" in
                                 one's own house
                                 from "siblings"
                                 who are father's
                                 brother's children

    wag lix liggum   "brothers of a dif-
    lix skat   ferent sort"—i.e.,
                                 father's brother's
                                 children

    gimxdimlixs-   father's brother's   (Rigsby MS:71)
      gedi'i   children

2) *-mgiet*   male   (I have examples of
                                                  these suffixes
   łxułm giet   son   only for people in
   gwislismgiet   nephew   descending gener-
   łems giedi   son-in-law   ations.)
   guxdagintum   grandson
     giet
   agwiłułumgiet   great-grandson

3) *-mhanaq*   female

   -hanaq
   łxułmhanaq   daughter
   łems hanaq   daughter-in-law
   gwislismhanaq   niece
   guxdagintum-   granddaughter
     hanaq

C. Compound Forms

Most relatives can be referred to by a compound form (see Beynon MS; Beynon's manuscript gives only compound forms, even
for such relatives as mother's brother or father's sister, for which
there are established Tsimshian terms). These are some examples:

stkagwii na'ai   mother's sister
łgułxw gigwii'   my sister's son
łguułxum hanaq   my sister's daughter
  giigwi
guxdagin łgiigwi   sister's daughter's
                          child
waks nigwood   father's brother
gimxtii nigwood   father's sister
łgułxm giet nibib   uncle's children
łgit nibibii   uncle's children,
                          used if ego is
                          much older than
                          they are; recipro-
                          cal is *wilxsitx-
                          witxw*. Used in-
                          stead of *gutxao'o.*

III. GENERAL TERMS:

ɫagadzo'ii dip (name)	"we're related to _____"	It is possible that this refers only to
ɫagacuul nigwoodii	"my father's relatives"	people within the house, but this needs checking (Rigsby MS:97).
wila'aisxw	"Closest people in your family"	*wilaisxw* used for brother-in-law was said to mean "to become in a family, to become part of your own family"
ptext	phratry	
'wilnada'l	"family," used only within the phratry	Does not include father's relatives.

Note: Generally, means people known to be blood relatives and can refer to several houses within the phratry. It thus is probably what Barbeau called "clan" (1929). These different houses may be linked houses, known to have split off from each other in one village; or the houses can belong to different villages if they are believed to have a common history. Kin terms used within the houses can be extended to the entire *'wilnada'l* in formal situations. It is not always clear whether the common history was created because the house adopted people from other houses into it, or vice versa. Houses in the *'wilnada'l* may adopt people from other houses in the same *'wilnada'l* if they marry into their village, or if the adopting house is dying out. Also members of different houses in the same *'wilnada'l* may *hawal* in larger amounts than other members of the phratry at feasts (see Adams 1973).

wilp	House
ɫiɫuugietit wilp xskogumlaha	the people of Skogumlaha's House
'nastik'eekut	"we are bothers and sisters"

gwats 'wil nisim	close relatives within the house	This and the above form were given when I asked for a word for a unit smaller than the House. The progression from large to small matrilineal unit goes *ptext, 'wilnada'l, wilp, 'nastik'eekut* or *gwats 'wil nisim*.
lip wil 'iiɬe'e	blood relatives—including one's mother and her siblings and their children and one's father, his siblings, and their children, "the ones you don't marry."	
gan niiyeetxw *gan djiidzwi*	plural distributive of grandfather and grandmother	*gan niiyeetxw* can be used for mother's father and father's father as well as for father's mother's brother and within one's own house.

Note: This is the term that is meant when someone says that so and so (a contemporary in age) is my grandfather; i.e., he is a member of one's mother's father's or father's father's house. (If he were in one's own house or father's house, he would be called by a sibling term or *gutxao'o*.)

The reciprocal is *guxdagin* Grandparents' brother or sister (HR:57)

gannigwood	father's house (plural distributive of father)	
g'ap *lip gapgapxwi* *nagap'apt*	blood relations on one's father's and mother's side relative, kinsman (HR:38)	Broader than *lip wil 'iiƚe'e* above. Used particularly for distant relationships. Used reciprocally

Note: Can be used for father's relations but not for a relationship to one's spouse's relatives; that is, the relationship must have begun in preceding generations. "Joined together" particularly for things that were once different or separate. For example, since ego's father's brother married a Fireweed, ego is Frog, her father is Wolf, the father's brother's child and ego are *nagap'apt.* Also a white thread and a red thread that are joined or rejoined, or "two trees are related because their roots are joined." The term can be used within the phratry for distantly related houses. Used particularly between children of brothers.

wilksitxwitxw or
   wilxsitxwitxw
   (sing)
wilksilaks (pl)
wilksibakw (pl)
   (Rigsby MS:77)
	"where you spring from or come from." Used for people in one's father's house.	The people can be of any age. Used particularly in connection with services performed for ego at feasts and on formal occasions.
		Can be used for people in father's *'wilnada'l* or phratry who do services for ego
		Used reciprocally only if both persons have fathers in the other's house (sometimes in the other's phratry).

tz'elaluuluq	Given as a possible reciprocal of *wilxsitxwltxw*	If a person's father has died, the person's *wilxsitxwitxw* can say, "He is our *tz'elaluuluq*." This would be used to call attention to the fact that the person sprang from their house and should not be made fun of or gossiped about.
dm clm dogoy ni-dit	"I'll adopt them as my nieces."	
dm gwisliswii loodit	Which term means adopt? (Rigsby MS:119)	

IV. TERMS OF ADDRESS

A. Regular Terms

My series is incomplete; I have added the more complete series from Hindle and Rigsby (1973).

ye'e	grandfather
tsiits	grandmother
biiý *bii'e* *biip*	uncle (address of *nibib*)
dada	aunt (address of *nixtaa*)
na'a	mother, husband's mother, wife's mother, father's brother's wife
Iguuglxw	child, also used for grandparent to grandchild

wilaisxw	brother-in-law
baap	father (informal), dad (HR:58)
baba	daddy, a child's word (HR:57)
o'os	cross-cousin (address of *gutxao'o*, HR:58)

B. **Special address terms of affection.** (See also Sapir 1920:270)

wex	brother, also used by father to son as a term of affection, can also be used between two boys who are good friends.	Hindle and Rigsby describe this as an ordinary address term. My informant, however, distinguished it from other terms of address as expressing affection, as did Sapir's.
doots	mother to son, father to daughter, term of address showing special affection, also can be used by woman to son of her sister. Can be used between boyfriend and girlfriend.	HR gives this as address form of *gimxdii* (HR: 58) as well as the address form of a man to his daughter.
diiqu	mother to daughter as sign of affection, also between girls as best friends.	HR gives *diikw* as address form of *xlgiikw*; used between female siblings and parallel cousins (HR:58) as well as between mother and daughter.
diiý	woman's father (HR:57)	

Painted Houses and Woven Blankets

Symbols of Wealth in Tsimshian Art and Myth

GEORGE F. MACDONALD

When Viola Garfield began field research for her monograph on the Tsimshian at Port Simpson on the north coast of British Columbia in 1932 all the old plank houses had been torn down and only the bleached corner posts of a single old house remained (Garfield 1939, frontispiece). Even though she was too late to see the elaborately painted house fronts of the Tsimshian in person, old photographs and the accounts of informants prompted her to comment in her later study of Tsimshian arts: "The most spectacular products were the paintings which covered the facades of houses and the timbers carved with symbolic figures, generally known as totem poles. Facade paintings seem to have been more popular with the Coast Tsimshian who made few carved columns compared to the numbers in Gitksan and Nisqa villages" (Garfield 1951:58; reprinted 1966).

Photographs taken just before the turn of the century show decorated plank houses indicating a tradition of house front painting that was the finest and most elaborate of any on the Northwest Coast. Within the past few years new evidence has turned up in archives and museums in various parts of North America which provides greater insights into this tradition of the Tsimshian than has been possible before. Indeed, two examples of house front paintings from Port Simpson stand among the major pieces of Northwest Coast art. Since neither of these pieces has been described or analyzed previously, it seems appropriate to offer this study in tribute to Dr. Garfield's major research commitment to Port Simpson and the Tsimshian.

This chapter will focus on specific ritual and ceremonial items that appear to have strongly influenced each other over a long period. These items are painted house fronts and Chilcat dance robes. Both are organized as a central panel with a smaller flanking panel on each side. Using the principles of structural analysis to reveal sym-

109

bolic relationships and mythological expressions, I will further suggest that these two items are part of a larger structure linked to frontlets, highly decorated storage boxes, and coppers.

There are two sources for illustrating Tsimshian house front paintings. The first consists of photographic records and historical drawings from various archives, and the other is the house fronts themselves that have been preserved in museum collections. To begin with the visual records, the earliest (Plate 1) is a painting by a native artist at Port Simpson, Fred Alexcee, who recorded scenes of village life that he witnessed during the 1860s and 1870s. In Plate 1 there are only two painted house fronts out of the six houses pictured. This suggests that house front paintings were relatively rare at Port Simpson even during this heyday of the village. In fact, to judge from the photographic evidence, the proportion is even less than that. There are records of scarcely more than a half dozen painted house fronts at Port Simpson, and this small number was compiled from several decades of records. The low proportion suggests that probably only the head chiefs of the four clans at Port Simpson were entitled to painted house fronts.

The earliest photograph of the village, taken in 1873 by Charles Horetzky for a railroad survey, shows the island portion of Port Simpson with but a single decorated house façade (Plate 2). In 1879, Israel W. Powell, the first Indian commissioner for British Columbia, paid an official visit to Port Simpson, complete with a photographer who recorded the same housefront shown in the Horetzky view, but in much greater detail (Plate 3).

In the house models or actual house front paintings that have been preserved, the earliest and most impressive is an example collected in 1875 by James G. Swan from Port Simpson (Plate 4), supposedly for the Philadelphia Exposition the next year, although probably not exhibited there. This 38-foot-long housefront lingered for many years in the storerooms of the Smithsonian Institution until rediscovered there by Norman Feder just a few years ago. There are two other partly preserved house fronts from Port Simpson about which little is known. The first is in the National Museum of Man collection in Ottawa and the second is in the collections of the University of British Columbia Museum in Vancouver. Several models of houses with painted interior screens were collected at Port Simpson, probably by James Deans for the Chicago Field Museum, and although they have now been reduced to simply the painted boards, they offer additional evidence that interior screens were also executed at Port

Simpson. Some comparable examples relevant to the Port Simpson paintings will also be discussed.

Although the sample is rather limited, these paintings are important because of the insights they provide to a number of structural principles of Northwest Coast Indian art. In a related article (MacDonald 1977), I discuss the Body-House-Cosmos conceptual model that seems to underlie the formal and iconographic aspects of a linked series of material culture forms on the Northwest Coast. Included in this paradigm is the human figure (often in the role of a dancer), the overall house structure (and its various component parts, including the house posts and painted screens), and finally the structure of the universe itself. This series of homologues is designed to link the individual to the powers of the cosmos. I further pointed out that the shaman plays a key role in Northwest Coast Indian culture through his economic role as an intermediary between the various Chiefs of Wealth that are thought to control wealth in their respective cosmic domains. The identities of the first ancestor, the first shaman, and the Chiefs of Wealth become merged into a single being associated with clan, power, and wealth.

Finally, there are the studies by Lévi-Strauss (1975, 1977) refining the structural analysis of Northwest Coast myths and the concept of a Chief of Wealth. The concept has various realizations along the length of the coast. Those he chooses to deal with are primarily Chiefs of the Sea. However, structurally simpler beings can be identified for each cosmic zone. These beings comprise a complicated network of chiefs and chieftainesses who control game, fish, and other forms of wealth, and to whom the human shamans and chiefs had to pay homage through songs and rituals. The main characteristic defined for the north coast Chiefs of Sea Wealth was their dedication to rewarding properly arranged exogamous marriages with various forms of wealth and to punishing those who indulged in incestuous or improperly close unions.

Lévi-Strauss (1977:13) examines many variants of the Sea Chief concept on the north coast, including Gonakadet of the Tlingit, Gonakada of the Haida, and Komokwa of the Bella Coola and Kwakiutl. In these tribes wealth results from sighting the Sea Chief. But the Tsimshian picture is much more complicated. Hakulak, a female sea monster, has a floating child who devastates the villages of its captors by eating the eyes of villagers at night, except for a brother and sister who escape.

Another Sea Chief that Lévi-Strauss investigates is Nagunak. The

Plate 1. A memory painting by Tsimshian artist Fred Alexcee of the plank house at Port Simpson about 1865. (Public Archives of Canada C-24250)

Plate 2. The island portion of Port Simpson photographed in 1873 by Charles Horetzky. At the left is the painted house front of Chief Sqa·gwet of the Eagle clan of the Gitando tribe. (Public Archives of Canada PA9137)

Plate 3. The painted house front of Chief Sqa·gwet with a Thunderbird design. Taken during the first official visit of the Indian commissioner of British Columbia to the north coast in 1879. (British Columbia Provincial Archives 88656)

Plate 4. A painted house front collected from Port Simpson in 1875 by James Swan, illustrating the Nagunak story of the Gispudwada clan. (Smithsonian Institution MNH2240)

anchor of Chief Dragging-along-the-Shore and his men lands on Nagunak's roof one night. Nagunak has their canoes brought to him at the bottom of the sea. Then Nagunak finds that Chief Dragging-along-the-Shore and his men are fellow killerwhale clansmen, and proceeds to give them a feast before the other Sea Chiefs and to present them with gifts. To Dragging-along-the-Shore he gives a house front painting and interior house compartment decoration, as well as wealth in terms of good luck in hunting animals. These things are given with the proviso that the recipient never again hurt any fish. Lévi-Strauss points out the unkindness of a gift that excludes sea creatures to a coastal people like the Tsimshian.

The chief's party is then provided with a magical copper canoe and returns home to its village. At home the party first appears to the chief's elder sister as a monster floating in the bay with living things on top of it. Eventually one of Dragging-along-the-Shore's men violates the prohibition against hurting fish by cutting open both sides of the mouth of a bullhead they had found stranded, but still alive, on the beach. Soon thereafter both the canoes and their occupants are sucked into a whirlpool where the two who disobeyed perish, while Dragging-along-the-Shore is taken back to live permanently in the house of Nagunak. Lévi-Strauss (1977:13) notes the ambiguous double imagery of Nagunak as a whirlpool in some instances and as a solid projecting reef in others. Among all the coastal variants of the story, this version is the only one that has such an ambiguous moral nature: on the one hand, Nagunak is the master of great wealth assuring the fortunes of those he favors; on the other hand, he places his beneficiaries under very strict and harsh conditions. Lévi-Strauss (1977:13) concludes that Tsimshian mythology has the richest range of gradations of the tribal variants of these Chiefs of Sea Wealth. I believe the same rich gradations and ambiguities apply to the symbolic content of Tsimshian graphic arts.

The Nagunak story that attracted Lévi-Strauss's attention is the same one Garfield chose to illustrate her examination of inherited powers and crests among the Tsimshian (Garfield 1951:42). The remarkable house front painting in Plate 4 seems to portray the Nagunak legend. The most distinctive feature of the chief in the center of the design is the series of small heads that surround his own head—much as Boas (1916:288) described the "mermaid children" who swim before Nagunak, and who are described as covering his back, and constituted his principal crest. These five small heads are like those forming the border around frontlets (Plate 5) and housefront paintings. These small heads vary from five to thirteen in

Plate 5. Tsimshian frontlet, or *amalait,* showing the "long nose" crest of the Sqa·gwet and Minisqu' house front paintings. (National Museums of Canada)

number for both the frontlets and the house front paintings. The two killerwhales on either side of the central figure on the house front painting represent an alternate appearance of Nagunak, since he is described in the feast episode as wearing the body of a killer-whale as his ceremonial garment (Boas 1916:288). Another of Na-gunak's crests consisted of two opposing killerwhales, joined at the nose, called Dashing-Against-Each-Other (Boas 1916:288).

Indeed, it may be significant that the holes in the dorsal fins of the killerwhales in the house front painting in Plate 4 are placed so as to interrupt the line separating the main design panel from the border design, becoming in themselves visual thresholds between different zones of the design. There is little doubt that the extreme extension of the dorsal fins beyond the design field emphasizes the symbolic association of the dorsal fin of the killerwhale as a world axis. There are several additional design features of the back of the killerwhale that appear to be significant in view of the myth of Na-gunak. The prominent figures of the animals whose heads form the joint marks on the dorsal fins of the killerwhales represent a land animal on the right side of the screen and an aquatic animal with both feet and fins on the left side. In both cases, care has been taken to show them as animals and not as fish.

On the snout of each killerwhale is an amorphous finned creature whose most distinctive attribute is its large mouth, which defies the usual conventions of mouth design by tapering off at both ends into the body of the killerwhale. This may be the bullhead whose mouth was cut open on both sides and then ridiculed by the chief's men.

The final comment on this house front relates to the two human figures being drawn down into the blowholes of the killerwhales, as described in the final paragraph of Boas's version of the story (1916:292). No doubt they simultaneously represent the men being blown out of the killerwhales (as when they rise from the house of Nagunak after the feast in a mountain of foam that turns quickly to fog).

It is clear that the major fields of this house front painting are the backs of the killerwhales. Remember that it was the elder sister of Dragging-along-the-Shore who first saw the returning canoe party and described it as looking like a large monster floating on the sea in front of the village. She also saw something on top of it that appeared to be alive and made a noise like a bell. In structuralist terms, I will argue that the backs of the killerwhales (which rise above the surface of the water as well as plunge down beneath it) represent mediating zones symbolized in the myths by reefs, whirlpools, and half-submerged beings. The killerwhale can be seen as a natural combination of these features. Its back is like a reef that can submerge, its dorsal fin is like the world axis, and its blowhole can both suck in like a whirlpool and spew out. The Haida describe a Sea Chief in Tsimshian territory who has no teeth and swallows his food whole, principally hair seals. After digesting his food for a few hours, he blows out the undigested bones and other parts with great force (Newcombe MS 1904–5).

In the house front painting in Plate 4 Nagunaks is depicted with his crown of small human heads, flanked on either side by manifestations of his alter ego, the killerwhale. Many structural contrasts are resolved in this particular painting, some of which have just been discussed. Another is the contrast between left and right in the design, where the forms and colors of the secondary and tertiary design elements are strongly contrasted between the killerwhales on the left and right sides. Also, the top of the housefront is zoned into a dozen small figures that are, at the same time, humans and killerwhale dorsal fins. Although each of these fins has the same value in the overall design, no two of them are identical. The doorway of the house is through the abdomen of Nagunak, suggesting an equation in which the whole house structure becomes the body of Nagunak as the Chief of Wealth, or of Dragging-along-the-Shore as primary ancestor, or, implicitly, of the primary shaman who went to reside permanently with Nagunak.

Let us now look at a set of house front designs of the Tsimshian and their neighbors which concentrate on thunderbirds. The first example (Plate 3) shows the painting as it appeared in 1879 on the house of Chief Sqa·gwet of the Eagle clan of the Gitando tribe of Port Simpson. It was somewhat larger than the Smithsonian house front (Plate 4), probably between 50 and 60 feet, and just as elaborate as the latter in design. The central figure (a front view of double profiles) surrounding the entryway is the thunderbird. Note that the huge beak with the hooked tip that shows in the Horetzky photograph of 1873 (Plate 2) is missing by the time of Powell's visit, when this picture was taken. The beak was over 20 feet long and was supported on the end by prop poles. The socket for the beak still shows clearly in the 1879 photograph. The general designation as a thunderbird is further supported by the prominent ears that project horizontally from either side of the bird's head. But, as Viola Garfield cautioned, specific attributes gave special covert meanings to the generally recognized figure. She states (1951:59):

> Carvers and painters developed a set of symbols by which the people recognized the various characters, incidents and plots that were represented. Illustrations of a few popular subjects became so conventionalized that carvings or paintings of them are readily recognizable whether they come from Yakutat or Vancouver Island. On the other hand, illustrations representing individual experiences could not be interpreted, even by a tribesman, without explanation from the owner or artist.
>
> In the process of graphic conventionalization, distinctive features of each oft-recurring story character were selected. The shape of the beak was the distinguishing mark of birds and of bird supernaturals.

Thus, while the previous house front painting suggested a specific myth as its inspiration, only a general identification of the present example as a thunderbird is possible, although a much more specific level of meaning must also have been intended by the artist.

In this painting, the eyes of the thunderbird each contain three human figures, while a single split human figure fills the space in its mouth. Over the head of the thunderbird is a row of eleven figures, which are almost identical to the twelve figures on the Smithsonian house front painting, suggesting that both paintings might be the work of the same artist. Flanking the central panel figure are much smaller profile birds on either side, which are also probably thunderbirds. Unfortunately, some elements of the design are obscured in the photograph by fences and by the spruce boughs that were erected in honor of Commissioner Powell's visit. It is regrettable that no portion of this house front has survived to allow a closer examination of the painting

The housefront paintings in Plates 3 and 4 both have frontal figures extending around the entryway of a house flanked by two profile figures, and a top panel with a host of small crested figures. In both designs the profile figures flanking the frontal figures vary greatly from the left to the right side in secondary design elements. The most striking difference between the two designs is that one is built around a human figure and the other around a thunderbird. The killerwhale house front, I would suggest, refers to wealth from the sea or underworld, while the thunderbird housefront refers to wealth of the upper world.

As Levi-Strauss notes (1977:13), the Gitksan describe a creature called Weneel who lives in the lakes and is the equivalent of Hakulak in the myths of the coast. He points out, however, that Barbeau's informants stressed the resemblance of this creature to the thunderbird (Barbeau 1929:105). It is illustrated as having a bird's head with a long recurved beak and a body covered with feathers. A relationship to the myth of the origin of mosquitoes is further implied by its similarity to depictions of mosquitoes by Tsimshian.

The next house front painting is from Gitlakdamsk, a Nishga village not far from Port Simpson (Plate 6). It belonged to Chief Minisqu' and was very similar to the thunderbird house front painting at Port Simpson, although simpler. The beak in this example appears to be even longer, more than 30 feet in length, with two sets of props to support it. The European style double doorway constitutes the body of the bird, while double U-shaped ears extend out from the sides of the bird's head. Above its head are eleven small human figures, the same number as on the Port Simpson house front. The central figure once again is larger than the others and extends down between the cleft in the forehead of the thunderbird.

Flanking the central design are two smaller thunderbirds on each side, which also have projecting beaks but, unlike the Port Simpson version, are depicted in frontal view rather than in the more traditional profile view of the figures on the side panels.

Two additional decorated house fronts warrant consideration here, since for the first there is evidence that it was at least influenced by designs at Port Simpson, if not actually done by a Port Simpson artist, and for the second there is substantial evidence that it was designed and executed by a Tsimshian artist under contract to a Tlingit chief.

The first example is the house front painting of Chief Gold (Plate 7), built just west of Skidegate around 1880 by this chief, who is credited with discovering gold on the Queen Charlotte Islands around 1850. It is known that Chief Gold visited Port Simpson during the time when the thunderbird house front was still standing. Chief Gold's house had virtually the only painted house front in the Queen Charlotte Islands. The design layout consists of the huge head of a thunderbird on the central panel, flanked on either side by thunderbirds in profile. There is no projecting beak attached to the central face, but directly above it is a sculptured thunderbird face (within a moon disk) which has a separately carved projecting and recurved beak. Although the sculpture was brought from Gold's house at Kaisun, and was originally intended as his mortuary plaque, it may have been considered a convenient substitute for a beak on this house front painting. While all the little human figures that characterize Tsimshian designs have been eliminated from this example, a single human figure, said to be the man in the moon, fills the mouth area of the thunderbird. The doorway to the house was inserted through the body of this human figure.

The Powell expedition also photographed a Bella Coola house front painting of comparative interest (Plate 8). The construction of the Bella Coola house front is very different from that of the north coast tribes. The central panel is composed of vertical planks that extend well above the roof line, while the side panels are composed of horizontal boards that more or less match the roof line. Nevertheless, the structure of the painted design is virtually the same as those on the north coast. The central thunderbird in this example is depicted in frontal view surrounding the doorway, flanked by smaller profile thunderbirds with ears. Between the ears of the central bird a human figure has been inserted, but it lacks the upper border of small figures of the Tsimshian examples. Like the Tsimshian examples,

Plate 6. The painted house front of Chief Minisqu' at Gitlakdamsk village on the Nass River. (National Museums of Canada 73-358)

Plate 7. "Moon house" of Chief Gold near Skidegate, Queen Charlotte Islands. Photographed by R. Maynard in 1884. (Chicago Field Museum 17344)

Plate 8. Bella Coola painted house front with a Thunderbird design. Photographed by O. Hastings in 1879. (National Museum of Canada)

Plate 9. Interior painted screen from Kitwankul village collected by Marius Barbeau for the National Museums of Canada. Barbeau identified the figure as a dragonfly. (National Museums of Canada 62244)

however, the apparent bilateral symmetry of the overall design is denied when the secondary design elements of the two sides are compared.

The Tsimshian authorship of the next example to be considered is well documented (Emmons 1926:24). It is not a house front painting, but rather an interior screen commissioned by the Tlingit chief Kate-tsu of the Whale House at the village of Klukwan. The artist who designed and carved the screen was a Tsimshian, but it may have been painted later by a Tlingit. A detailed history of the screen from the Whale House is provided by Emmons (1916).

The most striking feature of the screen is the myriad small human figures forming a frame around the central figure. Although common on Tsimshian screens, such figures are not found in Tlingit designs and thus stylistically mark the piece as Tsimshian. Although the side border of figures is missing on the right in Plate 10, early photographs (for example, see Reid and Holm 1975:21) show that the screen was complete at one time but that Emmons's drawing, taken from a photograph, leaves out what was blocked by an interior post. Originally the design included thirteen small figures of humans, with double fin designs on the sides of their heads,

Plate 10. The "rain wall" from the interior of the Whale house in the Tlingit village of Klukwan, said to have been carved by a Tsimshian artist.

which formed a border around the central figure. There were no flanking designs.

The small border figures reflect closely the huge central figure whose body consists of a doorway—marking a zone of transition—between the communal portion of the house and the chief's compartment. The central figure also has fins on its arms that are lacking on the small peripheral figures. Completely human representations fill the pupils of the eyes on the central figure, but whereas the thunderbird house front from Port Simpson had three human figures in each eye, the Whale House screen figure has only two, each of which has the false door design in the center of its body. All the joints in the arms and legs, as well as the ears and tail, nostrils, and mouth, contain small figures that are typical Northwest Coast designs. However, the addition of another fifteen frontal faces in the primary form lines of the head of the central figure is distinctive.

Emmons (1916:23) claims that the central figure, with outstretched arms, represents the rain spirit, while the small border figures are called "raindrops splash up," for they represent the splash of falling drops after they strike the ground. He says that the whole partition was called the "rain wall." Although I would not dispute this interpretation, and indeed will come back to it again shortly, I do think that the name "rain wall" tells only part of the story.

Almost certainly the figure is that of Gonakadet, the Tlingit Chief of Wealth, who was the subject of the first house post on the right side when entering Whale House. According to Emmons (1916:25): "Gonakadate was believed to be a great sea monster, half animal and half fish . . . generally shown with fore feet, a characteristic dorsal fin, and the tail of a fish, but again it is said that rising from the water it appeared as a beautifully ornamented house front. It brought good fortune to one who saw it." Curiously, he never specifically identified the "rain wall" figure as even a manifestation of Gonakadet, although, as we shall see, he does not hesitate to identify strikingly similar images in Chilcat weaving as Gonakadet. The best piece of evidence that the central figure on the "rain wall" screen is Gonakadet, however, is the small figure in its mouth. It is a double profile killerwhale with the characteristic curved dorsal fin pierced by a hole. As Emmons notes (1916:25), whales were the main food of Gonakadet.

Essentially then, the "rain wall" from Whale House at Klukwan and the killerwhale house front at Port Simpson both illustrated, in my view, the same mythological reference to Sea Chiefs of Wealth—

Plate 11. Three versions of Sea Chief Gonakadet

a. A Chilcat dance blanket identified by Emmons and Swanton as Gonakadet (after Emmons 1907:fig. 585a)
b. Design from the interior house screen of Chief Edenshaw's house at
   Kiusta, Queen Charlotte Islands, identified by Swanton as Gonakadet
   (after Swanton 1909:fig. 6)
c. A box front painting in the three-panel house front format, claimed by
   Boas to be a frog but probably representing Gonakadet (after Boas 1927:fig.
   246)

Nagunak in the Tsimshian example and Gonakadet in the Tlingit. A large interior screen representing the Haida version of Gonakadet also served to divide off Chief Edenshaw's compartment in his house at Kiusta on the Queen Charlotte Islands (Plate 11b).

As to the meaning of the "rain wall" design, there are many possible levels of interpretation. I would like to suggest a few for this screen that supplement rather than oppose other interpretations. After endorsing the one provided by Emmons's informants that the screen represents raindrops splashing up, I would point out the cosmological concept common to the north coast tribes, although specifically recorded by Swanton (1909:13) for the Haida, that the "shining strings of heaven" are attached to the axis mundi, or mythological world pole. If they are pulled during the candlefish or herring season, they cause hail, which is said to be candlefish or herring eyes falling down. A mythopoetic reference to the abundance of fish runs, the illusion to the splashing up of rain drops by Emmons's Tlingit informants is understandable. Throughout the Northwest Coast precise terms for symbols of wealth or power are avoided, and more circuitous terms or circumlocutions are used instead.

Swanton also recorded the Haida equation of the souls or spirits of fish with those of human beings. In a myth it is said: "At a place beyond the Land of Souls, and just visible from there, was the dwelling of a chief called Great-Moving-Cloud. He owns the dog-salmon; and when a gambler died, and his soul went to the Land of Souls, he always came over to gamble with him. Souls were bid against dog-salmon, and if the gambler won, there would be a great run of the latter fish; if he lost, there would be many deaths" (Swanton 1909:35). In another myth of the Haida, recorded by Swanton (1909:259), the hero goes out to slay Gonakadet for killing too many people and tells a friend to drown him in a hole on the beach where salmon heads are kept so that he can go down to make war on Gonakadet. The "rain wall" screen might even represent the "salmon-head hole" that led to Gonakadet's lair.

In the Tsimshian deluge story recorded by Boas (1916:346), two brothers go to hunt a whale that is causing floods on the Skeena River by overflowing the lake in which it lives. The elder brother seeks the whale in an underwater house but encounters only thunder, lightning, and hail. Next a large Grizzly Bear comes out of the carved screen in the middle of the rear of the house and asks the man to open its back. The bear turns into a carved box. Then a thunderbird comes from behind the carved screen and asks the man to put it into the box, where it becomes a drum. "Living Eyes" appears in turn from behind the screen in the form of hail and asks to be put in the box as well. The man takes the supernatural helpers and becomes a shaman with the following song (Boas 1916:349):

Every living fish, every living fish,
My supernatural power told me where every living fish is now.

He eventually leads the people to saltwater and teaches them how to catch halibut. Perhaps now we are approaching another level of meaning of house screens whereby the elaborately structured, three-panel depictions of cosmic animals such as thunderbirds and killerwhales refer to abstract concepts of wealth equatable with salmon and halibut, the staples of the north coast. In a slightly different dimension, these three panel screens with a central "chief" flanked by profile animals also signify wealth in human terms, as a numerical statement of the power and strength of a clan or lineage. The equation between fish and human souls found in myths helps to explain how "raindrops splashing up" can serve as a metaphor for a steady fish supply as well as for a strong lineage.

Another aspect of the large frontal designs that warrants comment is that when used on house screens they are placed on the threshold of the house. This is where the axes of the universe are thought to intersect for that household. Either as a house front screen or as an interior screen behind which the ceremonial regalia is stored, these main designs surround a doorway, a zone of transition into another world of sanctity. The significance of the appearance of initiates or dancers through the hole in the rear compartment screen captures such sanctity throughout the Northwest Coast culture area.

The creatures that are pictured surrounding these cosmic doors are the guardians of the doors. The two most common cosmic door guardians along the coast are unquestionably the thunderbird as the guardian to the upper world and the killerwhale as the guardian to the underworld. The dorsal fin of the killerwhale bears the hole, which is a symbol of the portal to the underworld ruled by the various Sea Chiefs. The thunderbird has a sky door through its body, either as an actual door, as in the thunderbird house front painting from Port Simpson (Plate 3), or as symbolized by a face, often with prominent teeth that represent the perils associated with passage through such cosmic doors.

A part of the Body-House-Cosmos model on the north coast is the form, in a structural sense, of the Chilcat blanket (see Plate 12): the same pentagonal form, with the same proportions, as a house front but reversed (MacDonald 1977). I should also point out that

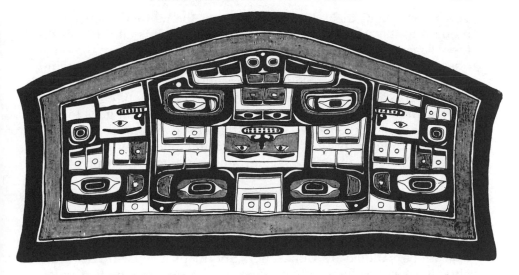

Plate 12. Chilcat blanket as a reversed version of three-panel house front design, depicting the "diving whale" in the center panel, flanked by thunderbirds on either side.

the fringe of the blanket has the same visual effect as the smoke from the hearth of the house, or, for that matter, the swan's-down at the top of the dancer's frontlet. I will not consider the designs on Chilcat blankets except to note that the atomized and recombined parts of animals in the designs are analogous to the ritual tearing apart and reassembly of the shaman as part of his initiation and blending with the universe. I would like to consider some of the significant motifs on Chilcat blankets.

Emmons devoted much time to the investigation of these motifs (1907:fig. 559) and produced a chart. He assigns three distinctive values to the white dots that occur within the black primary lines of the blankets. The first type of white dots may be classified as "holes," the second as "gambling stick ends," and the third as "raindrops." These classes can be considered to form a core group of symbols that have particular meaning to both the Haida and the Tlingit, as well as to the Tsimshian, as seen in the previous examples of myths.

This association between eyes, gambling sticks, water creatures, and wealth is frequent in the mythology of the area. Another Tsimshian example is provided by the story of "plucking out eyes" (Boas 1916:154–58). In it a prince marries a girl from the lake near Prairie

Town. One night their child is taken from the mother's house and brought to the father's village, where the child eats all the eyes of the villagers. To console the father and his sister, who are the only ones who escape the village alive, the supernatural mother compensates them with gambling sticks. With the sticks the father becomes very rich and the sister becomes Property Woman. The supernatural mother leaves the lake with her child and goes to the sea, where she becomes Hakulak, the female counterpart of Nagunak. A Tlingit version of the story accounts for the origin of Lenaxxidaq, the female Spirit of Wealth, and counterpart of Gonakadet (Boas 1916:746).

Emmons believed that the blanket named for the Chilcat division of the Tlingit was a Tsimshian invention, and he provided several Tsimshian stories to support that view. In the first story (1917:330) a girl who insults the bear chief is forced to marry him, but escapes in a canoe paddled by Gonakadet. She in turn must marry him, although he already has a wife. Forced to hide from the first wife, the girl spies on her and discovers the secret of making Chilcat blankets.

The link Emmons describes between Gonakadet and house fronts has already been noted. He illustrates a dance apron (Plate 11a) which he says represents Gonakadet rising out of the sea and which would be upside-down when worn. The central figure is shown flanked by two killerwhales with double dorsal fins. Over the head of Gonakadet are three small human faces. In all essential details this dance apron is the same as the Nagunak house front painting from Port Simpson and the "rain wall" from Klukwan. Emmons feels that Chilcat weaving originated from the painted skin apron of the shaman.

In support of the link between Chilcat blankets and house screens, Emmons (1907:345) related the story of the Tsimshian widow and her daughter who were starving at the end of a long winter. The girl sat staring day after day at the intricately carved and painted interior wall of their house, for they had not always been poor. Finally, the image took possession of her and she began to weave a copy. It was so successful that it provided her dowry. Her new father-in-law honored her work with a great feast that spread her reputation until the Tsimshian became the acknowledged weavers of the coast.

An early interesting example of a Chilcat dance blanket decorated with the image of Gonakadet is illustrated in Gunther's study of the Rasmussen collection (1966:204). In this blanket the figure of Gonakadet is upside-down and surrounds a rectangular doorway motif that would be against the dancer's neck; his head would project out of the design field, just as the initiated pass through or move out of the doorway in the "rain wall" screen.

Support for the above interpretations are also provided, I believe, in Viola Garfield's observations on Tsimshian blanket weaving (Garfield 1951:65): "Chilkat designs were usually arranged in three fields, similar to the layout of designs on other flat surfaces. A wide center field covered the back of the wearer. There was a narrower strip on each side which extended over the shoulder and was visible from the front. This was similar to the arrangement of painted designs on the front edges of skin robes."

Brief reference should be made to several other forms of material culture that are closely related to concepts of wealth on the Northwest Coast. Included here are the frontlets of the dancer, the highly decorated storage chests, and of course the ultimate symbol of wealth, the Northwest Coast copper. A Tsimshian frontlet or *amalait* (derived from the Tsimshian word for dance) is shown in Plate 5. Although much simplified because of its diminutive scale compared with a painted house front, it retains all the essential features of the thunderbird house front paintings at Gitlakdamsk or Port Simpson (Plates 6 and 3), including the border of small human faces and figures, the frontal faces in the eyes, the small figure in the "doorway" of the mouth, and the large projecting, hooked beak. From the structural perspective the eagle down that wafts from the top of the *amalait* during a dance is visually analogous to the smoke rising from the roof of the house, and the swaying fringe of the Chilcat dance blanket.

Storage boxes are containers or protectors of items of wealth. They clearly form part of the Body-House-Cosmos model, and are decorated accordingly. The example in Plate 11c is so close to a painted house screen that it should need no further explanation. Less obvious, although certainly more typical of Northwest Coast box designs, the box shown in Plate 13 depicts a finned creature that could be a Grizzly-Bear-of-the-Sea, or Gonakadet himself, in the center panel flanked by vestigial side panels with salmon-head joint marks and profile faces that barely suggest the side view of the central figure. The body of the main figure, however, is clearly in the form of a doorway in which the figure of some unidentifiable creature appears.

The copper as a Northwest Coast symbolic form of material culture can be interpreted as a cosmogram from a variety of perspec-

Plate 13. A carved and painted storage box from the north coast in which items of wealth and prestige were stored. (DeMenil collection)

tives (MacDonald 1977). The symbolic relationship of coppers to house front designs is supportable. The main difference is that the side panels of the house and screen design structures so far considered have been rearranged and placed below the center panel.

The example of a Tlingit copper in plate 14b displays in the main panel the figure of a bird with prominent ears (folded together over the head) and a sharply hooked beak. The bird's body has been reduced to wing joint marks on either side of an oval doorway that in turn has been incorporated into the figure of a crab. The lower panels contain a conglomeration of elements that are interpretable as profile figures, but have lost their original meaning and can only be loosely read as the wings of the overall bird figure.

CONCLUSION

Attention has been directed in this chapter to particular ritual and ceremonial items that I believe have strongly influenced each other in both design structure and decorative motif over a very long period. The two classes of objects of special interest were painted house

Plate 14a. Copper (University of British Columbia Museum of Anthropology)

Plate 14b. Tlingit copper in which the three-panel house front design is rearranged with the center panel at the top and the two lateral profile panels below (after Boas 1916:fig. 21).

screens and woven Chilcat dance robes. Other objects mentioned that appear to be structurally linked to the series include frontlets, decorated storage boxes, and coppers.

The design structure used for all of these consists of a central panel with two narrower flanking panels. The broad central one always displays the frontal (double profile) image of a "monster" figure in which a greatly exaggerated head is often surrounded by small human figures of faces. The mouth or body of the monster frequently contains a portal. It may be an actual doorway, an inlay of some other material, or a figure or head that is in the process of emerging from, or being swallowed by, the mouth of the monster.

The side panels are much narrower and contain profile figures that represent alternative or supporting images of the central figure. On box fronts, the side panel designs are often very narrow or perhaps vestigial, while on frontlets they have been eliminated altogether. On coppers the two side panels have been regrouped so that they are separated from the central panel by the characteristic T-shaped ridge of copper.

It appears that the monster design in question is not a crest, although it provides a structure into which crest elements can be fitted. It was noted that many of the house front paintings and woven Chilcat examples depict Gonakadet or related Sea Chiefs who figure prominently in the art and myth of the region as Chiefs of Wealth. Brief reference to the mythology of the north coast revealed intriguing links between doorways, water holes, water spouts, and floods; fish heads and eyes and "Living Eyes"; gambling sticks and wealth; and, last but not least, infants and human souls. The recent studies of Lévi-Strauss (1975, 1977) on the mythology of water spirits on the Northwest Coast also support this interpretation.

The chapter is essentially a test of the Body-House-Cosmos paradigm for Northwest Coast art and mythology proposed elsewhere (MacDonald 1977) and based on two forms of material culture—the painted house screen and the Chilcat robe. Although both of these forms are widespread on the coast, Viola Garfield's studies convincingly demonstrated that they achieved particular refinement among the Tsimshian.

Tsimshian Religion in Historical Perspective
Shamans, Prophets, and Christ

JAY MILLER

Given the thousands of pages we have on Tsimshian myths, crests, kinship, and economies, we really have next to nothing on religion. If defined as a relation with transcendence, the supernatural, or the extranormal, then Tsimshian religion traditionally focused on shamans, together with chiefs in their priestly guise as the bestowers of supernatural power to noble youngsters at Winter Ceremonials. Yet Boas (1916:473–77) devotes only four pages out of a thousand to shamanism, Garfield (1951:46–48) adds a few more, and Barbeau (1958) includes thirty pages on Tsimshian shamans in his one-hundred-page booklet. More material can be found in the Beynon notes, but *in toto* these are not impressive percentages for such a central feature of Tsimshian life and culture.

Aboriginal religion focused on the crucial concept of *haleyt* augmented by that of *naxnox*. Vastly simplifying, *haleyt* refers to controlled supernatural power expressed through simulations of desired state, while *naxnox* is unwieldy supernatural power associated with chiefly might, antisocial acts, and distinctive tendencies intended to instill fear into onlookers. *Haleyt* had continuous, legitimate usage, while *naxnox* was limited to masked performance and dramatic events held during the winter season.

During initial stages of Euro-Canadian intrusion, these concepts were challenged and demeaned. In their defense, several native prophets appeared who preached revisions, making the concepts more acceptable to the Evangelical Christianity that eventually superseded them. Of these prophets, the most famous was Bini, a Carrier Athapaskan who founded a line of imitators who also used his name. While accounts of Bini among the Tsimshian have yet to appear in print, Jenness (1943:550–59) discusses him within the Carrier context as the younger brother of Sisteyel and nephew of Sami, earlier prophets. Some of the appeal of Bini related to his position as chief of the Beaver phratry, strengthened further when he gave a large potlatch to dedicate his Fireweed totem pole in Bulkley Canyon. In fact, during his life he was best known as Kwiis, the Beaver chiefly name, only taking the name of Bini, and later of Samtelesa, after successive visits to the sky. He died about 1870, apparently from water—which he used for a curing—that had been poisoned.

At present all the older Tsimshian and many of the younger ones are devout Christians, the result of missionary work by William Duncan, Thomas Crosby, and others less well known. With their conversion, the Tsimshian came to publicly reject their previous beliefs as pagan and, as they say, "low class." Their native medicoreligious specialists were hounded into abandoning their practice by accusations that they were in league with the devil. Even now with a reawakened appreciation of their past greatness, the accepted translation of the word *swansk* (shaman, Indian doctor) is "witch doctor" or "devil worker." Of all the Tsimshian, only the Gitksan, somewhat insulated by their interior homeland, continue to recognize and patronize shamans who derive their power from the Christian God and who practice a Christianized shamanism. The Coast and Southern Tsimshian urge that shamanism be forgotten and sometimes go as far as to say that shamans were never all that important in the past anyway. Yet no matter how strenuous the denials, the subject of shamanism is not easily discussed at all without making the participants uneasy. Attitudes toward shamanism continue to run deep and be emotional. This became clear to me when I was showing the testament summarized in the "Conflict over Christianity" section of this chapter to several Tsimshian. Though they occurred in 1918, the events described in the testament could as easily have happened in the 1980s.

In homage to Viola Garfield, this paper is based on materials either collected by her in the field or sent to her by William Beynon and now stored in the Garfield Collection of the University of Washington Archives. These data have been sufficient to trace the history of religious change among the Tsimshian by describing the roles, duties, and privileges of specific shamans, by presenting two brief accounts of Bini, prophet-cum-shaman, and by summarizing the narrative of a woman brought to the brink of insanity by her personal conflict between her new Christian faith and her training to assume the shaman's power of her dead mother's brother.

THE TRADITIONAL: THE SWANSK

Garfield was fortunate to have among her principle ethnographic informants at Port Simpson a man called Niəsgane (died 1935), who was the only shaman in the community. But she was unable to broach the specific subject of shamanism with him, since he was on court probation from a charge of witchcraft and had to avoid any reference to this activity. Other members of the community were willing to discuss his career with Garfield as a warning for her to be careful while they were working together.

Among the people of the Nass and Skeena, Niəsgane had a reputation as a powerful curer, but they would call on him only in great secrecy. One woman he was treating said that he could see through her and would know if she disobeyed him, so she never did anything without his consent. He communicated with the dead who would send messages to their living relatives through him. On occasion, he was called upon to insure success in fishing and other pursuits.

Niəsgane's uncle Watimənloik (Without-Rising) was also a shaman. Although the position of shaman was not strictly hereditary, it was more likely for a boy to become a shaman if there was someone in the family to instruct him. The power of a shaman was called *səmhalait* (real power). This power came to a boy through a vision while he was isolated from the community. It was said that the house of Watimənloik and his mother has always possessed shamans of great power. As evidenced by the fact that both Watimənloik and his mother were initiated shamans, the Tsimshian recognized that both men and women could be shamans, although men more commonly filled the role. Before a shaman could be said to be with *haleyt* (power), he would have to be sick for such a long time that people became alarmed and sent for a shaman to find out what was the matter. The shaman would see that such a person was afflicted by the power and he would so inform the household. The father of the patient would gather in all the shamans, who would (each in turn) take the same rattle and begin the cure by singing a song that belonged to a former shaman of this house. Night after night they would continue to sing in order to strengthen the supernatural power of the patient-cum-shaman. These shamans received compensation for their labors every night of the cure.

Eventually the cure progressed to the point where the patient began to sing his or her own personal curing song. At this juncture, the initiate would be exhibited before his or her tribe. The shaman-to-be would then parade around the fire four times, singing the personal song, and then retire to bed. An initiate's father would distribute gifts to the guests, and the household feasted everyone as public confirmation of the power of the new shaman.

In curing, the shaman always had a young male assistant to beat the drum for him. Like the shaman, the young man was also compensated by the family of the patient. When a patient died, however, the fees were returned. If a shaman was not satisfied with the amount of compensation, he would not touch it or leave the house until the family increased the amount. Once he began the cure, the shaman wore eagle down and a crown of grizzly bear claws, a neck ring inlaid with carved bones, a fringed dancing apron, carried a carved wooden rattle in the right hand and an eagle feather in the left one, and wore either black or red face paint.

Widəlda'l (Gispawadwada crest, Gitsəm-ge·'lon tribe) was another great Tsimshian shaman. In his day, while the people were living on the Nass, there was danger of starvation. One of the important men of the Gilutsau tribe urged that they gather together gifts and give them to this shaman to see if the eulachon were going to come that year and provide salvation. The gifts were brought and placed before the shaman, who filled two vessels with water drawn from the Nass River. One bowl he placed at the entrance and the other at the back of the house, then he took a dried eulachon and cut it in two so there was a piece in each vessel, and finally he said to those watching, "When I start to dance around the house watch these vessels. As soon as any fish come to life call out." He danced three times around the house and called out, "If the fish do not come to life, then there will be no eulachon and the people will starve." Before he was half way around for the fourth time, one of the watchers called out, "The fish has come to life." The shaman then said to the Gilutsau people, "Get your eulachon nets and set them tomorrow, as there will be many eulachon," and there were!

Niəshaida (Grandfather of the Haida?), a great shaman of the Gitxała (Kitkatla) tribe was visiting the Ginax'angi·'k living in the house of Gamayam (Only Mocks). At this time there was concern over some tribesmen of Gamayam who were missing in a boat. They brought the shaman many gifts, so he took out his best paraphernalia, used only when the fee was large. He filled a bucket with salt water, covered his head, and looked into the water. He said, "I see they are not dead and will soon arrive home." He called a man to him and gave him a ceremonial cane, saying, "Take my cane and place it at the edge of the water on the beach. Do not allow the water to splash on the cane, but when it reaches this mark on the cane, look out toward the point, below the Eagle House, and you will see a canoe, then call out." The man went out and the shaman began to sing and dance until the man called out and announced the safe arrival of the lost men. The people rushed to the beach to welcome them.

A very powerful shaman was believed to have the power to avenge his own death. Kininook, a Tlingit shaman, was captured by a Tsimshian raiding party, which cut off his head. As blood spurted into the air, the body ran around until it became stuck in a stump and died. The Tsimshian took the head home fastened by its long matted hair to the crosspiece that held the sail of their canoe. They sneered at the face and spat at it. But then the head moved and fell into the water. Immediately, there was a storm that destroyed all but one of the war party, who reached home to tell the tale.

A shaman would never cut his hair because of the belief that his spirit helpers lived there and in the bone tube that was worn suspended about the neck. It was actually these spirit helpers who told the shaman about mishaps, the causes and cures for illness, and many things other people could not see or know.

Niəsbiɛns, another powerful shaman, once came to the man called Lagaxni·'tsk (To Each Side Looks) and said, "I was going along the creek at Gitsəmge·'lon when I heard a voice from underground. My spirit said to me, 'That is the soul of Lagaxni·'tsk which he lost here while hunting. Take it back to him.'" But Lagaxni·'tsk was by then a convert, so he replied, "Take my soul. I lost it long ago and it is spoiled now. Take it and use it, you will live a long time." Niəsbiɛns was angry, so he put the soul on his own head and kept it. Later Niəsbiɛns died and this soul died with him, but Lagaxni·'tsk felt no differently.

While some shamans did practice witchcraft (*halda'ugit*), anyone could use it to produce illness or death if they knew how. The only difference was that the witchcraft of a shaman was always more effective.

Personal belongings were the most potent means of producing ill effects. Hair, nail parings, or soiled clothes were secured and combined with plants and objects believed to have an evil influence. Incantations were said over these, and the specific evil intended for the individual was mentioned. For illnesses caused by witchcraft, the patient could only be cured if the shaman secured the personal belongings that had been used and washed them clean of the harmful intent. For this reason, until a few years ago, no washing was left out of doors overnight because of fear that it might be used for witchcraft. Even now, pieces are sometimes cut from garments left outside by people attempting witchcraft. The owners of mutilated laundry accordingly become at least nervous, if not ill.

THE TRANSITIONAL: BINI, THE PROPHET

It is presumed that sometime around 1800 a prophet-cum-shaman of the Carrier (Athapaskan-speaking) people named Bini preached an early revitalistic form of religion among the Tsimshian. After his death, he had several imitators who also used his name, which makes it difficult to sort out the different persons called Bini.

Bini's influence extended not only to the Tsimshian but also to other groups as far north as Haines, Alaska, and as far south as Vancouver Island and Rivers Inlet. His preaching was also known to interior Athapaskan tribes such as the Babines, Tahltans, and the Tinnehs.

Beynon thought that Bini might have found some inspiration for his sect from contact with a Catholic missionary at the Bear Lake Missions. Many of his teachings may be seen as related to the increased tensions and pressures brought on by initial Euro-Canadian settlement. The five commandments laid down by Bini were that his followers (1) be faithful to their home life, (2) not encroach on the hunting territory of another tribal member, (3) not murder, (4) respect the voice of the old people and chiefs, and (5) cease making war on one another.

According to one biographical account collected at Hazelton, Bini was a member of the Hagwilget village of Carriers, and he was known as a great hunter, gambler, and shaman. Many feats of magic were attributed to him, including the defeat of some very powerful witches. His hereditary hunting grounds were filled with all kinds of resources, so he was very wealthy. However, it happened that during one session of gambling he lost everything.

First he bet and lost his possessions, then his nephews, then his parents, and finally his wife and children. He had nothing, and so he left the village and entered the forest in deepest sorrow. His wife's family was very angry with him, therefore he hid and wandered around in the mountain forest without food for many days. At last he became so tired that he dropped from exhaustion and slept.

He slept for a long time and a vision came to him. A person dressed in shining white came to him and said, "You will come with me up into the hills, for I have much that I want to show you." Bini got up and, leaving his clothes behind, followed him. When they had gone some distance the man spoke again, "You will return to your people, tell them I have been sent down by the Chief of the Skies— you must teach your people to be good." As the person spoke, he made a motion of touching his forehead, then each shoulder, and then the middle of his breast. At each gesture, he repeated a foreign word. This he did many times. Then, turning to Bini, he said, "You will do this saying the same words when meeting with your people. You will speak to them in a strange tongue, which will be interpreted by one of your nephews." After saying this, the stranger went away and Bini fell forward upon the ground.

Meanwhile, people were searching for Bini. They found where he had left his clothes, but as it was a very cold time of the year, they had no hope of finding him alive. Yet they did find him barely alive, lying on the ground with his head buried in snow. They carried him to the village, laid him by a fire, and a shaman worked on him for two days before he showed strong signs of life. When he did revive, he spoke to the people in a strange language and acted differently. He taught the people new songs and dances, which the people repeated until they dropped from exhaustion. They were able to learn because Bini's nephew interpreted the strange language. Some people danced and rolled on the floor until they fell asleep from sheer exhaustion. Other people brought food to Bini's house for everyone. After many days of this, Bini delivered his five commandments and moved on to visit other villages. He always used an unknown language that was interpreted by his nephew. Bini went to the mouth of the Skeena, where others imitated him and spread the religion everywhere.

According to another biographical account collected by Beynon at Port Simpson, Bini came from the Hagwilget people before the arrival of Reverend Duncan among the Tsimshian. Bini was noted for the use of a strange tongue and a strange manner of singing. While singing and dancing, he carried a cross and made something like the sign of the cross over his head and breast. After visiting the old Tsimshian camp at Metlakatla, he returned to the upper Skeena. It was the Coast Tsimshian themselves who spread the religion when they went up the Nass for eulachon and met Tlingits, Haidas, Niska, and other tribes. Beynon's source felt that this was actually not a new religion, but rather it was a new form of *haleyt* dance which also included unintelligible songs, dancing, and rolling on the floor.

CONFLICT OVER CHRISTIANITY

In Garfield's notes is a testimonial taken from a woman at Port Simpson who during 1918 fought a personal battle between the part of herself that wanted to be a good Christian and the part that wanted to fulfill her traditional obligation to assume the spirit power of a shaman who had been her mother's brother. A probable strong influence on this conflict was its occurrence in 1918, the year of the great influenza epidemic throughout Canada that had such a devastating effect on the population. The woman appears to vacillate between the belief that as a Christian she could pray for her friends and loved ones during the epidemic but that as a shaman she could actually *do* something for them. The angst expressed by this woman reflects the pathos affecting many tribal peoples after contact.

As a girl, this woman accompanied her shaman uncle when he was called to cure patients. As his assistant and heir apparent, she would carry the box in which he kept his paraphernalia so that she and the power objects could gradually become familiar with each other. But one day her uncle had a vision of angels with wings pulling on ropes that made mighty bells ring. When the angels told him to pull the ropes, the bells would not ring. Then he knew he had done wrong, so he became a Christian, and was baptized "Samuel." Four years later he died. Some years after, his spirit came to the niece one night. She sent it away. A year later it came again and she heard her uncle's song, the most powerful expression of his power, and saw her uncle as a boy and as a baby. She prayed to God and the spirit and visions again went away. But about this time her husband died and she was alone. The spirit next made her desire a man: "The evil spirit sees me; no sweetheart, no man, no husband; a widow woman has a hard time." She was able to hold off the urge and continued to pray and read the Bible.

Over the next fifteen years she would sometimes hear the sound of a shaman's rattle in her dreams, but that was about all. In 1918 while she was working at the cannery at Kumeen, she was out alone on a trail when a wren flew into a stump and killed itself. The stump became a human face moving from side to side, and a nearby mountain became a giant grizzly bear.

She managed to make it home to her cabin before she collapsed, remaining delirious for the next nine days. The devil spirit tormented her in her dreams by taking her out in small boats or up the Skeena River to drown her. She managed to regain her composure by the ninth day and had her son take her to the hospital at Port Simpson. After four days in the hospital, she was given some big white pills that kept away the spirit for some time.

But it returned again. She actually had to wrestle the being around the floor of her cabin before she could throw it out. Another time, three children all dressed in red appeared to her and the eldest one said, "You are going to become a shaman or you will die." She said, "No, I have my own chief, God, and my own witness, the Bible." They grabbed and twisted her arms until she passed out. She revived and began to sing "I Am Coming to the Cross," but then lapsed into delirium for the next four days, during which islands, fish, seagulls, and a cat spoke to her. When the Evil One, the Devil, or the spirit came, it told her to take up shamanism and threatened her with drowning if she did not. Once her left hand became paralyzed. Another time, the spirit said: "You are a poor woman. Your sisters' children and your daughters' children will die because you don't take the power."

She received some help from the white man who supervised the cannery and had employed her as a net mender. When she went to his home, a caged blue jay there spoke to her, warning her that while she was away from her cabin every possible spirit would crowd into it. The blue jay offered to help her if she would ask the white man to release it, because, it said, "I do not want to speak English to the white man." Later the white man and his family invited her to supper. The wife read to her from the Bible and told her: "In my Father's house are many mansions. He will prepare for you. I don't want you to die with some crazy spirit. I am in the church. I am a Catholic and my husband is Presbyterian, so we each take one of our two sons into our own religion." The woman baked some Catholic bread with square marks on it, which everyone ate up. Not one crumb was left in the pan. The woman felt better by the time she got home.

During the night she had a vision of a man with long hair standing straight up. He tormented her until the floor of her cabin split open to reveal a glimpse of Hell. Her right hand spoke to her left hand about taking up the Bibles that the woman kept on each side of the head of her bed. At this the visitor left and the woman wept.

That Sunday she awoke to see tiny angels standing on the window curtain ruffle. Behind the angels stood women wearing nurses' caps. Soon she was strong enough to go back to the hospital in Port Simpson. Even while in her hospital room, she saw tiny devils everywhere: on the window, in the room, on the caps of the nurses.

These devils were, she said, "Marking all of the people we are taking from all over the world." She said of her meals, "The cook made me meat and to me it was mud; another dish was a boy; bread and butter was a flat fish like halibut; and peas were rats. One time there was a frog in my dish. The Evil Spirit caused me to see these things."

Visitors came to see her in the hospital with prayers and good wishes, but there were times she did not know they were even there. The doctor gave her pills and more pills. Yet still she was tormented by spirits, demons, and apparitions. Once the spirits demanded her to have intercourse with a specific man because she had led too pure a life. Again she was consumed by a desire for a man, but she prayed to God and kept control of herself. The doctor and other people tried to find a husband for her. The doctor said, "You are sick because no man has touched you since your husband died and your blood is too watery. A man changes a woman's blood and she his. You need a husband. You are sick because no man has touched you and changed your blood."

Finally, after further torment, she had a vision of a bright, shining youth who took her to Heaven where she saw the headdresses and white gowns worn by the Christian Tsimshians. With this she truly began to recover, but when she was released from the hospital and went to visit people in the community, she learned that many of the people whom she had recently seen in her vision of Heaven had actually just died in the 1918 flu epidemic.

She went back to the cannery to collect the money she had earned before her difficulties and reported: "I made over three hundred dollars in the cannery. God was good to me because He used me and I repented."

After this awesome experience, she remained afraid of drowning, as do most people who live along the coast, and she occasionally heard singing, but this always happened just before there was to be news of someone close to her.

SUMMARY

Through the years, Tsimshian religion has undergone some very significant changes but the belief in *haleyt* (power) has been maintained consistently by the traditionalist elders. While not all Tsimshian recognize the role and abilities of shamans, some still do consult practicing shamans in the inland villages. As shamans have thus continued to coexist with Christianity, so aspects of traditional Tsimshian culture have survived within the context of Euro-Canadian society. An accommodation has been achieved between the old and the new—an accommodation initially attempted by prophets like Bini. The revitalistic *haleyt* of Bini has faded from memory, but the two traditions (native and white) that he tried to syncretize live on.

PART II
The Neighbors

Tradition and Innovation

The Visual Ethnohistory of the Kasaan Haida

MARGARET B. BLACKMAN

In 1939 Viola Garfield and Linn Forrest began a survey of extant totem poles in Southeastern Alaska for the U.S. Forest Service. The results of their survey were published several years later in *The Wolf and the Raven* (1948). This publication represents only a portion of Dr. Garfield's data from that trip, focusing as it does on the Tlingit totem poles now located in Mud Bight Village, Saxman, Klawock, and Ketchikan totem parks. As I discovered during the course of my own ethnohistorical research, Dr. Garfield's unpublished field notes from 1939–40 also include significant documentary material on the Alaskan Haida settlement of Kasaan. Her careful notes attempt to correlate the findings of earlier surveys of Kasaan with information she obtained on Kasaan totem poles and houses from Kasaan informants. Accompanying her notes is an album she compiled of early Kasaan photographs, with captions identifying Kasaan poles and tying them into a plan drawing of the village done in 1926 by Herbert Krieger of the Smithsonian Institution.

Viola Garfield's notes and photographs have proved critical to understanding and interpreting the recent ethnohistory of Kasaan village, its settlement pattern and the sociocultural changes hinted at in visual documents from the closing decades of its existence. They have been essential to my research on the Kaigani Haida, and doubtless they will be rediscovered and used anew by other generations of Northwest Coast scholars.

During its occupation, numerous photographs were made of Kasaan that are now in museum and library archives. Taken by early tourists, amateur ethnographers and professional photographers, these photographs have been used now and then to illustrate an article (eg. Niblack 1890; Krieger 1927) or to accompany a museum exhibit, but never have they been considered the basic subject material for scholarly study. Yet such visual documents as those from

151

Kasaan can be powerful media for interpreting recent periods of culture history.

Historic photographs are of particular value in the study of North west Coast societies because they provide information on a period ignored in the ethnographic literature. Apart from the data on traditional cultures carried in the minds of their members, turn-of-the-century Northwest Coast cultures themselves generated little interest in early anthropological circles. Neither, for the most part, have contemporary scholars of the Northwest Coast turned to examine the heterogeneous but viable combination of traditional and Anglo-American features which made up turn-of-the-century Northwest Coast native life. Something of this culture and the processes of change at work within it can be discerned by investigating the photographic record of Kasaan village made between 1885 and 1903. Through these visual documents, socio-cultural change at Kasaan is seen in terms of architectural alterations, innovations in totem pole carving, syncretism in mortuary practices, and changes in settlement pattern. This essay discusses material acculturation as it has been gleaned from the photographic record and the implications of these material changes for the Kasaan Haida.

THE ETHNOHISTORIC DATA

The visual documentary record of Kasaan, numbering sixty photographs, dates from 1885 to 1903, just after the village had been abandoned. More recent photographs of Kasaan houses and totem poles have been taken, but in general have not contributed new information on the village. Kasaan was systematically and intensively photographed in 1885 by Ensign Albert Niblack, and in 1902 by C. F. Newcombe. Photographs taken of portions of the village in 1893 and 1899 by other photographers contribute information on the intervening years.

In addition to taking photographs, Ensign Niblack collected information on selected houses and totem poles. Thomas Waterman visited Kasaan in 1922 to collect information on Kasaan totem poles and houses from elderly Haida then living in nearby New Kasaan. Herbert Krieger of the Smithsonian stopped at Kasaan in 1926 and made a sketch map of the village during his survey of the Indian villages of Southeastern Alaska. In the early 1940s Goldschmidt and Haas, following shortly after Garfield, interviewed Kasaan informants about land tenure and resource utilization as part of their investigation of the possessory rights of southeastern Alaskan natives for the Indian Claims Commission. No further research efforts were directed at Kasaan until the summer of 1971, when the U.S. Forest Service and the Alaska State Museum sponsored the Kasaan Cultural Heritage Project in an effort to salvage certain remaining totem poles and to preserve for future generations information on Kasaan village (Laforet n.d.). As part of this project, the village site was surveyed by the Forest Service, totem poles in good condition were tagged for removal to Ketchikan for display, and Kasaan informants were interviewed. During the course of my fieldwork in southeastern Alaska in the summer of 1971, I was unable to interview the elderly Haida of Kasaan origin because they were employed in the Kasaan project. I was, however, granted access to the cultural heritage project material, and I spent a week during August 1971 at Kasaan village locating and measuring the remains of village features depicted in the early photographs.

Although research on Kasaan village over the years has been intermittent and brief, the combined research efforts and the photographic record comprise a sizeable compendium of data on recent Kasaan ethnohistory.

KASAAN VILLAGE: SETTING AND ETHNOHISTORY

The most northerly Haida settlement, Kasaan is situated in the upper reaches of Skowal Arm, a deeply incised storm-protected notch on the eastern coast of Prince of Wales Island (Fig. 1). Its southerly facing cedar plank houses, totaling thirteen in 1885, were constructed more or less in two rows located just above the extreme high tide mark. The village area, including the grave areas at the eastern and western ends, covered a cleared expanse of just over 1,000 feet, and the spruce-cedar-hemlock forest rose from behind the houses barely 200 feet away from the beach. The site itself rises in elevation from sea level to 70 feet at a ridge behind the village where several turn-of-the-century graves were located.

The occupation of Kasaan by the Haida probably dates to protohistoric times. The Queen Charlotte Haida villages of Dadens and Tcaaɫ, on North (or Langara) Island, were the original home of the Haida who emigrated to Alaska and displaced the southern Tlingit (Fig. 1).

Swanton's informants' versions of the migration recount a conflict which resulted in the abandonment of the North Island villages and the move across Dixon Entrance to Alaska (1909:89). Elderly Haida informants from the Northern Queen Charlottes, explaining the mi-

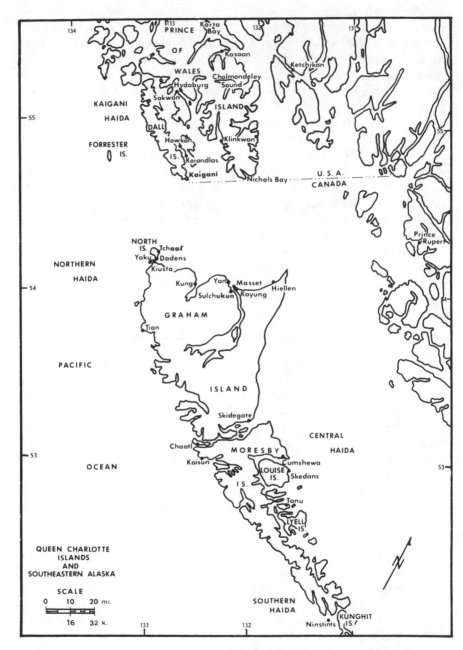

Fig. 1. Map of Haida territory

gration in the 1970s, noted that the North Island villages were quite close to two villages on Graham Island and suggested that there were insufficient food resources to supply all four villages. Swanton himself holds to this explanation for the Alaska migration, remarking, "It would appear that the people were increasing in numbers, and that this corner of the island was becoming over-populated" (1909:90).

The exact date of the migration is uncertain. Contemporary accounts have a mythical cast, the old people in both Masset and Hydaburg speaking of it occurring "just after the flood" and "before we had canoes." Several factors suggest a late protohistoric date for the move. Walter Young, the main informant for the Kasaan Cultural Heritage Project, noted that the first village in Alaska, established by the people who eventually settled Kasaan, was cleared with stone axes (Laforet n.d.). Thus one might conclude that the Haida were in Alaska before 1787, when iron tools were introduced in quantity to the Queen Charlotte Haida people. The move to Kasaan involved one intervening settlement, and historic accounts relate that by the time guns were first introduced to the Kaigani Haida in the 1790s, Kasaan was already an established Haida settlement. The kinship organization of the Kaigani Haida also suggests antiquity of residence in Alaska. Following the emigration to Alaska, the Kaigani lineages, which trace their origin to the Queen Charlottes, subdivided into a number of new sublineages. Similar to Tlingit custom, these sublineages were identified by their "house" of origin, and one of these, the Dark House People, traced its origin to a particular house site at Kasaan. The Tlingit influence on Kaigani Haida kinship and the Kasaan origin of at least one new sublineage lend additional support to a late protohistoric date for the Haida migration to Alaska.

Oral traditions of the migration note that the emigrants were members of four Raven moiety lineages (Taslanas, Yakulanas, Qoetas, Hauqewas) and three Eagle moiety lineages (Tcaałanas, Salandas, and Yadas).[1] From Cape Muzon on Dall Island where they were reported to first land, the immigrants divided, one group (Yakulanas, Qoetas, Hauqewas, Tcaałanas, Salandas) moving up the west coast of Prince of Wales Island, the other (Yadas, Taslanas) heading northward along its eastern shores. The former group eventually settled at Kaigani, Koiandlas, Howkan, Klinkwan, and Sakwan, and

1. Haida terms have been anglicized, retaining only the palatals, q and x, and the lateral spirant, ł.

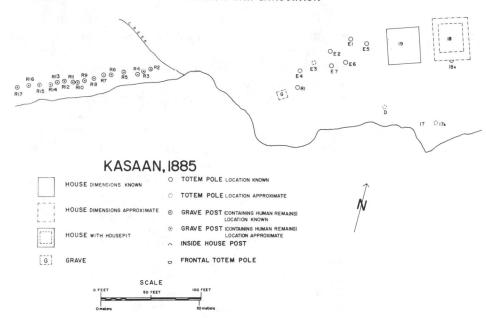

Fig. 2. Location of houses at Kasaan in 1885

the latter became the occupants of Kasaan (see Fig. 1). With the exception of Kaigani ("crab apple town") and Koiandlas ("muddy water") the historic Haida settlements in Alaska bear Tlingit names. While oral tradition is not clear on the question of Tlingit occupancy of these sites at the time of the Haida migration, numerous wars between Haida and Tlingit ensued subsequent to the settlement of southeastern Alaska by the former (Swanton 1905).

The Haida who followed the easterly route upon arrival in Alaska lived first on Chasina Island, just inside Cholmondeley Sound (Fig. 1). They cleared the village site of its forest cover with stone axes and fortified it, naming the settlement Chatchini for the humpback salmon creek located nearby (Laforet n.d.). From Chatchini they moved to Kasaan, a site whose Tlingit name translates as "pretty town" or "on top town."

Kasaan was favorably located for obtaining important resources. One salmon-spawning creek was within the site itself. Drinking water was available from this creek or from a smaller creek that ran between houses 4 and 6 (Fig. 2) at the other end of the village. Several species of berries grow in the village and were important to its inhabitants, who used to pick berries all along the shores of Skowal

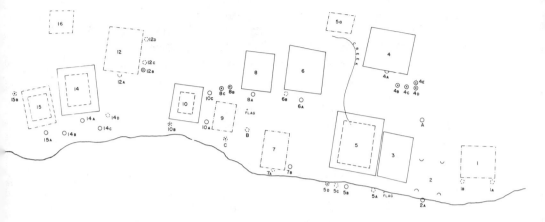

Arm (Goldschmidt and Haas 1946). A cod bank in front of the village was an important source of winter food for the Kasaan people (Laforet n.d.).

Traditionally the Kasaan Haida were resident in their village from late November until April, when they left for American Bay on Dall Island to hunt fur seal (and later to trade with European and American maritime traders who came there), or for Patterson Island, where they fished for halibut and collected seaweed (Fig. 1). Early June found the Kasaan people at Forrester Island, outside Dall Island, where Alaskan Haida from several villages gathered to collect bird eggs at lineage-owned nesting sites. Summer months and early fall were spent at fish camps in Karta and Nichols bays and at Cholmondeley Sound, where salmon were taken from the mouths of spawning streams. From these same campsites Kasaan men hunted beaver, mink, otter, and deer. During the summer months and into late fall, Kasaan women picked berries at the campsites and in the vicinity of Kasaan village itself.

From its founding, Kasaan was occupied by house owners of both the Raven and Eagle moieties, one lineage of each moiety comprising the original settlers. At some later point in its history, a few members of the Yakulanas (Raven) lineage moved to Kasaan and built houses. Members of a fourth group, the Skwaładis (Raven), were present at Kasaan at one time. This lineage or sublineage is not mentioned by Swanton in his "Families of the Haida" (1909:271–72), nor could Walter Young, the chief informant for the cultural heritage project, recall any members of this group; the name, however, is Tlingit.[2] According to informants interviewed in the 1940s by Goldschmidt and Haas (1946), the village site itself was among the property claimed by the Taslanas lineage: "Skowal Arm was claimed in the old days by Chief Skowal of the Raven [Taslanas] clan. . . . All his nephews were free to hunt, fish, and trap for mink, land otter and beaver in the Skowal Arm area" (pp. 150–51). Skowal was the first chief of the Taslanas lineage, the "town chief" [village chief] according to Swanton (n.d.). Skowal may have been accorded the position more because of his influence than because of any inherited right to the formal status of "town chief." Niblack (1890:328) in this regard comments, "As a young man his physical prowess, wealth and family influence made his tyrannical rule at Kasaan one long to be remembered." Although the status of town chief was an institutionalized role on the Queen Charlotte Islands, the comparative fluidity of Kaigani social organization in contrast is suggested in ethnohistorical data which document the movement of the locus of power from a lineage of one moiety to a lineage of the opposite moiety. According to Walter Young of Kasaan (Laforet n.d.), Negun, the Yadas chief, was at the time of the first smallpox epidemic in 1794 the most important chief in Kasaan. Sanaxed, also a Yadas, held this distinction at a later date. The Yadas chieftaincy passed to Gitkun and then to his heir, Kagwanshinga. By the time the first photographs of the village were made in 1885, Kagwanshinga was the lineage chief of the Yadas. Before his death in 1882, Skowal had been the chief of the Taslanas lineage, and during his tenure was acknowledged to be the most powerful chief at Kasaan. Peter Jones remarked in the 1940s, "He [Skowal] was chief of Old Kasaan Village" (Goldschmidt and Haas 1946:151). No important Yakulanas chiefs were resident in Kasaan.

Up to the time the first photographs of Kasaan were made, the ethnohistory of the village is sketchy. A "census" of the village was taken between 1836 and 1841 by John Work of the Hudson's Bay Company. At that time, 249 people were reported at Kasaan (Daw-

2. Florence Davidson of Masset recalled this group as a sublineage of the Yakulanas.

son 1880:173B). The first official census of the area was taken in 1880, and in that year only 173 people are listed for Kasaan (Petroff 1884). The 1890 census reports only 47 people (Porter 1893); although the population was declining, this total seems too low. Possibly the census was taken when a number of people were absent from the village.

Just after the transfer of Alaska to the United States, an Austrian, the Marquis Charles Vincent Baronovich, met and married the daughter of Chief Skowal. Baronovich lived in a white style house at Kasaan (House 5a, Fig. 2), and he established a fish saltery and trading post nearby at Karta Bay. By 1884 the saltery was packing and shipping 1,500 barrels of salmon a year (Skidmore 1885). Haida men from Kasaan were employed in the commercial fishing industry, and the Haida women cleaned and prepared the fish at Baronovich's saltery for packing and shipment. The saltery and occasionally the village of Kasaan itself were visited by mail and freight steamers of the Alaska Steamship Company. During the 1880s and 1890s, wealthy tourists boarded these steamers to get a firsthand view of the coastal Indian villages in southeastern Alaska.

The tourists on board the Alaska Steamship Company's ships sparked the trade in both traditional Haida artifacts and such nontraditional items as gold and silver bracelets bearing Haida designs. One late nineteenth-century Kasaan artisan advertised his skills on a sign at the front of his house: "Hyda John, Jewelry." Skidmore (1885:40), describing this trade in artifacts at Kasaan in 1883, remarks, "In one house an enlightened and non-skeptical Indian was driving sharp bargains in the sale of medicine men's rattles and charms, and kindred relics of a departed faith." With the growing interest in Indian curios in the 1880s, 1890s, and after the turn of the century, a number of totem poles, carved inside houseposts, and even two entire houses from Kasaan were sold to individuals, expositions, and museums.

Kasaan was never the site of a mission, perhaps in part because of Chief Skowal's alleged antipathy to missionaries. Niblack (1890:328) notes that Skowal "did much to keep his people to the old faith and to preserve among them the manners and customs of his forefathers." Nonetheless, Kasaan people came in contact with a number of other missions. They visited Reverend William Duncan's model Anglican community at Metlakatla; trading trips to the Hudson's Bay Company post at Fort Simpson brought them into contact with the Methodist mission there; and through trading ventures to Sitka, the Kasaan people were introduced to Russian Orthodoxy. Attendance at Haida feasts and potlatches at Howkan brought them face to face with the Presbyterians.

In October 1901 the Kasaan Bay [copper] Mining Company persuaded the leading men of Kasaan to relocate to the site of a proposed village in the vicinity of the mine. In exchange, the company offered permanent employment, a school and church, and assistance in laying out a new village (Jackson 1908). Removal to this village was accomplished during the next three years. By 1904 the village of Kasaan was completely abandoned and the new village of the same name, composed entirely of "white style" houses, was built on Kasaan Bay not far from the mine. Left to the elements, old Kasaan was partly destroyed by a fire in 1916. In 1937 the site was declared a U.S. National Monument.

KASAAN IN 1885

Figure 2 represents a plan drawing of Kasaan village as it appeared in 1885. The drawing is based on data from the U.S. Forest Service survey of the village site in the summer of 1971, my own measurements of Kasaan house features made during the same summer, and the photographs taken in June 1885 by Ensign Niblack. Houses are numbered from east to west, and the numerical designation of totem poles represents an attempt to assign poles distributed among the house sites to individual houses. Those poles identified only by capital letters defied assignment to house sites; most of these are mortuary poles. The numbered poles prefixed by R and E at the western extremity of the village refer to mortuary poles containing Raven and Eagle crests, respectively.

A summary of data by house given in Table 1 includes the name, owner, and lineage affiliation of each house present in Kasaan between 1885 and 1902, the totem poles associated with the house, and, where determinable, the length and width dimensions of the house.

In 1885 Kasaan contained eighteen houses, sixty-two totem poles, and three flagpoles. Houses were owned by members of three lineages, eleven houses belonging to the Yadas, three to the Taslanas, and two to the Yakulanas. Most of the totem poles were located on individual house sites, though twenty-four poles were associated with the two grave areas at the west end of the village.

By Haida standards, Kasaan in 1885 was a large village. Masset, on the northern Queen Charlottes, comprised approximately thirty-three houses by the mid-nineteenth century (Swanton's ethnographic baseline; Swanton 1909:290), and its plethora of totem poles was likened by nineteenth-century visitors to a forest of ship masts. But Masset as a nucleated multilineage settlement is unusual.[3] The Kaigani settlements of Howkan and Klinkwan, for example, were smaller than Kasaan, and the earliest photographs of these two villages, also taken by Niblack in 1885, indicate relatively few poles in contrast to the numbers at Kasaan. Sakwan and Koiandlas, also Kaigani, were even smaller than Howkan and Klinkwan, each having only eight houses.

The largest house at Kasaan in 1885 belonged to Chief Skowal (House 5; Table 1, Plate 1), and was comparable in size to that of Chief Weah, the town chief of Masset, whose house was aptly named Neiwans, the Monster House, because it was so large. Skowal's house had associated with it five totem poles, the largest number belonging to any house site at Kasaan. Again, only the house of the town chief of Masset, whose property included nine totem poles, was comparable. Skowal of Kasaan owned not one but two houses (Houses 4 and 5; Table 1, Plate 1), and associated with the former were also five totem poles. Thus the extremes of material wealth, expressed in house size and quantity of totem poles, are similar for the Haida settlements of Kasaan in Alaska and Masset in British Columbia.

In sharp contrast to the opulence of Chief Skowal, there were two Kasaan houses with no totem poles in 1885 (Houses 3 and 19). Though one of these houses had no measurable foundation features in 1971, the other house (3) occupied less than half the area of either of Skowal's two houses. Photographs of Masset and the other Kaigani villages clearly indicate that houses without totem poles were not a rarity among the Haida.

THE PATTERNS OF CHANGE

Architecture

By 1885 there were no Kasaan houses that conformed with regard to entryway to the description Swanton (1909:123) gives of the aboriginal Haida house. He notes, "The doorway to this house, as in all the older houses, passed through the pole itself. After contact with whites, a swinging door, cut at one side of the pole, took its

3. Swanton's list of houses for Masset (1909:290–91) indicates house owners of eleven different lineages were resident in Masset by about 1850.

TABLE 1
Summary of Data by House

Number	1	2	3	4	5
Name	?	?	Flicker House	House Climbing Up	Ribs of Killerwhale House
Owner	Jelu	Yełchangi	Kwałagundas	Skowal	Skowal
Lineage	Yadas	Yakulanas	Taslanas	Taslanas	Taslanas
Width × Length			31.5' × 43.0'	46.2' × 39.7'	49.0' × 58.0'
Proportions			.7325	1.163	.8448
Square Feet			1354.5	1836.14	2842
Totem Poles	1A,1B,1C	2A		4A,4B,4C,4D,4E	5A,5B,5C,5D,5E

Number	6	7	8	9	10
Name	House by Itself	Farthest Outside House	Brown Bear Nest House		Eagle Leg House
Owner	Kagwanshinga	Nastao	Xuchitlakdas		Kwiłans
Lineage	Yadas	Yakulanas	Yakulanas	Yadas	Yadas
Width × Length	38.5' × 43.5'		32.0' × 37.0'		31.0' × 38.0'
Proportions	.8850		.8648		.8157
Square Feet	1674.75		1184		1178
Totem Poles	6A,6B	7A,7B	8A,8B,8C		10A,10B,10C

	11	12	13	14	15
NUMBER					
NAME	?	Daybreak House		Eagle House	Valuable House
OWNER	Sonihat	Xiu	Ginida	Sanaxed	Negun
LINEAGE	Yadas	Yadas	Taslanas	Yadas	Yadas
WIDTH × LENGTH				38.7' × 45'	
PROPORTIONS				.8593	
SQUARE FEET				1740.15	
TOTEM POLES	11A	12A,12B,12C, 12D	13A	14A,14B,14C, 14D	15A,15B

	16	17	18	19	
NUMBER					
NAME		Grand House	House of Dead Man's Head	Sky House?	
OWNER	George Frank	Kidal	Sanxad	?	
LINEAGE	Yadas	Yadas	Yadas	Yadas	
WIDTH × LENGTH					
PROPORTIONS					
SQUARE FEET					
TOTEM POLES		17A	18A		

place." There were, however, six Kasaan houses in 1885 that were traditional in style except for the rectangular doorways that had been cut into their fronts (Houses 1, 3, 4, 5, 12, and 14; Plates 1, 2, 3). Five of these six houses were still occupied when Niblack photographed the village, and four of the five were located in the eastern section of the village. Six more Kasaan houses were traditional in construction (Houses 6, 7, 8, 10, 18, and 19; Plates 2, 3, 4), with the exception of their front façades. To the fronts of these "neotraditional houses" had been added pane glass windows, milled siding, scalloped trim, and in some cases paint.[4] One traditional house was in the process of having its face lifted when Niblack recorded the village on film (House 10; Plate 3).

The process of house façade renovation was fairly simple and did not necessitate extensive architectural alterations. One can reconstruct the procedure as follows. The inside houseposts and the two heavy roof timbers they supported were left intact, as was the traditional planked siding on the rear and sides of the house. Planked siding was removed from the house front, and the top and bottom plates that supported the planking were replaced by a lattice of two-by-fours. The old sheets of cedar bark roofing were removed, and rafters, which considerably heightened the roofline, were constructed upon the old roof timbers. The projecting ends of the rear upper plates were cut flush with the house posts into which they were mortised. With the addition of clapboard siding, windows, and a shaked roof, only the open smokehole at the roof peak of the house revealed its Indian occupancy. It is worthy of note that these alterations left the interior of the house unaffected.

House 6, which belonged to the highest ranking chief of the Yadas (Eagle) lineage in 1885, provides an interesting example of this remodeling process. In 1885 the false façade of this house, embellished with gingerbread trim, was flush against the tall frontal totem pole at its center (Plate 1). Ten years later, the once again renovated façade of House 6 was several feet behind the same pole (Plate 5). This suggests that the façade of the house in 1885 did not represent

---

4. The source of these materials is not indicated in any of the ethnohistorical data, but several likely possibilities exist. In 1883 the Haida village of Howkan erected a sawmill that provided lumber for constructing the white style houses encouraged by the missionaries. The Kasaan Haida frequented Howkan for potlatches and feasts and may have acquired both the ideas and materials for house alterations there. The town of Ketchikan, nearer to Kasaan than Howkan, is perhaps a more likely source of supply. A third possible origin for some of the building materials in use at Kasaan is the Northwestern Trading Company, established at American Bay in the early 1880s. The Kasaan Haida visited the company to exchange furs.

the true location of the original façade but was constructed in front of it. The dismantling and alteration of the house front was neatly avoided by merely erecting a false façade between the totem pole and the still intact original house front.

The remodeling of house façades at Kasaan and other Northwest Coast villages of the late nineteenth century also involved the construction of rectangular doorways and the addition of pane glass windows. Figures 3 and 4 depict the variety of façade decoration at Kasaan in 1885 and 1895. It is apparent from study of the photographs that none of these alterations served primarily utilitarian functions. In 1885, four houses at Kasaan had double rectangular doors symmetrically placed on either side of the frontal totem poles. Elsewhere there are precedents for double doors on Haida houses. Plate 6 shows this feature on a Haida house from the southern Queen Charlottes, where round doorways were still in use into the 1880s. The placement of these traditional round doorways is postcontact according to Swanton (1909:123); the similarly placed but rectangular double doorways on Kasaan houses represent the next logical step in material acculturation. The significance of the paired doorways is unclear, and this feature is not mentioned in the discussion of individual houses in the Kasaan cultural heritage project report (Laforet n.d.). A Masset informant, however, discussing her great uncle's house, which had an old doorway through the totem pole and a rectangular door to the left of it, remarked that the older door through the frontal pole was used by slaves, while the newer door was used by other members of the household. Possibly such ritual separation was also served by double doors on Kasaan houses, though, if it were, one wonders why door placement changes in the ensuing years after 1885.[5] On the other hand, such patterning may also be kin based. All Kasaan houses with double doors, for example, belonged to members of the Yadas lineage.

After 1885, double doors were no longer being added to Kasaan houses, and two houses that had sets of double doors in 1885 had altered their façades by 1895 to present a single, centrally placed doorway (Houses 6 and 14; Fig. 4). All other houses at Kasaan that were still occupied in 1895 had only the single doorway.

Pane glass windows, employed before 1885, increased in numbers

---

5. On the other hand, the change in door placement may have occurred *because of* the institution of slavery, which, by the end of the nineteenth century, had declined. Walter Young, in fact, noted that House 2A, built after 1895, was owned by a former slave of Chief Skowal's.

Plate 1. Near east end of Kasaan, 1885 (courtesy, Smithsonian Institution, no. 3874)

Plate 2. Middle section of Kasaan, 1885 (courtesy, Smithsonian Institution, no. 3883)

Plate 3. Near west end of Kasaan, 1885 (courtesy, Smithsonian Institution, no. 3886)

Plate 4. West end of Kasaan, 1885 (courtesy, Smithsonian Institution, no. 3873)

Plate 5. Panorama of Kasaan, 1893 (courtesy, Smithsonian Institution, no. 4320). House 6 is between houses 5 and 7, but is not labelled.

between 1885 and 1895. Those houses sporting two windows in 1885 which were renovated during the next ten years display four or more windows by 1895. As a comparison of Figures 3 and 4 indicates, there was considerable activity in house renovation between 1885 and 1895. The significance of these changes is not totally clear, but the patterns of architectural change seen at Kasaan are not isolated ones; similar changes could be cited for the villages of Masset, Klinkwan, and Sakwan. Elsewhere on the Northwest Coast the linkage between turn-of-the-century house façade alteration and the prestige system is documented in the ethnohistorical record. William Beynon (n.d.), for example, referring to the alterations in a Fort Simpson house, noted that windows were added to the front of the house "where everyone could see them."[6] The two windows that graced the front of Chief Weah's big house at Masset were placed so high above ground level that any view from inside the house was precluded.[7] While multiple windows allowed the entrance of light into the great dark houses, their main function was symbolic and not utilitarian. Several houses at Kasaan also have their windows positioned much too high for the occupants to look out; Skowal's house (House 5, Plate 5), which did not have a second story as the placement of windows might deceive one into believing, had a fifth window placed near the apex of the gable. House 3 at Kasaan presents an interesting example of window decoration. A rather small and unpretentious dwelling with no totem poles, it was owned by a lesser chief of the Taslanas. In 1885 the house was traditional appearing except for the centrally placed rectangular doorway. Perhaps unable to afford the added elaboration of siding, paint, trim, and multiple windows, this individual chose to add by 1895 only a single small window, centrally positioned above the door to the house (Fig. 4).

The timing of house façade renovation at Kasaan suggests that it usually occurred at the succession of a chieftainship. Skowal's house, for example, remained traditional (Plate 1) as the deceased chief lay in state within in 1885, but not long afterward the house front was drastically altered (Plate 5). This alteration and the erection of a new totem pole, which also appears in photographs of the house after

6. Ethnohistorical data do not indicate whether a potlatch was given, though the timing of some house renovations to coincide with succession to house chieftaincy suggests potlatching.

7. Photogrammetric measurements of this house revealed the windows to be more than six feet above ground level.

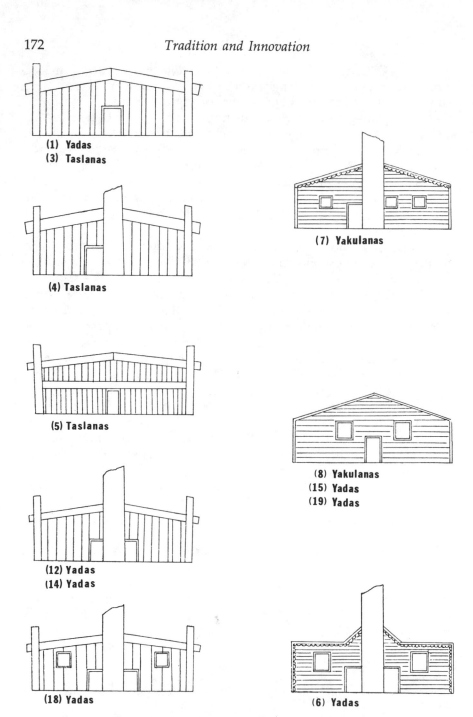

(1) Yadas
(3) Taslanas

(4) Taslanas

(7) Yakulanas

(5) Taslanas

(8) Yakulanas
(15) Yadas
(19) Yadas

(12) Yadas
(14) Yadas

(18) Yadas

(6) Yadas

Fig. 3. House façade decoration at Kasaan, 1885

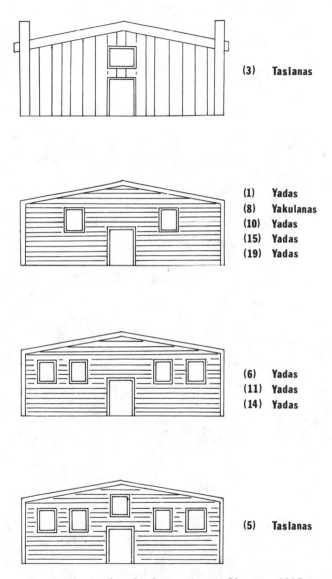

(3) Taslanas

(1) Yadas
(8) Yakulanas
(10) Yadas
(15) Yadas
(19) Yadas

(6) Yadas
(11) Yadas
(14) Yadas

(5) Taslanas

Fig. 4. House façade decoration at Kasaan, 1895

Plate 6. Haida village of Haina, ca. 1884. Note round doorway on house at right. (courtesy, British Columbia Provincial Museum, no. PN5571)

1885, probably coincided with the formal succession of Skowal's heir to the chieftainship.

Three "white man's style" houses had been built in Kasaan before the village was photographed for the first time, and all belonged to members of the Yadas lineage. These houses were relatively small compared with the native Haida houses, and no totem poles could be definitely assigned to their sites. The adoption of white style housing marks the disruption of at least three Haida cultural patterns: (1) the orientation of house to shoreline, (2) the link between house and lineage, and (3) the link between house ownership and rank as demonstrated through the housebuilding potlatch. Traditional Haida houses were built with their gable ends oriented toward the water (though house 17, Plate 4, departs from this norm); As white style houses were added to Haida villages, this pattern was no longer followed; of the four white style houses that were built at Kasaan, only one was traditionally oriented. The others were constructed with rooflines parallel to the water. These early white style houses had no special identity; as Table 1 shows, they had no Haida names marking them as dwellings that housed members of a given lineage. Furthermore, though there is no direct evidence from Kasaan, the adoption of white style housing by the Northern Haida at Masset brought about the demise of the grandest, most elaborate Haida potlatch—that connected with the construction of a traditional house. As I have argued elsewhere (Blackman 1977), this was owing, in part, to the difficulty of transferring the work of the housebuilding group (high ranking individuals of the housebuilder's own moiety) to the construction of a building totally different in concept and design.

On the other hand, some patterns were not seriously affected at first by the construction of white style housing. Again, turning to data from Masset, it is apparent that the first white style houses still sheltered extended families, and, except for the absence of the central fire (replaced by a stove), the housepit and surrounding platforms, personnel and goods were distributed in accordance with tradition throughout a single large room. A Masset missionary, writing to his superior in England in January 1894, remarked on the interiors of the "shapely wooden cottages": "The interior of the houses, it must be confessed, are not yet what one would wish to see them. The habits of the lodge are still in several cases retained, and the result in the more confined style of house is neither pleasant nor healthy" (Keen n.d.). He was referring here to sleeping and eating on the floor. Masset informants recalled that at feasts held in the early cottages, guests were seated on the floor around the perimeter of the single large room of the cottage which served as living room, kitchen, and dining room.

Flagpoles, Totem Poles, and Headstones

Flagpoles were another indicator of material acculturation at Kasaan, though as in the case of "white man's style" houses, they had distinctive Haida usages. Flags were first obtained by the Haida and other Northwest Coast groups from maritime traders in the nineteenth century, and were flown on occasions of ceremonial significance: at funerals, potlatches, feasts, weddings, and so forth. Chief Skowal's own flag is a prominent part of his funerary display recorded by Niblack on film in 1885. To these functions of flags, missionaries in the late nineteenth century added the designation of the Sabbath. Thus, in missionized Haida villages, flags regularly flew on Sundays. It is worth mention that the three flagpoles that appear at Kasaan in 1885 did not belong to the largest or most important houses. Only one flagpole was added to the village after 1885, and no flags appear flying from poles in the early photographs. While Garfield (1939) noted that potlatches were given by the Coast Tsimshian on the occasion of the erection of a flagpole, Masset informants denied that the Haida did the same, and no mention is made of a connection between flagpole raising and potlatching in the Kasaan ethnohistorical material.

Beginning perhaps a decade or more before Kasaan was first photographed, and continuing to about 1895, figures carved on some totem poles exhibited striking departures from tradition, in both style and content. In the 1885 series of photographs of Kasaan village there are two totem poles containing images of white men. Both poles, frontal poles to houses (poles 7A and 4A, Plate 2), relate legendary or real events important to the owner of the pole. According to Niblack (1890:326) pole 7A, which Garfield (n.d.) dates to 1877, relates the following story:

> Many years ago the wife of a chief went out in a small fishing canoe with her two children, near the summer camp, to get the pine [hemlock] boughs on which herring spawn. She drew her canoe up on the beach, warned the children not to go off. They disappeared. She called, they answered back with the voice of crows. The children never returned and it is said that white traders [represented by the bearded face at the top of the pole] carried them off.

Pole 4A commemorates events from Chief Skowal's own life, including the failure of missionaries to convert him to the Russian Orthodox Church. Raised in derision of the Church,[8] the pole depicts a Russian missionary, a saint, and the Archangel, Saint Michael (Garfield, n.d.). While pole 7A appears quite traditional in the execution of its carved figures, Skowal's pole (4A) is most unconventional, particularly in the use of scrollwork, the portraitlike representation of human faces, and the non-Haida looking eagle near the base of the pole.

In the intervening years between 1885 and 1893 a totem pole (13a, Plate 7) was raised at the west end of Kasaan by a woman of the Taslanas lineage in honor of her deceased husband, a white man from Victoria. With the inheritance he left her, she had a pole carved bearing her own Raven crest at the base and the figure of a white man in frock coat and top hat at the apex of the pole. Traditional Haida frontal poles frequently displayed the crests of husband and wife, with the house owner's crest at the base and the spouse's (usually the wife's) crest at the top of the pole. In the case of this individual, whose spouse was alien to the traditional Haida social system, the figure of a white man dressed in finery served as an appropriate identifying symbol. Garfield (n.d.) notes that the scrollwork along the side of this pole was regarded by the Haida as especially suitable for a white man. In this particular instance, the departure from tradition in totem pole carving is directly linked to a departure from traditional marriage patterns.

Totem pole raising continued at Kasaan after 1885. Within the decade after Niblack's visit to Kasaan, four large totem poles were erected. Only one of these (pole 13A, discussed above) was nontraditional in some aspects. The remaining three poles appear to be traditional in content and design. All were associated with either the alteration of a house front façade (5E, 1C) or with the construction of a new house (11A, 13A). Pole 13A belonged to a white style house built after 1899 and is the only totem pole so linked.

Poles were not only added to the village area during the last years of its occupation, but several were removed. Between 1885 and 1895, six poles were taken down, and all but one of these removals was

8. Barbeau (1950:406–7) cites two conflicting interpretations of the significance behind Skowal's pole. I have followed Niblack's interpretation (1890), since it is both earlier and more detailed.

Plate 7. Kasaan in 1902 (courtesy, British Columbia Provincial Museum, nos. E161 and E164)

linked to the renovation of a house.[9] One other pole was removed from Kasaan during the last years of its occupation. The frontal pole to House 17 was sold to Governor Brady of Alaska for the 1904 St. Louis Exposition (Garfield n.d.).

Changes in the Haida mortuary complex are reflected in the temporal sequence of Kasaan photographs. While four free-standing totem poles were added to the village area, only two new mortuary poles were raised between 1885 and 1895. At the same time these grave poles were being erected, other individuals who died were being buried in graves marked by tombstones in a cemetery at the near western edge of the village. No new poles or burials were added to the far western grave area of the village, suggesting that this was an old cemetery. Thirteen of the sixteen mortuary poles shown in

9. The sixth pole, B, could not be linked to a house site.

Niblack's 1885 photograph of this cemetery are topped by crest figures, all of which refer to individuals of the Raven moiety (Plate 8). This is the only clearcut example at Kasaan of the ritual separation of the matrimoieties. There is some suggestion from the photographs that the near western cemetery at one time contained mortuary poles exclusively for members of the Eagle moiety. Of the eight poles present in this cemetery four contain Eagle crests; the figures on three poles could not be identified, and one pole, relatively new in 1885, contained Yakulanas (Raven) crests (Plate 9). The presence of headstones marking graves of members of both moieties in the near western cemetery by 1885 indicates that ritual separation by moiety at death was no longer being practiced. Such separation was customary traditionally, according to Swanton (1909).

The 1885 photographs indicate that mortuary poles were erected among the house sites as well as in separately designated cemetery areas. Though the differentiation between the two cemetery areas at Kasaan may have been based on kinship, the relationship between these mortuary poles and those distributed among the house sites is unknown. No new mortuary poles were added to individual house sites after 1885.

Mortuary crest display at Kasaan took two new and interesting directions after 1885. Shortly before 1899 when a member of the Harriman Expedition photographed the near western cemetery at Kasaan, a mortuary pole in the form of a grizzly bear was erected here. The bear totem rested on top of a burial, and a gravehouse had been constructed over the bear and grave (Plate 10). The bear was a particularly poor example of Haida carving and suggests the decline of this art at Kasaan. Thomas Waterman wrote about this pole in 1922, "Large bear on gravehouse: fine condition, poor carving, augur holes for nostrils, lots of paint" (Garfield n.d.). In the case of the bear mortuary, the ancient practice of erecting a mortuary pole existed alongside the white man's earth burial and headstone. Less than ten years after the carving of the bear mortuary, Thomas Skowal—the successor to the Taslanas chieftainship—was memorialized at his death by a marble monument, carved in the shape of a killerwhale fin (Plate 11). Here a headstone marked the grave, but its content was distinctively Haida. The combination of mortuary pole, burial, and gravehouse is not common in the Haida area, while, after the turn of the century, the carving of crest figures on tombstones became a widespread practice among the Haida and other northern Northwest Coast groups.

Plate 8. Row of mortuary columns at west end of Kasaan, 1885 (courtesy, Smithsonian Institution, no. 3887)

Plate 9. Near west section of Kasaan graveyard, 1885 (courtesy, Smithsonian Institution, no. 3885)

Plate 10. Near west section of Kasaan graveyard, 1899 (courtesy, Smithsonian Institution, no. S43, 549A)

Plate 11. Thomas Scowal's marble headstone with Killerwhale fin, New Kasaan, Alaska (courtesy, Smithsonian Institution)

SETTLEMENT PATTERN: TRENDS AND CHANGES

Oral tradition relates that from its very founding Kasaan, unlike some other Haida villages (e.g., Koiandlas and Klinkwan, and Kiusta on the northern Queen Charlottes), was inhabited by householders of both moieties. Moiety division is not apparent in the allotment of house sites, members of both moieties being dispersed throughout the village. In other Haida villages occupied by house owners of both moieties, houses were sometimes aligned according to moiety membership (e.g., Yan, on the northern Queen Charlottes). At Kasaan the only indication of a ritual and physical separation of moieties is in the distribution of mortuary poles at the western end of the village. The photographic data from 1885 forward suggest that the pattern of separating individuals by moiety at death had ceased being practiced by the time Niblack visited and photographed the settlement.

In the Queen Charlotte Haida settlements of Masset, Kiusta, Kayung, and Skidegate the town chief's house was centrally located. It was said of Chief Weah of Masset, for instance, that he chose the site on which his house was built because "he wanted to have his house in the center of the town." This tendency is not evident at Kasaan. The arrangement of Kasaan houses, however, is not random. It follows a pattern noted in several Queen Charlotte and Kaigani villages (Kloo, Skedans, Chaatl, Kung, Klinkwan). Those most important individuals selected house sites on the flanks of the village (e.g., Houses 17, 4, 5, and 1), while the houses of latecomers or houses without chiefs were positioned in the middle of the village (Houses 7 and 8). Elevation of house site also seems to be related to rank. The houses of the highest ranking individuals (e.g., Houses 4 and 6) are located on higher ground than those of lower ranking people or are placed on prominences of land near the beach (e.g., House 17).

The photographs of Kasaan, and the ethnohistorical data gathered by Garfield (n.d.) and Laforet (n.d.) suggest that the expansion of Kasaan was from west to east. The shifting location of the Yadas chieftaincy before 1885 (Table 1) reflects this, as does the location in the eastern sector of Kasaan of the three houses belonging to the Yakulanas lineage, a group not originally resident in Kasaan. By 1885 the center of innovation and activity lay in the eastern section of the village. The two most important chiefs at Kasaan had their houses at this end of the village (Houses 6 and 5), and the tabulation of occupied/unoccupied houses for 1885–1902 (Table 2) shows that, in

TABLE 2

OCCUPIED/UNOCCUPIED HOUSES BY YEAR

	OCCUPIED			UNOCCUPIED		
	Traditional	Neo-Traditional	White	Traditional	Neo-Traditional	White
1885	1,3,4,5,14	6,7,8,15,19	5a,9,16	2,12,17,18	10	0
Sub-Total	5	5	3	4	1	0
TOTAL	13			5		
1895	3	1,5,6,8,10,11?, 14,15,19	5a,9,16	2,4,12,17,18	7	
Sub-Total	1	9	3	5	1	0
TOTAL	13			6		
1902	3	1,2a,5,6,8,10, 11,14	13,16	2,4,12,17,18	7,15,19	5a,9
Sub-Total	1	8	2	5	3	2
TOTAL	11			10		

the last years of the inhabitation of the village, its western portion contained more unoccupied houses than the eastern section.

CONCLUSION

Although the population of Kasaan in 1885 was reported to be only two-thirds of what it had been forty years before, the village was still a viable settlement in the 1880s and 1890s. Wealth and prestige were visually expressed by large houses and numbers of totem poles. Totem pole raising and attendant potlatching were still being practiced.

By the third quarter of the nineteenth century numerous intrusive elements and concepts had been incorporated into Kaigani Haida culture, appearing in the photographs as changes in domestic architecture, totem poles, and the mortuary complex.

White style houses were being constructed at Kasaan before the first photographs were taken. At the same time that some persons were building these houses, others opted to alter the fronts of their traditional Haida houses to resemble white man's style houses from the exterior. At least one person at Kasaan built a house on the traditional plan with a white man's style façade; this house was completed by 1899 (House 11; Plate 7). During the last years of Kasaan's occupation no traditional style Haida houses were built. The adoption of white style housing was significant because (1) it disrupted the traditional geographical pattern of arrangement of houses within the village, (2) it marked the end of the housebuilding potlatch, and (3) it represented a break in the association between house ownership and chieftainship and between house and lineage.

The alterations performed on the traditional Haida houses allowed a modicum of participation in the intrusive culture. House fronts mimicked the houses of whites. But, the forms of mimicry (the windows, the paint, the siding, the shaked roof) were exterior embellishments only. Housepits and the central fire still existed. The interior of the house continued to have one large room where feasts and potlatches could be held and where the distribution of goods and personnel remained largely traditional.[10]

While the decoration of Haida house fronts may have been in imitation of white style houses, it is possible that, at some level, these exterior embellishments were incorporated into the Haida social system. The suggestion that much of the patterning of material culture

10. This has been demonstrated for Chief Weah's house at Masset (Blackman 1972).

on house fronts is based on kinship and rank is tempting for several reasons. We know from the ethnographic literature on the traditional Haida that privileges, including the right to decorate possessions with lineage crests, were inherited in the matrilineal line. Boxes, feast dishes, horn spoons, gambling sticks, ceremonial blankets, and headdresses all had decorations that identified the moiety and lineage of the owner. According to Swanton (1909), before the introduction of totem poles, which of course identified the lineage of owner and spouse, house façades were painted with the crest figures of house owners. Some houses in the southern Queen Charlottes were so painted at the time the villages were first photographed in the 1870s. Thus the patterning that appears in late nineteenth century house decoration at Kasaan (Figs. 3 and 4) may represent an acculturative addition to the matrilineally specific display of privileges. The traditional display of crests also conveyed information on other aspects of Haida social organization. Swanton (1909:112) notes, "The crest system is . . . an heraldic device by which a man indicates his rank and position in the social scale." House façade decoration at Kasaan in the late nineteenth century probably also reflects this principle, representing a mechanism for expressing social position by the addition of rectangular doorways, siding, trim, and, most important, multiple windows.

An architectural deception directly borrowed from Anglo-American culture by Northwest Coast natives in the late nineteenth century was admirably suited to the expression of rank and the demonstration of quantity and expansiveness. This was the use of the false façade on house fronts, which, as in the case of House 6 at Kasaan, served to exaggerate the size of the house. The deception was carried to even greater extremes farther south at Kwakiutl villages, as Plate 12 from Alert Bay shows. Northwest Coast villages were meant to be seen from the water, and the false front on houses gave the illusion of greater size to one approaching a Northwest Coast village by canoe.

The incorporation of foreign elements and stylistic influences in carving was apparent at Kasaan at the end of the nineteenth century and is characteristic of other Northwest Coast societies. White men appear carved as figures on totem poles.[11] Scrollwork, the depiction of feathers on bird figures, and, at one Northern Haida village, flower motifs (Barbeau 1950:409) appear on totem poles. As with the use of windows, doors, and milled siding, the elements are borrowed,

11. Other examples can be found in Barbeau (1950).

Plate 12. Southern Kwakiutl house with false front, Alert Bay, 1901 (courtesy, British Columbia Provincial Museum)

but the conception is Haida. The motivations for erecting a totem pole and the meaning of the pole itself remained traditionally Haida despite the alien elements.

Although no missionary was ever resident at Kasaan, Christian burial practices had been introduced by the time the first photographs of the village were made. Picket fences surrounding burials appear in the 1885 photographs. Nonetheless, for a time the erection of mortuary poles was still practiced. Before the turn of the present century a compromise with Christian mortuary practices was effected and is shown in the combination of burial, mortuary pole, and gravehouse. By the time Kasaan was abandoned, earth burial and tombstones were the norm, though the stones might bear the crest of the deceased individual (Plate 11).

In 1885 Kasaan was a viable settlement of some 170 people, a village whose architecture and art reflected a heterogeneous mixture of old and alien elements, but whose outward face yet bespoke the strength of Haida tradition and culture. By 1902 no more totem poles were raised and no more houses had been built within the village. By 1904 the village had been abandoned. The houses were emptied of people and goods; the smokehole screens crumbled and fell to the fireplaces below. The remaining totem poles listed and grew patches of soft green moss as the forest gradually reclaimed them.

Kasaan is today a National Monument, an archaeological site with only a few totems and house features, but it survives in the childhood memories of elderly Haida like Walter Young, in the notebooks left us by Dr. Garfield, and in the visual images of early photographers.

Succession to Chiefship in Haida Society

MARY LEE STEARNS

In her classic study of Tsimshian society (1939), Garfield demonstrated a sensitivity, unusual for that period, to the distinction between ideal and actual behavior. Nowhere is this more evident than in her treatment of succession to chiefship. In examining this institution over time she raised the important issue of variability in modes of recruitment to high office.

In the strongly corporate, ranked social structure of the Tsimshian, there seems to be a high degree of determinacy in the transmission of status and property. "In general, the eldest man most closely related to the deceased holder of a name succeeds him" (Garfield 1939:178). More precisely, the eligible candidates in order of precedence include: own next younger brother, own eldest sister's eldest son, next younger parallel cousin, eldest house nephew, eldest man of a related house, and adopted man (1939:179). While outlining the normative rules, Garfield considers the distribution of actual cases: "In half of the instances recorded 'nephews' succeeded and in nearly as many 'brothers' took the names" (1939:179). "When the head of the house died . . . his own younger brothers already possessed important names and had established their reputations through potlatching and did not care to step up, although they could if they wished. Instead they usually agreed to a nephew taking the position" (1939:179). In other cases, however, it is clear that circumstances provided ambitious men with room for maneuver. "Since the theory and practice of inheritance are in conflict it is inevitable that jealousy, antagonism and controversy should at times enter into the succession to names, especially where these were financially or socially valuable to the possessor" (1939:179).

Illustrated with abundant case material, Garfield's study invites us to consider the relative importance of an automatic rule of hereditary succession, appointment of a successor by an incumbent chief, election of a successor by kinsmen, and validation of an illegitimate seizure of a name by potlatching. Although the latter mode has often been seen as a characteristic feature of political process in Northwest Coast societies, Garfield's data suggest that it was an infrequent occurrence among the Tsimshian. Turning to the neighboring society of the Haida on which I have focused my own research, I propose to pursue some of the questions raised by a rereading of Garfield's monograph.[1]

In studying political process we must consider the character of the political system, the nature of political goals, and the organization of groups competing for power (Burling 1974; Goody 1966). This analysis will reveal the structural contradictions in Haida society that affect recruitment to chiefship. We must inquire into the powers of the chief's office and its relation to the corporate structure: its uniqueness or otherwise, the kinds of leadership required, the relations of authority figures and their constituents. We will ponder the concomitants of modes of transferring office, the solutions selected by the society, and their consequences. Finally, we will assess the scope for individual achievement on the one hand and the limitations of competition on the other, seeking out the principles of Haida politics in ethnographic and historical data.

Haida society, like that of the Tsimshian, observes the rule of matrilineal descent, which, in each generation, creates sets of siblings linked to the senior generation by their mothers and to the junior generation by their sisters. For the Haida a group of such kinsmen constitutes the localized, property-holding corporation we term the matrilineage. This autonomous unit, referred to as "family" by Swanton (1905a) and "clan" by Murdock (1934; 1936), also performs juridical, political, and ceremonial functions.

Ethnographic data indicate that access to chiefship is obtained in one of several ways: (1) an automatic rule of hereditary succession; (2) appointment of a successor by the incumbent; (3) election by a lineage council; (4) setting up of a new unit after segmentation and, usually, migration; (5) competitive potlatching. Since the preferred determinate rule (1) and the indeterminate alternatives (2–5) resemble those recorded by Garfield for the Tsimshian, we must entertain the possibility that they are a response to certain shared structural features.[2] Jack Goody has argued that "the main types of succession, heredity, election and appointment, are found in all societies,

1. I should like to thank Wayne Suttles, Marianne Bölscher, Jay Miller, and Nancy Williams for their careful evaluations of an earlier draft of this paper. I am also indebted to Marianne Bölscher and Barry M. Gough for permission to quote their research data on Haida chiefship.
2. Such a comparison is beyond the scope of this paper.

but they occur in different combinations depending upon the kind of polity" (1966:39). Under what conditions is each of these modes operative in Haida society, and what is the political significance of the potlatch?

Haida society is segmental, to adopt the term Service applies to "the kinds of societies composed of equal and similar component groups (normally kin groups like clans and lineages)" (1975:70). The major segments, the matrilineages, are replicative and contraposed. There are no crosscutting allegiances or associations such as secret societies (Swanton notwithstanding, 1905a:156,160–61), and no paramount chiefs. Boundaries between segments are maintained by competitive relations including feud and potlatching. The framework for lineage interrelations is provided by the moiety principle which governs ceremonial exchange and military alliance as well as marriage.

Service's distinction between segmentary and segmental is useful here (1975:69–70). For the Haida fission and fusion are not the regular processual events which characterize segmentary societies. Rather, segmentation is a response to political, demographic, or economic pressures that is available under certain conditions, namely, the absence of external or superordinate political constraints. The reverse process, where small groups or survivors of war and disease join existing groups, is more accurately termed nucleation than fusion. I am rejecting Service's classification of "northwest coast" societies as chiefdoms for reasons which will become clear as we proceed (1975:66n, 75).[3]

Turning to the internal structure of the primary segment, we find that lineage members occupy a series of ranked statuses which entail differential access to authority and prestige. As head of the corporation, its senior member manages its properties, coordinates its activities, and represents its interests in external affairs. The core members, that is, the senior males and their sisters' sons, may occupy one or several houses depending on their wealth and numbers. Since postmarital residence is virilocal (avuncu-virilocal for men

3. We do not find, among the Haida certainly, the diagnostic feature of centralized redistribution but, rather, reciprocal exchange between coordinate units. There is no requirement for "overall coordination and redistribution in order to effectively hunt whales, net schools of halibut, or trap, smoke, and box salmon" (Service: 1975: 75). Leaving aside whaling, for which there is no ethnographic evidence among the Haida and which, in any case, is not a subsistence activity, these activities are carried out by domestic groups. Service's own distinction between domestic and political authority is important here (1975: 49–50). Finally, we cannot speak of chiefdoms unless both expressive and instrumental powers are vested in the same office.

who succeed mother's brother and marry his daughter), the household includes wives and unmarried daughters, young sons, and sisters' older sons along with other relatives and slaves.

While ownership of the economic resources is vested in the lineage, their exploitation is carried out by the household under its head, whom Swanton terms a "petty chief." "Usually each household had its own camping-ground on a salmon creek, where its smoke-house stood, and whither the people went in the spring to dry salmon and halibut, trap bear, gather berries, dig roots and make canoes, returning to town in the fall" (Swanton 1966:55).

The identity of the corporate lineage is expressed in the communal ownership of its estate—resource areas, townsites, and ceremonial privileges. Earlier writers had observed that the Haidas exercised strict proprietary rights over sections of coastline, salmon streams and halibut banks, tracts of land, seabird rookeries, berry patches, and so on (Dawson 1880:110B, 113B, 117–18B; Swanton 1905a:71; Niblack 1888:335). Even the townsite was a lineage property, conveying the prestigious status of "town chief" to the head of the dominant segment. While other lineages might take up residence only with permission of the owners and by accepting lesser status, the town chief had no authority over any group but his own. For their part, it seems that "guest" lineages did not usually compete with the owners for dominance. However, as Swanton points out, "The power of family chiefs living in a town belonging to another family depended largely on the number and wealth of their people. . . . [Some] might become more powerful than the ruling family itself, and in course of time supplant it" (1905a:69). The village, then, was not the political unit but simply the arena of political action.

Ownership of a town was distinct from ownership of surrounding land on the one hand (Swanton 1905a:71) and from resource areas on the other. In each of these instances, however, the lineage's property rights were established by prior occupancy or claim, purchase from previous owners, inheritance, or as compensation for injury in a legal settlement. Infringement of these rights was a serious matter, often provoking blood feud. Property transactions were certified by the myths and traditions which formed the charter of each corporate group.

That element of the corporate estate which most explicitly denotes the group's identity is its ceremonial privileges. Access to the names, titles, crests, songs, dances, and stories was closely guarded by the lineage head, who attempted to reserve the most prestigious for his

own use (Swanton 1905a:107–8, 117–21). Though nominally the cus-
todians of lineage property, heads came to regard the estate as personal property. Niblack commented on this tendency, "the ownership of a tract of land by a family has come, through being vested
in an individual or in the head of that family, to mean practically
individual ownership" (1888:335). In the corporate group, however,
the strain toward individual control of the estate and the monopoly
of privilege is countered by conflicting claims (Goody 1962:346–47;
1966:26).

Against the restricted access to power and authority entailed in
the principle of rank must be set the rights of all members to share
in the estate. Joint ownership implies equivalence, at least among
the senior sibling set from which the successor emerges, and that
equivalence stimulates competition for the highest status. Herein lies
the structural inconsistency which contributes to indeterminacy of
succession on the one hand and to lineage segmentation on the other.

The egalitarian ethos associated with the equivalence of siblings
affects the qualifications for political roles. Even when an automatic
rule of succession is posited, candidates are required to meet criteria
of achievement as well. Chiefship in Haida society is an ascriptive
role, in that high hereditary status is prerequisite. But, as Nadel
points out, "it seems that societies do not particularly care for such
frankness; in the case of numerous roles they prefer the illusion of
achievement, however small its real chances" (1957:40).

Niblack describes the chief's qualifications: "Good birth and wealthy
or influential family connections are the first requisites for an as-
pirant for the highest rank" (1888:372). Elsewhere he adds, "Personal qualities count for what they are worth in addition. General
recognition and consensus of opinion settle the question of rank.
That is to say, it is about what the individual can make it by all the
arts of assertion, bargain, intrigue, wealth, display and personal
prowess" (1888:250). Swanton insists that "success in amassing
property generally governed the selection of a new chief of the town,
the family, or the house. It might be the own brother, own nephew,
or a more distant relation of the predecessor" (1905a:69).

Other kinds of excellence were demanded of those who aspired
to or enjoyed high status. "The discipline that young men of high
family went through was thorough and severe. . . . it is always said
that a chief's son must excel others in living up to their ethical standards" (Swanton 1905a:70). However, rigorous discipline was prescribed for all members of an age or sex category. In describing puberty regulations imposed on girls Swanton concludes, "The

difference between the regulations observed by the child of the rich and those undergone by the child of the poor seem to have been mainly in the amount of property placed above them" (1905a:49). In requiring display of these qualities by candidates for high office, the illusion of achievement is introduced. But when persons of lesser status possess the desired qualities, they tend to promote the fiction of achievement and to strive for the same goals.

Although we can find considerable evidence that egalitarian values pervaded this society, it would be difficult to overestimate the importance of hereditary status. Dawson concludes a discussion of alternative modes of recruiting chiefs with the proviso, "In no case, however, does the chieftaincy pass from the royal clan to any of the lesser men of the tribe" (1880:119B).

The automatic rule of succession provides that the position of the deceased head passes to the next eldest brother, and down the line of brothers before descending to the next generation when the eldest sister's eldest son becomes eligible. In the words of my old informant Peter Hill, "You can't jump over a brother." The lateral transmission of office, characteristic of matrilineal societies, has significant consequences for the scope and nature of political participation in this society. Brothers are not only closest to the head in status but in age, so that a plurality of potential heirs is available at the same time. Corporate dynasties of siblings also exist in patrilineal systems, of course, but here father-son succession seems to be the rule. Collaterals are shuffled off out of the way by a variety of means. Younger brothers, for example, may be killed, exiled, or given posts where they can be kept under surveillance. In filial succession the incumbent can expect a breathing space, since a generation span diminishes the implicit competition between incumbent and heir. Various mechanisms lengthening this period have been described for African cases: the first wife may not be the Great Wife who bears the heir, the eldest son is ineligible to succeed, and so on (Goody 1966:32–39).

Fraternal succession, on the other hand, means that the implicit tension between incumbent and heir is focused on the adult sibling set rather than the nuclear family. Thus the segregation of political and domestic relations, which is said to undermine marriage in matrilineal societies (Schneider and Gough 1962:16–20), may actually foster solidarity in the domestic group. Such solidarity is reflected in the cooperativeness of husband and wife in ceremonial as well as economic activities, as illustrated for the Haida by Murdock's account of the hosting of a potlatch (1934:360, 371; 1936). This structural factor argues against Swanton's impression that wives would betray their husbands if loyalty to their own group required it (Swanton 1905a:62; Murdock 1934:371–72).

One solution to the problem of multiple heirs deriving from the equivalence of siblings is the proliferation of political roles. In the segmental society the uniqueness of high office is modified: each lineage has its own head. The position of town chief is unique within the village, but the opportunity in traditional times for lineage segmentation and migration to a new locale meant that even this highest status was not beyond the reach of ambitious, well-born men. The replication of households within the lineage opens up additional leadership roles at a lower level. Political participation is further broadened by allowing all those whose parents have potlatched—the *ya hét*, whom Murdock referred to as "nobles" (1934:360; 1936:18)—to act as electors of heads of their own units. Indeed, we can view the whole potlatching complex, which gives expression to a multiplicity of ranked names, titles, crests, and so on, as a vehicle promoting maximum political as well as social participation.

The factors stimulating competition for high office give rise to several indeterminate modes of succession. Dawson (1880:119B), however, appears to think that these alternatives are resorted to only when the automatic rule cannot be applied:

> The chieftaincy is hereditary, and on the death of a chief devolves upon his next eldest brother, or should he have no brother, on his nephew, or lacking both of these his sister or niece may in rare cases inherit the chieftaincy, though when this occurs it is probably only nominal. . . . Should all these means of filling the succession fail, a new chief is then either elevated by the consensus of public opinion, or the most opulent and ambitious native attains the position by making a potlatch, or giving away of property greater than any of the rest can afford. . . . This form may in reality become a species of election, for should there be a strong feeling in favour of any particular man, his friends may secretly reinforce his means till he carries his point.

Dawson, then, identifies the modes of succession as the automatic rule, election by consensus, and competitive potlatching.

Swanton's opinion that "success in amassing property" is the primary consideration was cited above. "The election seems to have been a foregone conclusion; but, in so far as any choice was exercised, it appears to have rested, in the case of a family or town chief, with the house chiefs, while the sentiment of a household probably had weight in deciding between claimants to a doubtful position in a single house. Only the town chief's own family had anything directly to say about his election" (1905a:69). It may be assumed that the "foregone conclusion" refers to the operation of the automatic rule. The value of this passage lies in its specification of the members of the unit concerned as the only eligible electors for an office.

An account given to me by Peter Hill emphasizes another mode, appointment. After stressing that "you can't jump over a brother" of a deceased chief, he adds that if there are several sisters, the eldest son of the eldest sister is the heir. "If the oldest nephew is no good, the chief may choose another one. Once the chief dies, his choice is law. Otherwise the family chooses the chief." Appointment and election are two aspects of a single process, the former requiring a powerful incumbent and pre-mortem selection of the heir. Election, on the other hand, is a post-mortem exercise, rests on consent of the constituents, and suggests that power is shared by a wider group (Goody 1966:15–17).

Before looking at the ethnographic evidence, we must first consider what kinds of leadership are required at each level of political organization. If administrative efficiency were necessary, as Service suggests (1975:75), the multiplication of overlapping political roles which we find in Haida society would be unworkable. We are, after all, dealing with a fishing and collecting society of no more than eight to ten thousand persons dispersed in villages of up to thirty houses along the coastlines of the Queen Charlotte Islands. Not only the small size but the segmental structure of Haida society precludes the institutionalization of power and authority over any units wider than the village.

Occasionally great chiefs were able to extend their influence over several villages. We catch glimpses of them in the journals of early visitors—Skutkiss mustering ten large war canoes with a party of two hundred to two hundred fifty men to make war on the mainland (Ingraham 1971:197); Douglas Connee ha [Gunia], described as head chief of the Parry Passage district, trying to persuade the great Tsimshian Chief Shakes to join the Kaigani leaders Kowe and Illtadza in war upon Comswas (Bishop 1967:84). In 1795 Illtadza told the fur trader Bishop that he and Kowe were "united under the command of the Huen Smokett, Douglas Connee ha" (Bishop 1967:81). In the 1860s an English mining engineer working in the southern area of the Queen Charlottes observed that all chiefs "seemed to consider themselves vassals to the great Chief of the Skiddans tribe" (Poole 1872:108).

Niblack, in discussing the exceptional case where a chief is able to extend his influence beyond his own village through war or the ownership of valuable lands, states that "in a strict sense, however, the village is the tribal unit. Alliances of tribes have always been only temporary, and no lasting federation has ever been formed" (1888:251). Dawson reported, "Among the Haidas each permanent village constitutes a chieftaincy, and has a recognized head chief" (1880:118B). "The village appears to be the largest unit in the Haida system of government, and there has not been any permanent premier chief, or larger confederacy or league of tribes. Such unions may doubtless have been formed from time to time for offensive and defensive purposes, but have not endured" (120B). Swanton concurs, "The largest body of people under one government among the Haidas were those in the same town. Although one family might own two or more towns, there were more often several families in one town; and, although all had their own family chiefs, one of these was chief of the town" (1966:56).

When we examine the content of the highest political roles, we find that they are almost entirely expressive, while instrumental power over resources and labor is vested in household heads. Most of the activities of the lineage head concern the administration of the ceremonial estate. He bestows names from the lineage fund of names and decides on the dances, songs, and masks to be used in a ceremony. He may draw upon the wealth not only of his own household but of related house heads to provide the feasts and entertainments which meet his obligations and proclaim his generosity. He starts the dances, leads the singing, and is seated in consideration of his rank. His assent and cooperation are required for the housebuilding potlatches which elevate junior members to the status of house chief. He symbolically initiates the season's activities, giving the signal to begin work on traps, move to fish camp, and so on. He has the right to the best portion of a whale washed up on the group's section of coastline and to a share of the spoils won by members of his war parties.

The head is said to settle internal disputes and, as representative of his group, to conduct trade, make alliances for war, negotiate claims for compensation, and enter into fictive kin relations with other lineage heads. In these activities too, his participation is often largely symbolic. A revealing illustration is provided by the following entry in a fur trader's journal: "the chief usually trades for the whole tribe; but I have sometimes observed that when this method of barter has been disapproved of, each separate family has claimed a right to dispose of their own furs, and the chief always complied with this request" (Dixon 1789:227). Whenever a lineage head is exercising any of his privileges, he can expect to be superseded by higher ranking chiefs and in particular by the town chief, who is also said to start the dances, lead the singing, and so on (Swanton 1905a:68–69)

The early ethnographic accounts stress the limitations on the chief's powers by heads of coordinate and lower level units. As Dawson notes, "The chief is merely the head or president of the various family combinations, and unless his decisions carry with them the assent of the other leaders they have not much weight" (1880:119B). Swanton provides corroboration. "The power of the family chief was thus a varying one, dependent on, and at the same time limited by, the number and power of his house chiefs" (1905a:69). "Declaration of war is said to have rested entirely with the family [lineage] chief, without reference to any family council; but it is quite certain that he must have obtained the acquiescence of his house chiefs if he intended the whole family to participate. In fact, the stories speak of meetings *en masse* to 'talk over' important questions" (Swanton, 1905a: 68–69, 56).

These passages raise questions about the process of consultation, which, as described by early observers, takes the form of a town meeting rather than a council of heads, though probably both modes were practiced. James Deans, a servant of the Hudson's Bay Company, reports that "councils of the tribe" were frequently called to decide an argument between individuals over use of a crest, payment of a debt, and so on (1899:22). Niblack refers to "household consultation or a meeting of the gens or of the chiefs" in which women have as much to say as men "on other than ceremonial occasions, and their advice is frequently followed, particularly in affairs of trade. In matters affecting one or more gentes or the village, representatives . . . meet more formally. They squat around or sit cross-legged, delivering formal speeches in turn, which are heard with rapt attention and approved of by grunts, murmurs, and uplifting of hands" (1888:253).

William H. Collison, the first missionary at Masset, described his reception in the great house of Chief Weah after he had declared his intention of bringing them the message of the Great Chief Above. "There was silence for several minutes. Then there arose a low mur-

muring consultation from all sides which gradually increased in volume during which the chief was in close consultation with his leading advisers. At length the loud tap of a stick by one of these caused silence and the chief arose to speak" (1915:106). The chief answered Collison, asking why the white men sent disease and drink long before anyone came to help them. When he faltered in his oration, he was prompted by one of his advisers, after which he resumed. Collison was then permitted to reply. He was answered by one of the subchiefs, whose remarks indicated that the missionary would be allowed to teach the children but the adults wanted to hold onto their old ways. His account continues, "Now that the consultation had ended the Haidas gave full vent to their views and groups of excited men were discussing the question in high tones and with vehement gestures, both within and without the lodge" (1915:108).

Here we see the town chief issuing a policy statement after consulting with his "leading advisers" in the presence of a large and vociferous public gathering. This function of articulating the views of constituents and fulfilling their expectations of the chiefly role is what we mean by expressive leadership. In a ranked society, expressive leadership calls for high hereditary status and the "chiefly" qualities of wealth, generosity, ambition, and personal prowess.

Instrumental leadership, as previously noted, is vested in house chiefs. It is these heads who actually coordinate the economic activities of their households after the ranking chief has symbolically opened the season. They also control military power. "Each house generally outfitted one canoe, in which the house-chief or his representative [usually sister's son] occupied the stern and was called war-chief" (Swanton 1966:57).

Instrumental roles clearly offer the greatest scope for achievement, particularly in the accumulation of wealth. Recruitment to these roles is subject to the same ambiguity that we noted for lineage headship. Of course, lineage and town chiefs are household heads as well and it behooves them to be the most powerful, wealthy, and aggressive in their town. It is only when they fail to stand first among the house chiefs that they are in danger of being supplanted by junior men. This does not mean, as Rosman and Rubel assert (1971:37), that "leadership within the town and lineage derives directly from leadership within a house." Rather, different powers are allocated to different status-roles. "The fact is," Swanton declares, "each Haida household was so complete in itself that all it required was a name and a certain amount of isolation to develop into an entirely independent family, and there was a constant tendency in that direction" (1966:55–56).

The seeds of segmentation are sown in the lineage's efforts to maximize its strength and prestige by establishing new houses. This might happen when a young man of high rank, assisted by his lineage, put up a carved totem pole and the rafters of his house. Receiving a name from the lineage list of names, he made "a grand feast and potlatch from his own house" (Niblack 1888:372). Alternatively, a house chief inherits his property from elder brother or mother's brother. Niblack describes a third method, arguing that even the handicap of lesser status can be overcome. "Chieftaincy is to a certain extent hereditary, but as it depends upon wealth, any *freeman* [emphasis mine] who can accumulate property may, by erecting a house and giving potlatches and feasts in honor of his ancestors, come finally to be the head of a household and be regarded as a petty chief or one of the principal men of the village" (1888:372). "The ambition of a life centers in the endeavor to accumulate enough property or wealth to enable a freeman to rise to the dignity of a petty chief" (Niblack 1888:324–25).

Swanton discusses the range possible in his role: "His actual influence among the house chiefs varied with the amount of his property; and it is easy to see how a successful house chief might overshadow the nominal head of the family and supplant him or come to found a new one" (1905a:69). It should be borne in mind that much of the competitive behavior described in ethnographic accounts refers to the efforts of junior men to improve their status by potlatching. This status rivalry should not be confused with competition for highest office, in which, as we shall see, public opinion imposes strict limits. Nor should we lose sight of the possibility that the passing of a title or headship from the house of the deceased incumbent may simply mean that the successor is a nonresident brother rather than a coresident nephew. An ethnographic example is the succession of Kitkun, house chief at Kloo, to the office of town chief, which had been held by his brother.

The establishment of new houses creates unnamed subdivisions in the lineage. Often members of these subgroups adopt distinctive features of dress for use at potlatches, saying, "The dress is between us" (Swanton 1905a:79). Thus distinctions are drawn which deepen until, perhaps, the final break occurs. Although demographic and economic pressures may be operating, segmentation in the lineage is usually conceptualized as the result of conflict. Indeed, competition between petty chiefs commonly provokes hostilities.

Feud breaking out between rival factions entails the expulsion of the weaker group. If sufficient numbers survive, they migrate to a new locale and establish their independence by acquiring title to the site and calling themselves the people of that place. They thereby obtain a name which is the diacritical feature of the autonomous lineage. This autonomy is preserved in subsequent relations by the maintenance of symbolic boundaries. Linking the lineage founder with some episode or character in tribal mythology gives a charter to the group and justifies its use of certain names, dances, songs, and stories. Related lineages retain the same crests but new exclusive ones are sought. Thus, at one bound, the house chief becomes lineage head and town chief. Whether his village can be maintained and prosper depends on his possession of the chiefly qualities of aggressiveness and shrewdness as well as on his ability to attract supporters. The warlike nature of competition in earlier times placed a premium on numerical strength. The prestige and power accruing to the head of a large and wealthy group prompted him to offer inducements to followers, who, in turn, are pleased to be identified with a powerful chief.

But if segmentation relieves the problem of a plurality of heirs by multiplying political roles, the costs are high. A group expelled from the village undoubtedly loses access to the lineage's economic estate, though the sources are not specific on this point. The size of all groups involved is diminished by partition and, in some cases, by the slaughter that accompanies feuding. A weakened group is vulnerable to further attack, its members risking death and enslavement. Survivors of such catastrophes are dispersed, taking refuge with kinsmen in another village or seeking the protection of a powerful chief by assuming the status of servants (Swanton, 1905a:100).

The structural contradictions in Haida society come into focus at this point. They arise from the conflicting principles of priority and equivalence which are inherent in the very nature of the corporate group. They are not to be confused with the breakdown of traditional authority (Stearns 1981: 53–54, 283–86). Social relations are ordered by the principle of priority: the first-born enjoys highest rank; first occupancy establishes title to property; first creation as certified in myths conveys highest prestige to a lineage, allegedly for all time. On the other hand, the principles of the solidarity of the sibling group and joint ownership of the estate imply equivalence.

The contradiction is expressed in relation to property. Chiefs, in the role of custodian, attempt to treat the corporate estate as personal property, appropriating its wealth and monopolizing its choicest ceremonial privileges. But the estate is subject to conflicting claims by household heads, who have access to resources and control the labor of their dependents. A partial resolution is found in the segregation of expressive and instrumental roles.

The contradiction in political terms is even sharper. The determinate rule of succession emphasizes priority, specifying the next eldest brother as heir. But a rule of lateral succession reinforces the equivalence of the sibling set. The result is a plurality of potential heirs available at the same time. With no structural requisite of a clearcut delineation of power and authority, the Haidas' solution to the dilemma of plural heirs is the multiplication of political roles by segmentation: lineage fission multiplies lineage headships; the migration of segments to new locales and the founding of new towns multiplies town chiefships; the setting up of new households multiplies house chiefships.

Underlying this proliferation of political roles is the normative conflict between the principle of hereditary right and an egalitarian ethos associated with the equivalence of siblings. The possibility of segmentation gives the appearance of social mobility, which stimulates competition. Its consequences are the geographic dispersion of new groups and the weakening of established groups, contributing to social instability. Counteracting these fissive tendencies are structural factors which encourage consolidation. Marriage is the most important. The practice whereby certain lineages consistently intermarry creates alliances of narrow range which are reinforced by potlatch exchanges and renewed in each generation by new marriages. The ritual dependence on father's sister at every phase of the life cycle binds intermarrying lineages in lifelong obligations to male members' children. The combination of matrilineal descent and virilocal residence while women continue to have a voice in their own lineages exerts strong pressures for coresidence. Only town chiefs were explicitly expected to "marry at a distance" (Swanton 1905a:68); others, presumably, tended to marry locally. Within the lineage group the head's monopoly of ceremonial privileges inhibited fission to some extent. To understand the interplay of these factors in the political arena we must examine some ethnographic evidence.

Analysis of the lineage composition of towns using Swanton's house lists compiled in 1900–01 shows several possible arrangements (1905a:282–95). The *single-lineage settlement* of one or several houses, where the highest ranking household head is also lineage head and town chief, is described by Swanton (1905a:66), Murdock (1936:16), and Drucker (1955:112) as the aboriginal type. Given the vulnerability of small, isolated settlements, the single-lineage village was a temporary form; there are no examples in Swanton's survey.

In the *multilineage town* the segment holding legal title is said to "own" the site, and other lineages of the same moiety enjoy residential privileges with its consent. The *composite town* is a multilineage settlement in which both moieties are represented; only this form is socially and ceremonially complete. Interlineage relationships imposed by exogamy and ceremonial interdependence exert great pressure for consolidation in composite towns. This pressure was increased by the operation of other factors during historic times. Thus a fourth form may be distinguished as the nucleating center fed by decimated groups from formerly dispersed lineages.

Figure 1 depicts the lineage composition of several Canadian Haida towns. Each bar stands for a moiety, its subdivisions indicating autonomous lineages, numbered according to Swanton's notations. The prefixes R and E denote Ravens and Eagles. It will be observed that the lineage of the town chief of each village, marked with an asterisk, is not always that with the greatest number of houses (for example, Kloo and Xaina). Because the houses were not all occupied simultaneously, the diagram is to some degree misleading. Oral traditions and other field data help to correct the picture.

The only multilineage settlement in the survey is Kiusta on northwestern Graham Island, an old Eagle town of three related lineages. At the time of Dawson's visit in 1878, the village had been abandoned but twelve houses and some carved posts were still standing (Dawson 1880:162B). Swanton identified three houses as belonging to the K'awas lineage (E21a) headed by Iłtine who was formerly town chief. Four houses belonged to the StA'stas (E21) under EdA'nsa, later known as Albert Edward Edenshaw. The other two belonged to the Hiellen-born StA'stas (E21c) who had accompanied Edenshaw to Kiusta (Swanton 1905a:293).

Oral traditions which I collected in Masset in 1962 tell that long ago (probably in the early 1840s) when the K'awas were living alone in Kiusta under their head Iłtine, a large party of canoes appeared offshore and attempted to land. The people rushed down to the beach and threw things at the visitors to keep them from coming ashore, but the chief came out and scolded them, saying that this was no way to greet friends.

"Why didn't the people want these others to land?"

"Well, they knew this man [Edenshaw] was going to try to take

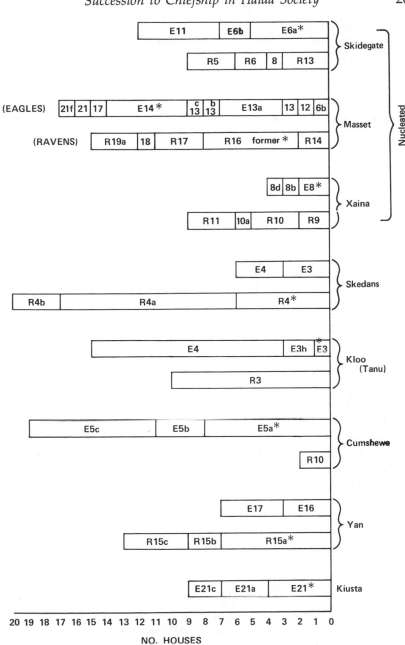

Fig. 1. Lineage composition of towns. (Source: Swanton 1905a:282–93)
NOTE: Asterisk indicates lineage of town chief.

over. But they let him come ashore and right away they built a huge house, called Story House, and their chief gave a big potlatch. And sure enough, when the old chief [Iłtine] died, this man grabbed the name and made himself chief."

This story was told by Morris Marks who in 1962 held the name Iłtine and was regarded by his friends as the "rightful chief of Kiusta." There are other versions of this tale which reflect the Masset people's attitude toward Edenshaw, but the account given here is most consistent with the archaeological evidence, the documentary sources, and the K'awas' own traditions.

Study of lineage genealogies (Swanton 1905a:93) throws some light on the matter. K'awas was reckoned as part of the StA'stas in that early time when they lived at Rose Spit. The group that broke away established its independence when it settled at Kiusta in an area abandoned by the Raven groups that had migrated to Alaska in the eighteenth century. The arrival of the StA'stas at Kiusta was seen by the K'awas as an attempt to reassert dominance. K'awas informants described Iłtine and Edenshaw as "distant blood relatives," but this may be, like the term "friends," a conventional way of referring to related lineages.

A story collected by Marianne Bölscher indicates the newcomers' status as guests. Her informant, whose mother's father was a K'awas, stated:

> Henry Edenshaw's father is not the chief of Kiusta. Kiusta was full when they [the StA'stas] tried to get in there. . . . Finally they [the K'awas] had a big meeting called together by Iłsqandas. She was taking care of the village. She must be the niece of the chief. They allowed others to stay there for a while. When they had the meeting they told Edenshaw to anchor way out while they had it. They just allowed him to stay there— didn't give him any land. [personal communication]

An interesting feature distinguishing this version from other accounts is the "chief woman" acting as caretaker of the village. This could only happen if no brother or sister's son were available when the old chief died. It does not mean that there were no eligible K'awas candidates, but only that the automatic rule could not be applied. Before the lineage council could act, Edenshaw seized the vacant office of town chief. A new head was chosen for the K'awas but title to the town passed to the StA'stas. Edenshaw's claim, based on his wealth, the number of his supporters, and his housebuilding and potlatching, was not recognized as legitimate at the time, nor subsequently, as we shall see.

In the case of Kiusta, a village occupied by one lineage became a multilineage town with the arrival of related groups. If newcomers respect the norms governing "guest" lineages, their presence strengthens the chief's hand. Given the nature of political process in this society, however, it is likely that competition with the owners was a common threat. Such a threat may be counterbalanced if the town chief can persuade his kin of the opposite moiety to move in. When Edenshaw was chief at Kiusta, he built a house intended for his young son (Swanton 1905a:125, 127). At maturity, however, this son, Cowhoe (Gau), became lineage head of the Middle Town People (R19) and town chief of Dadens across Parry Passage on North Island. The adjacent settlement of intermarrying lineages allows their heads to enjoy political independence and highest status while maintaining close relations.

Adjacent settlement was also practiced by the Pebble Town People (R9) and the Sea Lion Town People (E9) whose villages were close by on Skidegate Inlet. Sections of both lineages used to camp along the north side of the western entrance to Skidegate Channel in the region called Stasa'os. Intermarriage was frequent and the children born to Raven women were called Those Born at Stasa'os (R11). Children of Eagle women also took the place name, becoming the Stasa'os Town People (E10). The related groups subsequently migrated together and shared the same villages (Swanton 1905a:83). With the establishment of coresidence by affinal kin, multilineage towns become composite, as we see again in Cumshewa.

Cumshewa was an old Eagle town belonging to the Witch People (E5). This large group had segmented into three lineages, each taking the name of the part of town where it was localized. The town chief's lineage, the Low Ground People (E5a) was represented by eight houses. The High Ground People (E5b) had three houses and the Up-Inlet People (E5c), eight (Swanton 1905a:97). Here lineage segmentation was not commemorated by traditions of hostility, nor were any branches forced out of the village. A large number of Low Ground People accompanied a "chief woman" to the west coast when she married a chief of the Pitch Town People (R12). Later, in the general exodus from the west coast, this group, after long wanderings, returned to Cumshewa with their spouses of R10 and R11.

One house in Cumshewa belonged to a man of the Sqoaladas of the west coast (R10) who had married the sister of the town chief. He raised a house in his wife's town rather than going back to his

own people at Tasu Harbor. The other R10 house may have belonged to a sister's son or other kin of the original colonizer. It might
be thought that the head of a "guest" lineage would have little hope
of gaining influence in such a situation. Given the norm of status-
equivalence of spouses, however, the brother-in-law of a great chief
would not occupy an inferior position among the lineage heads of
a town. Since he was not a political threat, he may well have played
the honored role of "peacemaker," for which I have evidence at
Masset.

Composite towns, as a glance at Figure 1 will show, are characterized by large lineages, each of several houses. In his population
estimates for 1836–41, John Work lists 286 persons with 20 houses
for Cumshewa, 439 persons and 30 houses for Skedans, and 545
persons and 40 houses for Kloo (cited in Dawson 1880:173B). Swanton speaks of a tendency to feudalism. There are references to strong
chiefs and vast properties. Groups are ranked. Class distinctions are
recognized. Poor families, termed *alg*A, provide servants whose status is "only slightly higher in the social order than slaves" (Swanton
1905a:69, 70). "Chiefless groups," usually absorbed in some "higher
family," include the People of McKay's Harbor (R4b), who were won
in a gambling game, and, at Kloo, the "low class" Common Food-
Steamers (E3b) (Swanton 1905a:79, 96).

With the emergence of hierarchical organization, political relations
are stabilized. Lineage segmentation is inhibited, although unnamed subdivisions develop (Swanton 1905a:79). When fission does
occur, the new group is not expelled from the village but allocated
a junior position on the status scale. There are echoes of challenges
to the town chief's authority, but, on the other hand, we noted Poole's
observation that the chiefs in his neighborhood considered themselves "vassals to the great chief of the Skiddans tribe" (1872:108).
Similarly, Douglas Connee ha was described as head chief of the
Parry Passage district (Bishop 1967:81).

What Figure 1 depicts is the cumulative archaeological evidence
of settlement. At Skedans, however, a few of the houses belonging
to the dominant Peninsula People (R4a) were abandoned because
successive chiefs preferred to erect new houses at their accession.
Of the six houses belonging to the "guest" lineages E3 and E4,
Swanton suggests, "it is not improbable that they were left behind
by the Kloo people when they moved from Skedans rather than by
subsequent settlers from Kloo. . . [although] a chief often had houses
in several towns, especially if there were a branch of his family there"
(Swanton 1905a:67). Significantly, the migrating Eagle lineages are

dominant at Kloo, where the town chiefship is vested in Those Born at Skedans (E3). Swanton sees this group, represented by a single house at Kloo, as a "later developed aristocratic branch" of E4, the Town of Dji'gua People (1905a:96).

The highest office clearly does not rest on the force of arms, or even of numbers, in these old established towns. The history of the succession at Kloo reinforces this point. Swanton tells how the "future chief of Kloo lived with his people at Skedans before attaining his majority and succeeding to the chieftainship at Kloo" (1905a:96). The first chief at Kloo belonged to E3 but was killed by members of R3, the "guest" lineage in his town. While the deceased chief's successor was growing up at Skedans, four chiefs of the related E4 lineage were heads of the town successively. One may infer that the short tenure of these chiefs is linked to their bloody wars as recorded in the tales (Swanton 1905b). When the determinate heir came of age, the chiefship reverted to E3. This chief was succeeded by "his two nephews conjointly. When the Kloo people sent to Skedans to ask which of them was the better, they said that these two were equally good; and to avoid jealousy and further trouble, they were both taken" (Swanton 1905a:97). In this instance the automatic rule of succession is applied with an interesting twist: "jealousy and further trouble" are avoided by dispensing with the competitive potlatch. The consensus of the "Kloo people" settles the issue. As for the dual chiefs, no better evidence could be found to illustrate the points that high office is concerned with expressive leadership, and that there is no perceived need for administrative efficiency. The case also testifies to the stability of political relations in a long-established composite town.

A case showing how motives for separation of residence conflicted with pressures for consolidation is that of the west coast peoples who were forced to abandon their villages. The Pebble Town People (R9) had migrated to the inhospitable west coast during their bloody wars with R5, as recorded in the traditions (Swanton 1905a:82–83; 1905b). For whatever cause, war or disease, the remnants of these lineages were not able to maintain themselves in isolation and were forced to return to Skidegate Inlet in about 1850. They "made a race" for the site of Old Xaina on the western end of Maude Island near the present-day village of Skidegate. According to Swanton, "The first to go were the Pebble-Town-Eagles (E8) whose chief consequently became chief of the town; and the chiefs of two old West Coast towns, *unwilling to take a subordinate position* [emphasis mine], moved back to the sites of the Inlet towns their ancestors had once occupied, and put up houses. They seem to have hoped to draw their families with them, but, if so, they were disappointed; and Xaina was only abandoned when the people all moved into Skidegate'' (1905a:84).

Swanton lists thirteen houses for Xaina. The lineage of the town chief of E8 is represented by two houses while two other Eagle lineages have one house each. The Ravens, in contrast, have a total of nine houses. These buildings are all contemporaneous and represent the actual distribution of strength. Here again, superiority of numbers does not confer political dominance. Swanton is persuaded that priority of occupancy was the legitimating factor, but Dawson notes that the head of E8 negotiated with descendants of the ancient owners, then living at Skidegate (Dawson 1880:168B). In any case, the chiefs who were not pleased with this arrangement set themselves up in rival towns rather than contest the title.

One of the oldest and most important towns on the north coast is Masset. Its history goes back to the dispersion of the Raven lineages from the legendary Story Town at Rose Spit (Swanton, 1905a:78, 84–90). Settled first by the Skidaqao (R16), the village has been a crossroads for the movements of Raven and Eagle lineages, possibly for centuries. Swanton's house lists, which record five Raven lineages occupying fifteen houses and ten Eagle lineages with seventeen houses, appear to show the composition of the town in the mid-nineteenth century before the arrival of the missionary and the final amalgamation of northern groups. This inference is based on the fact that the lineages of Yan, Yatza, Kung, and others are not included in the Masset list.

The extreme heterogeneity of the village, dating from a period before the disastrous depopulation, gives a very different tone to political relations. Masset already shows characteristics of the later nucleating villages—many small, weak lineages with small property holdings. In contrast to the four or five lineage heads of typical composite towns, there are at least fifteen heads, more after nucleation, contending for status in this village. Swanton's list for Skidegate also shows this pattern. No wonder that the ethnographic accounts of the late nineteenth century lay such stress on competition as the dominant mode of political action. We must now ask whether this emphasis is justified. Of course, in the segmental society, the characteristic feature of political process is the contraposition of corporate groups. But their interaction is concerned at least as much with reciprocal exchange—of spouses, gifts, services, and status recognition—as with rivalries of chiefs and headmen.

We have been considering how political relations reflect variations in lineage association. Our analysis suggests that realignment of power relations is possible in the multilineage town as exemplified by Kiusta and in the nucleating center as in Xaina. But in the composite town as represented by Kloo, political relations are apparently so stable that we find no challenge to the hegemony of the entitled lineage even though its chief is slain by members of the opposing "guest" lineage and a kind of regency is established by the related lineage during the minority of the determinate heir. Before concluding, prematurely, that determinate rules of succession apply in the stabilized situation, whereas the fluid states of segmentation and nucleation open the door to indeterminate modes, we must examine some data for Masset. Unfortunately, we do not have the rich case material that Garfield was able to gather for the Tsimshian during the 1930s. In the 1960s, however, I was able to collect details about the town chiefship which may throw some light on this question.

When I first went to Masset in 1962 I began to hear about the great Raven chief Sígai who had passed the title and the town to his *son*. The event was considered remarkable by informants because it "broke the custom" of matrilineal succession. It was still providing fuel for rivals who wished to challenge the legitimacy of the current hereditary chief. This chief, William Matthews, gave the following account of his predecessor's appointment.

Chief Sígai, the head chief of Masset, married the sister of Skil ta qá dju, who was the Eagle chief of a village called S⁽ʿ⁾ulju kun across Masset Inlet. "Our grandmother got a son, first born." He grew up with his "uncle" whom he expected to succeed as town chief of a village of perhaps two hundred persons. He married the daughter of the town chief of the west coast village of Tian and came back to his father's village. "He was very popular with his father's tribe members. He got lots of property by hunting. His father made a big feast. He called people from Yan, Kayung, Hiellen, Sangan, all the towns around. When all the guests were here, the chief made a speech. He said, 'I got a son. He's very popular here. He's a good hunter and has slaves of his own. I don't want him to be a common member of this village. I give him this village.'"

Other informants believed that Sígai's son had already assumed his uncle's place as chief of the Eagle lineage, Sᵉadjuga′ lanas, and of the town, Sᵉ ulju kun. After the great feast where he was named heir to his father, Skil ta qá dju moved across the inlet to Masset, bringing several households with him. Upon assuming his position, he took the name of Weah. Swanton refers obliquely to this matter. He remarks of the Sᵉadjugał Town people, whom he refers to as E14, "In former times it was considered a rather inferior division; but very recently its chief has become town chief of Masset, *by sufferance of the people, and owing to his personal popularity*" (1905a:101, emphasis mine). Although the title to the town "jumped clans" (moieties in our terminology), Weah did not inherit the symbolic properties of his father's lineage. The name Sígai was passed down the matriline. Nevertheless, Sígai's own prized crest, the grizzly bear, which was exclusive to the Raven moiety and never claimed by Eagles, was ascribed to Weah by customary usage. This signifies that the town chief has come to stand for the entire community; there has been an extension of his expressive, though not of his instrumental, powers.

At first, the succession of a son to the highest political status in a matrilineal society seems extraordinary. On the other hand, Goody has observed that "sons usually have a role of greater political importance under uterine succession than sister's sons in agnatic ones (e.g., in the Trobriands, Bemba and Ashanti)" (1966:30). With virilocal residence a son belongs to his father's household until puberty and shares in his prestige. Reference was made above to Swanton's statement that chiefs' sons were expected to excel (1905a:70). By this standard the appointment of Skil ta qá dju must have been acceptable to the Haidas. He was a close kinsman of the great Chief Sígai and a town chief in his own right. He had married the daughter of an important chief and amassed wealth on his own, had slaves, and was extremely popular with the people of the village.

The last element, his popularity, may have been decisive. This interpretation is supported by the fate of a contemporary of Weah's whose achievements seem to express the values of Haida society equally well. But, instead of cultivating support, Edenshaw apparently repeatedly outraged public opinion and in return was denied the recognition he so relentlessly sought. An important feature of Haida politics highlighted by these cases is the consensual basis of the chief's authority. As we examine additional evidence we shall see that it confirms the testimony of early observers, quoted above, about the weight of public opinion.

At Kloo we saw that the chiefship passed temporarily into the hands of a junior lineage but reverted to the senior line when the prescribed heir became available. No such reversion occurred in Masset. In the traditional account which I have published elsewhere

(Stearns 1981:230–31), the office of town chief of Masset passed from Sígai's son to his sister's son Harry Weah and thence to his sister's son William Matthews. The claim of the latter chief to be the "fourth and last Weah" thus presented a puzzle. There are allusions in the literature to another Chief Weah. Swanton had attributed the name "Wia" to the E21c lineage (1905a:290 #13). It seemed plausible that the name assumed by Skil ta qá dju at his accession had belonged to his father's father. More confusing is the missionary Collison's reference to an incident before his time in which an old Chief Weah had drowned while on a journey with his young nephew "See-gay" (1915). The Weah who received him in 1876 was also an old man and there was never any question that he was Sígai's successor.

In receiving the story of Weah's appointment from Chief Matthews' widow in 1979, Marianne Bölscher recorded an important new element. "Chief Weah-going-to-be's brother had a house here and he traded the house with his brother" in order to give the new chief the idealized central place in the village. This information explains and is supported by Swanton's attribution of House 13, "Na yū Ans," to "Wia" and House 20 to Skil ta qá dju (1905a:290). The possibility that the great Weah had a younger brother who succeeded him is confirmed by an original document turned up by Marianne Bölscher during field work. Its author was the factor at the Hudson's Bay trading post in Masset.

"June 1st, 1869

I would say the death of Wiha is much lamented by all his people. His brother assumes his name and I find him to be an exception. He is well disposed and likes to see the whites come among them. He is of great service to me in trade. He has great influence among his people. I find him to be trustworthy in every particular. Hudson Bay Trading Post

W. F. Offutt in Charge" [punctuation added]

This information never emerged in any of the long discussions of Haida history and chiefship which I held with old informants over twenty years ago. In view of their willingness to share their recollections with me and the reliability of that corpus of data, it seems unlikely that William Matthews, Peter Hill, Joshua Abrahams, Morris Marks, George Jones, and others would have concealed these interesting facts if they had known of them. Of course, the "forgetting" of persons and the telescoping of genealogies is not uncommon. I often found that informants did not at first remember a child or other relative whose existence I learned of in church and agency records. "Structural amnesia" in this instance does not indicate that the events occurred beyond the reach of memory, for Edenshaw's actions, which can still provoke controversy, took place a generation or more earlier. We conclude instead that the fraternal succession of the younger Skil ta qá dju was considered unremarkable. The public's approval, documented in Offutt's letter, is further evidence of the legitimacy accorded the appointment of the original Weah.

When Acting Chief Weah died in 1883 without naming a successor, two candidates for his position were put forward. Weah's "family" preferred the sister's son Harry while the other E14 house chiefs favored Paul Ridley. Paul was "prominent" in Masset, which meant that he was "a big man, polite, obliging, good-natured, and wealthy," in the words of his brother's son, Peter Hill. The "family" (probably Weah's household) considered Paul too distantly related. I could never obtain any description more precise than that he was "a blood relation of Weah's on his mother's side and a cousin of Harry's." For their part, the "subchiefs" of the lineage maintained that Harry was not wealthy enough to be town chief of Masset. At the potlatch held to decide the merits of the candidates, "the family produced things so Harry could prove he was worthy. Harry couldn't do this for himself. Paul didn't need help." After prolonged consultation, the sister's son was installed in the town chief's house, his opponent's merit, wealth, display, and personal achievement notwithstanding. This case is instructive because it shows us the interplay of the automatic rule, the electoral council, and competitive potlatching. Had Harry been a more impressive candidate, it is unlikely that Paul would have been considered at all. What we see, then, is not the operation of the automatic rule of succession but the council's affirmation of the hereditary principle over demonstrated achievement.

Long before Harry Weah assumed the office of town chief, the period of dispersed lineage settlement had come to an end. His disappointing performance of the role contributed greatly to its declining prestige during the period of nucleation. He was not prosperous and there is no record that he hosted any memorable feasts. His personal behavior resulted in his being banned from the church. At feasts given by rivals he was deliberately slighted when the seat of honor and invitation to speak first were given to someone of lesser rank.

Much of the esteem reserved for persons of chiefly status and qualities was bestowed upon the Edenshaw family, descendants of Albert Edward Edenshaw, who had claimed to supersede even Chief Weah. Claims to highest rank by Edenshaw's children and grandchildren on the basis of their paternal ancestor's achievements, however, were (and are, even today) contested by many villagers. Edenshaw's case allows us to explore the possibilities and limitations of competition as a method of achieving highest rank.

We met Edenshaw earlier at Kiusta, where he had challenged the authority of the current owners and established himself as town chief. We catch later glimpses of him in logbooks and journals of traders and mariners. With a reputation as "the only Indian we met with that seemed to have made a distinction in his own mind between a passage fit for canoes, and one where a large vessel can pass" (Hills 1853, quoted in Gough 1981:12), he was sought after as a pilot. Implicated in the attack on the trading schooner *Susan Sturgis*, Edenshaw was detained on board the warship H.M.S. *Virago*, sent to investigate the incident (Gough 1981). It was Chief Weah who actually seized the vessel in Masset Harbor in 1852. Edenshaw was credited with saving the lives of the crew by persuading Weah to offer them to the Hudson's Bay Company at Fort Simpson for ransom. A marble monument, which stands in the village to this day, was erected by whites in recognition of this service. Nevertheless, Edenshaw, who had been aboard the *Susan Sturgis* as pilot, was suspected of planning the attack and sharing in the plunder.

During his detainment on the *Virago*, several officers recorded their impressions of him. James C. Prevost, commander of the *Virago*, described him as "decidedly the most advanced Indian I have met with on the Coast: quick, cunning, ambitious, crafty and, above all, anxious to obtain the good opinion of the white men" (Prevost 1853, quoted in Gough 1981:8). William Henry Hills, chaplain of the *Virago*, gave his colored impressions of Edenshaw's character and circumstances in the early 1850s.

> He has great good sense and judgment, very quick, and is subtle and cunning as the serpent. Unfortunately like all his countrymen he has no perception of right and wrong, but what self interest dictates: he is ambitious and leaves no stone unturned to increase his power and property. He is now about thirty-five years old; his father dying while he was young—left him poor, at the head of a weak tribe, only safe from the attacks of their neighbour on account of their poverty, which made them not

worth attacking: to better this he contrived to marry a woman nearly 50 years of age, who is a high Chief of the Kigarny tribe, inhabiting the coast opposite the North coast of Q. Charlotte, one of the strongest of the North west tribes of Indians. Backed by such influence he is able to remove his people to Nadun [Kung], close to the powerful Masset tribe, where with the advantage of a good harbour and making his people cultivate the ground he hopes to attract vessels. He also talks of trading with the other tribes for furs in the same way as the Hudson's Bay Company, and then selling them to them, or to the highest bidder; should he carry out this idea he will prove an awkward customer for the H.B.C. to deal with. He talks very intelligible English; and is a very sharp hand at driving a bargain. [Hills 1853, quoted in Gough 1981: 11–12]

By all accounts Edenshaw would seem to possess the qualities for which Haida chiefs received renown: intelligence, leadership, ambition, industry, wealth, and headship of an important lineage. In 1852 when Captain Rooney of the *Susan Sturgis* engaged him as pilot, he was chief at Kung near Naden Harbor. Kiusta was behind him. At the time of Dawson's visit in 1878, Edenshaw had moved his people to another new village at Yatza on the exposed northern coast of Graham Island (Dawson 1880:162–63B). Later he built a house at Masset, the only one there recorded in Swanton's house lists as belonging to the StA'stas. In all, he was credited with four house-raisings and seven to ten potlatches.

Yet, his successful bid for the town chiefship of Kiusta was never fully acknowledged. A description of the head of the K'awas lineage as the "rightful heir of Kiusta" implies that Edenshaw's action was not seen as politically legitimate, at least by other important factions (Stearns 1981:227). Certainly he challenged the norm that "guest" lineages did not compete with the owners of a town for dominance. We saw that when the head of E8 established his claim to Xaina by the recognized rules of priority of occupancy and purchase from previous owners, rival chiefs set up their own towns.

The charge by some villagers that Edenshaw was "never chief of anything" seemed no more than an extreme statement of opposition to his claims. The noteworthy passage quoted from Hills' journal, recently unearthed by Barry Gough, raises questions about Edenshaw's status and that of his lineage. We have assumed that as head of a group which Swanton listed as one of the three Eagle lineages that "stood first" (1905a:70), Edenshaw's high rank was indisputable. On the other hand, Hills' contemporary account of the young chief as head of a poor, weak group, scrambling to improve his position by a strategic marriage and by his relations with whites is more consistent with the picture that emerges from Kiusta. The K'awas stories depict Edenshaw and his party as a band of renegades. The people apparently found it difficult to concede much importance to a group whose head was thirty years old or younger and had no village of its own. Marianne Bölscher points out that informants always emphasized that old Edenshaw was "from Skidegate," implying that his group was only an offshoot of the StA'stas (personal communication). There are no traditions respecting a "rightful chief" of the StA'stas, however. It may well be that the high prestige that the StA'stas enjoyed in Swanton's time was due to, or restored by, Edenshaw's exploits. His own hereditary status within the group does not seem to have been questioned.

He steps forth from the journals as a loner and entrepreneur. His bearing moved Hills to exclaim extravagantly, "He would make a Peter the Great, or Napoleon, with their opportunities" (Hills 1853, quoted in Gough 1981:11). Clearly he was a man of arresting presence. One imagines him as being of imposing proportions, like Chief Weah, but Hills describes him as standing "about 5 feet 7 ins., with a shade of yellow in his complexion, hazel eyes rather small, and broad features. Square and high shoulders and a wiry form" (Hills 1853). This description easily fits his son Henry at the same age, a man whose photographs convey the aloof, assured demeanor of the highest ranking Haidas.

Old Edenshaw had a strong following made up of kinsmen and slaves, but there is no evidence that it included any important subchiefs. It seems that he generally spurned alliances with other Haidas, seeking from outsiders the recognition and approval that the native society accorded to others. Even his dress bespoke this choice. "Wears his hair in European style, and whenever we saw him was always dressed very neatly; quite different from the usual Indian style that rejoices in gaudy colours: his dress consisted of a blue cloth travelling cap, white shirt, and black silk handkerchief, blue cloth monkey jacket, white waistcoat, blue cloth trousers and boots; and every article fitted as if made for him" (Hills 1853).

It may have been Edenshaw's commerce with whites and his attempts to use their approval to bolster his claim to be the "greatest chief of all the Haidas" that offended certain contemporaries. Even today we find that while the Haidas honor achievement in the outside world, they do not allow this kind of prestige to be translated into internal authority (Stearns 1981:106, 116–17, 296). In contrast to Sígai who ensured the widest possible public support for the appointment of his son by inviting "all the towns around" to a "big feast," Edenshaw did not build an unassailable constituency in his own society. While he worked within the values of his culture, he exaggerated them.

We might explain the outcome of Edenshaw's quest as a demonstration of Parsons' formidably phrased point that "competitive allocation cannot operate without institutionalization of a set of norms defining the limits of legitimate action, particularly . . . with regard to legitimacy of means of attaining the goal" (1951:118). In Haida society, norms defining the limits of competition are not explicit. They inhere in the people's sense of fitness (Stearns 1981:228, 266). Their attitude toward moderation is expressed in a text collected by Swanton. "Then he [Raven] acted like one of a high family who never eats much" (1908:306). Thus, gluttony and other forms of excess are only to be expected of commoners, but high-born people ought to have a sense of balance. Because the norms are implicit, they cannot effectively regulate competition. Haida society can afford this apparent oversight because competition is not a primary mode of recruitment to high office. It is a secondary measure for choosing between candidates who meet ascriptive criteria.

We began this paper by asking under what conditions indeterminate modes of succession are operative. We found that in many cases more than one rule applies. For example, the election of sister's son Harry Weah over the more distantly related but wealthier Paul Ridley demonstrates the primacy of ascriptive criteria. The fiction of achievement, however, is maintained by the kin group's material support in the potlatch. In other instances the operation of a rule is masked. It must have been a common practice for chiefs to designate one of their brothers or nephews as heir in circumstances which would be classified as determinate succession. It is only when the preemptive heir is an unlikely candidate, such as the chief's own son, that we see appointment as a separate mode.

Appointment, as we noted earlier, is testimony to the power of the incumbent, to his undisputed right to name his successor. We find such power ethnographically in the composite town where the chief's strong position is reinforced by tradition, as at Skedans and Kloo, or by the weakness of "guest" lineages, as at Masset. Far more common than appointment is the convening of an electoral council of the group concerned to select or confirm a successor. Occasionally the council will be called upon to adjudicate the claims of contenders in a potlatch. The sentiments of the broader public which participates in such affairs are an influential factor and may be decisive. We saw that public opinion granted legitimacy to Weah despite his irregular descent and withheld unanimous approval from Edenshaw in spite of his achievements.

Parsons argues that "both appointive and selective allocation are associated with primacy of achievement-orientation over ascriptive" (1951:118). However, there are apparently no exceptions to the requisite of high hereditary status for chiefs and lineage heads. Nor is there any basis for correlating modes of succession and varieties of lineage association in towns. The choice of successor remains an internal lineage affair, even in composite and nucleated settlements where the town chief exerts expressive leadership over the entire community. What we have, then, are not alternate rules of succession but variations on the basic rule of hereditary allocation.

The indeterminate modes of appointment, selection, and competition are secondary principles, providing the necessary flexibility in a political system which requires that candidates possess both high rank and "chiefly qualities." Achievement becomes a primary principle in the remaining mode of attaining high office: setting up a new unit by segmentation and possibly migration. Here the leader is self-selected and his success rests on his ability to recruit followers and thus ultimately upon his chiefly qualities.

Segmentation is a means of multiplying high offices during periods of stable or expanding population when the frontiers are not closed by external political constraints. The expectations of social mobility fostered in these circumstances cannot be sustained when population declines and the frontier is closed. But the political style is maintained in the round of potlatches. The political significance of the potlatch lies less in the assertion of claims than in the public's power to reward those who best express the values and support the norms of the society.

We are accustomed to think of the ceremonial elaboration and the artistic achievements of Northwest Coast cultures as a response to the social leisure afforded by abundance and the seasonal cycle. Perhaps we should also consider the proliferation of political activity as another expressive mode deriving from social leisure.

Negation In Haida

Carol M. Eastman

~~~~~~

The Haida are neighbors of the Tsimshian and, like them, have a language which represents a linguistic anomaly on the Northwest Coast. Professor Garfield's numerous references to the neighboring Haida in her Tsimshian studies reflect her general interest in all the peoples of the Northwest Coast. Giving of this knowledge, she has been helpful to me in my fieldwork among the Haida of southeast Alaska.

In her contribution to the book *The Tsimshian: Their Arts and Music* (1951; republished in 1966 as *The Tsimshian Indians and Their Arts*), Garfield includes comparisons of Haida culture (social and political organization, religion, art, oral literature) with her ethnographic account of the Tsimshian while noting the dissimilarity of both the Haida and Tsimshian languages to other Northwest languages and to each other. With regard to the Haida and Tsimshian languages, she states: "In a consideration of the Tsimshian and their place in the Northwest Coast area, language is a factor of prime importance. Linguists have not been able to relate the Tsimshian language specifically to any other, either of North America or Asia. Tsimshian lacks functional tone which is characteristic of all neighboring Nadene speakers, excepting Haida" (p. 6).

The linguistic affiliation of each of these languages is still not known. In fact, it appears that Haida is not Na-Dene after all. Lately, fieldwork has begun anew in an effort to describe the languages so that ultimately their genetic relationships might be known. Since 1972, I have been working on the southeast Alaskan dialect of Haida as spoken in Hydaburg with a number of students and Haida consultants.

It is my purpose here to describe the process of negation as it occurs in various types of sentences and constructions in the language. In recent years a number of linguists have been concerned with negation as a linguistic process common to the world's languages. Studies within the framework of transformational/generative grammar have been concerned with negation in English in an effort to understand the grammatical and semantic nature of negation in general.

Jackendoff (1969; 1971), and earlier Klima (1964), make a distinction between *sentence negation* and *constituent negation*. The distinction has to do with the semantic *scope* (range of meaning) of the negative particle used in these grammatical constructions. If a negative particle or word extends over a whole sentence, we may say it figures in sentence negation, e.g., "I won't catch the fish" versus "I will catch the fish." Here the negative particle (the contraction of "not" added to "will") has sentential scope in that it negates the entire subject and predicate of the positive form of the sentence. On the other hand, when negative particles have a narrower range, they are said to effect constituent negation, e.g., "I will not catch the fish" (as in, that is, "I will—positively—not catch the fish" versus "I will catch no fish"). The difference between sentence and constituent negation has to do with the scope of the negative in the surface structure of an utterance. Thus, negation is a process involving syntactically determined semantic scope.

Note that in English "I will not catch the fish" is ambiguous. That is, the negative particle "not" may be interpreted as having either sentential scope or be restricted to a single constituent—such as, predicate or V(erb).

Sentential: I will not catch the fish
               NEG + I will catch the fish.

Constituent: I will not catch the fish.
               I will + NEG catch the fish.

Figures 1 and 2 show the two underlying structures of the ambiguous sentence "I will not catch the fish": the different interpretations may be accounted for by different positions occupied by the negative particle in the deep or underlying structure (phrase marker) of the sentence (Lakoff 1969).

In Figure 1 the negative particle (NEG) extends over the whole S(entence). In Figure 2 it is restricted in scope to the transitive verb (Vt) and its object (NP).

An explanation of negation in English, at least, also needs to account for why the sentence with the contraction of the negative is not ambiguous and the one using the full particle "not" is. A still different position, again based on an analysis of English and gleaned from an observation by Bach (1968:96ff), holds that "there is a re-

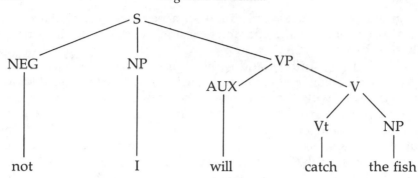

Fig. 1. Sentential

lationship between what is negated and the stress" (Sgall, Hajičová, and Benešová 1973:78). Performance factors such as stress and intonation and the context of spoken discourse are more and more being used to study negation. That is, the context in which phenomena or linguistic processes such as negation are used (performed) and the way in which the processes are used are becoming important components of linguistic analysis.

Very little that has been published on Haida describes or analyzes negation in that language. Harrison (1895) considers what he labels

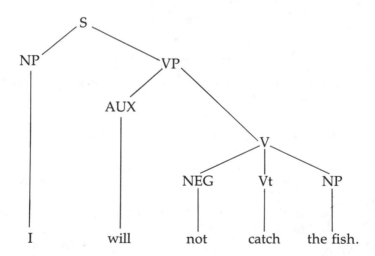

Fig. 2. Constituent

a *negative conjugation* which is employed with "regular" verbs. He also sets up a category of "irregular" verbs and notes that they fall into a number of conjugations, but he does not provide examples of the use of a negative with any of these verbs. In addition to the negative conjugation, Harrison also gives a list of negative particles (1895:150). Swanton (1911:251) mentions a negative modal suffix ǥAŇ (Masset ⁿAŇ) which he claims is always preceded by the negative particle ǥAm. In a section on interjections, Swanton (1911:266) includes some negative expressions. In what follows, a description of the process of negation in Haida will be made by stating what the various negative grammatical particles are and what their semantic scope is in Haida utterances.

From the analysis to be presented here, it appears that in Haida, as in English, both constituent and sentential negation occur; the two types differ with respect to where in a sentence the negative particles occur (their syntactic position) and with respect to their range of meaning (their semantic scope).

Sentential negation in Haida involves prefixing a negative particle /ʔaŋ/ to a verb's tense, aspect, or mode particle (that is, to the category AUX or Auxilliary). In some cases, a negative word may also occur in the sentences in addition to the negative particle which appears in the verb. Constituent negation, on the other hand, involves placing a negative word before the elements included in its scope. The actual semantic range (scope) of the negative word is delimited by suprasegmental factors such as stress, pause, or intonation. Compare this result to Klima's analysis of negation in English (1964:316):

> The principle grammatical notions developed in this study concern the scope of negation (i.e., the structures over which the negative element has its effect) and the structural position of the negative element in the sentence. The scope of negation varies according to the origin of the negative element in the sentence (over the whole, over subordinate complementary structures alone, or only over the word containing the negative element). A single independent negative element, whose simplest reflex is *not*, is found to account for sentence negation; its scope is the whole sentence, but because that element is mobile and capable of fusing with other elements (for example in *nobody*), its ultimate position and form have great latitude. When the negative element originates in other constituents . . ., the scope of negation is restricted to structures subordinate to those constitu-

ents. However, granted the differences due to varying scope, it was found that the phenomena connected with negation could be described grammatically on the basis of a single negative element.

In Haida it appears that both constituent and sentence negation as distinguished by Klima occur—yet they involve distinct grammatical elements, the former characterized roughly by /gəm/ and the latter by the /ʔaŋ/ prefix to AUX. The differences in semantic scope parallel those found in English.

The data from Haida presented below were gathered from speakers of the dialect spoken in Hydaburg, Alaska (on Prince of Wales Island), and in Seattle, Washington. Speakers of the Hydaburg dialect (also known as Kaigani Haida) today live primarily in Hydaburg or Seattle, with many spending part of the year in each place.[1] Geographically "in-between" on the Queen Charlotte Islands of British Columbia, at Masset and Skidegate, are the Canadian Haida, who speak those dialects respectively. Masset is the dialect described in Harrison's Grammer, while Swanton analyzed Skidegate. From what we know so far, the dialect of Hydaburg seems to be more like Masset than Skidegate yet distinctly different in its own right. In fact, in Hydaburg speech, some speakers differentiate between usages derived from speech at Old Kasaan (Blackman, this volume) versus Kaigani-Alaskan Haida settlements prior to amalgamation at Hydaburg in the early twentieth century under the auspices of the Presbytery of southeast Alaska.

The linguist working on Northwest Coast languages in the 1980s is faced with certain transcription problems. Linguistic erosion makes comparing today's Haida with the Haida of Swanton and Harrison difficult and the transcription systems used by them are frequently confusing and hard to interpret. Swanton used the script encouraged by Boas to be used by all BAE (Bureau of American Ethnology) researchers, Harrison used a Latinate attempt at phonetic spelling, and today we use the International Phonetic Alphabet. With regard to equivalences, Eastman and Aoki (1975) compared Swanton, Harrison, and Sapir's symbols for Haida sounds in the dialects they

1. I wish to give special thanks for help with both data and analysis to my students Elizabeth A. Edwards, Daniel Vaughan, Robert Welsch, and Paul Aoki, and to my consultants Lillian Pettviel, Alice Kitkoon, and Bertha George. Small grants from the Melville and Elizabeth Jacobs Foundation (Whatcom County Museum, Bellingham, Washington) and the University of Washington (Graduate School Research Fund, Sea-Alaska Haida Project) aided this research.

each analyzed with the symbols for what they found necessary to use to record Hydaburg speech. Note that Swanton used *A* for what is a high lax rounded back vowel /U/ or a schwa in Hydaburg and a schwa /ə/ in Skidegate. He used Ñ for the IPA "eng" or "engma" ("tailed *n*") /ŋ/. Except for what is directly quoted from other sources, IPA symbols are used in the examples throughout this paper. The /U/ symbol for a high back lax vowel appears as a /U/ in italic; both forms refer to the same sound.

We will now look at negation in Haida. Sentence negation generally occurs inflectionally as anaphora. That is, negation is marked in verbs and refers coreferentially (or anaphorically) to a negative word (most often *gUm*) elsewhere in the sentence. Constituent negation involves the use of negative words without concomitant marking in the verb. We will examine the context for using semantically negative words and discuss briefly the use of the negative in yes/no questions and statements of fact.

SENTENCE NEGATION: THE ANAPHORIC NEGATIVE

As reported elsewhere (Eastman, Welsch, and Vaughan 1975:115), negation with verb inflection is a relatively straightforward process. It involves the infixing of a particle *ʔaŋ* before tense and aspect markers. The use of *ʔaŋ* in Hydaburg speech parallels Harrison's negative conjugation in Masset and the negative modal suffix reported by Swanton (Skidegate *gAN*, Masset *ʿAÑ*). The *ʔaŋ* in Hydaburg then, after orthographic conversion, is the same as the Masset particle. We have also found, in accord with Swanton, that the negative verbal word generally does require an obligatory *gUm* (*gəm*, Swanton *gAm*) preceding it. The *gUm* "no, not" particle will be discussed in the next section along with semantically negative words. Where *ʔaŋ* occurs, *gUm*, then, will precede it. As will be seen below, *gUm* often occurs, as well, without an *ʔaŋ* particle suffixed to the predicate root. Thus, *ʔaŋ* stands in an anaphoric relation to *gUm* in the contexts where it occurs.

The use of *ʔaŋ* appears to be limited to the indicative and interrogative moods. It is infixed between the predicate root (simple or derived) and the indicative or interrogative tense/aspect marker (Eastman, Welsch, and Vaughan 1975:113).

The following sentences illustrate the use of *ʔaŋ*

(1) gəm dəŋ gUtaʔaŋsaŋus   Aren't you going to eat (something)?

(gəm 'not' + dəŋ 'you' + gU
'implied object' + ta 'eat' + ʔaŋ
'neg' + saŋ 'future' + us 'interrogative')

(2) gUm adaɫ čInai dəŋ taʔaŋgən   You didn't eat the fish yesterday.

(gUm 'not' + adaɫ 'yesterday'
+ čInai 'the fish' + dəŋ 'you'
+ ta 'eat' + ʔaŋ 'neg' + gən
'past')

(3) gUm di lamgaʔaŋgən   I'm not drunk.

(gUm 'not' + di 'I-stative pronoun' + lamga 'drunk' + ʔaŋ
'neg' + gən 'present')

It should be pointed out here that the *verb* as a category in Haida
is broadly conceived. Adjectival and nominal as well as verbal predicate roots are inflected for tense/aspect. What is said here regarding the anaphoric negative applies also to such inflected roots. For
example:

(4) xat kiɫhUl gusus gUm la laʔaŋ   She does not speak the Haida
     (Haida + language + she +   language well.
     speak +s 'subordinate marker'   (lit., She is not good, she
     + gUm 'not' + la 'her' + la   speaks the Haida language)
     'good' + Ø 'unmarked time' +
     ʔaŋ 'neg')

Note here that the position of *gUm* limits the scope of the sentential negation (ʔaŋ) in this compound sentence, i.e., Haida-lan-
guage-she-speaks (positive constituent)-negative scope marker (*gUm*)-
her-good-(ʔaŋ) neg. (negative constituent). In compound sentences
such as these each constituent is also a sentence.

ʔaŋ further appears to be limited in that it occurs mainly with
active verbs, optionally with neutral verbs, and rarely with stative
verbs. The categories active, neutral, and stative refer to verbal word
types. An active verbal word contains an active pronoun, an optional object, and a predicate root + tense/aspect suffix.[2] A neutral
verbal word differs from an active one in that there is no optional

2. See Eastman, Welsch, and Vaughan (1975) for more detail on Haida verbal
word subcategorization. See also Welsch (1975) for an account of the active and
stative (or inactive) pronoun series in Hydaburg Haida.

object but, instead, an obligatory particle *gu* preceding the predicate root serving as an implicit object of sorts. For example:

(5) ƛao guta   I eat.

                                    (ƛao 'I-active pronoun' + gu 'implicit object' i.e. "something" + ta 'eat' + ∅ 'unmarked tense/aspect')

A stative verbal word differs from an active verbal word only in that it employs a stative (inactive) pronoun. The negated constituent of the compound sentence (4) is an example of the rare use of sentential negation with stative verbal words (i.e., gUm (not) la (inactive pronoun her) la (predicate adjective) ʔaŋ (neg.)).

In our research, verbal words which may be considered "active" seem to coincide with the majority of verbs, while "stative" forms include predicate adjective and nominal or copula constructions. Thus sentence negation as defined by use of both *gUm* and *ʔaŋ* is most often restricted to active sentences, while stative and (optionally) neutral forms usually employ a constituent type of negation. Neutral forms are relatively rare. Therefore, sentence (6) is an acceptable alternate form for (3):

(6) gUm di lamgagəŋ   I'm not drunk.
                                    (gUm 'not' + di 'I-stative' + lamga 'drunk' + gəŋ 'present')

Note, however, that the formation of the negative with neutral verbal words using either *ʔaŋ* or *gUm* or both is often precluded on semantic rather than syntactic grounds. Consider the following ungrammatical sentences compared with (5) above:

(7) *gUm ƛao guta
(8) *gUm ƛao gutaʔaŋ

When asked if (7) and (8) are grammatical, our consultants replied that there would be no point in saying that: why would anybody say "I don't eat"? One would say instead:

(9) ƛan ƛao guta   (ƛan 'never' + ƛao 'I' + gu 'implicit object' ta 'eat')

ƛan will be mentioned below along with *gUm* as a semantically negative word with a range of occurrence similar to that of *gUm*. The unacceptability of *gUm* here in favor of *ƛan* seems to be associated with the occurrence of the *gu* 'implicit object' in such rare constructions. It appears that to negate a sentence such as "I eat," it is more correct on semantic grounds to say "I never eat" than "I don't eat." To use *ʔaŋ* here would convey the sense of *"I not eat," that is, "I (active) do carry out the action of not eating (something)." "I carry out the action of never eating something" is grammatical or proper instead. In the final section of this paper some conjectures will be made regarding restrictions on the use of *gUm* in relation to *ƛan* in certain sentences.

Klima, in his analysis of English, described a similarity in sentence negation between the use of *not* (*gUm* in Haida) and *never* (*ƛan*) which we also corroborate here. He called *never* a negative preverbal adverb and distinguished it from nonnegative preverbal adverbs such as *always, surely,* and *usually* by observing that "the negative preverbal adverbs as a class are grammatically different from the other pre-verbal adverbs, and . . . the particle *not* is grammatically the same as the negative pre-verbal adverbs (e.g., *never*) in this respect" (1964:262). Thus *gUm* in active sentences (with *ʔaŋ*) and *ƛan* in neutral sentences affect sentence negation in that the scope of negation extends over the entire sentence.

In English, sentence negation is structurally characterized "as resulting when *neg,* the subject Nominal and the Predicate are 'in construction with' one another and are directly dominated by S(entence)" (Klima 1964:303). See figure 1 above. This definition includes both declarative and interrogative utterances in English and seems to apply as well in Haida when negation is employed involving an active verb.

It may be said then that the anaphoric negative particle *ʔaŋ,* as it occurs regularly with active verbs in the indicative and interrogative, serves to negate the action, while gUm and other semantically negative words serve to negate the object or complement particle or word. *ƛan* "never" as a negative adverb of time may serve as both complement and negation in a sentence.

The use of words such as *ƛan* and *gUm* alone to effect negation will be seen more clearly below when we examine the use of semantically negative words in other contexts. In sentences such as (1), (2), and (3) above, where both *gUm* and *ʔaŋ* are used, both the verb and its object or complement may be considered to be negated. That is, the scope includes the whole sentence. It seems to be the case that when active verbs in the indicative and interrogative are negated, the intent is to negate both the action and its object/complement. Sentence (4), in contrast, presents the relatively rare case of the anaphoric negative being used where the predicated root is an inflected adjective. Had *la* "good" been used as a complement instead and "speak" as the verb, it is unlikely that the anaphoric negative would have been used.

Consider the next sentences:

(10) adaⱡ gUm dəman dəŋ kʔatuja   Didn't you sleep well yesterday?
(adaⱡ 'yesterday' + 'not' + dəman 'well' + dəŋ 'you-active' + kʔat 'sleep' + uja 'past-interrogative')

(11) adaⱡ gUm činai aⱡ tauja   Didn't I eat the fish yesterday?
(adaⱡ 'yesterday' + 'not' + 'the fish' + aⱡ 'I-active' + ta 'eat' + uja 'past-interrogative')

(12) sinλa gUm la dUŋ gUlaŋ(w)uja   Why didn't you like him?
(sinλa 'why' + 'not' + la 'him' + dUŋ 'you-active' + gUla 'like' + ʔaŋ 'neg' + uja)

In (10) and (11), negation is accomplished employing only *gUm* and not both *gUm* and *ʔaŋ* as in (12). Thus (10) and (11) might more properly be glossed respectively as

    (a) Did you sleep *not well* yesterday? [adverbial negative]
    (b) Did I eat *not fish* yesterday? [nominal negative]

while (12) may be interpreted as glossed with both the verb and object marked for negative—that is, involving the whole sentence in scope. In contrast, the *gUm* in (10) and (11) negates an adverb (*well*) and a noun (*fish*) respectively. These sentences serve as examples of Constituent Negation (as described by Klima) in that the scope of negation does not extend over both the nominal and the predicate. This may be seen by demonstrating in English that when the negated constituent is removed from the sentences, *different* sentences result whose difference is greater than that between positive versions of negative sentences. For example:

    (a') Did you sleep yesterday?
    (b') Did I eat yesterday?

When both an object and a complement occur in a sentence, the placement of *gUm* in terms of word order determines the negative emphasis rather than its scope. For example:

(13) gUm wEd xagia ļ da?aŋwaŋ   They don't have a dog *now*.
                                 (not + now + dog + they +
                                 have + neg + waŋ "3rd pl.
                                 present")

In (13) the sense is "Not now (is when) they don't have a dog" as opposed to "Now, not a dog (is what) they don't have." If the latter were to be the sense conveyed, the *gUm* "not" would precede *xagia* "the dog" rather than *wEd* 'now.'

Constituent Negation: Semantically Negative Words

In his discussion of Haida negation, Harrison (1895:150) lists the negative particles for Masset Haida as: *Kāhano* "no," *Kum* "not" (our *gUm*), *chiKiang* "by no means," and *Kum tliku Klingē Kānggaangung* "not at all." In the expression for "not at all" we have what looks like a sentence containing both *gUm* and *?aŋ*, as discussed above. *Kāhano* is described as the negative answer to a question. For example, "Did you see James?" Answer: "No."

Swanton provides the following examples of negative words (1911:266): *āya* "no!"; *î* "don't!"; *ga'o ano* or *gō'ano* "no!"

In addition to the *gUm* and *Xan* mentioned above, in our data we also have: *ganu~ga?anu* (cf. *Kāhano* and *ga'ano* or *gō'ano*); *ulaŋ*; *gˀe~ge*; *aiya* 'I don't know.'

In this section we will examine some of the contexts for the use of such negative words. As stated earlier, the negative word *gUm* "not" generally occurs in sentences that also contain the inflectional negative *?aŋ* used with most active verbal words. In fact, for Haida, this is how sentence negation is most generally defined.

Consider as well the following sentences:

(14) gUm lak iskinUŋ   Don't wake her up.
                             (not + her + boundary marker
                             + wake up)

(15) gUm git ista Xlŋən   I don't want it.
                             (not + git 'thing' + do + I-ac-
                             tive + Xlŋən 'want')

(16) adaX gUm gin X nlXlnsan   Tomorrow I am not going to
                             drink.
                             (tomorrow + not + thing 'in-
                             animate' + I-active + nlX
                             'drink' + future)

(17) adaⅼ gUm tanai dəŋ *k*Iŋs
 Won't the bear see you to-morrow?
 (tomorrow + not + the bear + you + *k*Iŋ 'see' + s 'future interrogative')

(18) gUm k'iu dəŋ *k*Iŋgəŋ
 Don't you see clams?
 (not + clams + you + see + gəŋ 'present')

(19) gUm k'iwai λUŋ *k*Iŋgən
 Didn't you see the clams?
 (not + the clams + you-active pl. + *k*Iŋ 'see' + gən 'past')

(20) gUm k'iwai λUŋ *k*Iŋaŋgən
 You didn't see the clams.
 (not + the clams + you-active pl. + 'see' + 'aŋ 'neg' + gən 'past')

(21) gUm di lamga
 I am not drunk.
 (not + I-stative + be drunk + Ø 'unmarked time')

(22) gUm gutsgia
 It's not wolves.
 (not + wolves + definite)
 (cf. *gutsgia* 'the wolves')

(23) gUm di xiaⅼ gai'aŋ
 I do not dance well.
 (not + I − stative + dance + fat, i.e., 'good' + neg + Ø 'unmarked time') (cf. (4) above)

(24) di xiaⅼ'alaŋ
 I am not a dancer.
 (I-stative + dance + 'alaŋ)

Sentences (14) to (23) illustrate a sample range of occurrence of *gUm* in our data. As the examples here and those used earlier show, *gUm* comes at the beginning of a sentence or clause except when it occurs with other negative particles (see below) or where nonnegated adverbs or interrogative words are used, as in sentences (10), (11), (12), (16), and (17).

Sentences (14), (21), and (22) provide examples of *gUm* as used to negate sentences that are in the imperative, employ stative verbal words, or are predicate nominals respectively. Example (14) contains gUm as a particle negating a constituent rather than a whole sentence, as we saw with (10) and (11), for example, "Wake up not her." In sentences (21) and (22) whether constituent or sentence negation is intended is impossible as well as unnecessary to decide, since the "meaning" is the same either way. Note that sentence (21) is yet another form of (6) and (3), further illustrating this point with regard to stative forms.

Sentence (19) as compared with (20) bears some comment. Sentence (20) "You didn't see the clams" is a straightforward example of the anaphoric negative. Sentence (19) "Didn't you see the clams?" containing an active verb in the past interrogative would also be expected to form the negative with *gUm* and *ʔaŋ*. And one would expect the sentence to contain the past interrogative particle *uja*. On the surface, (19) might seem to be an alternate form for (20). What appears to be the case is that in order to say "You didn't see the clams" the anaphoric negative particle as well as *gUm* is obligatory. In the absence of the interrogative particle (marked for tense) it is possible to ask negative questions using *gUm* + noninterrogative tense/aspect marker. Such structures are questions in English, but in Haida they are more properly statements contrary to fact which in discourse require a response. That is, in Haida there is no point in saying "You did see *not* clams" except to clear up a misunderstanding by evoking a response such as "I *did* see salmon."

Thus *gUm* may be used with an active verb marked for tense/ aspect to elicit responses in structures which in English would be considered interrogative. Compare sentences (19), (20), and (25) to illustrate this:

(19) gUm kʔiwai λUŋ *k*Iŋgən   Didn't you see the clams?
                                    (not + the clams + you + see
                                    + past)

(20) gUm kʔiwai λUŋ *k*Iŋaŋgən   You didn't see the clams.
                                    (not + the clams + you + see
                                    + neg + past)

(25) gUm kʔiwai λUŋ *k*Iŋaŋuja   Didn't you see the clams?
                                    (not + the clams + you + see
                                    + neg + past interrogative)

In sentences (20) and (25) we have examples of sentence negation as described above. In sentence (19) *gUm* occurs but the verb is not marked negative, although it is inflected for tense. In (19) the scope of *gUm* includes only the sentence nominal: (19) "not clams—you did see" versus (20) "not the clams you didn't see" and (25) "not the clams you didn't see?"

In the previous section we mentioned *Xan* "never" as a semantically negative word with a range of occurrence similar to *gUm* differing in content as "never" versus "not." Another negative word is common in Haida, $g^ʔe$ (g^ue~ge). The closest translation in English is "no." It always occurs in a complete sentence and as such differs from *ganu*, which we have found, in accord with Harrison, to be the negative answer to a yes or no question in Haida. In contrast, *ganu* is used alone. For example, Speaker 1: "You're afraid of bears?" Speaker 2: *ganu* ("no"—period).

We know little about the word *ulaŋ* other than that it, too, is said to mean "no." The negative used in sentence (24), *ʔalaŋ*, which behaves as a negative copula, may be related to *ulaŋ*. Compare sentence (24) with (23), where the anaphoric negative is used with the unmarked tense to say "I do not dance well." Note the verbal use of the usually adjectival *gai* "fat" or "good." Our analysis is only tentative with regard to (24), but it may be that the *ʔal* in *ʔalaŋ* is a nominalizing particle and the *aŋ* a negative.

Sentence (26) shows a positive copula or predicate-nominative construction where there appears to be a nominalizing particle *asʔa*:

(26) dUŋ xiaɫ gai asʔa   You are a good dancer.
                            (you + dance + fat i.e. 'good'
                            + asʔa) (i.e., you + good dance
                            + nominalizer)

If our analysis of (24) *di xialʔalaŋ* is correct, we may have a case of the negative *ʔaŋ* used nonanaphorically. However, until we have more evidence, it seems best to regard *ʔalaŋ* as a negative word used in copula (i.e., predicate nominative or predicate adjective) constructions.

The following sentences illustrate the use of g^ue:

(27) g^{u}e gəm tangai di   No, I'm not afraid of bears.
     ɫkuagUŋgəŋ   (no + not + the bears + I-sta-
                              tive + ɫkuagUŋ 'be afraid' +
                              present)
(28) g^{u}e gəm ɫ giujuʔaŋgəŋ   No, I'm not listening.
                              (no + not + I-active + giuju
                              'hear' <giu 'ear' + neg +
                              present)
(29) g^{u}e Masset a di gutkaʔaŋgəŋ   I'm not anxious to go to Mas-
                              set.
                              (no + Masset + to + I-stative
                              + gut 'want' + *ka* 'go' + neg
                              + present)

Finally, the following sentence provides an example of a negative word as an idiomatic expression:

(30) *aiya*   I don't know.

YES/NO QUESTIONS AND NEGATIVE FACTS

In this section we will discuss briefly what we have observed to be a reluctance to employ a negative in general except for the anaphoric negative in the contexts described. For example, to ask questions such as "Aren't you eating fish?" one would say:

(31) čin dUŋ ta   (fish + you + eat + unmarked
                                     time).

Note that there is neither a negative nor an interrogative marker here. It seems that this would be interpreted as a question. According to our consultants, the declaration would never occur in discourse, since if it were obvious that you are eating fish, the fact would go unstated. To ask if someone is not eating fish would be equally senseless. So, sentence (31) (literally, "You eat fish") would be interpreted as a sentence to which a yes or no response to the truth or falsehood of the stated fact would be given. The response to (31) may be either of the following:

(32) gaʔanu   No.
(33) aŋ   Yes.

Sentence (31) is a question only insofar as it is a statement to be affirmed or denied, and its form is a positive statement. When such a question is affirmed, the word *aŋ* is used. Its distribution is much like that of *gᵘe* as well—that is, it also may occur in sentences. For example:

(34) aŋ tan di ƛkuagəŋ   Yes, I'm afraid of bears.

Sentence (35), on the other hand, contains no negative marker, but the tense is marked for the interrogative.

(35) adaƛ činai dəŋ taʔas?   Aren't you going to eat fish
                                     tomorrow?
                                     (or 'Are you going to eat fish
                                     tomorrow?' i.e., the fish + you
                                     + eat + ʔas 'future interroga-
                                     tive')

Yes and no questions when marked for tense do take the interrogative form but are not inflectionally marked for negative. Compare sentences (31) and (35) with (17), where *gUm* is used. It appears that yes and no questions are asked positively—(31) and (35)—and that it is also common to ask yes and no questions positively involving negated objects and complements: (17) "Tomorrow, not the bear will you see?"

Thus, the anaphoric inflectional negative does not regularly occur with yes or no questions. As we saw in sentence (1), it may occur when the question calls for a sentential response:

(1) gəm dəŋ gUtaʔaŋsaŋus   Aren't you going to eat (something)?

That is, the expected reply to sentence (1) is a sentence that would make the object explicit: "Yes, I'm going to eat salmon" or "No, I'm not going to eat anything."

Finally, we have observed a tendency in Haida to make positive statements rather than negative ones in order to assert a fact. It is considered better to say what something is to get around saying what it is not. For example:

(36) ḷ I tʔamju   She is thin, small (i.e, lost weight)

We asked our consultants how one would say "She isn't thin," and the response was:

(37) ḷ gayagəŋ   She is fat (ḷ 'she' + gaya 'fat' + present).

The expected negative for (36) would be *gUm ḷ I tʔamju*. We were told that this is "broken Haida" and would not be said. Such definite negative utterances are considered impolite, while an overt statement of fact such as "She is fat" is acceptable.

We asked what someone would say if a person was neither fat nor thin. The response (somewhat jocularly) was, "You wouldn't mention it!"

Rather than saying "I will not see you again," one might say:

(38) ƛan dUŋ ƛ kIŋsan   I will never see you again. never (again) + you + I + see + will (i.e., Never again will I see you)

Sentence (38) is a possible statement of fact (e.g., if the speaker decided not to see the person again, or if the speaker was going blind).

On the other hand, the statement "I will not see you again" where *gUm* would be used (or both *gUm* and *ʔaŋ*) reports a prediction which the speaker has no control over, and thus would not properly be said.

It also appears to be the case that certain temporal statements resist negation. For example, in an effort to elicit the sentence "She didn't wake up until dusk" we got:

(39) siŋyes ƛu ḷ skIŋgən   Dusk + at + she + awoke + did (lit., She awoke at dusk)

and for "She didn't wake up for three days" we got:

(40) sIŋ lgUnəƛ ƛu ʔu ḷ skIŋgən day(s) + she + at + is/when + she + awoke + did (lit., She awoke in three days)

And, finally, in our investigations we have found no evidence so far of contradiction of fact in Haida. Although sentence (19), *"Not the clams* you did see," is possible, we get no utterances of the type "No, you *did* see the clams" or "No, I *am* glad to see you." It appears that in Haida one says "Yes, I am something" or "No, I am not something"—see (27), (28), and (29)—but not "Yes, I am not" or "No, I did so."

Summary and Conclusion

In the foregoing analysis we have looked at the process of negation in Haida and noted that it is possible to analyze it, as many have advocated for English, from the point of view of the semantic scope of negative particles. If the verb is included in the scope of negation, we have a case of sentence negation, if it is not included we may note to which constituents of the sentence negation applies. Negative words used in constituent negation (e.g., *gUm*, *ƛan*) may also be, and often are, used for added emphasis in sentence negation (e.g., with *ʔaŋ* prefixed to AUX or the tense/aspect marker).

Our analysis here based on data gathered working with consultants necessarily represents the speech of Haida speakers today. More recent analyses of negation than Klima (1964) have to do with the formal analysis of negation in linguistic theory and are of little help in a descriptive analysis of negation as a process used by speakers such as this one. However, it is becoming more and more the case that analyses of aspects of language such as negation, interrogation, and the like require that attention be paid to semantic or intensional aspects of performance (language use). What people won't or wouldn't say in Haida aids our understanding of the process of negation in general as well as facilitating a description of where negative particles are placed (in terms of word order) and of what scope they have in an utterance in Haida in particular. Our work with Haida so far also backs up the idea (which is certainly intuitively pleasing) that negative particles of a constituent type (i.e., excluding the *ʔaŋ* prefixed to AUX or tense/aspect) may function as emphasis markers as well as to delimit less than sentential scope. For example:

Negative emphasis

(41) gUm halgwa tau gut ḷ ˙Xa-xu   No, emphasis − last night −
     jaŋ + aŋ + gən + gwa   food − box − he − break pl.
                                      objects continuously − neg −
                                      past − definite. *No*, he *did not*
                                      break food boxes last night

                                      vs.

Constituent negative

(42) gUm halgwa tau gut ḷ ˙Xa-xu-   He did not break food boxes
     jaŋ+gən   last night (i.e., He did break
                                      food boxes *not last night*).

                                      vs.

Sentential negative

(43) halgwa tau gut ḷ ˙Xa-xu-   He did not break food boxes
     jaŋ+aŋ+gən   last night

                                      vs.

Positive

(44) halgwa tau gut ḷ ˙Xa-xu-   He broke food boxes last night
     jaŋ+gən

However, it is still the case, as Klima pointed out, that "the grammatical relationship between the particular constituent structure of *neg* and its scope has not yet been formulated; that is, it has not yet been demonstrated that the *full scope* of the negative pre-verbal particle [*ʔaŋ* in Haida] over the whole sentence and the *reduced scope* of the negative affixes [the independent particles *gUm* and *˙Xan* in Haida] over certain dependent sentence-like structures is one and the same phenomenon and that the differences in the two result naturally from the relationship of these two instances of *neg* to other constituents in the sentence" (1964:296).

For English, Klima concludes, as we noted earlier in the chapter, negation can be "described grammatically on the basis of a single negative element" (1964:310) whose reflex is *not* despite the differences in scope (sentential or constituent). From what we know so far in our analysis of Haida we must conclude that to describe negation in Haida it is necessary to distinguish (1) a negative element used in sentential negation (*ʔaŋ*), (2) other elements used in conjunction with *ʔaŋ* and also independently in constituent negation (*gUm* and *χan*), (3) negative words (e.g., *gʷe* and *ganu*), and (4) a general tendency to avoid using negation for contradiction or assertion—that is, to avoid sentences of the type used in English such as "She's not fat" or "No, she is pretty," favoring instead "She's skinny" and "She is pretty," the latter in answer to someone who says, "She is ugly."

Haida remains an anomaly on the Northwest Coast, but a resurgence of interest in it, as well as in Tsimshian, by descriptive linguists may yet help to categorize and classify these groups on the Northwest Coast. In the meantime, research on these languages is helping us to understand processes common to all languages.

A Reevaluation of Northwest Coast Cannibalism*

JOYCE WIKE

Cannibalism (anthropophagy) assumed some prominence in early historical sources on the native Northwest Coast of North America as it has in later ethnographic studies of religion and ceremonialism of the region. Information gathered from the two periods does not agree. Ethnographers portrayed a distinctive kind of ceremonial cannibalism (Boas 1897; Drucker 1940; McIlwraith 1948). In these ceremonies, unclean, dangerous food was ingested in a great personal display of supernatural prowess aided on occasion by the use of counterfeit corpses and legerdemain. In contrast, early explorers and traders sensed no artificiality in the man-eating they reported for the region; sometimes as far south as the Oregon coast, but generally from Vancouver Island northward through Prince William Sound. On the west coast of Vancouver Island, victims were frequently young; also slaves were evidently fattened with future consumption in mind. Both epicurean and famine incentives were mentioned. Apparently there was a market or some kind of formal exchange in human flesh as well as a lunar ritual involving cannibalism (Martínez MS 30 September 1789; Ingraham MS 1789; Wagner 1933:160–62; Suría 1936:275).

The purpose of this study is to compare and reconcile the impressions of actual cannibalism of the late eighteenth century with the ceremonies studied one hundred years later under their Kwakiutl names, the *hamatsa* and *hamshamtses*.[1]

This study aims to elucidate the characteristic features, meaning, historical depth, and distribution of this unique, geographically isolated occurrence of institutionalized cannibalism. The general conclusions of ethnologists are confirmed in the face of a substantial

---

*I am grateful to Audrey Christophersen, Professors Laura Casari, James Gibson, the late Preston Holder (University of Nebraska-Lincoln), Patricia Rieper (Nebraska Wesleyan University), and William Jacobsen, Jr. (University of Nevada-Reno) for their assistance.
1. These and all other native terms used in this paper are anglicized.

challenge by the historian Cook (1973:190–91, n. 7). Furthermore, evidence from Cook's study of Northwest Coast history alters the argument presented by this author earlier (Wike 1962). In the present study, the following claims are made:

1. Based on information accumulated by Spaniards at Friendly Cove, Nootka Sound, and reported by Cook (1973), ceremonial cannibalism, as portrayed in ethnographic descriptions, was present in the Nootka area in the late eighteenth century.

2. Native behavior, interpreted by early observers as proof of enthusiastic cannibalism, suggests instead that human flesh was being proffered to visitors in a form considered by the *hamatsa* to be especially deadly.

3. Ritual cannibalism existed as early as the sixteenth century in the Northwest according to Kwakiutl traditions which had not been recorded when Boas determined that the *hamatsa* was relatively recent in its dispersal (Boas 1921, 1897). Other signs that ceremonial cannibalism was not a recent phenomenon have been pointed out elsewhere (Drucker 1940:22; Codere 1966:448–49; Goldman 1975:89).

A Nootka Cannibal

The most detailed, reliable information about Northwest Coast life in the late eighteenth century is from Friendly Cove on Nootka Island (at the entrance of Nootka Sound on the northeastern part of Vancouver Island's western coast). Friendly Cove was not the "very snug harbor" it appeared to be in Captain Cook's brief glance in 1778 (Beaglehole 1967:303; cf. Drucker in Moziño 1970:6). Nevertheless, it was occupied for a span of two thousand years (Folan and Dewhirst 1969). The cove is readily accessible from the sea and convenient to wood and fresh water. Just as important as its accessibility was the consistent hospitality offered to strangers by the Moachaht Nootka people whose summer residence, Yuquot, was there. No serious conflict marred relations between the Moachaht Nootka and the Europeans until the seizure of the ship *Boston* in 1803 other than some trouble with a trader, Hanna (1785), and the killing of a famed war chief, Kelekem, by the Spaniards (1789).

For six years beginning in 1789, visitors to the area and newcomers (including the Spanish during intermittent occupations) came into close contact with the Moachaht. Our knowledge for this period is limited to records of contact between various officers and relates to the highest-ranked chief. This head chief, Tsawasep (Harpooner) has become known under the name of Maquina (Moon), a title of Kwak-

iutl origin (Curtis 1916:8, 69). Like other Northwest Coast aristocrats, he held additional appelations—eight more according to
Ingraham (MS 1789). Maquina was head chief of the largest of the
four tribes in the Nootka confederacy (Drucker 1951:220). As the
holder of this position, he was the architect of a policy of cultivating
friendship with Europeans in order to secure social and economic
benefits (Moziño 1970:31; cf. Vancouver 1798; 2:307–8). Although he
had to be in a strong position to seize the new opportunities for
trade and ceremonial exchange presented by the European presence, Maquina evidently needed to improve his status militarily and
economically in the broader region. Possibly part of Maquina's economic problem was that whales were becoming rare in Nootka Sound
(Meares 1790:125) and whaling was the major preoccupation of the
Nootkan chiefs. Where whales continued to be numerous (to the
south in Clayoquot Sound), people were also more numerous and
prosperous under the powerful chief Wickananish (see Howay
1941:69; Wagner 1930:149; Ernst 1952:101–2). Wickananish was related to Maquina both affinally and consanguineally. In their
personal lives the two were alternately foes, rivals, and allies. Yet
farther south there was another mighty chief, Tatoosh, who dominated the environs of Cape Flattery.

In his dealings with Wickananish and the newcomers, Maquina
exploited a close alliance with the Nimkish Kwakiutl who could be
reached by a chain of streams, lakes, and a trail northward across
Vancouver Island from Maquina's winter village, Tahsis. Insight into
Maquina's status is essential background to Nootka history, for it
shows how he might have come to have many rivals and enemies,
and it suggests how, thereby, he was granted the honor of being
THE *hamatsa* of his time.

All the late eighteenth-century evidence for the existence of a *hamatsa*-like ceremony applies to Maquina. Most significant is the way
he is portrayed eating raw human flesh with the technique and
mannerisms of the later cannibals (Cook 1973:190, 296). A ceremonial event consistently featuring him is pieced together below,
although there is no way to determine whether a single type of
ceremony or one or more occasions are involved. Some details of
the event were supplied by children who escaped being Maquina's
victims by fleeing to the Spaniards or who were ransomed to save
them from this fate (Cook 1973:190, 296, 314, n. 100). Sometimes
guns were paid by the Spanish to the Indians to rescue children.
Victims asking for deliverance and any sellers who represented them
had no reason to minimize the horrors they faced. Occasionally,

when children were being purchased, the Indians asked if the Spaniards wanted them to eat.

Meares, who had a reputation among his contemporaries for inaccuracy, claimed to have learned about Maquina's behavior from the subchiefs second and third below him in rank in 1788 (Meares 1790:255–56). The distinguished warrior Kelekem, who was killed by the Spaniards the next year, claimed he was "averse to human flesh" but Maquina was not and killed a slave "every moon."

It is not easy to judge the probity of Meares himself. He (1790:132) mentioned having seen the journal of Mackay/Mackey (Waldron MS), the surgeon from the *Captain Cook*, who lived in Maquina's house for a year in 1786–87. There is some reason to suspect that Meares may have used Mackay's journal (which was subsequently lost) in order to provide detailed descriptions of Nootkan culture, including reports of Maquina's propensity for human flesh.

Assuming for the sake of argument that the available reports do refer to a single ritual of Maquina's, we can piece it together from the following sources: Meares (1790:255–56; based on Meares: Espinosa y Tello 1930:103–4; Wagner 1933, with reference to the year 1788); an anonymous Franciscan and an unspecified informant with reference to 1789 (Cook 1973:190); some Indians to Eliza (with reference to 1790 from Cook 1973:296); from a child to Eliza (ibid.); an interrupted account by Hoskins (with reference to 1792 in Howay 1941:289).

In the reconstruction below, the details from Meares's account are followed by the letter M. The other sources are marked by Uk (unknown), Ad (adult), or Ch (child).

MAQUINA'S RITUAL CANNIBALISM

A slave (M) or war prisoner was chosen (Uk, Ch) from a group or selected at random (M, Ch) by Maquina, blindfolded (M, Ch) or with his eyes closed (Ad). The group comprised younger prisoners of war (Uk), boys fattened (Uk), children (Ad, Ch) or children purchased for the purpose (Ad). They stood in a circle around him (Uk) or were pursued by him (M, Ad). This took place in his home (M) before spectators who were only men (Uk), including warriors (M), only the most valiant of these (Ad), and subchiefs (M, Uk). The inferior chiefs sang a war song (M), danced around the fire (M), fed the fire with oil (M), prior to the main action by Maquina who held a club or "instrument" (Ch). He then clubbed the victim, quartered and cut the body into strips, separating flesh from bones, and ate it raw "in great mouthfuls, shouting and making fearsome gestures" (Ad), slit open the abdomen, cut off the arms and ate the flesh (Uk), cut up the body in pieces and distributed them to his guests (M).

As mentioned previously, Meares was told that the ceremony was held monthly; Vancouver (1798; 1:290) received the same impression. In 1792, Boit understood that it occurred rarely, only on very special occasions (Howay 1941:387). Eliza (Cook 1973) learned that a total of eleven children had been killed by Maquina after being raised to seven or eight years of age. Maquina's son informed Moziño that cannibalism was limited to preparations for warfare (Moziño 1970:22–23). José Cardero's identical information is obviously from Moziño (Espinosa y Tello 1930:104; Wagner 1933).

These representations of Maquina's alleged cannibalism show a significant resemblance to the ritual cannibalism recounted in the nineteenth century. Maquina's handling of the bodies likewise appears ritualistic, and thus seems divorceable from implications of epicureanism or gluttony. The youthfulness of his prey may be explained by the ceremonial purity attributed to infants and children. A Nootka ritual practiced to attract drift whales sometimes employed infants (Boas 1930:267) and boys (Curtis 1916) as well as corpses. According to this line of reasoning, the flesh of children would constitute the "food" least unclean and therefore most desirable for the supernatural cannibal—and least dangerous to the cannibal's natural self. The impression of pitilessness that was cultivated by Northwest Coast warriors might well have been enhanced by the selection of immature victims. It would seem likely, too, that being small, children were ideal candidates for theatrical manipulation. In a famous trick at the Saint Louis Exposition, the Kwakiutl, Charles Nowell, and his friends, chose an African pygmy to be "devoured" by a *hamatsa* before a horrified audience, then they subsequently restored him to life (Ford 1941:186–90).

It is interesting that the ethnographic record contains few hints that children ever formed a substantial part of a ceremonial cannibal's feast although the historical sources are strong on this point.

Elsewhere in the area Maquina's behavior was replicated by a distinguished Haisla chief. The Haisla are a northern Kwakiutl people in the region where ceremonial cannibalism was believed to have originated. In a "famed incident" between 1855 and 1875, a Haisla chief was presented with two child slaves by a Tsimshian counterpart during the Haisla chief's first *hamatsa* dance (Olson 1940:177). The Haisla initiate seized and bit the children, eating their flesh until they died. At a later period, according to missionaries (Lopatin 1945:86), some Haisla cannibals tried to carry off an infant and a child. At Wrangel in Stikine Tlingit territory, a missionary persuaded fifty *hamatsas* to release two girls already badly injured; one was subsequently recaptured and killed (Crosby 1914:173).

Other than the Haisla and Tlingit episodes, the slave killings reported ethnographically in connection with nineteenth-century ritual cannibalism involved solitary adults surprised on the beach or killed suddenly during a *hamatsa* or *hamshamtses* performance (Boas 1897:439; McIlwraith 1948:108–9; Curtis 1915:239). Thus there is no real basis for comparison with Maquina's alleged modes of selection. The mention of his club or clubbing is one of the rare references anywhere to the ceremonial use of this kind of·weapon or instrument so widely identified as a "slave-killer" in museum collections (cf. Gunther 1960:271–72, 1972:60).

The most striking similarity between Maquina's performance and that of the *hamatsa-hamshamtses*, the consumption of raw flesh in a characteristic way, was rationalized in a fashion that sets Northwest Coast cannibalism apart from other traditions of ceremonial anthropophagy. Typically, in ceremonial anthropophagy, the cannibal incorporates some attributes of the slain. In contrast, on the Northwest Coast, a supernatural being has already been incorporated in the *hamatsa*. It, not the human, is actually the eater. The ceremonial for the initiate was designed to tame and dislodge this man-eating spirit (cf. McIlwraith 1948:79, 115, pl. 5).

The notion that a supernatural being or animal has inhabited the person who undertakes cannibalistic behavior is part of a widespread system of beliefs on the Northwest Coast associated with the even more widely dispersed guardian spirit complex. The being or tutelary takes over, replacing or supplementing normal personal faculties at special times of ceremonial or personal need. The appetite of this supernatural creature is frequently expressed in bizarre, inhuman cravings such as the yearnings of the "cannibal" for mummified corpses, or raw living flesh obtained by biting others, even biting oneself (McIlwraith 1948:110) and killing slaves or recent war captives.

The cravings were fulfilled in order to pacify the creature. In the same category with the wish to consume raw human flesh, the Bella Coola placed the desire to eat fresh, raw salmon out of season—or the desire to eat living dogs (ibid., 108). The Haisla considered the flesh of dogs as well as humans to be unclean and poisonous, so that onlookers were impressed with the ability of performers to survive (Olson 1940:176). In a Tsimshian myth, some cannibal dancers tried to kill a shaman and drive away his supernatural power by feeding him cooked human meat. He managed to feed it to them instead and they died immediately (Boas 1916:334–35). In everyday life, some animals were not eaten by the Tsimshian because those animals ate corpses (pp. 501–2). The Kwakiutl understood that relatively fresh cadavers were likely to be poisonous, whereas old, mummified corpses were not (Jacobsen 1884:50). Nonetheless, the Kwakiutl *hamatsa* made sure that no part of the corpse was ever digested (Curtis 1915:228).

There seems to be only one ethnographic reference to any cooking of humans. Around 1867, following a *hamshamtses* performance which he witnessed when he was in his teens, George Hunt was told by a Nawiti (Newettee) chief that the group of cannibals had boiled and eaten all that remained of a slave's body after the dance had ended (Curtis 1915:241). The experience of visitors in the late eighteenth century with roasted human parts and the various expressions of enthusiasm for cannibalism conveyed to them by their hosts will be explained below by reference to this deadly-flesh motif. My suggestion is that the offering of body parts as food to Europeans was a covert attack on—or a testing of—them in the pattern reflected above in the myth of the cannibal dancers' attack on a Tsimshian shaman.

DEADLY HANDS

The Kwakiutl belief that the ingestion of certain body parts caused sudden death illuminates some remarkably uniform experiences of the early traders and explorers with so-called Nootka cannibalism. The Kwakiutl *hamatsas* "must not eat the hands and feet. It is believed that . . . they would die immediately" (Boas 1897:441). Curtis (1915:224) understood that palms and soles produced the deadly effect. Human hands, dried or roasted, were offered for sale on more than six separate occasions, sometimes with heads or skulls. This took place over a period of fourteen years commencing with the visit of Captain Cook four years after the initial authenticated appearance of Europeans in the vicinity in 1774. Other body fragments are rarely specified except for some limbs—the arms of a man (Hunter 1940), children's arms and legs (Cook 1973:296). There are indefinite references to "other body parts" (Moziño 1970:22–23) and "human bones" (Ingraham MS 1789). Hunter reported finding "some bodies" in a basket covered with leaves.[2]

There is evidence that poisonous appendages were offered by the Indians to the Europeans not simply as a way to profit from the sale of useless by-products and test European vulnerability but also as a means of expressing mischief for whenever the native traders are identified, it is as strangers to the area. Otherwise it might seem that the souvenir-hunting of Captain Cook's men transformed a chance offering into suitable trade goods. Such receptivity on the part of the Indians to European demand is common in the maritime fur trade (Wike 1947). The presence of skulls or heads could suggest that hands were simply another form of trophy.[3]

The first references to the offering of human appendages to Europeans appear in the records of Captain Cook's expedition during the month spent in Resolution Cove (Bligh Island, east of Friendly Cove) in 1778. Ships were repaired there, and some exploring in the vicinity included a visit to Friendly Cove. In the official journal, as originally published in 1784, Cook noted (II, p. 271): "But the most extraordinary of all articles which they brought to the ships for sale were human skulls, and hands not quite stripped of the flesh, which they made our people plainly understand they had eaten, and indeed; some of them had evident marks that they had been upon the fire."

Zimmerman (1930:71) noted seeing "dried human flesh which they ate with relish and which they wished us to try. We traded with

2. A letter from W. [A.?] Hunter (1940), dated November 21, 1786, from Macao Road refers to Nootka cannibalism as follows: "We found the people answer Capt. Cook's description of them so accurately that I shall say nothing of them except to clear the doubt that they are cannibals. We have reason to suppose it is only their enemies they eat for we found some bodies deposited in a basket lying on the ground covered with leaves. They are excellent curers for some of our Gentlemen carried some heads with them which kept perfectly dried. One day they brought the head and arms of a man they had just kill'd & offered them for sale."

3. The reports of the Cook expedition may also be of interest in showing that any Mexican inspiration for the Nootka attention to hands would have to come as a result of the 1774 Spanish voyage. Although Middle America is not mentioned in Quimby's catalogue (1948) of potential foreign influences, it should not be ruled out. A Mexican Indian who deserted from the Spaniards in 1792 was suspected of slaying one of their boys, who was mutilated in a fashion suggestive of cannibalism (Cook 1973:377–78). The hands, feet, and head of victims who had been sacrificed by the Maya were reserved for the priest and his assistants (Thompson 1966:283, quoted by Harner 1977:132). I am indebted to Michael Harner and Robert Anthony Holder for directing my attention to the only reference to this combination I have seen in the ethnological literature. Mayan practice, of course, is assumed to be cognate with Mexican.

them for several dried human hands which we took back with us to England." Rickman (1781:242) itemized a head, arms, and limbs. Captain Cook's remarks quoted above were taken from the journal of the surgeon Anderson (Beaglehole 1967:cxcviii–cci). Beaglehole (1967:297) cites the following quotation from the journal of a man named Bayly (March 30, 1778): "We bought 3 or 4 human hands which they brought to sell, they appeared to have been lately cut off as the flesh was not reduced to a horny substance but raw. . . . they made signs that they were good eating, and seemed to sell them to us for that purpose or at least all of us understood them in that light. They likewise brought on board two or three Human Skuls (sic) and offered them to sale. . . . our Surgeon bought one of them."

Another person, Edgar, bought a hand from a man (April 25, 1778): "and then desir'd him to Eat it, which he would not do, I then offered him more Iron & Brass than wou'd have purchas'd one of their most Elegant dresses, if he would eat part of it, all which offers he treated with Great Contempt & departed in Great anger" (ibid.).

The American who traveled with Cook, John Ledyard, suggests that some effort was made to communicate censure to the Indians: "The first boat that visited us in the Cove brought what no doubt they thought· the greatest possible regalia, and offered it to us to eat; this was a human arm roasted" (Ledyard 1783:73). Ledyard and "many others" tasted it out of curiosity and then "intimated to our hosts that what we had tasted was bad, and expressed as well as we could our disapprobation of eating it on the account of its being part of a man like ourselves."[4]

In 1786, James Strange out of Bombay on leave from the East India Company was offered three hands and a head (Strange 1928:27). In this instance, the donor was prepared to demonstrate his wares. Maquina introduced Strange to a celebrated warrior who had slain twenty-eight men during the previous ten months. Strange identified this warrior as "Clamata." It is likely that he actually was Kelekem. Strange said that he would not know what to do with the items offered for sale. Clamata (Kelekem?) explained that they were to be eaten: "My hero now gave me ocular demonstration, & very composedly put one of the hands in his mouth and stripping it through his teeth, tore off a considerable piece of the flesh, which

4. Reports from the Cook voyage are problematic. Cook's own journal simply lists "even human skuls [sic] and hands" brought to trade. Ledyard relied heavily on Rickman (1781), whose first published account of the expedition was a "fanciful and ridiculously exaggerated production" (Beaglehole 1967:ccv, ccix, 297).

he immediately devoured, with much apparent relish."

Strange was horrified. Kelekem reassured him by insisting that he would eat neither Strange nor his friend, Mackay (the ship's doctor), who was left behind in the household of Maquina. Kelekem explained: "But the hand he had then Eaten was the hand of his Enemy whom he had killed in War, & that the Eating of it was a deed acceptable in the Eyes of Heaven, to which he at the same time pointed." This explanation fits in very well with Boas's comments regarding the symbolism of the cannibal ceremony (Boas 1897:664, in 1940:383). Although Strange rejected the goods, his narrative of the incident closes with some ambiguous remarks indicating that others of the visitors may not have done so: "This kind of Traffic was always carried on with seeming secrecy, and an apparent fear of being Detected by their Own Countrymen & they therefore Watched the occasion of parting with their Goods, at a time when their Companions were otherwise busied. . . . they were never purchased, but at a most exorbitant rate" (Strange 1928:27).

The next recorded incident (1788) was believed to involve the mummified hand of a Englishman brought to Meares's ship along with furs for sale by visitors who had just entered the cove (Meares 1790:124). The visitors were driven away after one was seen wearing an article identified as belonging to an officer of the *Imperial Eagle* who had been captured and killed by the Quinault (or Quileute, near the mouth of the Hoh River, on the Washington coast). The innocence of the visitors with regard to the fate of the officer was established by Maquina, who knew "that the article came indirectly into the donors' possession in the way of trade, from the natives of Queenhythe, which was the very place where Mr. Miller and his associates had been murdered. But the chief did not attempt to deny that the hand had belonged to one of our unhappy countrymen; and from his manifest confusion in conversing on this subject, and various other concurring circumstances which will be related hereafter, we were very much disposed to believe that Maquina himself was a cannibal. There is, indeed, too much reason to apprehend that the horrible traffic for human flesh extends, more or less, along this part of the continent of America" (pp. 124–25).

One "concurring circumstance" was the time Kelekem, the hand-eater (above), and another chief of lower rank, claimed that Maquina, and not they, was cannibalistic. Once Maquina, after accidentally injuring himself, expressed pleasure at the taste of his own blood and confessed that he had recently killed and eaten a slave. Meares reports that on hearing this he threatened Maquina with death if there were a repetition (Meares 1790:257).

Ingraham mentions that an attempt was made to sell him "the perfect hand of a child about three years old which appeared to have been on the fire" (1789, MS letter in the form of a summary for Martínez). Ingraham stated that people eventually stopped bringing the hands and "human bones" because the Europeans were horrified.

The Spanish presence in 1789 brought intensified efforts to stamp out any signs of cannibalism. Nevertheless, a cooked child's hand was brought to the packet boat *San Carlos* and also "other limbs prepared in the same manner" were offered elsewhere (Moziño 1970:22–23).

In contrast to such experiences is that of the Vancouver expedition. No purchase of human relics is noted. Jewett did see several dried hands which the Indians indicated were very nice eating (MS marginalia, Vancouver 1:270, lines 10–26). It is not clear whether Jewett is speaking of the Klallam or the Nootka in this instance. A recently severed hand was tossed into Lieutenant James Hanson's boat from a passing canoe in Nootka Sound in 1792 (Meany 1915:64–65). Hanson's experience was perhaps an expression of defiance as much as an insult, threat, or warning to the people of Hanson's party and the other Europeans.

By 1792 Moziño had expressed the belief that human sacrifice was no longer carried out; he speculated that this was either because of disapproval and threats or because of a lack of prisoners due to the peace enforced by the Spaniards (1970:40). Records indicate that traders understood that the killing of a slave as part of the Clayoquot Nootka first-whale ceremony had no connection with cannibalism (Howay 1941:76; Curtis 1916:38).

The Ceremonial Setting

John Jewitt lived for two years as Maquina's slave after the seizure of the *Boston* in 1803. He was told that Maquina had abolished ceremonial killing in the Wolf Ritual (Jewitt 1896:206). Nootka who have read Jewitt's account believe that he and his fellow survivor were conducted through the Wolf Ritual (Drucker 1951:391, n. 92; Ernst 1952). The emphasis of this ritual on the training of warriors would fit with the cannibalistic displays of Maquina and his followers. From Jewitt's remarks it appears that such displays were being replaced by self-torture; indeed, he never mentions cannibalism (1896; 1931).

During the nineteenth century, the Wolf Ritual was the major

Nootka winter ceremonial along with the activities of a separate curing society *tsayeq*. Among the Nootka, the sponsorship of the Wolf Ritual ceremony was the prerogative solely of a head chief. Ceremonial details and equipment were his lineage possessions. Nootka aristocrats could be measured according to the number of wolves they were entitled to use to spirit away initiates in the ceremony. One noted ancestor was remembered as a forty-wolf man (Ernst 1952:66, n. 11).

The Nootka winter ceremonial was conservative; in effect it stood apart from ceremonial developments that swept the southern Kwakiutl in the nineteenth century. Myths detailing the origin of the southern Kwakiutl winter ceremonial suggested to Boas that it once resembled the Nootka ritual (Boas 1966:257–59). The similarity was greatly reduced after the appearance of a new supernatural sponsor: Baxbakwalanuxsiae, "Man Eater at the Mouth of the River" (Goldman 1975:10) or "Cannibal at the North End of the World." Boas equated the introduction of this spirit to the winter ceremonial with the inception of ceremonial cannibalism. The Kwakiutl proper received Man Eater's myth and rituals in the first half of the nineteenth century through a series of marriages with the Rivers Inlet people in whose territory the spirit had originated (Boas 1932).

Fortunately for the hypothesis being developed here, it can be shown that ceremonial activity involving the *hamatsa* had to do with more centrally located groups to the south at a time earlier than was apparent at the initial early stages of Boas's research. In many places, the new *hamatsa* simply supplanted (in prestige and importance) a similar but precedent form, *hamshamtses* (Boas 1897:463, 1930:99; Curtis 1915; Drucker 1940:229; Goldman 1975:89; cf. Codere 1961:448). Around 1866 the replacement had not yet taken place at Newettee on northern-most Vancouver Island. The affinity of the *hamatsa* and *hamshamtses*, however, is established by the personal experience of George Hunt, who as a young man saw *hamshamtes* society members kill and "devour" a slave. This was the time (mentioned earlier) when he was told that the remaining parts of the slave had been prepared and eaten afterward—the sole reference to any cooking in relation to the ceremonies (Curtis 1915:240–41).

Twenty years later, when Boas visited Newettee, both dances were present, as is evidenced by his description of 1895 (Rohner 1969:39; Boas 1897:612–13). As late as the early 1920s only two lineage heads of the Kwakiutl proper (Fort Rupert peoples) held the right to *hamatsa* performances, whereas ten out of the total of eighteen were, or had the right to be, *hamshamtses* (Boas 1921:795–801, 825–35).

The most impressive case for an ancient *hamatsa* is contained in some traditions of southern Kwakiutl other than those at Fort Rupert. One marriage history covers twenty-three generations of the leading Gwasela family of Smith Inlet. The Gwasela (northernmost of the southern Kwakiutl) placed their first *hamatsa* ceremony at the time of their initial performance of a winter ceremonial (Boas 1921:836–91; cf. Goldman 1975:213–14). According to their reckoning, this would be in the last quarter of the sixteenth century (Boas 1921:848–51). Along with two slaves "as food for the cannibal," it came to them from the Nakwadax of Seymour Inlet, their neighbors to the south (p. 850). The succeeding head chief, a youngest son, also received a cannibal dance—from the head chief of the Noxunts Owikeno Kwakiutl (directly north), who also gave a present of two slaves whose fate was not mentioned (p. 856).

In the early nineteenth century a *hamatsa* dance was received from the Bella Bella along with four slaves—one of whom was eaten in the performance (p. 861). The subsequent history of the ceremony shows that the Gwasela were in ceremonial contact with the Kwakiutl proper. By means of sorcery, their head chief killed the father of the Gwasela initiate in retaliation for the breaking of a copper. The dance was said to be put into the father's burial box and never performed again (pp. 861–62).

A substantial traditional time span both for the *hamatsa* of the southern Kwakiutl and for the custom of eating slaves as part of it is supplied by the Gwasela history. The aristocratic present of slaves for the purpose is reminiscent of the Tsimshian gift to the Haisla chief in the mid- or later nineteenth century. Such gifts could easily have been misinterpreted by the eighteenth-century observers as an epicurean market or exchange.

The Gwasela marriage history illustrates the dynamics of the winter dance exchange, which was one element in a network binding the Northwest Coast together. According to their history, the Gwasela "married all over the world" (p. 854). Some of their southern neighbors complained of the Gwasela, "In olden times [they] had many dances and did not want to give them to the other Kwakiutl tribes who desired to obtain them through marriages" (Boas 1897:490).

Boas did not apply this record, collected after 1916, to the question of the antiquity of ceremonial cannibalism. Apparently he did not consider the matter after his 1895 reconstruction of the growth of secret societies (Boas 1897, in 1940:379–83) except in brief analyses ancillary to his study of mythologies and some comments accompanying a description of the Kwakiutl winter dance published posthumously (1966:257–59).

The people of the coast were in a severe crisis when Boas visited in the 1880s. Their physical survival was placed in some doubt by the continuing toll of epidemic and endemic disease and a birthrate drastically reduced by venereal infection. Their territorial rights, religion, and other fundamental beliefs were under attack. They were being "saved" even further from the winter ceremonial and potlatching, after European intervention called a halt to "deadly warfare, cannibalism, and head-taking." In British Columbia, participation in these practices became misdemeanors under the Indian Act of 1876. The first winter dance Boas observed (at Newettee) was performed under the threat that a gunboat would appear (Rohner 1969:33). The threat was evidently discounted, although Newettee had been bombarded a generation before (Codere 1961:459). In 1865 the village at Fort Rupert was destroyed in reprisal for a slave-killing by the *hamatsas*.

Jacobsen believed that the bombardments and threats inspired the *hamatsas* to substitute corpses for living bodies (1884:50–51). There is no traditional reference to outside pressures bringing about this change. The retaliation following the death of the slave cited by the Fort Rupert Kwakiutl is the subsequent annihilation of the *hamatsas* by the curse of their victim's widow (Boas 1897:439), not the loss of their homes. Corpse-eating was not stopped by threats nor by the conversion of prominent people to Christianity (as in the north), but instead became covert in 1892 when six *hamatsas* died from eating parts of a cadaver that allegedly had been poisoned (Curtis 1915:242–43).

Ceremonial cannibalism on the Northwest Coast apparently ended with these allegations of poisoning just as the historical record began with some trials of the cannibals' poison on a few Europeans. For the writer the appearance of cultural consistency is not, however, the most telling support for this interpretation: it grew out of an undirected examination of *all* the early references to cannibalism. There was no selection of data and it has all been presented or cited here. Further, a simple explanation of the hand theme illuminated a variety of different circumstances, one good test of sound theory. In significant contrast to this variation, the hearsay descriptions uniformly portrayed the cannibal devouring raw or living flesh in the manner of the ritual performer. His unlikely achievement does not fit nutritional or epicurean modes. Could these have coexisted as the Spaniards believed? One can't say categorically, but not if every form of cannibalism was so dangerous. The final episode above shows the danger was real, yet a powerful few may have engaged in other forms. Great power meant the ability to violate specific taboos safely and to override the hazards that blocked lesser men. Tradition and custom did not necessarily limit the actual deeds of prominent chiefs and great warriors. They needed to demonstrate superhuman capacities in order to survive, and to secure, maintain, and extend their privileged status and by extension sometimes the well-being of their people or town. Others should hesitate before turning against, or confidently facing in combat, adversaries who possessed these unnatural appetites and skills. These individuals exploited and created attitudes of horror and fear, which must have matched many of the sentiments brought by the Europeans.

Europeans have traditionally recorded sentiments and expressed views on the subject that make it difficult to learn the truth about cannibalism wherever it may have existed in pre-European contact times. On the one hand, the humanitarian representatives of this cultural tradition suppress such customs with logic or force whenever they can. On the other hand, as colonialists they benefit from exaggerated disclosures of the sanguinary aspects of native life to rationalize and justify their own destructive or exploitative response to it. The Northwest Coast has been no exception to this treatment. This paper has been one more consequence of the Europeans' consistent concern with this matter, which has unwittingly produced nuances of insight and detail that are rarely preserved for the ethnohistorian.

Northwest Coast "cannibalism" must have grown out of beliefs similar to the *windigo* complex molded by the distinctive property and status system. In this system human life was equated with wealth. The ownership of human beings led naturally to their destruction or consumption like other valuables—food or goods—in occasional public affirmation of the overwhelming abundance of familial holdings enhanced by great marriages and the fruits of war. The performer must have been comforted by a sense of the personal continuity of his supernatural gifts with those of remote ancestors even though he afterwards carefully regurgitated all that was swallowed (Curtis 1915). Actually he did not gain nourishment by devouring others. He was only pacified. It may seem naive for the anthropologist to accept dates for this continuity with the past on the basis of oral traditions yet the reader might well conclude from this treatise that the record maintained by European observers is not more accurate and trustworthy than the carefully coded and memorized formal "Wail of a Gwasela Woman."

SUMMARY

Visitors to the Northwest Coast in the late eighteenth century received the impression that gustatory cannibalism was associated with warfare and slavery. Ethnographers found only the type of ceremonial anthropophagy widely known for its fictive nature under its Southern Kwakiutl name, the *hamatsa*. The known behavior of this ritual Cannibal matched that portrayed in the hearsay accounts of explorers and traders in key ways that are incompatible with apparent signs of epicureanism. These signs have been explained differently on the basis of a detailed examination of historical data and of the lore surrounding the *hamatsa*.

The enthusiastic offering of certain human body parts must have been both a test of the eighteenth-century visitors and an attack upon them, for the body parts were considered lethal in the ceremonies performed a century later. The existence of the ceremonies and associated beliefs at the earlier time is suggested by formal oral history, which shows that eligibility to perform the *hamatsa* was a treasured marriage gift as far back as the sixteenth century.

As interpreted here the hand motif of the early historical record signifies a belief in real cannibals and cannibalism on the Northwest Coast. Regardless of the dimensions of its practice this belief was a cultural fact. For this reason the first missionaries hesitated to perform the Eucharist. Some anthropologists, even Northwest Coast specialists, label ritual aspects of other cultures counterfeit or sham that would be symbolic expressions in our own culture, rather as if the practices of the Eucharist proved that Christ never existed or that his followers lacked true spiritual conviction. Because of brilliant stagecraft Northwest Coast ceremonialism has often been treated in this way.

The efforts to demonstrate that cannibalism was a Northwest Coast cultural fact can also be directed to the general conclusion that cannibalism is not a valid cultural category. A tremendous range of custom and belief has been lumped together by ethnologists on the basis of one common element, ethnocentrically weighted, that humans eat one another. Surely the vision of the regurgitating cannibal is far removed from the usual connotation of the term. "Cannibalism" should follow "totemism" into the analytical scrap heap for reasons much the same.

Individual Psychology and Cultural Change

An Ethnohistorical Case from the Klallam*

L. L. LANGNESS

In a short story published in the Seattle *Town Crier*, Viola Garfield has her main character, Niasauta, end on the following pessimistic note: "The Supernatural Power has gone far away across the world and will never return to us during the sacred season. The good and strong ways of our ancestors will be forgotten and our people will die" (1933:29).

Like all the anthropologists who worked with Northwest Coast Indians, Garfield was deeply concerned with what had and was happening to them as a result of their prolonged contact with Europeans. Certainly there was just cause for concern. This concern was inevitably and properly transmitted to her students, and several of us had our first fieldwork experience with Northwest Coast groups and with the subject of culture change. In this chapter I would like to deal with a postcontact reform movement (Voget 1956; Wallace 1956, 1973) that occurred among the Klallam on the Olympic Peninsula, and with the individual and group dynamics that appear to have brought it about. I will attempt to demonstrate that although much of the change that occurred can be understood in terms of social and cultural forces, a more complete understanding must also consider the motives of particular individuals. Although I will keep it to a minimum, some preliminary ethnographic and historical description is necessary.[1]

*The fieldwork on which this chapter is partly based was conducted in the summers of 1958 and 1959 and was made possible by grants from the Department of Anthropology, University of Washington, I would like to thank the department and the university, and also Ms. Jill Korbin, Dr. Robert B. Edgerton, Dr. John G. Kennedy, Dr. Harold Levine, and Ms. Gelya Frank, for commenting on an earlier draft.
1. For those who would like more detailed information, see Gunther (1927; 1972) and Langness (1959). Since this paper was written, the federal government has conferred tribal status on the Jamestown Klallam (*Federal Register* vol. 45, May 30, 1980).

KLALLAM ETHNOGRAPHY

Aboriginally the Klallam occupied a strip of territory on the southern shore of the Strait of Juan de Fuca extending from the mouth of the Hoko River on the west to Port Discovery Bay on the east. Within this territory there were between ten and thirteen villages, some of which were surrounded by palisades of logs for protection from warlike neighbors. There were also a few Klallam living on Vancouver Island at Saanich, Sooke, and Beecher Bay.

Linguistically and culturally the Klallam are most closely related to the Salish peoples of southern Vancouver Island (Barnett 1955), and they were a variant of better-known Northwest Coast groups such as the Kwakiutl (Boas 1909), Tsimshian (Garfield 1939), Tlingit (Krause 1956), Haida (Swanton 1909), and others. Before European contact the Klallam must have numbered about 1,500 and perhaps a few more. They were known as a fierce group and just prior to contact had slightly extended their territory to the east as far as Port Townsend by defeating the Chemakum. They called themselves by a name which translates as "strong people."[2]

Physical features of Klallam life were probably not dramatically different from those of the early American settlers on the Olympic Peninsula. Klallam villages were built on the shore, near the water, in a single row fronting the beach. These villages were never very large, probably seldom having more than ten to fifteen houses. The houses were constructed of cedar planks and varied in size from the large potlatch house, which might be fifty by two hundred feet, to smaller ones approximately twenty by thirty feet. These villages were permanent, although the Klallam traveled extensively and left them frequently to follow the salmon runs and to gather other foods.

Like all Northwest coast tribes, the Klallam depended for their sustenance primarily on seafood. Hunting was not as important as fishing, but each village usually had at least one man who was known as a hunter. There was a clear division of labor by sex: the men did the fishing, hunting, raiding, and canoe building; the women gathered roots, berries, and shellfish that could be obtained without actually fishing.

Large quantities of food were dried and stored each year, although food of some kind was always fairly easy to obtain. The

2. All of the ethnographic description and information comes either from *Klallam Ethnography* (Gunther 1927) or from my own fieldwork and interviews with older Klallam informants.

Klallam smoked salmon, clams, halibut, and other fish, and stored various dried berries and roots. Although horticulture was totally unknown, they did not live at subsistence level but consistently produced a relatively large surplus, which was used for potlatching. It is probably reasonable to assume that this economic base and relative abundance tended to minimize the potentially deleterious effects of contact with a technologically superior culture.[3]

The Klallam had more than sufficient food and vast resources at their disposal. They manufactured baskets, twine, rope, and wove blankets. They made boxes of cedar for storage, small canoes, paddles, dishes, spoons, and cradles; but in no case, it seems, did they develop these crafts as highly as did the people to the north. They manufactured only items essential for everyday living and bartered extensively with other tribes for things they did not produce or items of better quality.

Their weapons for warfare and hunting consisted of the bow and arrow, lance, harpoon, and war club. Deerskin and elkskin were worn in double thickness for armor. The material products of Klallam culture were given up quickly, with few exceptions, once they were compared with items of European and American manufacture.

There were certain other features of Klallam life that might be seen as important in facilitating friendly relations and trade between Klallam and whites. Like Americans, the Klallam valued physical strength. Children were often massaged to make them straight and slender, and they were encouraged to swim often and to run and exercise on the beach. Boys and girls played together until about twelve years of age. Much of their play revolved around duties they would perform as adults. Furthermore, men and women of light complexion were considered by the Klallam to be very attractive. They also valued athletic contests of many kinds. Shinny, tug-of-war, wrestling, foot-racing, and lifting contests were held throughout the year, particularly at potlatches. Many were held for gambling purposes, and gambling was common and popular aboriginally.

Facts of Klallam social structure are not well known. Those that are known indicate that rank and the achievement of rank were important distinguishing features, as they were in other Northwest Coast groups (Drucker 1965). This fact is of considerable impor-

---

3. Although to my knowledge it has not been systematically reviewed, the history of contact between Northwest Coast groups and American settlers seems to have been considerably less traumatic and warlike than in most other parts of North America.

tance, I believe, for the proper understanding of the reactions of the Klallam to white civilization.

There were three classes of people—a high class, commoners, and slaves. The high class consisted of chiefs, their immediate families, and relatives. High-class standing depended to a certain extent on birth, but it was possible for a commoner to rise to this status if he was wealthy enough and gave potlatches. A high-class person could lose his status if he did not remain wealthy and failed to give pot-latches. There was never the rigid distinction between the classes of the Klallam that there was among those of the more northernly groups. Slaves were taken in raids, but slavery, like other institutions of Northwest Coast cultures, was not as highly developed by the Klallam as other groups. Slaves were never very numerous. There was little distinction between master and slave for economic tasks, slaves did much the same work as their masters, ate the same food, and were generally treated well.

People of high class wanted their children to marry outside the tribe in order to establish political ties. If this could not be arranged, village exogamy was preferred. Low-class people could not marry outside the village or tribe because they could not give the necessary feasts, thus they married within the village, avoiding close kin ties if possible. Marriage with northern rather than southern tribes was apparently preferred. At marriage the groom's family would bring food and gifts to the family of the bride, and later the bride's family would reciprocate.

Polygyny was practiced, but only the wealthy were able to participate. Both the levirate and sororate were practiced, as was primogeniture. Residence was most frequently patrilocal. There was no individual ownership of land. Houses belonged to individuals but only as long as they were known to be living in them.

The Klallam had a system of bilateral descent, and, according to Gunther (1927), there was an absence of clans or moities. Personal names were used in address, kin terms were seldom employed. Names belonged to families and would be passed down, but only after some time had elapsed since the demise of the last person who had the name. Thus a boy might be named for a grandfather but not for his father. When a name was given, there was a feast for the relatives. If it was a particularly wealthy family, a potlatch might be held. Certain names carried prestige: there were names recognized as high class and others known to be definitely lower class.

Villages appear to have consisted of a number of related families, the wealthiest and most influential man being recognized as headman. If a headman gave many potlatches and became well known outside his own village, he could be recognized as a chief. Chiefs held little political power and did not control the movement of the village for purposes of fishing or hunting. If a chief or an influential headman decided to move to a new location, however, it is quite likely that the rest of the villagers followed him.

Chieftaincy was contingent on wealth and the ability to give potlatches. By potlatching, a man would become known to other villages and tribes and this fame influenced the people of his own village to recognize him as their leader. An eldest son usually succeeded his father to the position of chief, but there were exceptions. Klallam chiefs depended on public opinion to enforce their decisions and frequently gave advice, but it was not always accepted.

EARLY CONTACT

When Juan Perez reached Nootka in 1774 he found the Indians there already in possession of bits of iron and copper, presumably taken from wrecked vessels that had drifted to the coast. Captain James Cook reached the Northwest Coast by 1778, and also during these years several others touched on it (Meany 1916). In view of the extensive and frequent contacts between the Indians of Puget Sound, doubtless the Klallam knew of the presence of whites before they came into direct contact with them. It appears that the Klallam had made direct contact by 1789: "So far as the records at present available disclose Captain Gray in the *Washington* in March, 1789, marked the furthest advance of the trader within the Straits of Juan de Fuca when he reached Klallam Bay. In 1790 Quimper reached Port Discovery; in 1791 Elisa made his way into the Gulf of Georgia and examined its shores as far as Cape Lazo" (Howay, 1915:83). There were Klallam settlements at both Port Discovery and Klallam Bay, and according to statements given to Gibbs (1877;239), one of these ships did communicate with the Klallam and gave them presents of knives, buttons, and copper.

Vancouver made contact with the Klallam in 1792 and remarked on their indifference to him (he, of course, believed himself the first to visit). He traded them copper, trinkets, and knives. They offered to sell him two children (Gibbs 1877:228).

These first relations served to introduce some European goods to the Indians, acquainted them with whites, and opened the way for the extensive fur trade that followed. In 1825 Fort Vancouver was established on the Columbia as a trading post (Meany 1916). Although the Klallam knew of its existence, there was no extensive traffic between them and the fort.

The only serious military incident between the Klallam and the whites seems to have been in 1828 when a number of Klallam, two of whom had been serving as guides for five white men, murdered them and took possession of their equipment. This apparently was sparked by the ill treatment accorded the two Klallam guides by one of the whites (Curtis 1913:24). In any case, a party of approximately sixty men from Fort Vancouver visited the Klallam and attacked the first group they found, killing seven people (men, women, and children) and burning the house. Then, in conjunction with a ship, they attacked the Klallam village at Dungeness with cannon and muskets and destroyed it with fire. They also plundered several canoes and other Indian property. A total of twenty-five Klallam were reported killed (Ermatinger 1914:197; also Dye 1907).

In 1832 a trading post and agricultural settlement was established at Nisqually. It is recorded in the records of Nisqually House that the Klallam were trading skins and game there by 1833 (Farrar 1915). The records kept between May 1833 and April 1835 show that Klallam visited there at least nine times, in every case to trade furs. A trading expedition was made to Klallam territory by this company during the same period. These records indicate that on several occasions the Klallam did not follow through with the trade because they believed the rate of exchange to be unfair. On these occasions they retained their furs and expressed their intention to wait for some competitive trader.

By 1847, when Paul Kane visited Nisqually House, there were six thousand sheep and two thousand cattle there. As an agricultural station it had proved very successful (Kane 1925:142). We can assume that the Klallam traded extensively with Nisqually House for the entire period and by this time were serving occasionally as guides for visiting travelers. The Klallam must have been impressed by the accumulating wealth in the form of cattle, goods, and agricultural products.

Kane's book indicates clearly that slavery was still practiced, that the Klallam by this time had largely given up bows and arrows and were in possession of guns, that duck netting was still common, shamanism was being practiced, and shell money was still valued. He gives an excellent account of the performance of a shaman curing a Klallam girl (Kane 1925:156–62). At least one of the Klallam villages he visited was still fortified and was inhabited by about two hundred Klallam. He was received there with cordiality and made sketches of some of the inhabitants (p. 158).

In 1850 the first settler arrived at Port Townsend. In the same year a Klallam chief, the Duke of York,[4] was taken to San Francisco by a ship captain. He returned very impressed with what he had seen of the whites there (Swan 1859). In 1851 four more settlers arrived at Port Townsend and the first one arrived on the Sequim prairie at Dungeness. By 1853 sawmills were already in operation at Port Gamble and Port Ludlow and two more settlers were in the vicinity of Dungeness. The settlement at Dungeness was known as Whiskey Flats, and for good reason; liquor was sold freely to the Indians, who were numerous, far outnumbering the whites. There could not have been more than three of four cabins at this time, and these were of crude construction, little better than those of the Indians (Meany 1916).

The ethnographer, George Gibbs, visited the Klallam in 1855. According to his report (1877), they numbered 926 at the time of his visit, although this census is believed by Eells (1886:612) to have been low. Even so, their numbers had doubtless been significantly decreased through intemperance and disease, as Gibbs claims. From Gibbs's account it appears that the Klallam were still raiding their neighbors, bows and arrows and war clubs had virtually disappeared, the potato was being cultivated, the fur trade was almost extinct, slavery and the potlatch still existed, and many tools and utensils of European manufacture were being used.

In 1855 the Klallam, along with the Skokomish and Chemakum, signed a treaty with the whites in which they agreed to give up their land in return for reservations and governmental support. They were to be moved to the Skokomish reservation (at the southern tip of Hood Canal) at government expense and given aid in the form of rations and instruction. This move was never carried out, however, and most of the Klallam simply remained where they were.

In 1856 there were numerous Indian difficulties around Puget Sound, and Fort Townsend was established about three miles from the town of Port Townsend. There were no great disturbances after this time, however, and the troops garrisoned there took part in only a few minor incidents connected with Indian affairs (Cowell 1925).

4. Many of the Klallam had been given the names of royalty, and some less distinguished names, by the earlier whites, who had difficulty in pronouncing the Indian names. Among these were the Duke of York, the Duke of Clarence, the Duke of Wellington, King George, General Taylor, Lord Jim Balch, John C. Calhoun, Jenny Lind, the Prince of Wales, Queen Victoria, and many others.

In 1859 there were three hundred whites and two hundred Klallam in Port Townsend. Some attempt was made to curb Indian drunkenness, and the Duke of York, whose trip to San Francisco had so impressed him with the strength of the whites, was chief of the Klallam there and did much to promote peaceful relations (Swan 1859).

A lighthouse was built at Dungeness in 1857, and at this time there were about thirty-five settlers in the vicinity. Five years later Dungeness was still hardly an impressive settlement, with just a few white residents living in crude cabins, only two horses and wagons in the community, and even oxen were rare (Lotzegesell 1933:265, and Weir 1900:123).

The dominance of whites had by no means been established at this time. For example, Mrs. Lotzgesell writes: "Bands of Indians would pay visits to the early settlers, go through their homes and fields and anything that attracted their attention was taken without opposition. If a farmer grew potatoes the band would dig a sack for each member and walk off with the usual 'ugh'" (1933:269). Caroline Leighton reports: "Yesterday, as we sat there, we received a call from two Indians in extreme undress. They walked in with perfect freedom, and sat down on the floor" (Leighton 1884:20).

Allen Weir, reminiscing about the same period of time, says: "John Allen went to Victoria in 1861 and while away his squaw wife at Dungeness was killed. On his return, blaming the Indians for the death of his squaw, Allen shot an Indian. The next day the Indians were arranged in war paint on one side of the Dungeness River, and the white men of the settlement (a little more than a handful compared with the Indians) were gathered on the opposite bank prepared for the worst. Fortunately the affair was patched up without further bloodshed by John Allen paying the relatives of the dead Indian a sum of money" (1900:120). Also according to Weir there was smallpox among the Klallam at about this time. There is no account of how serious it was (1900:120).

In 1859 Klallam county was formed. In 1860 the first election was held, with a total vote of 90. In 1861 the first school opened for three months at Dungeness. In 1863 the first Sunday school class was held and the first lumber building was erected. In 1864 a narrow road was cut from Port Angeles to Sequim. The first postmaster was appointed in Sequim in 1866. There were at this time only two buildings, a post office and a school. In 1866 the first school district was established with a total of 69 pupils (Lauridson and Smith 1937; McDonald 1952). In 1867 Dungeness was the county seat and the largest community in Klallam county. Also in 1867 an election was held in which 116 votes were cast.

In 1869 the last act of intertribal warfare involving the Klallam occurred. A band of over thirty Tsimshian, men, women, and children was massacred on the Dungeness spit by a group of about twenty Klallam men. The rationalization for this massacre was the abduction of two Klallam women by the Tsimshian several years earlier. After some hesitancy, and some discussion of what the whites would think about it, the raid was carried out following the traditional pattern. The Tsimshian were all murdered and mutilated with the exception of one woman who pretended to be dead. One Klallam was killed and this brought about a great deal of bickering between the murderers, who finally threw away their trophies and went home in dejection. These men were apprehended and placed at hard labor on the Skokomish reservation (Curtis 1913:19–25). They were not detained there very long, however, and the punishment was not considered by them to have been severe.

From the period of initial contact to 1862 the number of Klallam decreased somewhat, but the census figures do not indicate a rapid decrease (Gunther 1927:181). From 1862 to 1878 this decrease became far more pronounced—from 1,300 persons in 1862 to only 597 in 1878.

During the years 1862 to 1875 a fairly large number of Klallam lived near Dungeness, and it is known that liquor and disease were taking a heavy toll. By 1873 the Dungeness Klallam were reported to have degenerated into such a state of drinking, bickering, petty thievery, and fighting that the white residents of Dungeness threatened to have them removed to the reservation. Balch, the chief, is known to have been a heavy drinker before reforming in 1873 (Eells 1886:30, 67). This period of conflict and disease appears to have been the lowest point in their history, and it led to a somewhat unusual development, the creation of a new Indian community—Jamestown.

JAMESTOWN

For two years previous to 1875 the Klallam in Dungeness had been living on a hillside above the town. They were asked to move from that location, presumably by the owner, and they moved to a sandspit north of town. They were then asked to move from there, and were finally threatened with removal of the reservation. In an unprecedented move, James Balch, the chief, decided they should buy some land and create their own community. Accordingly, he and two others visited the approximately 250-acre site that was to become Jamestown, decided favorably, and then collected the $500 purchase price. Twelve individuals contributed various sums of money and the land was purchased in 1874. Balch contributed a large part of the purchase price and the deed was made out in his name. The group was well established in Jamestown (named after Balch) by 1875.

One of the men who had accompanied Balch to see the place earlier had talked to the owner and found a good farming site. He soon cleared part of this site and planted potatoes. The rest of the people made fun of him but he had a good crop and soon all the people got together and began to clear more land. This was difficult work because the ground was full of cedar stumps that had to be burned and removed by hand (Gunther 1927).[5] Potatoes, oats, wheat, and turnips were planted and soon a few horses, chickens, swine, and cows were acquired. Cherry, pear, and apple trees were planted. Some of these may have been a gift from the Reverend Eells. Almost all the families had gardens and some planted cash crops, although these were very small.

As nearly as I can discover there were between 120 and 140 members of the group that founded Jamestown. Most of those who contributed to the purchase price were young men, but it is said that many old people were attached to the group when it settled in the town. For the most part they were parents and relatives of the purchasers. Initially everyone built wherever they chose, and many who had not actually contributed to the purchase also built on the land. Soon, however, the area was surveyed and divided according to the amount each had contributed to the purchase price. But, no one, including noncontributors, was asked to move.

The village was laid out in traditional fashion, a single row of houses with entrances facing the water. At each end of the village was a large house—one belonged to Balch, the other to a man called Lame Jack. In between were several smaller houses. These houses were built with gabled roofs and in the fashion of the whiteman instead of in the old style with shed roofs. Most were built with sawed lumber procured from a nearby sawmill. And most of the houses had windows, locks, doors, and floors.

5. The land had recently been logged and then used as a temporary right-of-way for similar operations. The owner had consented to sell it provided he could keep the deed until he finished logging in that vicinity.

One of the first things that occurred directly as a result of buying Jamestown was a change in marriage customs. It was soon called to the attention of these new landowners, presumably by the whites at Skokomish, that if they wanted their children to inherit the land, it would be necessary for them to marry in the manner of the whites. In 1876 Eells married eleven couples in Jamestown. He gives the following interesting account (1886:107–8):

> In 1876 I was called upon to marry eleven couples at Jamestown. All went well with the first ten, the head chief being married first, so that the others might see how it was done, and then nine more couples stood up and were married with the same set of words. But the wife of the other man was sick with the measles. She had taken cold and they had been driven in, but had come out again, so that she was as red as a beet. Still they were afraid that she would die, and as I was not to be there again for several months they were very anxious to be married so as to legalize the children. She was so near death that they had moved her from their good house to a mat-house, which was filled with smoke. The fire was thrown out, and soon it became less smoky. She was too sick to stand, and only barely able to sit up. This, however, she managed to do in her bed, which was on the ground. Her husband sat beside her and took her hand, and I married them, measles and all. She afterwards recovered.

These people were not actually forced to marry in the manner of the whites, nor were existing polygynous marriages broken up, but no new polygynous marriages were being permitted by the agent at Skokomish.

There was much more to Jamestown than simply buying the land and planting crops. Balch, for unknown reasons, had very progressive ideas for the new community. One of the first small buildings to be erected was a jail. This jail was used for some years, primarily as a punishment for drinking. Balch, after his own reform, disapproved of drinking and regularly either heavily fined or jailed those who were found inebriated (Eells 1886:67).

As far as can be determined, Balch took these judicial powers upon himself and enforced them with the consent of the others. There was no Indian agent for ninety miles, no Indian policeman, and no whites to enforce law and order in Jamestown. They were, of course, subject to the law of the Indian agent at Skokomish, but there seem to have been very few, if any, instances of his intervention in the affairs of Jamestown.

During the first few years these Indians were not given help by the government. Eells writes (1886:200): "The Indians there had at first no help from the government, because they were not on a reservation. They had, however, some worthy aspirations, and realized that if they should rise at all they must do so largely through their own efforts."

In March 1875 Balch visited the Skokomish reservation and appeared very anxious to obtain religious instruction. This was unusual in that he was not a Christian, nor had he ever shown much interest in Christianity. The Congregational missionary, Reverend Eells, was delighted and gave him some instructions, a Chinook hymn, and a few bible pictures. Balch returned to Jamestown to hold prayer meetings (Eells 1886:201).

After this "training," Balch instigated religious meetings which were held in the best kept homes each Sunday. In 1877 the people of Jamestown began to think about building a church. This idea, stemming from Balch and the people, was quickly approved by the agent at Skokomish and by Reverend Eells. Construction was started immediately. Reverend Eells, who dedicated the church in 1878, gives the following description of this event (1886:202):

> About a hundred and twenty-five persons were seated in the house: ninety Klallams, ten Makah Indians, and twenty-five whites. The house is small, sixteen by twenty-four feet. It was made of upright boards, battened and white-washed. It was ceiled and painted overhead. It was not quite done, for it was afterward clothed and papered and a belfry built in front, but it was so far finished as to be used. Although not large or quite finished, yet there were three good things about it: it was built according to their means, was paid for as far as it was finished, and was the first church-building in the county. Its total cost at that time, including their work, was about a hundred and sixty-six dollars. Of this, thirty-seven dollars and fifty cents were given by white persons, mostly on the reservation, four dollars were given by Twana Indians, and some articles, as paint, lime, nails, windows, and the door, came from their government annuities, it being their desire that these things should be given for this purpose rather than to themselves personally. It was the first white building in the village, and had the effect of making them whitewash other houses afterward.

In 1880 there were six hundred white residents in Klallam county, but the only church in the county was the one at Jamestown, built by the Klallam and with a membership composed mostly of Klallam. The deacon of the church was a Klallam. This is all the more interesting in that Balch never actually became a Christian nor did a majority of the other Klallam who attended. One white who lived near Jamestown remarked to Eells in 1880, "It is a shame, it is a shame! that the Indians here are going ahead of the whites in religion affairs. It is a wonder how they are advancing, considering the examples around them" (Eells 1886:208).

Along with the construction of the church in 1878 came a desire for a school. There was no provision for a school (except at Skokomish) in the treaty, but, according to Eells, the Jamestown people argued their case so effectively that the government provided them with a schoolteacher in that same year. The church building was used as a schoolhouse and attendance fluctuated between fifteen and thirty. By 1883, when the white schoolteacher resigned, one of the Klallam was able to keep the school going for a year until a new teacher was found (Eells 1886:206).

In about 1885 Shakerism was introduced to Jamestown (Gunther 1949:43).[6] At first, this movement involved all the members of the community, young and old alike, but the younger members soon lost interest. The older people were seriously involved, however, and Shakerism was soon so firmly established that a newer and much larger church was constructed. One of the first Shaker ministers was the previous deacon of the original church.[7] There is little doubt that curing was the most important feature of this new religion. The number of Shaker members who attended the regular Sunday service was much lower than the number who attended the curing ceremonies. Shaker ceremonies became very important in the social life of the people but had little effect on the economic life of the community.

6. My three best older informants at Jamestown all agree that 1885 is too early for this to have happened. I was unable to establish a precise date, but they all also agree that it was definitely before 1900. Since Barnett (1957:58) claims that the Reverend Eells successfully inhibited the Shaker movement in this area until about 1891 when the implications of the Dawes Severalty Act became recognized, it would seem that the early 1890s is the most likely date.

7. According to Barnett (1957:61), Shakerism was introduced to Jamestown by the Skokomish, who had been invited there to cure Annie Newton of some unknown illness. They were successful and she and her husband (who went by the name of Billy Cook) both became converts. Billy Cook had been the deacon and Annie had been one of the staunchest members of the previous church.

Village life in the years 1875–90 was a curious mixture of old and new. Writing a "progress report" about 1883 Eells mentions that many had abandoned the old way of smoking salmon and had begun salting it. Flour, potatoes, and sugar had become indispensable. Such products as rice, beans, coffee, tea, butter, salt, lard, spices, and crackers were also used. In the gardens, corn, peas, beans, onions, turnips, beets, carrots, parsnips, cabbages, and raspberries were raised. The villagers kept a few cows but apparently did not use much milk.

Their houses were all built after the "white" style, with many having floors and stoves. They had beds, tables, chairs, benches, cupboards, and a few had rugs, clocks, brooms, and mirrors. Some of the rooms were papered, and sawed lumber, locks, and windows had been purchased. Dishes, knives, cups, forks, lamps, and buckets were common. Brushes, combs, and soap were in use. Native articles for war and hunting had almost entirely disappeared. In fishing, however, the Klallam still used many of the old style articles and saw no advantage to giving them up. They preferred their canoes to European boats but had added oarlocks to some of them. Eells reported that he had never seen an Indian in native garb but the women were slow to take up wearing shoes. European measurements of length and quantity were being used. There were outbuildings in the form of latrines, stables, cellars, and woodsheds (Eells 1886).

Along with the innovations of the church, school, and jail many traditional customs were still in evidence although most likely no longer normative by this time. Social classes among the Klallam were still recognized but were breaking down. Different classes no longer lived in separate parts of the village. Puberty rites for girls were observed, but the tattooing that had previously been common was rapidly disappearing. The cradling of children continued but without the former head deformation. A few men continued to have more than one wife, but no new polygynous marriages were taking place. Blood money was still demanded on occasion, people still sought and received "power," and shamans were still active both malevolently and benevolently. Potlatching and the secret society were maintained. Eells gives an account of a fairly large potlatch which featured a secret society initiation in Jamestown in 1878 (1883:137–47). The last secret society initiation held by the Klallam was in Port Angeles in 1893 and was attended by people from Jamestown (Williams 1916:296).

Sometime between 1887 and 1892 Balch was killed by a white man in an altercation over the price of a canoe trip. Apparently Balch changed his mind and wanted more money than originally stated for transporting the man to Port Discovery. The white refused to pay and Balch jumped overboard trying to upset the canoe. The man then struck Balch on the head with a paddle and killed him. Since this was considered to be a private affair, it apparently created no ill-feeling between Indians and Europeans. There was no successor to the chieftaincy after Balch's death. Although two or three different men attempted to be chief, no one would listen to them, and they had no particular effect on the life of the community.

In about 1894 several new families moved to Jamestown from Washington Harbor and some of them soon bought land there. One was a Shaker minister, William Hall, who became important in the Shaker movement and had considerable influence on the other members of the community. His nephew, Jacob, who came to Jamestown at the same time, was also to have considerable influence in the community.

Jamestown was flourishing from 1900 to 1910 and was one of the most important Indian settlements in the area. Farming had increased in importance and three of the villagers had begun dairying. In 1902 a modest crabbing industry was started by Fred Hall. He employed six men and they sold crab to the City of Seattle. They had a contract to furnish so many crab a day. The crab were taken to Dungeness by canoe, picked up there by boat, and transported to Seattle. Many of the men worked for wages on farms and sawmills. Some of the women went by canoe to a nearby cannery and supplemented the family income. By this time a few of the men were hiring out their teams as well as themselves and in this way earned additional money. Fishing of all kinds was still by far the most important activity.

In about 1910 the government built a school immediately adjacent to Jamestown. One of the teachers, Johnson Williams, was a Klallam man born and reared in Jamestown. Williams went to school in Jamestown and later attended the Cushman Indian School of Tacoma. He then returned to Jamestown to teach. A few other Klallam boys at this time were enrolling in the Cushman School, after completing the five years of schooling available in Jamestown.

Some of the young people were learning to play the banjo, violin, and other instruments. They had dances frequently, usually in someone's home, and they waltzed and did the two-step and the schottische. They had an excellent community baseball team that traveled to Port Gamble, Port Townsend, Skokomish, and other places to play. This activity was important to them and they took great pride in having good players and a winning team. All the young people spoke English at this time and in some homes it was the only language spoken.

Up to this time the people of Jamestown still came to the flats of Dungeness annually for the salmon run. This was an important source of salmon for their own use. These salmon were salted and stored in barrels. The women still returned regularly to the customary places to gather "china slipper" shellfish, roots, berries, and the like; but they did this less often and gathered smaller quantities than previously.

It was not until around 1910 that fishing laws and regulations became of any importance to the Klallam. Spearfishing was suddenly made illegal and other restrictions were enforced that closed the Dungeness River to the Indians. This interfered seriously with their economy and aroused a great deal of bitterness. Fishing laws had been enacted before then, but the Indians had either been exempt or ignored. Now, however, the laws were enforced.

Farming had become more important but only three or four persons had sufficient acreage to reap any profit. The Klallam all depended on their gardens, the fish, and what money they earned working out. Even with the new laws, the Klallam remained well fed and relatively prosperous.

About 1910 Jacob Hall and another young man, David Prince, purchased European-made fishing boats. These were twenty-six feet long and there was a great deal of pride in them. The boats were used for commercial fishing, which was becoming more and more important. When William Hall died, his nephew Jacob took over the crab industry. In 1917 the government dug a well for the people of Jamestown and Jacob Hall had the first hot and cold running water in the community. He also had the first bathtub. Electricity was introduced about this time and Jacob Hall soon had the first telephone, which he used for his crab business. In 1918 he was the first to own an automobile, which became immediately popular even though there were no roads for automobile travel. The other villagers often rented it for rides, and they began to throw rocks and gravel in the wagon ruts to make them suitable for cars. By 1924 there were several automobiles in the village and the wagon tracks were rapidly being transformed. Jacob Hall also introduced the first washing machine, he squared off the end of a canoe and added the first outboard motor, and at some point he brought in the first lawn mower (he was probably also the only one with a lawn, although I am not certain of this).

In 1921 the government school at Jamestown was abandoned for reasons of economy and the children began attending school with the white children at Sequim. There was considerable resistance on the part of the whites and the Klallam came to have bitter thoughts about it.

Jamestown was apparently like many small rural communities by the 1920s. There were few links to the Indian past—a few old canoes and what remained in the memories of the oldest survivors. The census taken in 1923 revealed that 76 persons resided in Jamestown, which, at its peak, had about 150 residents. The decrease was from outmigration as well as illness and death.

After 1930 Shakerism declined rapidly. The older generation was disappearing and the younger people were not interested. When the Shaker church burned in 1940, there were only six Shakers, including Jacob Hall. They made no attempt to have a new church. Several young men from Jamestown left the village to serve in the armed forces during World War II. After the war they returned to find very little to do. Small farms were no longer profitable; the standard of living had changed; it was easier to work for wages, which were high; fishing was not profitable because of increased competition; and people began drifting away to the cities, where they could find work.

INDIVIDUAL PSYCHOLOGY AND CULTURE CHANGE

There can be little doubt that the creation of Jamestown was a conscious, rational attempt on the part of a group of American Indians to alleviate tensions and dissatisfactions stemming from culture contact. As such it might fit Voget's classification of "reformative nativism": "In contrast with dynamic and passive nativism, reformative nativism is a relatively conscious attempt on the part of a subordinate group to attain a personal and social reintegration through a selective rejection, modification and synthesis of both traditional and alien (dominant) cultural components. No synthesis, of course, is ever so consciously conceived or programmed that it falls directly in midstream" (1956:250).

It might also be seen as a "revitalization movement," following Wallace: "We refer, here, to revitalization movements, which we define as deliberate, organized attempts by some members of a society to construct a more satisfying culture by rapid acceptance of a pattern of multiple innovations" (1970:188).

However classified, the creation of Jamestown simply may have resulted from the fear among the Klallam of being placed on a reservation, away from their home territory, and among people with whom they had formerly fought. It would be difficult to invoke economic deprivation as an important factor because they seem to have been relatively well off and materially successful. Sociologically viewed, they were being slowly deprived of status, but their relations with the surrounding whites after the settlement of Jamestown seem to have been for the most part quite satisfactory. Culturally, there were momentous changes and Klallam values and practices were under heavy pressure. Slavery and the taking of heads were repugnant to the whites, as were polygyny and head deformation. Native religious ceremonies and the key institution of the potlatch were being denigrated. Their puberty and marriage ceremonies were not approved of, nor were most of their traditional manners and customs. None of this, however, is a sufficient explanation for what happened at Jamestown. Why, for example, did the Klallam feel the need for a jail, a church, and a school? This is especially difficult to understand given that the whites in Klallam county had no such institutions. And why the rigid prohibition and the conscious attempt to adopt items of European culture of all kinds? Why were certain individuals so obviously in the forefront of innovation and change?

It has been common for students of culture change to speak of the "feeling states" of those involved. For example, the "mood" of an individual in situations of this kind, according to Wallace (and depending on the particular situation), "will be one of panic-stricken anxiety, shame, guilt, depression, or apathy" (1970:189). In his review of articles on culture change up to 1952 Keesing wrote of groups that undergo such change: "So far as they feel superior, in relation to groups and individuals with whom they are in contact, their culture may be held to the more firmly, or change may go further with little tension. By contrast, to the extent that groups and individuals come to feel themselves inferior, lose confidence in their basic sources of security, power and prestige, and so lapse in morale, the way is opened to extensive and even drastic change" (1953:89).

The concept of inferiority has been invoked or accepted as a motive for change by Mannoni (1956), Hagen (1962), and many others, and is clearly implied in further categories such as Barnett's "disaffected," "resentful," and "dissident" (1953). Granted that inferiority is not precisely defined and not easily separated from other feelings such as guilt, inadequacy, impotence, insecurity, and others (Brachfeld 1951; Brenner 1955), it is sufficiently well understood to be useful here. As a psychological term it can be defined as "a diminution of the ego and its activities, characterized by an affective state of negative order, of which the subject is not always conscious, although his conduct is profoundly influenced by it" (Brachfeld 1951:291).

It is my contention that both James Balch and Jacob Hall suffered from such feelings and were thus motivated to take the course of change they did. What is of unusual interest in this particular case is that Jacob Hall's feelings of inferiority were not so much a result of contact with Europeans as they were a result of a personal handicap, and his innovations were more the result of his idiosyncratic competition with another Klallam than his desire to emulate Europeans. Since the evidence for Balch's feelings of inferiority is both limited and speculative, and must be postulated from the contact situation in general, let us begin with him.

Some idea of the relationship between Indians and whites in the period prior to Jamestown might be seen in the following: "Lord Jim was one of the principal chiefs. He was saucy, cunning and utterly unscrupulous. When George Davidson first arrived at Dungeness, Lord Jim undertook to make him pay two-bits for a drink out of the Dungeness River. Davidson's foot came up rather suddenly and collided with Mr. Indian's chin, and the latter recovered consciousness an hour or two later" (Weir 1900:120).[8]

That this was not an unusual occurrence can be seen in the Duke of York's remarks to Governor Stevens at the signing of the treaty: "I hope the Governor will tell the whites not to abuse the Indians as many are in the habit of doing, ordering them to go away and knocking them down" (Gates 1955:55).

There was also a degrading practice of giving "letters of recommendation" to the Indians: "Lord Jim is very intelligent and can speak English quite well. He took a great deal of pride in showing me some papers he had received from different whites, principally sea captains. I was much amused at their contents, for most of them abused him without reserve, calling him a liar, a thief, a drunkard

---

8. Weir gives the impression that this happened to the same James Balch who was later killed in the squabble over the canoe, but I believe he has confused James Balch, the founder of Jamestown, with his father, Lord Jim. In any case the incident provides some insight into the situation, and James Balch must have been aware of it whether it happened to him or to his father.

and a gambler. Some of them were curious literary productions, abounding in flowers of speech. Lord Jim, of course, imagined these certificates of his rascality to contain nothing but praise, and begged me to add mine to the number, which I think will help him as much as any of the others" (Kautz 1900:12).

The titles that had been given the Indians were themselves derogatory, and although they were obviously not aware of this at the beginning, they were intelligent enough to understand it later. They were treated as children, as if they had no rights, prerogatives, or even common sense. This paternalistic attitude comes across nowhere more clearly than in the following excerpt from Governor Stevens's speech to them at Point-No-Point (Gates 1955:56):

> The treaty was read to you last night. You have talked it over. We will now consider it. I think the paper is good, and that the Great Father will think so. Are you not my children and also children of the Great Father? What will I not do for my children and what will you not do for yours? Would you not die for them? This paper is such as a man would give to his children, and I will tell you why. This paper gives you a home. Does not a father give his children a home? This paper gives you a school? It gives you mechanics and a Doctor to teach and cure you. Is not that fatherly? This paper secures your fish. Does not a father give food to his children? Besides it says you shall not drink whiskey and does not a Father prevent his children from drinking the *fire water*. Besides all this, the paper says you shall be paid for your lands as has been explained to you. In making this paper I knew the Great Father was good to his children, and did not wish to steal their lands.

James Balch, as chief, had to be aware of the situation and can probably be said to have represented the feelings of the Jamestown Klallam as a group. It is an almost classic instance of what Edgerton has described as "disillusionment in culture contact" (1965). But here, with the success of Jamestown, the process of disillusionment was slowed down or even stopped for a time.

Certain facts of James Balch's life must be considered in addition to the general situation portrayed above. First, Balch became chief under unusual circumstances (Gunther 1927:262):

> When Lord Jim died the village as well as the tribe as a whole was without a chief. Jim had a son, James Balch, then a young

man. In those days the Klallam used to go to Skokomish for government rations. During one of their gatherings there at which the Skokomish, Chehalis and Tszaiwamish from the vicinity of Shelton were also present Stitai'xten (Sam Johnson) from Dungeness let it be known that he would like to be recognized as chief of the Klallam. He was the wealthiest man in the village and had many potlatches to his credit. The agent asked if Stitai'xten was in direct line for the chieftaincy. The people answered that he should not have it, because James Balch, the old chief's son, was with them and that he should be appointed. The agent then told them that they should line up with the one whom they wanted as chief. All the men from Dungeness, six in number, joined Stitai'xten. Balch was still a very young man and the people hesitated to choose him. Mrs. Solomon's mother rose and mentioned the places from which all the assembled people had come, saying, "What is the matter with you, people of Skokomish and you Tszaiwamish and Chehalis and everybody else, this boy is Telesmi'ten's grandson; he is your own child." So all the people mentioned stood up with James Balch. The line doubled many times behind him, so Balch was elected.

Not only was Balch young when he became chief but he had not won the right to be chief by potlatching. In the context of the aboriginal culture he was in this way inferior to Sam Johnson and others. But the institution of the potlatch was under attack by the whites and was disappearing. Balch is known to have been against potlatching after the formation of Jamestown. Not only is it likely that Balch had feelings of inferiority about the relative illegitimacy of his position but he was probably also an opportunist.

More important for the argument being made here, however, is that James Balch was a heavy drinker until 1873, when he suddenly quit for reasons that are unknown. It would seem likely that Balch felt guilty (and hence inferior) over his drunkenness, which explains his desire for a jail and his militant antidrinking stance later on. He was certainly aware of the consequences of drinking for his people: "The Klallam head chief has said that five hundred Indians have been killed by the saloons of Dungeness within twenty years. This is probably an exaggeration, but not a very wide one. The diseases consequent upon licentiousness and consumption have caused the death of many" (Eells 1887:613).

In the case of Jacob Hall there is considerably more information with which to characterize his individual psychology. He was born, with a rather pronounced hunchback, at Port Discovery about 1886. His mother died soon afterward. He was brought to Jamestown by his father while still very small, almost an infant. He had no brothers or sisters, or at least none that lived. His father insisted that he work, even when he was a small boy, and he was kept busy fishing, cleaning crab, repairing crab traps, and doing other odd jobs. He attended the Jamestown School, where he learned to read and write and, according to both himself and others, was a precocious student. About 1900 his father remarried, and Jacob did not get along well with his stepmother. In 1902 his father started the crab business which Jacob was to be involved in for most of his life. He attended the Cushman Indian School in 1908–9 when he was over twenty. He nearly finished the eighth grade but quit to return home when his father died. In the early 1920s he served in the Klallam Tribal Council and in 1922 he married. Jacob's wife was a woman from a good family near Tacoma, a high school graduate, and a musician of sorts. She gave birth to two daughters before she died four years after marriage. Only one of the daughters survived childhood. Jacob was one of the most active Shakers even after the church burned in 1940 and tried to keep the others interested but to little avail.

All his life Jacob Hall was an extraordinarily active innovator, a hard worker who constantly tried to be a leader in the community. In addition to the material innovations he made (mentioned previously), he also attempted to influence the life style of the community. He tried to set an example of how married people should live so that the others, in his words, "could learn things from Jake and his wife." Jacob knew the proper way to conduct meetings and insisted that they be so conducted. He attempted to organize the community to buy the government school, turn it into a community center, and dedicate it to the "boys in the service" (he failed at this). He was proud of his ability as a public speaker and seldom passed up an opportunity to perform. In his younger days he was quite a good singer and would sing to his wife's piano accompaniment. When his wife died, he raised his daughters largely by himself, introducing formula and baby food to the community in the process. As an active Shaker he traveled widely trying to cure illnesses and proselytize. Even though the Klallam were dispersed and not well organized, Jacob often spoke of "his tribe" and was active in whatever political affairs presented themselves.

Most of the facts of Jacob Hall's life are well known and confirmed by other members of the community. To understand his feelings of inferiority it is necessary to understand his personal distortion of history and also his egocentrism. First, and very important, is his physical handicap. Although it was common knowledge in the community that Jacob had been born a hunchback, and although Jacob had been told by various doctors that the condition was congenital, he consistently stuck to his story of having fallen out of a wagon and onto a stump when he was three. He used to say, "When they picked me up they didn't straighten me out and I just grew like this. If they had pulled me out I would have been all right." Jacob claimed to have worked on the surrounding farms when he was younger, putting up hay, pulling stumps, and so on, but others agreed that he did very little such work and was physically unable to do it. This is not to say that he did not work hard all of his life as he claimed. He did, but he worked mostly at fishing, gardening, and other activities at which he was not so handicapped. He also usually claimed to have graduated from the eighth grade at the Cushman School but, as noted previously, he quit before he finished. At times, in conversations with me, he would slip into rather farfetched distortions. Once, for example, he told me he had witnessed the signing of the treaty with Governor Stevens. He claimed to have known the Duke of York fairly well, which seems entirely unlikely, although I do not know when the Duke actually died. He may have baked salmon for President Roosevelt at Port Townsend as he claimed. But whether such claims are true or not is not as important as that he did make them and more. Jacob sought always to call attention to himself and to demonstrate how important he was. He failed in his attempt to take on the name "Chief White Feather" as the others ridiculed him.

Jacob moved an elaborate (by Jamestown standards) house that had belonged to his father by raft from Dungeness to Jamestown. Although this was unusual, by itself it would be of little significance. But it became part of Jacob's plan to have all the Klallam visit Jamestown and the house to "come and learn how to live." He often called attention to his house, pointing out that it was the only one like it in Jamestown. He added to it so it was considerably larger than anyone else's. It was to this house that the hot and cold water, the bathtub, and the lawn mower came.

To understand Jacob it is also necessary to understand his competitive relationship with a lifelong Klallam friend, David Prince. They were the same age, Jacob having been born in the spring and David in the fall. David was born on a small island just east of Port Townsend and for much of his early life had only his dog to play with. Although David occasionally visited Jamestown as a child and played with Jacob, he did not move there until about 1900. David Prince was in many ways the opposite of Jacob. He attended school less than a year and could barely read or write. He was an enormously powerful man and an exceptionally hard worker. He cleared most of his own land and often worked long hours in the hayfields. He was a strong swimmer, whereas Jacob never learned to swim. Although David did own one of the first boats along with Jacob, he cannot be said to have been an innovator. Whereas Jacob was constantly calling attention to himself, David was basically shy and even reticent. Jacob was a "joiner," David was not. The Princes lived in the same house for over fifty years, making no improvements and basically unconcerned about such things. Finally one of their sons decided they should build a new one, which they did. Although he was a Shaker for a short time, David had little or no interest in religion. He served briefly on the tribal council when he was younger but did not find it to his liking. Similarly, unlike Jacob, David had little interest in politics either local or national.

Both David and Jacob were primarily fishermen for the greater part of their lives and they often fished together. They were very close friends and thought highly of each other. Even so, their remarks about each other are often revealing. In my first interview with Jacob he said, "David Prince is the same age I am. . . . We was raised and grew up together. He was a powerful man. Oh! he was strong. He used to pick me up and run with me and dance up and down. We grew up and were together most of the time. My father would make me work—clean the crab and crab traps and he would be there waiting all that time." But at the same time Jacob repeatedly pointed out to me the difference in their backgrounds. His ancestors, he reported, were all upper-class Klallam, whereas David's mother was lower class. He said this was "one mark against David." This comment is particularly interesting in that no one but Jacob seemed to be at all interested and David was a highly respected member of the community. Similarly, although Jacob was raised partly by David's wife's parents, and thus was very close to her, he often alluded to her lack of education and essentially unfavorable comparison with his own wife. Jacob's intent was not malicious. He was not trying to cast the Princes, whom he clearly loved, in a bad light. He was emphasizing his own worth.

David Prince, although he acknowledged his greater physical strength and spoke occasionally, and rather lovingly, of "poor Jake," made no other comparisons. He admired Jacob and acknowledged that he had indeed done all of the things he bragged about—the first car, and so on. He pointed out how Jacob had always worked hard, how marvelous it was that he had been able to overcome his handicap, how fine a public speaker he was. David was totally unaware of any competition between himself and Jacob. But not so with Jacob. When speaking with me, Jacob often alluded to his competition with David. He cut off the canoe and added an outboard "so he could beat David." He secretly raced his boat home against David's so recklessly that on two occasions he almost capsized. He boasted of taking more crab than David and knowing more "secrets" of crabbing.

Jacob also thought of himself at times as a martyr. He reported that Amy Allen "couldn't take it any longer and broke down" when participating in some university research program, so he volunteered to go, "because they had to have someone." When speaking of his experience with the doctors he reported: "The doctors use my x-ray to teach with. I wouldn't be ashamed or embarrassed. I offered them my body if it would do any good." He quit school at Cushman "because I knew we just wouldn't make it if I didn't go home." When he was ridiculed for trying to be Chief White Feather he said, "they just don't understand." When coming into Jamestown with some others, he had to be "chief boat captain" because he was the only one who "knew how to get in." He reported that when his wife died, "it was a terrible burden" but he managed by himself. When telling me about visiting a boy in the hospital he said: "I guess it was my fault that he died. When I went to see him he was so lonesome and wanted to come home with me. But he couldn't and when I left he cried so hard he busted a blood vessel or something. He died, I guess it was really my fault that he died." He even put visiting the Princes in this context: "I have to go to the Princes now, you know they can't get around anymore." Although there is a grain of truth in some of these statements, it is the consistent style of presentation of self that is significant. I think it is safe to conclude that Jacob Hall did feel inferior, particularly in relation to his friend David Prince, and these feelings drove him to compete for success in the best way he could. The result of this was innovation, culture change, and his personal satisfaction.

Here is a case in which two individuals, one a chief and one a "marginal man," both contributed significantly and in similar ways to culture change in the same community. But whereas James Balch seems to have been driven by the inferior position he and his people had slipped into in relation to whites, Jacob Hall's motives were far more personal and complex. Without an understanding of both the group and the individual dynamics involved no understanding of what led to the creation, growth, progress, and decline of Jamestown would be complete.

"Niasauta mused before his fire," Garfield wrote. "Winter no longer was a season of potlatches" (1939:29).

Coast Salish Concepts of Power

Verbal and Functional Categories*

WILLIAM W. ELMENDORF

Several recent anthropological studies of religion have stressed instrumental aspects of religious subsystems, as well as the relations of these subsystems to other features of total social systems. Twenty years ago Miller's study "Cultures as Religious Structures" (1964) pointed to the need for examining the rubric "religion" in specific cases, not only as myth, belief, and ritual per se, but also as these involve linkage with other aspects of the society under examination. More recently Glick defined a "religion" as "a people's . . . beliefs and practices having to do with controlling extra-human power and applying it to the service of human needs and purposes" (1973:226).

This latter formulation, although apparently intended as a general etic statement, would accord almost exactly with data from specific cultures of the Northwest Coast area. In treating certain religious concepts of this region comparatively, Viola Garfield indicated, as long ago as 1947, a need to examine systematically "the manner in which various stresses in social systems have affected relationship to supernatural beings" (MS 1947). Garfield's paper dealt with the varying forms assumed by guardian spirit beliefs and practices in different kinds of northern Northwest Coast societies, particularly those of the Tsimshian and Kwakiutl.

It is these emphases, on guardian spirit beliefs as key religious concepts, on their instrumental and social-integrative aspects, and on the need to define these concepts in terms of their total func-

*Some of the research on which this chapter is based was funded through a grant from the National Science Foundation (GS-36784), here gratefully acknowledged. An earlier version was presented in the session on Cognitive Studies at the 72nd Annual Meeting of the American Anthropological Association, New Orleans, November 30, 1973. I take pleasure in addressing this study to my former teacher and colleague, Viola Garfield, and am honored to have it included in her Festschrift volume.

tional context, that have motivated the present study. This purports to treat (on a narrower topical and territorial basis than Garfield's paper) specific aspects of a religious system of a Coast Salish people in western Washington. These people, the Twana Indians of the Hood Canal region, shared many features of religious and social culture with other Coast Salish groups, so that some of this analysis may apply to aboriginal conditions over a wide area of western Washington and southern coastal British Columbia.

The present treatment is not properly a comparative one, however, except in the special sense of intra-system comparison discussed by Tyler (1969:15).[1] As with Tyler, it is here maintained that descriptive adequacy for comparability between systems rests on the adequacy of prior intra-system analysis. Hence, this attempt at an integrated picture of certain Twana religious ideas might furnish a basis for later inter-societal comparison with other similarly analyzed systems in other parts of the Pacific Northwest.

NATURE OF POWER

In fieldwork conducted some years ago on aboriginal Twana culture it became clear that a dominant feature of what I described under the rubric of "religion" (Elmendorf 1960:480–539) was the notion of power, obtained and maintained through ritual practices, and used to serve human ends. This core aspect of Twana native religion covered all means for mobilization of sources of power external to human individuals, which might then become controllable by these individuals and contribute in essential ways to performance of their social roles. The agreement of this formulation with Glick's definition is close, and it should be stressed that it was derived earlier, independently, and in an emic analysis of one specific cultural system.

1. Tyler's remarks are worth citing in this connection, since they bear directly on the method of treatment in this paper: "Those who insist that no fact has meaning except by comparison are right, but the implication that comparison can occur only between similar facts from different systems does not follow. It is much more pertinent to compare similar, but not identical facts within the same system. This is not so much a total abandonment of the comparative method; it is a matter of priorities. Comparisons between systems can only be useful if the facts compared are truly comparable, and we cannot know what facts are comparable until the facts themselves are adequately described. When this is achieved, the units of comparison will be formal features rather than substantive variables" (Tyler 1969:15). Comparability in this sense rests on a systemic definition of the position and relationships of "substantive variables" within the systems being compared.

Among the Twana, as with most neighboring peoples, the most important source of power was a class of personified entities, of the sort usually designated since Benedict's study as "guardian spirits" (1923). I shall continue to use this term as a label of convenience for the class of power-conferring entities, although it is both ethnocentric and descriptively misleading in reference to native Coast Salish concepts. As a first approximation, however, we may say that to the Twana, power is conferred on human beings by guardian spirits. True, the culture recognizes other sources of power, also obtained through ritual means, but guardian spirits appear to have been overwhelmingly the most important power source.

The native notion of power forms the principal conceptual basis of all goal-directed instrumental activities. An emically acceptable analysis of this concept would consider both verbal statements of cultural participants as to the nature of power and observable behavior based on or in accord with the statements. Here I have tried to bring both kinds of data to bear on the problem of determining native Twana conceptual categories related to power and to the uses of power.[2] For this culture we may make a series of defining statements regarding power, inductively derived from and summarizing a wide range of ethnographic data:

1. "Power" denotes all means for affecting and controlling the physical or social environment in ways not directly attainable or immediately practicable through technology.

2. Power may attain results beyond the reach of technology, although power and technological means are often combined as mutually supporting instruments of control or manipulation.

3. Power tends to be specific to particular effects; that is, there are kinds of power that correlate generally with kinds of effects or manipulations of the environment.

4. Power is never innate or inherent in human beings, but human individuals may obtain power. And most differences in social performance among adult human individuals are due to differences in their powers and in their abilities to control power.

"Power," then, as I apply it in this Twana context, is something distinct from the Tylorian term "spirit." We may say that spirits appear to people, usually in special types of vision experiences, and grant them powers, which then become manifested in the social roles

2. An earlier attempt at formulating Twana power concepts appeared in a study of victimizing magic (Elmendorf 1970:152–54), which also dealt with specific aspects of the shaman's role.

of those receiving these powers. Thus spirits are the sources and media of conveyence of powers to human recipients, but they are not themselves those powers, and the two categories are thus to be distinguished. This distinction seems satisfactory from a preliminary ethnographic analysis, and it does enable us to make meaningful statements in English about a range of Twana ideas and behaviors.

POWER TERMINOLOGY

If we take account of work in cognitive anthropology, we should ask how the Twana Indians themselves conceptualize (or formerly conceptualized) such situations. Here, the first thing we note is that native terminology does not show any neat correspondence with the above definitions and distinctions. In particular, there appears to be no single Twana-language synonym for the English term "power," as used here. Furthermore, the most general key native terms covering the conceptual domain of power and the uses of power do not distinguish between guardian spirit as a power-conferring entity and the power obtained from a guardian spirit. Examples of these general terms follow:

1. *swádaš*. Shaman's guardian spirit, or power from such a spirit. More precisely, a class of guardian spirits conferring power to become a shaman, and that power itself; such power is specifically to diagnose and cure illness, and to implement a variety of sorcerous and victimizing activities. A shaman is *bəswádaš*, literally "having *swádaš*."

2. *c'šált*. Layman's or nonshaman's guardian spirit, or power from such a spirit. The derivative term *bəsc'šált* refers to "one having guardian spirit power" but not a shaman. A grammatically related word is *c'ášalt* 'to dream,' but there is little semantic relation. Layman's guardian spirit power is not acquired by dreaming, although dreams may, at times, indicate the relations of the dreamer to a guardian spirit.

3. *s'alíx^w*. The experience of encountering or getting power, in a vision granted by a guardian spirit to one seeking such power. The term is a nominalized form of a verbal stem *'alíx^w* 'to encounter a guardian spirit, to experience a guardian spirit vision, to obtain power in a spirit vision.' The spirit or power may be either *swádaš* or *c'šált*.

4. *bəsdá'b*. Having power from a guardian spirit, or one having such power. The term does not indicate whether the spirit, or power, is shamanistic or not. Linguistically, the form is peculiar in being an apparent derivative of a stem **dá'b*, which does not seem to ap-

pear otherwise in Twana, but which is probably cognate with words for "shaman power" in several other Coast Salish languages.

Failure to distinguish spirit from power also recurs in the word *sk'al·é*, translatable either as 'dangerous supernatural being (not a guardian spirit)' or as 'dangerous supernatural power (not conferred by a guardian spirit).' Thus a good deal of terminology suggests that Twana speakers did not distinguish verbally between certain animistic beings and the powers that these beings might exert, or grant to human beings.

At this point we may recall Goodenough's caution to the effect that "people have concepts that are not represented by the vocabulary of their languages" (Goodenough 1956 [reprinted 1970:112]).[3] In the present case there are indications that conceptual distinctions not directly indicated by certain key terms may nevertheless be inferred from a total verbal and behavioral context.

I would stress this point of total context, as crucial in the kind of conceptual analysis attempted here. Behaviors and behavioral patterns directly relatable to lexeme sets are of course essential in determining objectively the semantic features of the lexeme sets as systems. If we consider the whole range of Twana behaviors relating to power, we see that the above set of general terms denoting indifferently spirit or power is actually a limited subset of a larger body of terms involved in this particular domain of the aboriginal culture. Some of these other subsets do appear to indicate a spirit-versus-power distinction not reflected in the general terms. Cross-comparison of all these terminological subsets, together with consideration of their behavioral referents, then make it clear that the distinction of "spirit" and "power" is a Twana one, and not something imposed a priori from outside the cultural system being investigated.

POWER AND SPIRITS AS CATEGORIES

In the four-term set above, two terms distinguish as exclusive classes shaman from lay or nonshaman powers/spirits, while the other two, referring to vision encountering and to "ownership" of a spirit/power, do not make this distinction. A possible arrange-

---

3. On this point of concepts not represented in vocabulary, Goodenough had earlier (1956:209–10) stressed the point in discussing "concepts not lexically objectified." It was given expanded treatment by Berlin, Breedlove, and Raven (1968) with reference to "unnamed taxa." Cf. also the cautions on terminologies and the structuring of semantic domains expressed by Fjellman (1975:120).

ment of semantic relations within this term set might be as shown in Figure 1:

A vision encounter (*s'alíx*^{w}) may involve reception of either shaman power (*swádaš*) or lay power (*c'šált*), and in either case, after establishing rapport with and control of the power, the human recipient is power-owning (*bəsdá'b*). This last term subsumes two classes of power owners, but it coexists with specifying terms for such owners (*bəswádaš* and *bəsc'šált*) according to whether the power is shamanistic or lay. As will be seen below, details of the vision experience and of subsequent procedures for establishing control of power do differ according to whether shaman or lay power is concerned. The dichotomy of shaman and lay powers and power-relations therefore appears a basic one, both terminologically and in associated ritual practices. But before looking at this ritual dimension of Twana power acquisition, some further details of terminology should be noted.

While the general terms discussed above do not distinguish "spirit" from "power," other aspects of Twana verbal behavior do show that such a distinction was made. The distinction appears not only in mutually exclusive term sets, but even more clearly in ritual patterns and in social role differences.

The Twana seem to have thought of "a power" as a specific function of "a spirit" in a specific relation with a human individual, a

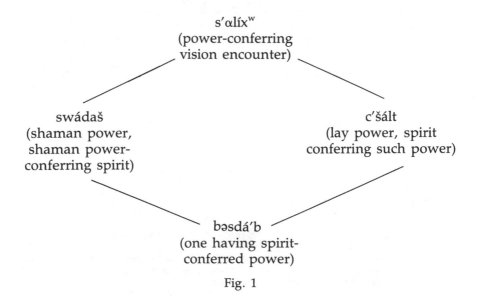

s'αlíx^w
(power-conferring
vision encounter)

swádaš
(shaman power,
shaman power-
conferring spirit)

c'šált
(lay power, spirit
conferring such power)

bəsdá'b
(one having spirit-
conferred power)

Fig. 1

particular way in which a particular spirit might enable a particular human being to produce a particular environmental effect. Many such effects, or the means of producing them, were classed together by certain common features under a common name, denoting a certain kind of power without reference to the identity of its source.

Spirits, or power-granting entities, were likewise named, but the two lexical sets are different. The names of kinds of powers are not coincident with names of specified guardian spirits. In fact, different spirits might grant the same kind of power, or the same spirit (as named) might grant different powers to different human recipients (*bəsdá'b*). Thus "powers" and "spirits" turn out to be separable components in a total Twana lexical, conceptual, and behavioral context.

This result, however, does not indicate a structure closely corresponding, even lexically, with the fundamental English language distinction of attributes ("powers") and entities ("spirits"). Rather, the organization of this Twana semantic domain seems to involve the following: (1) no *general-term* distinctions of powers versus spirits; but (2) *specific-term* distinctions, embodied in two distinct sets of lexemes denoting, respectively, kinds of powers and kinds of spirits.

Names of powers fall under the fundamental shaman/lay dichotomy. That is, there were kinds of shaman powers and kinds of lay powers, and the two categories do not overlap. The classification of shaman powers is a simpler one than that applied to the powers of nonshamans, which fell into a series of at least a dozen named classes. This reflects the social role association of laymen's powers; *swádaš* essentially determined one kind of role, that of shaman, while *c'šált* powers applied to most other important or striking role distinctions. (See Elmendorf 1960:485–91, 499–500.)

Spirit names cannot be separated into two exclusive sets, corresponding to the shaman/nonshaman power division. In this respect the statement above, that swádaš and c'šált represent mutually exclusive classes of both powers and spirits needs modification. A very limited number of spirits did grant only shaman power, but others were known to have granted, to different human recipients, powers falling under the shaman and several nonshaman power categories. Examples are Cougar (*k'awác'ap*) spirit, known to have conferred, in different *s'alíx^w* experiences, shaman power and land-game hunting power (*astálax̣*), and Wolf (*dušúyay*) spirit, which could grant in separate vision encounters land-game hunting, hand-game gambling (*slahál*), or war (*sčálaq*) powers. Many named spirits could grant two or more categories of nonshaman powers.

I think enough has been said to demonstrate that from even an exclusively lexical analysis, provided the lexical net is cast widely enough, an emic Twana distinction of "powers" and "spirits" can be made, and this despite the consistent failure of the language to furnish any dichotomous general term distinction corresponding to the English one. It also seems, however, that lexicon does not in this instance completely or adequately reflect cultural structure, and that to gain a clearer notion of the Twana spirit and power categories, they must be analyzed in a wider context which includes ritual procedures, social roles, and certain other elements of belief relating guardian spirits to mythology.

POWER RITUALS AND SOCIAL ROLES

Ritual procedures involving acquisition, control, and use of spirit power fall into a sequential pattern of five principal stages, in which each stage may itself consist of a series of sequential events. The five-stage structure applies alike to shaman and to lay powers, but details of ritual procedures differ in these two classes. The list below shows the sequence patterns for (A) nonshamanistic and (B) shamanistic powers.[4]

A. Normal lay (c'šált) pattern:
   1. Training for quest
   2. Guardian spirit questing
   3. Vision, encounter with spirit, conferral of power
   4. Suppression or dormancy period
   5. Winter illness, recall, exhibition, control (the spirit dance complex), leading to activation of power-enabled role
B. Normal shaman (swádaš) pattern:
   1. Training for quest
   2. Guardian spirit questing
   3. Vision, encounter with spirit, conferral of power
   4. Bodily possession, uncontrolled manifestations of power, control procedures, purposive "novice" use
   5. Direct use of controlled power in diagnosis and curing, or in victimizing (sorcerous function)

Comparative analysis of the shaman and lay power ritual sequences shows that shared by both are (1) training by an older men-

4. A more detailed analysis of these sequence patterns and of the relations of myth beings and power-conferring spirits is given in Elmendorf 1977.

tor, (2) questing, (3) spirit vision-encounter, (4) acquisition of a specific power, and (5) role determination on a power basis. These features seem common to the two patterns, although numerous specific details may vary within each feature. Exclusive to the lay sequence are the postvision dormancy period and the complex of spirit-dance procedures, while only the shaman sequence shows the features of continuous bodily possession by and control of the vision-conferred power, and the special power functions of diagnosis, curing, and sorcerous victimizing. Although many other details differ, it is sequence stages 4 and 5 that diverge most markedly in these two ritual patterns.

In this five-stage analysis, stages 2 through 4 can be considered "liminal" in the sense originally defined by van Gennep (1960:21) and also discussed by Victor Turner (1964). During these stages the person in process of acquiring power is in various ways withdrawn from society, in a special numinous state, and hedged about with ritual restrictions and prescriptions. With stage 5 the power owner returns to normal social functioning, though in a new and role-enhanced status. Thus these ritual sequences appear to be, in native terms, the means by which persons come to assume socially functional adult statuses. And these statuses can, many of them, be denoted by the terms for special classes of powers, discussed above. In Twana native culture, power structure is equated with social structure; the social role system is mirrored in the power system in a manner very like that adumbrated by Garfield (1947) in her paper cited earlier.

POWER, SPIRITS, AND MYTH

If powers are, as we have seen, in one sense labels for various sorts of social functionings, what of the separate terminology denoting kinds of spirits or power-conferring beings, which constitutes a lexical set distinct from designations for power classes? Here we must recognize another dimension of Twana culture, that of myth, in which an earlier myth world (*sábu*) gave way through a period of world change (*sp'əláč'*), the term for which literally denotes the capsizing of a canoe, to the world of the present day. (For details see Elmendorf 1960:535–36; 1961:1–37.) The names of guardian spirits are those of myth-age beings, many of whom have survived into the present world as animals, but some as creatures neither animal nor human. In either case, the vision-experienced and power-conferring manifestations of these beings are reflections of their myth-age characteristics, rather than of their present-day ones.

Hummingbird, in the myth world, was a formidable killer; in the present world he can function in a vision encounter as a donor of war power (*sčálaq*), although the Twana are perfectly aware that no one today is ever harmed by an actual hummingbird. The vision experience thus appears to be a temporary withdrawal into the *sábu* myth world, in the course of which the spirit myth-being confers power later manifested in the present world as social performance.

The two categories, spirit and power, thus seem to be mediated through a ritual structure which joins the ancient myth world with present-day human society. Ultimately, the distinction of the spirit and power categories rests conceptually on the roles of myth beings and their relation to the roles of human beings.

The integration of this myth-spirit-power system may be suggested in Figure 2.

CONCEPT DEFINITION AND FUNCTIONAL CONTEXT

In conclusion, I think that this admittedly sketchy and ethnographically specific analysis does bring out a few points of general ethnological relevance. One is simply a further demonstration, if any further demonstration is needed, of the sometimes subtle dangers of imposing categories from one system on another. I am sure that some of the difficulty in semantic analysis of the sorts of term sets and concepts discussed here has arisen, at least in part, from tacit, purportedly etic but actually ethnocentric imposition of categories from outside the system being investigated. This is the pitfall which cognitive analysis has attempted to bypass during the past twenty years. However, obvious subtleties and difficulties attend any headlong attack on the problem of deriving emically meaningful

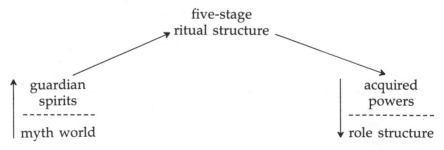

Fig. 2

structural categories from analysis of lexical domains. It seems that only in a wider than lexical context can the apparent contradictions in certain areas of Twana religious terminology be resolved.

This wider context turns out to include not only relevant lexemes and their denotata, but also relevant features of myth, ritual, and social role structure. Without such a context, within which the intra-systemic comparisons discussed by Tyler (1969:15) can be made, one could not set up an adequate emic analysis of Twana spirit and power concepts. Terminology alone proves to be insufficient, recalling Keesing's (1972:314) stricture that a decade and more of cognitive studies have made it increasingly doubtful that "the labeled lexical categories of a language reveal directly the cognitively salient pieces into which a people segment their world of experience." Doubt on this matter has been often expressed since the 1956 statements of Goodenough cited in footnote 3, and the point may be taken as proved in the negative. In the present case, it is only from analysis of systemic relations within a total terminological, ideological, ritual, and social context that we can discern how certain "cognitively salient pieces" of this particular culture are, so to speak, put together.

A Little More than Kin, and Less than Kind

The Ambiguous Northwest Coast Dog

Pamela Amoss

~~~~~~

To the Northwest Coast peoples from the Tlingit in the north to the Yurok in the south the domesticated dog was an ambiguous being that could be interpreted as belonging to either category—animal or human being. According to de Laguna, among the northernmost Tlingit at Yakutat, "Only the dog occupied an anomalous position" (1972:824). At the southern end of the Northwest Coast culture area the Yurok saw the dog as "so close to man that there is risk of the line between them being effaced" (Elmendorf and Kroeber 1960:99). Northwest peoples recognized that the dog was closely related to wild Canidae, wolves, foxes, and coyotes. At the same time, dogs lived in the human household, shared human food, and as companions in the hunt took mankind's part against the beasts of the wild. Depending on whether the principles of classification were functional or morphological the dog could fit into the human or animal category.

The position of the dog in a native classification system is important, because, as Durkheim (1915:165) and following him Lévi-Strauss (1962a:16; 1962b) have argued, a classification is more than a device to organize experience; it is in some ways a replication or representation of the significant social units of the human group that created it. Building on the work of Durkheim and Lévi-Strauss, Leach (1972) and Douglas (1966) have suggested that animal classifications as representations of human organization are not limited to societies with totemic clans, but are probably a kind of human universal.

Given the importance of the classifications as a device to keep one's thinking about nature straight, and perhaps one's thinking about society as well, Mary Douglas has argued that creatures whose classificatory status is uncertain, either because they fit into none of the existing classes or because they can fit into more than one, represent a challenge to the whole culturally created construction of reality (1975:27–45). She shows that such unthinkable beings are handled in a limited number of ways: some few may be successfully ignored, some can be rammed into one procrustean category or the other, but perhaps the most interesting are those that are set apart and made the focus of ritual elaboration. The ritualization not only protects people from the dangers inherent in the anomaly but also harnesses its power. Douglas claims that it is this kind of solution that has produced the common and widespread phenomena anthropologists call "taboos." Such is the case of the extraordinary African pangolin (spiny anteater), eccentric in both form and function, which the Lele elevated to the status of a sacred symbol and solemnly consumed in an esoteric rite (Douglas 1975:36). Such is also the case of the animals that are peripheral to the categories of pet, barnyard domesticate, and wild beast in Burmese and English animal taxonomies (Leach 1972). And such is the case of the Northwest Coast dog. Unlike the English and Burmese, Northwest Coast peoples had only one domesticated animal—the dog. They did not designate a special class comparable to "domestic animal" for it, but let it remain as a most aberrant member of the animal category—morphologically a beast, functionally a member of the human world.

The intermediate position assigned the dog made it a source of power and danger which might be suitably exploited in ritual and myth. As an ambiguous being, the dog had a special affinity for other marginal beings. As something whose position between the human and animal poles remained negotiable, the dog served a ready metaphor in myth and ritual for ambiguous human relationships. In a broader perspective, the dog's liminal status provided a device to highlight the distinction between the human and nonhuman spheres, or between culture and nature. In this paper I will explore the symbolic functions assigned to the dog by looking at its place in myth, belief, and ritual.[1]

The symbolic significance of the dog seems on casual inspection

1. Although I have found inspiration in Lévi-Strauss's analysis of Northwest Coast myths (1971), I am not emulating his approach. He looks at the meaning of myths to illuminate their general structure; I am looking here at myths and rituals to clarify the meaning of only one symbol, the dog. Although my goals are different, I have taken license from Lévi-Strauss to examine myth, ritual, and belief, and to take evidence from all three sources (1964:4). Like him, I believe that the "infrastructure is primary"; that is, myth and ritual must always look to the realities of economy and ecology to find the metaphors in which the realities of human relationships are expressed. I have described the economic role of the dog elsewhere (Amoss 1975:16–17), and I will only allude to it here when it is directly related to my argument.

to be very diffuse, but all the different roles played by the dog can be derived from the logical possibilities of the dog's intermediate position—a position made the more peculiar by the presence of closely related wild Canidae in the region. One myth in particular demonstrates the native view of the dog as a kind of mediator between the worlds of men and animals. The Cowlitz and Humptulip people south of Puget Sound recount how Dog lived with his brothers, Wolf and Coyote. In those days the brothers had fire, and Dog was left at home to tend to it. Wolf and Coyote, through their carelessness, put out the fire and sent Dog to beg fire from people who lived nearby. The people welcomed Dog into their house and gave him baked camas to eat. (The storyteller noted that Dog's paw still shows a little hollow at the base of the pad where they put the camas.) Dog decided to stay with the people and never returned to his brothers. So Wolf and Coyote are without fire and Dog lives with people still. Wolf and Coyote have not forgiven him for deserting them, and that is why wolves and coyotes will kill dogs if they get a chance (Adamson 1934:307). This story succinctly delineates the intermediacy of the dog's position—allied to men in culture (symbolized by the cooking fire and the cooked camas) and allied to wolves and coyotes in nature (represented by the sibling tie).

The Uses of Ambiguity: Defense and Offense

Dogs were valued because in addition to their practical services as sentinels for the village they offered special protection against a number of supernatural dangers. Ghosts, witches, and "land otters" were all hostile beings much feared. They all shared with dogs the characteristic of indeterminancy. Because dogs were also liminal or ambiguous creatures, they had the power to detect these perils. Witches, although ordinary human beings in one sense, were anomalous because they threatened the social unit from within by the practice of their sinister arts. Seemingly friends, they were really enemies. Among the Tlingit, Tsimshian, and Haida to the north (de Laguna 1972:702, 832), and the Coast Salish Klallam to the south (Gunther 1927:299), dogs were often spirit helpers of shamans because they could quickly identify witches. To the Tlingit, land otters were highly ambiguous beings: although they looked like animals, they were really people who had drowned and suffered a kind of aquatic change into "land otter men." Once transformed they haunted wild places hoping to entice other people away and change them into land otters. Land otters could make themselves look like people, even like a person's closest relative, and often deceived the unwary into following them. But no matter how clever a disguise they assumed, dogs were never fooled (de Laguna 1972:832).

All along the Northwest Coast, ghosts of people who had met death through illness or accident (other than drowning) often came back to their relatives, and their unseen presence was universally feared. It was ghosts of the recently dead who returned to bother their kinsmen, and these were still liminal beings, because they were no longer part of the community of the living but not yet committed to the society of the dead (Hertz 1950). The fear of ghosts, corpses, corpse pollution, and places where the dead were deposited can all be derived from the danger of the liminal state through which the recently dead are still passing. Here again, the dog was able to recognize the liminal spirits and warn the living against them. When dogs stared off into space barking furiously, people knew there were ghosts around and took appropriate precautions.

Paradoxically, although dogs as spirit helpers helped shamans unmask witches practicing secretly within the community, the dead bodies of dogs served Tlingit and Haisla witches as a powerful source of magic (de Laguna 1972:730; Lopatin 1945:76). Dog corpses were functionally equivalent to human corpses, which both groups also used to make maleficent magic, but the bodies of dead dogs were believed to be even more powerful than the remains of dead people. One of De Laguna's Tlingit informants phrased it aptly, "You can't keep a dead dog in your possession or they will tie you up for witchcraft. A rotting dog is stronger than a dead person" (1972:730). Why a rotting dog was stronger than a dead person was not explained, but I would suggest that the additional strength may have come from the cumulative liminality of death added to the already indeterminate position of the dog.

The intermediate position of dogs allowed them to stand for people under certain special conditions. In most cases the possibility of equating dogs with people was strongly resisted (as we shall discuss below in relation to the danger of talking dogs). There was, however, at least one case in which the possibility of substituting dog for person had a positive value. After there had been a death in the house, the Tlingit were careful to·allow the ghost of the deceased no chance to find its way back in. They made a special opening in the house wall through which they moved the body, and before closing the opening they pitched a dog out through it. Either a dead dog or a live one would serve, because, as Tlingit people explained to Swanton, they wanted the lonely ghost to seize the spirit of the dog instead of the spirit of a human kinsmen (1908:430).

There is another ritual use of dogs practiced by a number of Northwest groups that can be interpreted as equating dogs with people: spirit-possessed initiates performing the Dog Eater Dance would seize a dog and devour it alive. Because the significance of this ritual and the myths associated with it are complex, I will defer discussion until later.

THE DANGERS OF AMBIGUITY: DOGS WHO TALK

One of the most interesting consequences of the dog's ambiguous position was a conviction that dogs might try to usurp human prerogatives. Northwest Coast people believed it was possible for dogs to talk, but most of them found the prospect very frightening. The Tlingit, Bella Coola, and probably other northern groups, and the Chinook and Yurok in the south, believed that a talking dog portended death to its master (de Laguna 1972:833; McIlwraith 1948:55(I); Jacobs 1960:343; Elmendorf and Kroeber 1960:46). Anecdotes from Bella Coola and Tlingit describe the horrible consequences of encounters with talking dogs. The only remedy was to kill the dog immediately. It was believed that a softhearted person who hesitated to kill his pet would suffer a dreadful fate.[2]

Interestingly enough, however, a few Northwest Coast groups found a talking dog to be a portent of good fortune. The Puget Sound Salish and the Tillamook believed a dog only spoke to you if he planned to give you his spirit power (Turner 1973; Jacobs 1936). In this case the dog was identified with the realm of nature, because should a bear, wolf, deer, bird, sea mammal, or some other creature of the wild speak to a person, the significance would be the same. The distribution of this interesting reversal of the more general attitude, if we ignore for the moment the anomalous Tillamook (a Salish-speaking enclave cut off from their cousins by the Chinook), is roughly coterminous with the distribution of shearing dogs for wool (Howay 1918). Elsewhere on the coast the only contribution dogs made to the native economy, aside from their universal functions as scavengers and sentinels, was helping the hunters bring down game. (The groups that kept dogs for wool also kept some for hunt-

---

2. The emphasis placed on the dangers from talking dogs suggests that speech was judged crucial to human status. In support of this contention we find that the Salish-speaking Tillamook to the south of the Chinook warned a young mother not to let a dog lick her baby's mouth, because they believed that the dog would steal the infant's words and the child would have trouble learning to talk (Jacobs 1935).

ing, but land hunting seems to have been of less importance to most of the groups that used dog wool.) When we compare the different interpretation of the talking dog in the two sets of societies, those that used dogs only for hunting and those that used them for hunting and for wool, it is tempting to argue that where dogs only serve as hunters and sentinels people see them as closer to human beings and therefore more likely to usurp essential human prerogatives. In hunting, communication between the hunter and his dog is necessary to success, and the more adept the dog is at mastering simple communication the more valuable he is, and at the same time the more "human" he is. The dog's role as sentinel also depends on communication: the dog "tells" the people something is coming. On the other hand, where dogs are primarily valued as the source of a product, their fur, they are seen as closer to wild animals that are also exploited for the products of meat, hides, and wool. To the Coast Salish, who kept them for wool, dogs may have seemed closer to the wild pole, and therefore, perhaps, a talking dog was seen not as a threat but as an opportunity.[3]

DOG AS METAPHOR

The dog as an ambiguous, intermediate being offers an ideal symbol of ambiguous human relationships. Just as the dog's perplexing status is a conceptual problem, the arrangements among human beings which muddle categories that should be kept distinct also pose a problem. Paramount among such irregular relationships are incest and cannibalism. Lévi-Strauss argues that incest and cannibalism are conceptually related, since both substitute an inappropriately close object for an appropriately distant one. In support of his logic he shows that often in myths of the New World a sexual appetite for kin develops into a gustatory hankering after kind, so that we see incestuous young women who end up as cannibalistic ogresses (Lévi-Strauss 1971:238). On the Northwest Coast, dogs are prominently featured in both cannibalistic rituals and in myths about incest.

3. Kroeber (1941:12) first noted that the fear of talking dogs seemed to have a broad if erratic distribution in North America (Yurok, Hupa, Yana, Pomo, Papago, and Shawnee), and hypothesized that with better information more examples would emerge. He also suggested that so far-flung a trait must reflect either historic connections at a very ancient level or some common causal factor at work in all the societies showing it. We will not be concerned with the wider distribution here but only with the variations within the Northwest Coast region.

First, let us look at the dog as a victim of cannibalism. In the northern Northwest Coast there is a widespread ritual, one of a series of winter ceremonial performances restricted to the members of a privileged sodality, called in English the Dog Eater Dance. During this performance the initiate became possessed by the society's tutelary spirit and devoured dogs.[4] Since the idea of eating dogs was repugnant to aboriginal Northwest Coast people, this feat was proof of the terrible power of the spirit which could drive the possessed dancer to so preternatural a deed.

There are parallels between the performances of the possessed Dog Eaters and the cannibal dancers who are driven by an irresistible craving for human flesh. Both novices were wild, both had to be restrained by force, both were excited by certain sights and sounds: the Tsimshian referred to dogs as "beasts of the field" during a performance of the Dog Eaters, lest the novice be driven into a frenzy by hearing the word "dog" (Boas 1916:551). Both novices bit their victims: in the case of the Dog Eaters the victims were live dogs; in the case of the cannibals, either a human corpse or a live fellow villager.[5] The Bella Coola myths that explain the origins of the Dog Eater Dance describe how the first Dog Eater received the power and the dance from the wolves (McIlwraith 1948:116 II). Wolves are the enemies of dogs and wolves eat dogs. In this instance the wolf can be seen as a prototype of the cannibal, since it is devouring an animal—the dog—to which it is closely related. When a person inspired by the spirit of the wolf eats dogs, he is eating a creature that is symbolically equated with both the animals, as a relative of the wolf, and mankind itself, as the companion of man and defender of his interests against the beasts of the wild. Thus the Dog Eater is a cannibal from either perspective.[6]

The Dog Eater performance was found among the Tlingit (Swanton 1908:436), the Haida (Swanton 1908:171), the Tsimshian (Garfield 1939:303), Haisla (Lopatin 1945:84; Olson 1940:175), Heiltsuk (Olson 1955:337), Bella Coola (McIlwraith 1948:102 I), and, rather differently interpreted, among a small number of Coast Salish groups and along the Columbia among Upper Chinook, where it may have

---

4. Whether or not the dancers actually ate live dogs is still in dispute. But the uninitiated were supposed to believe that they did.

5. Arrangements were usually made with the victims in advance, and they were later compensated.

6. Stanley Walens (1981:109) interprets dogs as representing hunger "repressed and socialized," in contrast to wolves who represent hunger as a primal destructive force.

been a recent addition (Elmendorf 1948; Collins 1974:177; Walles: entry of 5/23/1845; Gunther 1927:281–82; Smith 1940:92; Duff 1952:261). It was far more widely distributed and therefore probably more ancient than the more famous Cannibal Society, which seems to have been a specifically Heiltsuk development that spread to some neighboring groups (Boas 1895), Southern Kwakiutl (Boas 1966:258), Bella Coola (McIlwraith 1948:102 II), and Coast Tsimshian (Garfield 1939:293).

Although in the sources I have consulted there is little direct evidence to support the symbolic equation of incest with cannibalism on the Northwest Coast, there is evidence for the equation of sexual relations with hunting and, by extention, with eating. Hunting rituals and beliefs vary in detail, but in general outline are common to the whole coast. The hunter's wife, or, among the Kwakiutl in some cases, his mistress, represents his quarry. The Kwakiutl text is quite specific: when the hunter dreams he has lain with a woman, he knows the time has come to go out to hunt (Boas 1921, pt. 1:642). Thus sexual relations symbolize securing game. Further evidence, also suggestive, is the association of the Dog Eater, who is the prototype of the cannibal, with the wolf, who is at the same time the very model of the successful land hunter.[7] The kinship between wolf and dog often expressed in myth as a sibling relationship makes the equivalence between the myth of wolves who eat dogs nicely parallel with the incest relationship: one has only to substitute sexual congress for eating.

Inconclusive though the ethnographic and ritual evidence for cannibalism as a symbolic equivalent for incest may be, when we add to it evidence from mythology we can build a better case. First, I will show how the dog can stand for a close kinsman in a disguised discussion of incest. By far the most widespread story that features dogs as principal performers is the Dog Husband story, which is found all the way from the Tlingit (Krause 1956:184–85), Haida (Swanton 1905b:252), and Bella Coola (McIlwraith 1948: 642 I), through the Kwakiutl (Boas 1895:401) and Nootka (Sapir and Swadesh 1939:55), to the Coast Salish (Gunther 1925:162), and appears again among the Tillamook (Jacobs 1935, 1959:22).[8]

The essentials of the story are as follows: the daughter of a high-

7. For an illuminating exploration of the logical equation of dogs with women and wolves with men among the interior Athapaskan, see Henry Sharp's article (1976).

8. For a brief discussion of the Dog Husband myth and its distribution, see Boas (1891). For inventories of examples, see Gunther (1925:160) and Thompson (1929:347).

class man has a lover whose identity she does not know because he comes to her only after dark and never speaks. To her dismay, she discovers that he is a dog. She is already pregnant and soon delivers a litter of puppies. The number she bears depends on the version, but often there are four or five males and one female, who, in many versions, is half dog and half human. Disgusted, the young woman's relatives pack up all their tools and provisions and move away, leaving her alone to die with her offspring. Only one person takes pity on her, and hides some coals for her to rekindle the fire. In the north this person is usually a kind-hearted slave; in the south, her grandmother or uncle. Alone with her puppies, she builds a fire, makes a shelter, and forages for food. Depending on the provenience of the story, she digs clams or wild potatoes, or gathers mussels, or fishes at night by torchlight. Whenever she is out she can hear singing coming from the shelter where she has left her puppies. Her male children have cast off their dog skins and are dancing and singing in their human form, while their sister watches from the door so they will not be caught by their mother. The mother, however, props her cedar-bark cape up with her digging stick on the beach and approaches the house by a circuitous route. When she sees her sons in human form, she seizes their dog skins and throws them into the fire so that the boys cannot resume their canine form. She upbraids them bitterly for deceiving her when she has been working so hard to feed them. They promise to reform and soon become proficient in human skills—hunting, fishing, whaling, canoe building, and so forth. Her one benefactor among the villagers, seeing the smoke rising from her house, returns to investigate. There is the deserted woman with her house full of food; as one narrator put it, "Ah, her house, crammed full, ready to burst, brimful with dried meat!" (Jacobs 1959:24). When the rest of the people learn that she is wealthy and that her sons are really people, they return and she is reconciled with her family. In some versions, however, she is implacable and destroys every one who deserted her, sparing only her benefactor.

To support my contention that the dog represents a close kinsman, with whom sexual relations were forbidden, there is another myth, much more limited in distribution, which is very similar to the Dog Husband story.[9] The Nooksack Coast Salish version opens with a high-class girl who has a lover whose identity she does not

---

9. Versions are noted from the Nooksack (Amoss 1955; Fetzer 1950), the Cowlitz (Adamson 1934:226), and Coos (Jacobs 1940:50).

know because he comes to her only at night, does not speak, and always leaves before morning. She marks his back with red paint, and the next day she sees that the man who has the paint on his back is her brother. (For purposes of the story he may have been either brother or cousin, because both are equally forbidden and both are covered by the same kinship term.) In this case it is the shame the lovers themselves feel that forces them into exile, rather than the response of angry relatives. They run away together and seek refuge in the woods, where they build a house and where the woman bears a child who is endowed with special supernatural powers. He grows very fast, and one day tells his parents that they look very much alike. Found out by their own child, they are again shamed. They tell him that he must go to his grandparents' home. As he leaves he turns for a last look at his own home and sees thick smoke rising from it. He realizes that his parents have set fire to the house and taken their own lives. He returns to his grandparents' village and eventually becomes a culture hero.

In both myths the forbidden or unnatural union is punished by separation from the group, either by self-imposed exile or desertion. In both cases the offspring of the union are superhuman and ultimately bring wealth to their communities. I take the close equivalence of these two myths to be an indication that for the group that told the Dog Husband myth, dogs represented the companionable but sexually forbidden insiders, in contrast with the wild animals that represented dangerous but marriageable outsiders.[10]

Both the incest myth and the Dog Husband myth are concerned with the problem of relations between the in-group and the out-group, and the significance of these relationships in the pressing business of making a living. To explain what I mean we should look at the Dog Husband story in contrast to the numerous and very widespread stories about marriages between human beings, male or female, and various wild animals.

10. While discussing the Dog Wife myth (Tillamook, gathered by Jacobs 1959:24), Lévi-Strauss (1971:519) alludes to the Dog Husband myth in passing, and identifies it as a "transformation of brother-sister incest." The relationship between the Dog Husband and the Dog Wife stories is close, in that the offspring of both unions are very powerful. This supports my belief that the ambiguous relationship is not only dangerous but powerful. Otherwise the plots of the two stories are not parallel. There is another story from Clackamas Chinook (Jacobs 1950:168) in which a man marries a bitch, but I exclude it from consideration here because he kills his wife before she can bear any offspring.

Subsequently, Lévi-Strauss changed his interpretation (1982:211), and now equates the Dog Husband theme with "marriage too far," i.e., the opposite of incest.

There are several kinds of wild animal marriage tales (Boas 1916:747–62). Here we shall only be concerned with those in which the final outcome is favorable to the human partner because the animal spouse supplies his mate and his affines with food. Food, or wealth derived from food, is the payoff for the relationship. The kinsmen and fellow villagers of the human spouse are enriched by plentiful supplies, either of the animal itself if it is a commonly used food species like the sockeye salmon, or by the food the animal eats if it is an animal such as the sandhill crane, which lives on some of the same food people eat (Jenness 1955:13–20; Suttles 1975:74). In the Dog Husband story, initially the heroine's relatives try to deprive her of all food and even the means to cook it. When she forces her children to relinquish their dog personae, they begin to provide her, and eventually her kinsmen, with food. But although she must humanize them to make them productive, once the transformation is made they are more proficient than the average hunter. They are supernaturally potent. Although the process is different, the results are the mirror image of each other. By crossing the barriers either internally or externally, or as Lévi-Strauss might put it, by contracting marriages that are either too close or too distant (1971:177), people release the power in chaos—power that can both destroy and enrich. In both Dog Husband and wild animal marriage stories, the power released by crossing the boundaries and breaking the taboos is directed well and redounds to the good fortune of the community.

The dilemma represented by marrying outside versus marrying inside the local group was of immediate concern to the people who told these stories. Suttles (1960) has suggested that exogamous marriage was a strategy employed by Coast Salish people like the Nooksack to get and keep access to a variety of food resources. Unfortunately, it required sending young women and occasionally young men off to villages where they might be practically strangers (Collins 1974:109; Snyder 1965:386). The elderly Nooksack man who told me the incest story commented afterward that sometimes people allowed cousins to marry because the parents feared their children would be mistreated if they married into distant villages.

The Dog Husband myth, which casts the dog in the supporting role, also emphasizes ambiguity and the resolution of ambiguity as a literary device for developing the plot. The story turns on a pair of misunderstandings about whether actors are dogs or people. The husband is really a dog, although the woman thinks he is a man. The children, on the other hand, are really people, although the woman and her outraged kinsmen think they are dogs. In both cases the crucial problem for the heroine is to resolve the ambiguity, which she does by practicing a deception of her own. In discovering her lover's real identity she surreptitiously rubs him with red paint and then during the day looks to see who shows traces of the paint on his back. In the case of the children, the singing and laughing she hears when she is away from the house suggest human activity, but when she returns she always finds only puppies. She deceives them by propping her cape up on her digging stick and sneaks back to surprise them in their human form. The confusion visited on her is of magical origin, but the solutions are strictly human inventions which celebrate the success of human cleverness in bringing this dangerous ambiguity firmly into the service of culture. In some versions the last child, a female, is half dog and half human. She represents the irresolvable paradox, because not only is she half and half, and not only does she serve as the watchman whose job it is to prevent the mother from transforming her brothers, but she herself cannot be transformed.

The incest myth also emphasizes the ambiguous relationship which the irregular union creates. In the Cowlitz story collected by Adamson (1934:226), the child does not tell his parents how much alike they look, but he dances outside his house and sings:

> "My mother is also my auntie!
> My father is also my uncle!"

As a final point on the subject of dogs as symbols used in metaphors of ambiguous relationships, let us look again at the symbolic equating of cannibalism and incest suggested by the hunt rituals and the spectacle of the wolves who devour their cousins, the dogs, in the Dog Eater ceremonial. I have argued that the Dog Husband myth represents incest, and therefore it seems reasonable to suggest that an equation between the Dog Husband myth and cannibalism would be further evidence for equating incest and cannibalism. One version of the Dog Husband myth collected by Boas among the Heiltsuk begins with a young woman who traveled from place to place giving birth to infants who were turned into rock formations. Finally she came to Northern Kwakiutl territory, where she gave birth to a litter of puppies. Following the usual course of the myth, she burned their dog skins and turned them into men. She transformed all but one, who managed to get his skin back on before she destroyed it. The young men then announced what human work they would perform for their mother, and the last one, the dog, announced that he would be her dog and protect her from the illnesses caused by spirits. The other brothers performed their chosen vocations and made their mother very wealthy. Then they went off into the woods, presumably to seek more spiritual power. While they were there they encountered Baxbakwalinuxsiwae, the maneating spirit of the woods, who taught them the Cannibal Dance performance. When they returned to their homes, they brought the Cannibal Dance with them (Boas 1895:401).

By tying together the Dog Husband, which we have already argued is a transformation of the incest myth, and the Cannibal Dance, this story offers tentative support for the other less explicit suggestions that among the Northwest Coast people incest and cannibalism were treated as symbolic equivalents, both representing the seeking of satisfactions, whether sexual or gustatory, too close to home.

METAPHORS FOR MEDIATION

Dogs serve as symbols of mediation in the opposition between the domains of man and beast, or, as Lévi-Strauss has expressed it, between culture and nature (1971:468). As I have already explained, dogs make ideal symbols for human actors in ambiguous relationships such as incest. Having rules against incest and cannibalism is an essentially human characteristic, so that scenarios in which dogs play incestuous actors or cannibal victims can also be seen as representations of the oppositions between a state of nature and a state of culture. In this connection we should look at the use of fire in some of those myths where dogs are featured as principal actors. Dogs and cooking fire are intimately associated in the myths of large areas of western North America. Lévi-Strauss has developed an analysis of the transformations between western North America and eastern North America in the relationship between dogs and fire (1971:468–9). In northern California Dog played the role of Prometheus, bringing fire to human beings (1971:103). Farther north, in the Northwest Coast region, the relationships have changed, and although Dog and fire are still associated, Dog is no longer the one who brings fire to men; he rather comes to men asking for fire, as we noted above in the Humptulip and Cowlitz myth of Dog and his brothers.

The hearth fire played a prominent part in the development of the Dog Husband plot and a lesser but still significant role in the plot of the incest myth. In Dog Husband, fire was the means by which the dog children became human. Earlier it was the fire hidden by her benefactor that saved the young woman's life and allowed her to survive and humanize her children. By emphasizing how careful the relatives were to extinguish all the fires, the story makes it clear that she and her children had been cast out of the human group. The fire was the essential element in the dramatic climax of the story when she burned the dog skins. By destroying their skins she committed her sons to a productive human existence.

The story indicates that before she transformed them they spent their time playing at being people, dancing and singing while their mother was out digging clams to feed them. (Significantly, some versions point out that she fed them only raw food.) Once changed, they had to take up the responsibilities of culture. And again, it was fire, or the smoke from it, that let her benefactor know that she had succeeded in turning her shame into victory.

Although in most versions the dogs are neutral about the fire and play no part in keeping it going, in some versions it is the dogs who find the hidden clam shell in which the benefactor has concealed the coals, and in one the Dog Husband himself keeps the fire going while the woman is working (Jacobs 1959:22). In the incest story, fire is the means by which the lovers take their own lives. In both cases fire represents the power of the state of culture which operates to "dis-ambiguate" the situation created by the irregular unions.

SUMMARY

Northwest Coast people exploited the logical possibilities inherent in the domesticated dog's ambiguous position, to make the dog a metaphor for ambiguous human relationships, an intermediary to other marginal beings, and a device to emphasize the distinction between the ways of beasts and the ways of human beings. Within the larger Northwest Coast area, variations in the economic role played by the dog were reflected in differences in his role in ritual and belief. Among the Coast Salish, where dogs were kept for fur as well as hunting, a talking dog was a positive manifestation of power, whereas elsewhere on the coast, where dogs were used only for hunting, a talking dog also meant supernatural forces at work, but very destructive ones.

APPENDIX

Angoon village, about 1900. Angoon is best known from de Laguna's *The Story of a Tlingit Community* (1960), which relied heavily on Viola Garfield's history of Angoon's clans (1947). (Vincent Sobolef Collection, Alaska Historical Library)

Łingit 'ani

Remembrances of Angoon for Viola

The proud houses of Angoon
Stand gaunt and paintless,
Stripped by storms of years,
And gaze across the straits
With empty windows
Like sightless eyes.

The broken boardwalk
Marks the trail
Once traced by the Beaver
When he led the people
To this village site
On the narrow isthmus.

Here the raging tides of Kootznahoo
Offered safety from foes,
The Brown Bear's Fort a refuge.
And Raven's Halibut Rock
Hides under the "fighting waters"
Only to permit the potlatch guests
To leave Raven's House.

The carved Raven and Bear
That glorified the houses of the chiefs,
The spouting Killerwhales,
Meeting each other, snout to snout,
Upon the facade of another,
All are torn down, destroyed,
Or painted over in shame.

Few still live who can recall
The potlatches by which
The houses and the people of Angoon
Obtained their names and honors.

I-ša'n di yeł,
I-ša'n di gutš!

The White man's world engulfs you.
And if the Tlingit children
Can no more return to old Angoon,
So, too, Viola, neither you nor I,
Can ever step again
Upon the same shingle beach
That once we knew and loved.

Frederica de Laguna
November 13, 1975

Viola Edmundson Garfield

A brief look at her life shows Viola Garfield as both a product of her time and far ahead of it. The first in her farming family to strive for higher education, she chose a field that combined an academic career with the rigors of fieldwork at a time when women were still a small force in the world of scholarship. At Columbia she knew and worked with other women who were to help shape modern anthropology: Ruth Benedict, Elsie Clews Parsons, Gladys Reichard, Ruth Bunzel, and Margaret Mead. Her name is linked with the Northwest as inextricably as the others are with the Southwest or Samoa.

Viola Edmundson was born at the close of the nineteenth century, December 5, 1899, on an Iowa farm near the farms of both sets of her grandparents. In 1905 her father moved his family west to join a brother already established on Whidbey Island in Washington. School on the island was a small two-story building in Coupeville with one teacher for some forty students. Viola started school twice because the first year she was too frightened to walk alone past a field of cows along the way. The following year she and her younger sister were able to walk together for mutual protection.

Eventually Viola thrived in the small school, skipping the fourth grade and finishing as valedictorian of her graduating class of eight in 1918. Her address to her class, "The Education That Caused German Children to Go to War," shows an already developed concern for cross-cultural work, education, and world issues.

Although she remembers only three books in her childhood home—the Bible, *The Sky Pilot* (a Methodist novel), and an encyclopedia—she early valued reading and set her sights on college and a teaching career. In her sophomore year of highschool, in pursuit of her goals, she took a job housekeeping for an island family named Pratt, where she had access to a library of some 2,000 books and the example of Mrs. Pratt, the county school superintendent. After graduation she remained for a time on the island to earn tuition money. Her own family's financial outlook had brightened by this time. They were able to move to a small homestead at the edge of town, large enough to hold the six children now in the family. Here they had a garden, orchard, barn, and some livestock, with the benefit of fresh milk, cream, eggs, fruit, berries, and vegetables. The first tiny house that they had lived in since arriving in Coupeville then became a chicken coop.

By saving her salary, Viola was able to enter the University of Washington in 1919, but her experience there was short-lived since money ran out in her second year. After earning a teaching certificate from the Normal School in Bellingham, in 1922 she began teaching fourth grade in New Metlakatla on Annette Island, Alaska, a settlement of about five hundred Tsimshian Indians. She was now an employee of the Bureau of Indian Affairs.

Her experience as a BIA teacher in the Tsimshian village affected her profoundly. There had been a few Salish Indians living in Coupeville when she was growing up, but she had had little or no contact with them. Besides herself and the five other BIA teachers assigned to New Metlakatla, the only whites living on Annette Island were the cannery watchman and his wife and son. She puzzled over events and behavior she witnessed in the village and in the classroom, becoming ever more curious about the Tsimshian, whom she had begun to admire. She noticed that the Indian children would not compete for attention or for rewards. She realized that they thought in terms of the group and not of their own self interest, and that they avoided showing up another classmate or causing another to be laughed at. She took pleasure in ignoring the school superintendent's instruction to punish a child speaking the Tsimshian language.

She learned something of Tsimshian mythology and culture from an elderly Tsimshian man who frequented the teachers' quarters to tell stories of Raven, the trickster/culture hero, and of the old customs. At a village wedding, which she remembers as a high point of her social life, she discovered that the Tsimshian traced their kinship through the mother. Back at the University of Washington some years later, she would recognize the arrangement in anthropological terms as a matrilineal kinship system and write a description of it for her dissertation.

Despite her growing sense of ease in the Alaskan community, Viola decided to return to Seattle at the end of her year's assignment in order to resume her own studies. Yet it was not until 1927 that she was able to reenter the university. Again short of money, she worked at the Seattle Chamber of Commerce, and it was there that she met Charles Garfield, an Alaskan sourdough active in Chamber affairs and in the Fur Exchange. They were married in 1924.

Finally, three years later, she was able to return to the university to take her degree in sociology. There she met a recently arrived anthropologist, Melville Jacobs, a student of linguistics trained by

Franz Boas, who was familiar with the few publications on Tsimshian mythology and society by Boas and his colleagues. Jacobs rekindled her interest in the Tsimshian when he introduced her to Boasian studies of the Northwest. By 1931, when she received her B.A. in sociology, she had given her heart to anthropology.

After returning to New Metlakatla for research on Tsimshian marriage patterns by clan, class, and race for a master's degree in sociology, she went on to study with Boas himself for the Ph.D. degree. Boas had special affection for the Northwest, where his long association with the Kwakiutl had begun in the 1880s. He found in Viola Garfield a willing and highly capable aid to him in his research on coastal art. While at Columbia she continued her work on the Tsimshian, with her first field trip devoted almost entirely to investigating the art of woodcarving, which she describes in articles on the making of a raven rattle and a box design (1955).

She spent her summers enrolled at Columbia earning the credits necessary for the degree. For the rest of the year, she and Charles lived in Seattle where she worked as a teaching assistant at the University of Washington. From 1932 to 1937 she found time to go north on several occasions to do comparative fieldwork among different Tsimshian groups, collaborating with William Beynon, a Tsimshian and self-trained ethnographer who had assisted Boas, Marius Barbeau, and others before her.

Beynon was the son of a Tsimshian woman who had instilled in him a great respect for his own culture. Beynon's family came from the Nass River and he belonged to the Nass branch of the Wolf clan through his mother. He eventually became chief of that clan. Like George Hunt, the Kwakiutl famous for playing a critical role in the research of Boas and of photographer Edward S. Curtis (among others), Beynon was a knowledgeable and careful informant, versatile in his talents.

"Beynon was always working," Garfield wrote. "When he was helping me work on Tsimshian art, he was also redoing the notes that Henry Tate had given Boas for the old Tsimshian mythology. Beynon was rewriting them in the then 'modern' orthography. He also showed me notebooks he had filled with information on the Gitksan totem poles. . . . He also worked with Marius Barbeau. Barbeau's books are almost all Beynon's work."

Before World War II the requirement for a doctoral degree at Columbia was not only the writing of a dissertation and its approval by committee, but the actual publication of the work. Garfield finished her dissertation in 1935, but did not receive her degree until

Tsimshian Clan and Society appeared in the University of Washington Publications in Anthropology series in 1939. She then joined her former teachers as a full member of the faculty of the University of Washington, where she was to teach for the remainder of her career.

The anthropology program at the university, which Melville Jacobs had inaugurated in 1927, was originally set up to be a center for regional research. Before Jacobs' arrival, anthropology had been taught only sporadically at the University of Washington, beginning with J. P. Harrington, long associated with the Bureau of American Ethnology, who taught a summer course in 1910. It gained firmer ground, though it remained a part of the sociology department, when T. T. Waterman taught from 1918 to 1920. Following him, Leslie Spier and Erna Gunther spent a year at the university as visiting faculty. With Melville Jacobs' appointment as the first permanently employed anthropologist, anthropology and sociology became separate departments.

Jacobs was able to persuade Erna Gunther to rejoin the faculty in 1929. She specialized in the Puget Sound Salish and the Makah of Cape Flattery, as well as in the material culture, ethnobiology, ethnohistory, and arts of the entire region. Jacobs himself recorded the languages, folklore, and cultural traditions from native peoples along the lower Columbia River and regions farther south in Oregon. Verne Ray, a later addition to the program, studied tribes of eastern Washington and defined characteristics of the Plateau Culture Area. By joining the department, Garfield added expertise on the northern matrilineal societies. Eventually, this nucleus of the anthropology department became internationally known for its Northwest Coast specialization.

All of the early Northwest scholars—most of them, like Viola Garfield, students of Boas—perpetuated the Boasian dedication to ethnographic detail and native texts, long after it began to be replaced by more selective theoretical orientations within general anthropology. The great virtue of Boas's legacy is that the Northwest has come to be considered one of the best known ethnographic areas in the world. In early studies of kinship and mythology, French anthropologist Claude Lévi-Strauss relied on Tsimshian examples drawn from the works of Boas and Garfield. His well-known, often controversial publications have helped to awaken interest in the Tsimshian and have encouraged a new generation of "Tsimshianists" from Canada, France, Australia, and the United States.

Works by Viola Edmundson Garfield

1939   "The Potlatch." Seattle Grade Club Magazine 15(3):12.

1939   Tsimshian Clan and Society. University of Washington Publications in Anthropology 7(3):167–340.

1940   The Seattle Totem Pole. Seattle: University of Washington Press.

1944   "Indian Arts and White Materials: III. Totem Poles." Indians at Work (with Ruth Underhill).

1945   "A Research Problem in Northwest Economics." American Anthropologist 47(4):626–30.

1947   "Historical Aspects of Tlingit Clans in Angoon, Alaska." American Anthropologist 49(3):438–52.

1948   The Wolf and the Raven (with Linn Forest). Seattle: University of Washington Press.

1951   "Anthropological Research in Southeastern Alaska." Proceedings of the Alaskan Science Conference of the National Academy of Science. National Research Council Bulletin 122:44.

1951   Meet the Totem. Sitka: Sitka Printing Co.

1951   "The Tsimshian and Their Neighbors." In The Tsimshian: Their Arts and Music (with Marius Barbeau and Paul Wingert). Vol. 18 of the American Ethnological Society Numbered Publications.

1951   "Anthropological Research and Publications" (with Wilson Duff). Anthropology in British Columbia 2:2–13.

1952   "Survey of Southeastern Alaska Indian Research." Selected Papers of the Alaskan Science Conference, pp 20–37. Arctic Institute of North America.

1952   "Anthropological Research and Publications" (with Wilson Duff) Anthropology in British Columbia 3: 5–9.

1953   "Possibilities of Genetic Relationship in Northern Pacific Moiety Structures." American Antiquity 18(3):58–61.

1953   "Contemporary Problems of Folklore Collecting and Study." Anthropological Papers of the University of Alaska 1(2):25–37.

1955   "Making a Bird or Chief's Rattle." Davidson Journal of Anthropology 1(11):155–68.

1961 (ed.) Symposium: Patterns of Land Utilization and Other Papers. American Ethnological Society Publication.

1962 (ed.) Symposium on Language and Culture (with Wallace L. Chafe). American Ethnological Society Publication.

1963 (ed.) Symposium on Community Studies in Anthropology (with Ernestine Friedl). American Ethnological Society Publication.

1966   The Tsimshian and Their Arts (with Paul S. Wingert). Seattle and London: University of Washington Press.

1967   "Tsimshian." In Encyclopedia Britannica.

1980   The Seattle Totem Pole. Seattle and London: University of Washington Press. (Revised and expanded from 1940 edition)

Works Cited

Abbott, Donald N., ed.
1981   *The World Is As Sharp As a Knife: An Anthology in Honour of Wilson Duff*. Victoria: British Columbia Provincial Museum.

Ackerman, Charles
1975   "A Tsimshian Oedipus." *Proceedings of the Second Congress of the Canadian Ethnology Society*, National Museum of Man Mercury Series 28:67–84.

Adams, John W.
1973   *The Gitksan Potlatch: Population Flux, Resource Ownership and Reciprocity*. Toronto: Holt, Rinehart and Winston of Canada.

Adamson, Thelma
1934   *Folk Tales of the Coast Salish*. American Folklore Society Memoir 27.

Allen, Glover M.
1920   *Dogs of the American Aborigines*. Bulletin of the Harvard Museum of Comparative Zoology 63:432–517.

Ames, Kenneth M.
1976   "Stable and Resiliant Systems Along the Skeena: The Gitksan/ Carrier Boundary." Paper presented at the 9th Annual Conference of the University of Calgary Archeological Association, November 4–7.

Amoss, Pamela
1955   Unpublished field notes.
1975   "Ancient Man's Best Friend." *Pacific Search* (November), Seattle.

Averkieva, Julia
1971   "The Tlingit Indians." In *North American Indians in Historical Perspective*, edited by Eleanor Leacock and Nancy Lurie. New York: Random House.

Bach, Emmon
1968   "Nouns and Noun Phrases." In *Universals in Linguistic Theory*, edited by Emmon Bach and Robert Harms. New York: Holt, Rinehart and Winston.

Barbeau, Marius C.
1915–57 Unpublished field notes. Centre for the Study of Canadian Folklore, National Museum of Man (Ottawa).
1917   Review of *Tsimshian Mythology* by Franz Boas. *American Anthropologist* 19(4):548–63.
1928   *The Downfall of Temlaham*. Toronto: Macmillan.
1929   *Totem Poles of the Gitksan, Upper Skeena River, British Columbia*. National Museums of Canada Bulletin 61.
1950   *Totem Poles*. Vol. 1. National Museums of Canada Bulletin 119.

1954   " 'Totemic Atmosphere' on the North Pacific Coast." *Journal of American Folklore* 67:103–22.

1958   *Medicine Men of the North Pacific Coast.* National Museums of Canada Bulletin 152.

Barnett, Homer

1938   "The Nature of the Potlatch." *American Anthropologist* 40(3):349–57.

1953   *Innovation: The Basis of Cultural Change.* New York: McGraw-Hill.

1955   *The Coast Salish of British Columbia.* Studies in Anthropology Monograph 4. Eugene, Ore.: University of Oregon Press.

1957   *Indian Shakers.* Carbondale, Ill.: Southern Illinois University Press.

Bauman, Richard, and Joel Sherzer, eds.

1974   *Explorations in the Ethnography of Speaking.* London: Cambridge University Press.

Beaglehole, J. C., ed.

1967   *The Journals of Captain James Cook on His Voyages of Discovery.* Vol. 3, pt. 1: *The Voyage of the* Resolution *and* Discovery, *1776–1780.* Cambridge: Cambridge University Press for the Hakluyt Society.

Benedict, Ruth

1923   *The Concept of the Guardian Spirit in North America.* American Anthropological Association Memoir 29.

Berlin, Brent, D. C. Breedlove, and P. H. Raven

1968   "Covert Categories and Folk Taxonomies." *American Anthropologist* 70 (2):290–99.

Beynon, William

1941   "Tsimshians of Metlakatla, Alaska." *American Anthropologist* 43 (1):83–88.

n.d.   "Ethnographic and Folkloristic Texts of the Tsimshian." On deposit, Boas Collection, American Philosophical Society, Philadelphia.

n.d.   "Tsimshian Kinship Terms." On deposit, Boas Collection, American Philosophical Society, Philadelphia.

n.d.   "Processes of Change from Matrilineal to Patrilineal Inheritance." On deposit, Boas Collection, American Philosophical Society, Philadelphia.

n.d.   Tsimshian Notebooks. Nos. 1–5. Centre for the Study of Canadian Folklore, National Museum of Man (Ottawa).

Bishop, Charles

1967   *The Journal and Letters of Captain Charles Bishop on the North-West Coast of America, in the Pacific, and in New South Wales, 1794–1799.* Edited by Michael Roe. London: Cambridge University Press.

Blackman, Margaret B.

1972   "Nei:wɔns, the 'monster' House of Chief Wi:ha: An Exercise in Ethnohistorical, Archaeological, and Ethnological Reasoning." *Syesis* 5:211–25.

1977 "Ethnohistoric Changes in the Haida Potlatch Complex." *Arctic Anthropology* 14:39–53.

Blackman, Margaret, and Susan Kenyon

1976 *A Guide to Contemporary Northwest Coast Scholars and Their Works.* Compiled for the Northwest Coast Studies Conference, Simon Fraser University, May 12–16.

Boas, Franz

1889 "Letter to Horatio Hale, and Preliminary Notes on the Indians of British Columbia." *Northwestern Tribes of Canada.* Report of the British Association for the Advancement of Science 4.

1890a *The Nootka.* Second General Report on the Indians of British Columbia for the British Association for the Advancement of Science.

1890b *Northwestern Tribes of Canada.* Report of the British Association for the Advancement of Science 6.

1891 "Dissemination of Tales among the Natives of North America." *Journal of American Folk-lore* 4:13–20.

1895 *Northwestern Tribes of Canada.* Report of the British Association for the Advancement of Science 10.

1897 *The Social Organization and the Secret Societies of the Kwakiutl Indians.* Report of the U. S. National Museum for 1895.

1898 *The Mythology of the Bella Coola Indians.* Publications of the Jesup North Pacific Expedition 1:25–127.

1902 *Tsimshian Texts.* Bureau of American Ethnology Bulletin 27.

1909 *The Kwakiutl of Vancouver Island.* American Museum of Natural History Memoir 8 (2):301–522.

1911 "Tsimshian." In *Handbook of American Indian Languages,* edited by Franz Boas. Bureau of American Ethnology Bulletin 40:283–422.

1912 *Tsimshian Texts.* New Series. Publications of the American Ethnological Society 3.

1916 *Tsimshian Mythology.* Thirty-first Annual Report of the Bureau of American Ethnology.

1920 "The Social Organization of the Kwakiutl." *American Anthropologist* 22 (2):111–26.

1921 *Ethnology of the Kwakiutl.* Thirty-fifth Annual Report of the Bureau of American Ethnology.

1930 *Religion of the Kwakiutl.* Columbia University Contributions to Anthropology 10, pt 2. New York: Columbia University Press.

1932 *Bella Bella Tales.* American Folklore Society Memoir 52.

1940 *Race, Language and Culture.* New York: Macmillan.

1966 *Kwakiutl Ethnography.* Edited by Helen Codere. Chicago: University of Chicago Press.

1974 *Indian Legends of the North Pacific Coast of America.* [1895.] Translated by Dietrich Bertz. Victoria, B.C.: British Columbia Indian Language Project.

Boit, John
  1941   "Log of the Second Voyage of the *Columbia.*" In *Voyages of the Columbia to the Northwest Coast 1787–1790 and 1790–1793*, edited by F. W. Howay, pp. 363–431. Boston: Massachusetts Historical Society Collections.

Brenner, Charles
  1955   *An Elementary Textbook of Psychoanalysis.* New York: Doubleday.

Brachfield, O.
  1951   *Inferiority Feelings in the Individual and the Group.* New York: Grune and Stratton.

Brown, Dorothy Lewis Gordon
  1968   Personal communication. Kitkatla, British Columbia.

Brown, Robert, ed.
  1896   *The Adventures of John Jewitt.* Edited and with an introduction and notes by Robert Brown, Commander of the First Vancouver Exploring Expedition. London: Clement Wilson.

Buchler, Ira, and H. Selby
  1968   *Kinship and Social Organization.* New York: Macmillan.

Burling, Robbins
  1974   *The Passage of Power.* New York and London: Academic Press.

Burridge, Kenelm
  1973   *Encountering Aborigines: Anthropology and the Australian Aboriginal.* Toronto: Pergamon Press.

Carpenter, Edmund
  1975   "Collecting Northwest Coast Art." In *Indian Art of the Northwest Coast*, Bill Holm and Bill Reid, pp. 1–27. Seattle: University of Washington Press for Institute for the Arts, Rice University.

Chagnon, Napoleon A.
  1977   *Yanomamo.* New York: Holt, Rinehart and Winston.

Codere, Helen
  1961   "Kwakiutl." In *Perspectives in American Indian Culture Change*, edited by E. H. Spicer. Chicago: University of Chicago Press.

Collins, June M.
  1952   "The Mythological Basis for Attitudes toward Animals among Salish-speaking Indians." *Journal of American Folk-lore* 65:353–60.
  1974   *Valley of the Spirits.* Seattle: University of Washington Press.

Collison, W. H.
  1915   *In the Wake of the War Canoe.* London: E. P. Dutton.

Conklin, Harold G.
  1969   "Ethnogenealogical Method." In *Cognitive Anthropology*, edited by Stephen A. Tyler. New York: Holt, Rinehart and Winston.

Cook, Captain James, and James King
  1784   *A Voyage to the Pacific Ocean ... for making discoveries in the northern hemisphere to determine the position and extent of the west side of North America, its distance from Asia and the practicability of a northern passage.* 3 vols. London: G. Nicol and T. Cadell.

Cook, Warren L.
1973   *Flood Tide of Empire: Spain and the Pacific Northwest, 1543–1819.*
New Haven: Yale University Press.
Cove, John J.
1976   "Back to Square One: A Re-Examination of Tsimshian Cross-Cousin Marriage." *Anthropologica* 18:153–78.
Cowell, Ray T.
1925   "History of Port Townsend." *Washington Historical Quarterly* 16 (4):284–89.
Crosby, Thomas
1914   *Up and Down the North Pacific Coast by Canoe and Mission Ship.*
Toronto: Missionary Society of the Methodist Church (Young People's Forward Movement Department).
Curtis, Edward S.
1913–16 *The North American Indian.* Vols. 9, 10, and 11. Norwood, Mass.: Plimpton Press.
Dawson, George M.
1880   *On the Haida Indians of the Queen Charlotte Islands.* Report of Progress for 1878–79, Geological Survey of Canada, Montreal.
1888   *Notes and Observations on the Kwakiool People of the Northern Part of Vancouver Island, and Adjacent Coasts, Made During the Summer of 1885, with a Vocabulary of About Seven Hundred Words.* Proceedings and Transactions of the Royal Society of Canada for the year 1887, vol. 5.
Deans, James
1899   *Tales from the Totems of the Hidery.* Archives of the International Folklore Association 2.
Dewhirst, John. See Folan, William J.
Dixon, George.
1789   *Voyage Round the World.* London: J. Stockdale and G. Goulding.
Dorsey, G. A.
1897   "The Geography of the Tsimshian Indians." *American Antiquarian and Oriental Journal* 19:276–82.
Douglas, Mary
1966   *Purity and Danger.* London: Routledge and Kegan Paul.
1975   *Implicit Meanings.* London: Routledge and Kegan Paul.
Drucker, Philip
1939   "Rank, Wealth, and Kinship in Northwest Coast Society." *American Anthropologist* 41 (1):55–65.
1940   "Kwakiutl Dancing Societies." *Anthropological Records* 2 (6):201–30.
1950   "Culture Element Distributions, 16: Northwest Coast." *Anthropological Records* 9:157–294.
1951   *The Northern and Central Nootkan Tribes.* Bureau of American Ethnology Bulletin 144.

1955   *Indians of the Northwest Coast.* Garden City, N.J.: American Museum Science Books.

1965   *Cultures of the North Pacific Coast.* San Francisco: Chandler and Sharp.

Duff, Wilson

1952   "The Upper Stalo Indians." Master's thesis, University of Washington.

1959   *Histories, Territories and Laws of the Kitwancool.* Anthropology in British Columbia Memoir 4. Victoria: British Columbia Provincial Museum.

1964   *The Indian History of British Columbia.* Vol. 1: *The Impact of the White Man.* Anthropology in British Columbia Memoir 5. Victoria: British Columbia Provincial Museum.

1965   "Thoughts on the Nootka Canoe." British Columbia Provincial Museum, Report for the year 1964.

Dumont, Louis

1957   *Hierarchy and Marriage Alliance in South Indian Kinship.* Occasional Paper of the Royal Anthropological Institute 12.

Dunn, John A.

1970   "Coast Tsimshian Phonology," Ph.D. dissertation, University of New Mexico.

Dunn, John, and L. Dunn

1972   "An Equivalence Cycle for Kitkatla Kin-Status Terms." *Anthropological Linguistics* 14 (6):240–54.

Durlach, Theresa Mayer

1928   *The Relationship Systems of the Tlingit, Haida, and Tsimshian.* Publications of the American Ethnological Society 2.

Dye, Eva Emery

1907   "Earliest Expedition against Puget Sound Indians." *Washington Historical Quarterly* 1 (2).

Eastman, Carol M., and Paul Aoki

1978   "Phonetic Segments of Haida." In *Linguistics and Literary Studies in Honor of Archibald A. Hill.* Vol. 2: *Descriptive Linguistics,* edited by M. A. Jazayery, E. C. Polomé, and W. Winter. The Hague: Mouton.

Eastman, Carol M, Robert Welsch, and Daniel Vaughan

1975   "On Tense and Aspects of Aspect in Haida: Hydaburg Dialect." In *Lektos,* edited by Robert St. Clair. Special issue: Papers from the Tenth International Conference on Salishan Languages.

Edgerton, Robert B.

1965   "Some Dimensions of Disillusionment in Culture Contact." *Southwestern Journal of Anthropology* 21 (3):231–43.

Eells, Myron

1883   "The Potlatches of Puget Sound." *American Antiquarian* 5(2).

1886   *Ten Years' Missionary Work at Skokomish.* Boston: Congregational Sunday School and Publishing Society.

1887   *The Twana, Chemakum and Klallam Indians of Washington Territory.* Annual Report of the Smithsonian Institution 1:605–81.

Ellis, William
1782   *An Authentic Narrative of a Voyage Performed by Captain Cook and Captain Clerke in His Majesty's Ships* Resolution *and* Discovery . . . *including a faithful account of all their discoveries, and the unfortunate death of Captain Cook.* 2 vols. London: Robinson.

Elmendorf, William W.
1948   "The Cultural Setting of the Twana Secret Society." *American Anthropologist* 50 (4):625–33.
1961   "Skokomish and Other Coast Salish Tales." Pts 1–3. *Washington State University Research Studies* 29:1–37, 84–117, 119–50.
1970   "Skokomish Sorcery, Ethics and Society." In *Systems of North American Witchcraft and Sorcery,* edited by Deward E. Walker, Jr. Anthropological Monographs of the University of Idaho 1.
1977   "Coastal and Interior Salish Power Concepts: A Structural Comparison." *Arctic Anthropology* 14(1):171–208.

Elmendorf, William W., and A. L. Kroeber
1960   *The Structure of Twana Culture with Comparative Notes on the Structure of Yurok Culture by A. L. Kroeber.* Washington State University Research Studies 28.

Emmons, George T.
1907   *The Chilcat Blanket.* Memoirs of the American Museum of Natural History 3(4).
1916   *The Whale House of the Chilkat.* Anthropological Papers of the American Museum of Natural History 19(1).

Ermatinger, C. O.
1914   "The Columbia River Under Hudson's Bay Company Rule." *Washington Historical Quarterly* 5 (3):192–206.

Ernst, Alice Henson
1952   *The Wolf Ritual of the Northwest Coast.* Eugene: University of Oregon Press.

Espinosa y Tello, José, ed.
1930   *A Spanish Voyage to Vancouver and the Northwest Coast of America in 1792.* Translated and with an introduction by Cecil Jane. London: Argonaut.

Farrar, Victor J.
1915   "Journal of Occurrences at Nisqually House." *Washington Historical Quarterly* 6 (3):179–97.

Fetzer, Paul
1950   Unpublished field notes on Nooksack.

Finlay, M. I.
1968   "Slavery." In *International Encyclopedia of the Social Sciences,* edited by David L. Sills. New York: Macmillan and Free Press.

Fjellman, Stephen
  1975   Review of *Structures in the Subjective Lexicon* by Samuel Fillen-
          baum and Ammon Rapoport (1971). *American Anthropologist* 77
          (1):120–21.
Fodor, J. A., and J. J. Katz, eds.
  1964   *The Structure of Language*. Englewood Cliffs, N.J.: Prentice-Hall.
Folan, William J., and John T. Dewhirst
  1969   "Yuquot, British Columbia: The Prehistory and History of a
          Nootkan Village." *Northwest Anthropological Research Notes* 3:217–
          39.
Ford, Clellan S.
  1941   *Smoke from Their Fires. The Life of a Kwakiutl Chief*. New Haven:
          Yale University Press.
Fox, James J.
  1971   "Sister's Child as Plant: Metaphors in an Idiom of Consanguin-
          ity." In *Rethinking Kinship and Marriage*, edited by Rodney Need-
          ham. ASA Monograph 11. London: Tavistock Publications.
Frachtenberg, Leo J.
  1913   *Coos Texts*. Columbia University Contributions to Anthropology
          1. New York: Columbia University Press.
Garfield, Viola
  1933   "The Dog-Eaters." *Town Crier*, December 16, pp. 28–29. Seattle.
  1939   *Tsimshian Clan and Society*. University of Washington Publica-
          tions in Anthropology 7 (3):167–340. Seattle: University of
          Washington Press.
  1945   "A Research Problem in Northwest Indian Economics." *Amer-
          ican Anthropologist* 47 (4):626–31.
  1947   "Notes on Elaborations of the Guardian Spirit Concept by
          Northwest Coast Tribes." Paper presented at the 46th annual
          meeting of the American Anthropological Association, Albu-
          querque, December.
  1951   "The Tsimshian and Their Neighbors." In *The Tsimshian: Their
          Arts and Music*, Viola E. Garfield, Paul Wingert, and Marius Bar-
          beau. Publications of the American Ethnological Society 18.
Garfield, Viola, and Linn Forrest
  1948   *The Wolf and the Raven: Totem Poles of Southeastern Alaska*. Seattle:
          University of Washington Press.
Garfield, Viola, and Paul Wingert
  1966   *The Tsimshian and Their Arts*. Seattle: University of Washington
          Press. (Reprint of *The Tsimshian: Their Arts and Music*, 1951, AES
          18.)
Gates, Charles M.
  1955   "The Indian Treaty of Point No Point." *Pacific Northwest Quar-
          terly* 41 (2):52–58.

Gennep, Arnold van
    1960   *The Rites of Passage.* Chicago: University of Chicago Press. (Originally published 1908 as *Les Rites de passage*).
Gibbs, George
    1877   *Tribes of Western Washington and Northwest Oregon.* Contributions to North American Ethnology 1:157–242.
Glick, Leonard
    1973   "The Anthropology of Religion: Malinowski and Beyond." In *Beyond the Classics? Essays in the Scientific Study of Religion,* edited by Charles Y. Glock. New York: Harper and Row.
Goldman, Irving
    1975   *The Mouth of Heaven: An Introduction to Kwakiutl Religious Thought.* New York: John Wiley and Sons.
Goldschmidt, Walter, and T. H. Haas
    1946   *Possessory Rights of the Natives of Southeastern Alaska.* Washington, D.C.: U.S. Government Printing Office.
Goodenough, Ward H.
    1956   "Componential Analysis and the Study of Meaning." *Language* 32:195–216.
    1970   *Description and Comparison in Cultural Anthropology.* Chicago: Aldine.
Goody, Jack
    1962   *Death, Property, and the Ancestors.* Stanford: Stanford University Press.
    1966   "Introduction." In *Succession to High Office,* edited by Jack Goody. London: Cambridge University Press.
Gough, Barry M.
    1981   "New Light on Haida Chiefship: The Case of Chief Edenshaw." Unpublished manuscript.
Greenberg, Joseph H.
    1966   *Language Universals.* The Hague: Mouton and Co.
Gumperz, John J.
    1975   "Foreword." In *Sociocultural Dimensions of Language Use,* edited by Mary Sanches and Ben G. Blount. New York: Academic Press.
Gunther, Erna
    1925   *Klallam Folktales.* University of Washington Publications in Anthropology 1 (4):113–70.
    1927   *Klallam Ethnography.* University of Washington Publications in Anthropology 1 (5):171–314.
    1949   "The Shaker Religion of the Northwest." In *Indians of the Urban Northwest,* edited by M. W. Smith. New York: Columbia University Press.
    1961   "A Re-Evaluation of the Cultural Position of the Nootka." In *Men and Cultures,* edited by Anthony F. C. Wallace. Selected Papers of the Fifth International Congress of Anthropological and Ethnological Sciences, Philadelphia, September 1–9, 1956. Philadelphia: University of Pennsylvania Press.

1966   *Art in the Life of the Northwest Coast Indians*. Catalogue of the Rasmussen Collection in the Portland Art Museum, Portland, Ore.

1972   *Indian Life on the Northwest Coast of North America as Seen by the Early Explorers and Fur Traders During the Last Decades of the Eighteenth Century*. Chicago: University of Chicago Press.

Haeberlin, Hermann
1924   "Mythology of Puget Sound." *Journal of American Folk-lore* 37:371–438.

Hagen, Everett E.
1962   *On the Theory of Social Change*. Homewood, Ill.: Dorsey Press.

Halpin, Marjorie Myers
1973   "The Tsimshian Crest System: A Study Based on Museum Specimens and the Marius Barbeau and William Beynon Field Notes." Ph.D. dissertation, University of British Columbia.

Harner, Michael
1977   "The Ecological Basis for Aztec Sacrifice." *American Ethnologist* 4 (1):117–35.

Harrison, Charles
1895   *Haida Grammar*. Proceedings and Transactions of the Royal Society of Canada 1 (2):123–226.

Haswell, Robert
1941   "Log of the First Voyage of the *Columbia*"; "Log of the Second Voyage of the *Columbia*." In *Voyages of the* Columbia *to the Northwest Coast*, F.W. Howay. Massachusetts Historical Society Collections 79.

Hertz, Robert
1960   *Death and the Right Hand*. Glencoe, Ill.: Free Press.

Hewitt, George Goodman
n.d.   "Notes" in copy of Vancouver's *Voyage*. Provincial Library, Victoria, B.C.

Hills, William Henry
1853   Journal manuscripts 1436/1. Mitchell Library, Sydney, Australia.

Hindle, Lonnie, and Bruce Rigsby
1973   "A Short Practical Dictionary of the Gitksan Language." *Northwest Anthropological Research Notes* 7:1–61.

Howay, F. W.
1915   "Some Remarks upon the New Vancouver Journal." *Washington Historical Quarterly* 6(2):83–89.

1918   "The Dog Hair Blankets of the Coast Salish." *Washington Historical Quarterly* 9(2):83–92.

1941   *Voyages of the* Columbia *to the Northwest Coast 1787–1790 and 1790–1793*. Massachusetts Historical Society Collections 79.

Hunter, W.
1940   *Letter from W. Hunter Regarding Voyage of the Vessels* Captain Cook

and Experiment *to the Northwest Coast in the Fur Trade,* A.D. *1786.* White Knight Chapbooks, Pacific Northwest Series 2.

Hymes, Dell
1974   "Ways of Speaking." In *Explorations in the Ethnography of Speaking,* edited by Richard Bauman and Joel Sherzer. London: Cambridge University Press.

Ingraham, Joseph
1789   *A Description of Nootka Sound and an Indian Vocabulary, Addressed to Don Estephen Joseph Martinez Commander of His Most Catholic Majesties Ship* Princesa, *1789.* Archivo General de la Nacion, Mexico City. MS. copy in the Bancroft Library, Berkeley, California.
1971   *Journal of the Brigantine* Hope *on a Voyage to the Northwest Coast of North America, 1790–92.* Edited by Mark D. Kaplanoff. Barre, Mass.: Imprint Society.

Jackendoff, R.
1969   "An Interpretive Theory of Negation." *Foundations of Language* 5:218–41.
1971   "On Some Questionable Arguments about Quantifiers and Negation." *Language* 47:282–97.

Jackson, Sheldon
1908   Letter to Harlan Updegraff, January 17, Kasaan. Alaska Division, record group 75, National Archives, Washington, D. C.

Jacobs, Elizabeth
1936   "Tillamook Ethnography." Unpublished typescript.
1959   *Nehalem Tillamook Tales.* Eugene: University of Oregon Press.

Jacobs, Melville
1940   *Coos Myth Texts.* University of Washington Publications in Anthropology 8(2):127–260.
1960   *The People are Coming Soon.* Seattle: University of Washington Press.

Jenness, Diamond
1955   *The Faith of a Coast Salish Indian.* Anthropology in British Columbia Memoir 3. Victoria: British Columbia Provincial Museum.
1943   *The Carrier Indians of Bulkley River, Their Social and Religious Life.* Bureau of American Ethnology Bulletin 133.

Jewitt, John R. See also Brown, Robert.
1931   *A Journal Kept at Nootka Sound.* Reprinted from original 1807 edition, with introduction by Norman L. Dodge. Boston: C. E. Goodspeed.

Kane, Paul
1925   *Wanderings of an Artist among the Indians of North America.* Toronto: Radison Society of Canada.

Kasakoff, Alice
1974   "Lévi-Strauss' Idea of the Social Unconscious: The Problem of

Elementary and Complex Structures in Gitksan Marriage Choice." In *The Unconscious in Culture*, edited by Ino Rossi. New York: E. P. Dutton.

Kautz, Frances
1900   "Extracts from the Diary of Gen. A. V. Kautz." *Washington Historian* 1:115–19, 181–85.

Keen, J. H.
1894   Letter, January 10, Church Missionary Society Archives, London.

Keesing, Felix M.
1953   *Culture Change*. Stanford: Stanford University Press.

Keesing, Roger M.
1972   "Paradigms Lost: The New Ethnography and the Old Linguistics." *Southwestern Journal of Anthropology* 28:299–332.

Kenyon, Susan
1976   "The Nature of the Nootkan Local Group: Kinship and Descent on the West Coast of Vancouver Island." Paper presented at the Northwest Coast Studies Conference, Simon Fraser University, May 12–16.

Klima, E. S.
1964   "Negation in English." In *The Structure of Language*, edited by Fodor and Katz. Englewood Cliffs, N.J.: Prentice Hall.

Kobrinsky, Vernon
1975   "Dynamics of the Fort Rupert Class Struggle: Fighting with Property Vertically Revisited." In *Papers in Honour of Harry Hawthorn*, edited by Vernon Serl and Herbert Taylor. Bellingham, Wash.: Western Washington State College.

1976   The Tsimshianization of the Carrier Indians. Mimeograph copy.

Krause, Aurel
1956   *The Tlingit Indians*. [1885.] Translated from the German by Erna Gunther. Seattle: University of Washington Press.

Kroeber, Alfred L.
1934   "Yurok and Neighboring Kin Term Systems." *University of California Publications in American Archaeology and Ethnology* 35:15–22.

1941   "Culture Element Distribution: Salt, Dogs and Tobacco." *Anthropological Records* 6:1–20.

Lakoff, G.
1971   "On Generative Semantics." In *Semantics*, edited by Steinberg and Jacobovitz. Cambridge: Cambridge University Press.

Laforet, Andrea
n.d.   "Cultural Heritage Project, Report on Kasaan." Juneau: Alaska State Museum.

Laguna, Frederica de
1972   *Under Mt. St. Elias: The History and Culture of the Yakutat Tlingit.*

Smithsonian Contributions to Anthropology 7, pts. 1, 2, and 3.

Langness, L. L.
1959 "A Case of Post-Contact Reform among the Clallam." Master's thesis, University of Washington.

Lantis, Margaret
1938 "The Alaskan Whale Cult and Its Affinities." *American Anthropologist* 40 (3):438–46.
1953 *Nunivak Eskimo Personality as Revealed in the Mythology.* Anthropological Papers of the University of Alaska 2 (1).

Lauridson, G. M., and A. A. Smith
1937 *The Story of Port Angeles.* Seattle: Lowman and Hanford Co.

Lave, Jean, Alex Stepick, and Lee Sailer
1977 "Extending the Scope of Formal Analysis: A Technique for Integrating Analysis of Kinship Relations with Analyses of Other Dyadic Relations." *American Ethnologist* 4:321–39.

La Violette, Forrest E.
1961 *The Struggle for Survival.* Toronto: University of Toronto Press.

Leach, Edmund
1971 *Rethinking Anthropology.* 2nd ed. London: Althone Press.
1972 "Animal Categories and Verbal Abuse." In *Reader in Comparative Religion*, 3rd ed., edited by Lessa and Vogt. New York: Harper and Row.

Ledyard, John
1783 *A Journal of Captain Cook's Last Voyage to the Pacific Ocean ... 1778–1779.* Hartford: Nathaniel Patten.

Leighton, Caroline
1884 *Life at Puget Sound, 1865–1881.* Boston: Lee and Shepard.

Lévi-Strauss, Claude
1963 *Totemism.* Boston: Beacon Press. (Originally published in 1962 as *Le Totemisme aujourd'hui.*)
1964 *Le Cru et le cruit.* Paris: Librairie Plon. (English translation: *The Raw and The Cooked* 1969.)
1966 *The Savage Mind.* Chicago: University of Chicago Press. (Originally published in 1962 as *La Pensee sauvage.*)
1969 *The Elementary Structures of Kinship,* rev. ed. Boston: Beacon Press.
1971 *Mythologique: L'Homme Nu.* Paris: Librairie Plon.
1975 *La Voie des masques.* Editions Albert Skira, 2 vols. Les Sentiers de la Creation, Geneva. (English translation: *The Way of the Masks.* Seattle: University of Washington Press, 1982.)
1977 "Les Dessous d'une masque." *L'Homme* 13(1):5–27.

Lopatin, Ivan
1945 *Social Life and Religion of the Indians in Kitimat, British Columbia.* University of Southern California Social Science Series 26.

Lotzgesell, George
1933 "Pioneer Days at Old Dungeness." *Washington Historical Quarterly* 24(4):264–70.

MacDonald, George F.
1977   "Cosmic Equations in Northwest Coast Indian Art." In *The World Is As Sharp As a Knife: Essays in Honour of Wilson Duff*, edited by George Abbott. Victoria: British Columbia Provincial Museum.

McDonald, Lucille
1952   "Dungeness was 'Whiskey Flat' in Early Days." *Seattle Times*, magazine section, December 14, p. 2.

McFeat, Tom
1966   *Indians of the North Pacific Coast*. Seattle: University of Washington Press.

McIlwraith, Thomas
1948   *The Bella Coola Indians*. 2 vols. Toronto: University of Toronto Press.

McKelvie, A. B.
1946   *Maquinna the Magnificent*. Vancouver, B.C.: Vancouver Daily Province.

MacLeod, William
1925   "Debtor and Chattel Slavery in Aboriginal North America." *American Anthropologist* 27 (3):370–80.
1928   "Economic Aspects of Indigenous American Slavery." *American Anthropologist* 30 (4):632–50.

McNeary, Stephen
1976a   "Tsimshian Matriliny as an Instrument of Alliance." Paper presented at the Northwest Coast Studies Conference, Simon Fraser University, May 12–16.
1976b   "Where Fire Came Down. Social and Economic Life of the Niska." Ph.D. dissertation, Bryn Mawr College.

Mannoni, O.
1956   *Prospero and Caliban: The Psychology of Colonization*. Translated by Pamela Powesland. New York: Praeger.

Mauss, Marcel
1954   *The Gift*. New York: Free Press.

Mayne, R. C.
1862   *Four Years in British Columbia and Vancouver Island*. London: J. Murray.

Meany, Edmond S.
1914–15   "A New Vancouver Journal." *Washington Historical Quarterly* 5:129–37, 215–24; 6:50–68.
1916   "Northwest Historical Syllabus." Excerpts from Washington Historical Quarterly, April 1912 to October 1916.

Meares, John
1790   *Voyages Made in the Years 1788 and 1789, from China to the North West Coast of America*. London: Logographic.

Menzies, Archibald
1923   *Journal of Vancouver's Voyage*. Edited by C. F. Newcombe. Archives of British Columbia Memoir 5.

Miller, Jay
    1980   "High-Minded High Gods in North America." *Anthropos* 75:916–19.
    1981a   "Moieties and Cultural Amnesia: Manipulation of Knowledge in a Pacific Northwest Coast Native Community." *Arctic Anthropology* 18(1):23–32.
    1981b   "Tsimshian Moieties and Other Clarifications." *Northwest Anthropological Research Notes* 16(2):148–64.
Miller, Robert J.
    1964   "Cultures as Religious Structures." In *Symposium on New Approaches to the Study of Religion,* edited by June Helm. Proceedings of the Annual Meeting of the American Ethnological Society, 1964, Seattle: University of Washington Press.
Morgan, Lewis H.
    1870   *Systems of Consanguinity and Affinity of the Human Family.* Smithsonian Contributions to Knowledge 17.
Moziño Suarez de Figueroa, José Mariano
    1970   *Noticias de Nutka.* Translated by Iris Higbee Wilson. Seattle: University of Washington Press.
Murdock, G. P.
    1934   "Kinship and Social Behavior among the Haida." *American Anthropologist* 36:355–85.
    1936   *Rank and Potlatch among the Haida.* Yale University Publications in Anthropology 13. New Haven: Yale University Press.
    1949   *Social Structure.* New York: Macmillan Co.
Nadel, S. F.
    1957   *The Theory of Social Structure.* London: Cohen and West.
Needham, Rodney, ed.
    1971   *Rethinking Kinship and Marriage.* ASA Monograph 11. London: Tavistock Publications.
Nelson, Edward W.
    1899   *The Eskimo about Bering Strait.* Bureau of American Ethnology Annual Report 18, pt. 1. Washington, D.C.
Newcombe, Charles F.
    1904–5   "Notes on a Trip to the Queen Charlotte Islands." Manuscript in the British Columbia Provincial Museum, Victoria.
Niblack, Albert
    1890   *The Coast Indians of Southern Alaska and Northern British Columbia.* U.S. National Museum Annual Report for 1887–88.
Nowell, Charles. See Ford, Clellan S.
Olson, Ronald
    1936   *The Quinault Indians.* University of Washington Publications in Anthropology 6 (1).
    1940   "The Social Organization of the Haisla of British Columbia." *Anthropological Records* 2 (5):169–200.

1954   "Social Life of the Owikeno Kwakiutl." *Anthropological Records* 14 (3):213–59.

1955   "Notes on the Bella Bella Kwakiutl." *Anthropological Records* 14 (5):319–48.

1967   "Social Structure and Social Life of the Tlingit in Alaska." *Anthropological Records* 26:1–123.

Parsons, Talcott
1951   *The Social System.* New York: Free Press.

Petroff, Ivan
1884   *Alaska: Its Population, Industries, and Resources.* Tenth Census of the United States, vol. 8.

Poole, Francis
1872   *Queen Charlotte Island.* London: Hurst and Blackett.

Porter, Robert
1893   *Report on Population and Resources of Alaska at the Eleventh Census: 1890.* Eleventh Census of the United States, vol. 8.

Prevost, James C.
1853   "Report to Rear Admiral Fairfax Moresby." Admiralty Papers, Public Record Office, London.

Quimby, George I.
1948   "Culture Contact on the Northwest Coast, 1785–1795." *American Anthropologist* 50 (2):247–55.

Reagan, Albert B., and L. V. M. Walters
1933   "Tales from the Hoh and Quilleute." *Journal of American Folklore* 46:304–5.

Reid, Bill, and Bill Holm
1975   *Form and Freedom: A Dialogue on Northwest Coast Indian Art.* Seattle: University of Washington Press for Institute for the Arts, Rice University.

Rigsby, Bruce
1969   "Some Linguistic Insights into Recent Tsimshian Prehistory." Unpublished manuscript.

n.d.   Unpublished fieldnotes.

Rohner, Ronald P., ed.
1969   *The Ethnography of Franz Boas.* Chicago: University of Chicago Press.

Roquefeiul, Camille de
1823   *Journal d'un voyage autour du monde* ... 2 vols. Paris: Ponthieu.

Rosman, Abraham, and Paula G. Rubel
1971   *Feasting with Mine Enemy: Rank and Exchange among Northwest Coast Societies.* New York: Columbia University Press.

Ruyle, Eugene
1973   "Slavery, Surplus, and Stratification on the Northwest Coast." *Current Anthropology* 14:603–31.

Sanches, Mary, and Ben G. Blount
  1975   *Sociocultural Dimensions of Language Use.* New York: Academic Press.
Sapir, Edward
  1915   *A Sketch of the Social Organization of the Nass River Indians.* Museum Bulletin 19, Anthropological Series 7. Ottawa: Canada Geological Survey.
  1920   "Nass River Terms of Relationship." *American Anthropologist* 22 (2):261–71.
  1921   "Vancouver Island Indians." In *Encyclopaedia of Religion and Ethics* 12:591–95, edited by James Hastings. Edinburgh: T. and T. Clark.
  1955   *Native Accounts of Nootka Ethnography.* Indiana University Research Center in Anthropology, Folklore and Linguistics Publication 1, Bloomington.
  1966   "The Social Organization of the West Coast Tribes." In *Indians of the North Pacific Coast,* McFeat. Seattle: University of Washington Press. (Originally published in 1915.)
Sapir, Edward, and Morris Swadesh
  1939   *Nootka Texts.* Philadelphia: Linguistic Society of America.
Scheffler, Harold W., and Floyd Lounsbury
  1971   *A Study in Structural Semantics: The Siriono Kinship System.* Englewood Cliffs, N.J.: Prentice-Hall.
Schneider, David M., and Kathleen Gough
  1962   *Matrilineal Kinship.* Berkeley and Los Angeles: University of California Press.
Seaburg, William R.
  1982   "Guide to Pacific Northwest Native American Materials in the Melville Jacobs Collection and in Other Archival Collections in the University of Washington Libraries." University of Washington Libraries, Seattle, Washington.
Service, Elman R.
  1975   *Origins of the State and Civilization.* New York: W. W. Norton.
Sgall, Petr, Eva Hajičová, and Eva Benešová
  1973   *Topic, Focus and Generative Semantics.* Kronberg Taunus: Scriptor Verlag.
Sharp, Henry
  1976   "Man:Wolf :: Woman:Dog." *Arctic Anthropology* 8 (1):25–34.
Simpson, George
  1847   *Narrative of a Journey Round the World, During the Year 1841 and 1842.* 2 vols. London: H. Colburn.
Skidmore, E. Rahamah
  1885   *Alaska: Its Southern Coast and the Sitkan Archipelgo.* Boston: D. Lothrup and Company.
Snyder, Sally
  1965   "Skagit Society and Its Existential Basis: An Ethnofolkloristic Reconstruction." Ph.D. dissertation, University of Washington.

Sproat, Gilbert M.
1868   *Scenes and Studies of Savage Life.* London: Smith, Elder.

Stearns, Mary Lee
1981   *Haida Culture in Custody: The Masset Band.* Seattle and Vancouver: University of Washington Press and Douglas & McIntyre.

Steinberg, D. D., and L. A. Jacobovits, eds.
1971   *Semantics: An Interdisciplinary Reader in Philosophy, Linguistics and Psychology.* Cambridge: Cambridge University Press.

Strange, James
1928   *James Strange's Journal and Narrative of the Commercial Expedition from Bombay to the Northwest Coast of America* ... Madras: Government Press of India.

Suria, Tomas de
1936   "Journal of Tomas de Suria." Translated and edited by Henry R. Wagner. *Pacific Historical Review* 5:234–76.

Suttles, Wayne
1951   "The Economic Life of the Coast Salish of Haro and Rosario Straits." Ph.D. dissertation, University of Washington.
1960   "Affinal Ties, Subsistence and Prestige among the Coast Salish." *American Anthropologist* 62 (2):296–306.
1975   "An Alternative to the Empty Stomach." Unpublished manuscript.
1978   "Native Languages of the North Pacific Coast of North America" [map]. Portland, Oregon: Cameron Suttles.

Swadesh, Morris
1943   "Motivations in Nootka Warfare." *Southwestern Journal of Anthropology* 4:76–97.

Swan, J.C.
1859   Articles in the *San Francisco Bulletin*, May 10 and May 19.

Swanton, John R.
1905a   *Contributions to the Ethnology of the Haida.* American Museum of Natural History Memoir 8 (1).
1905b   *Haida Texts and Myths: Skidegate Dialect.* Bureau of American Ethnology Bulletin 29.
1908   *Social Conditions, Beliefs and Linguistic Relationships of the Tlingit Indians.* Bureau of American Ethnology Annual Report, no. 26.
1966   "Social Organization of the Haida." In *Indians of the North Pacific Coast*, edited by Tom McFeat. Seattle: University of Washington Press.
1911   *Haida.* Bureau of American Ethnology, Bulletin 40 (1): 205–82.
n.d.   "Materials relating to the Haida . . ." National Anthropological Archives, catalogue no. 4117-a, Smithsonian Institution, Washington, D.C.

Teit, James
1898   *Traditions of the Thompson River Indians of British Columbia.* Memoirs of the American Folklore Society 6.

Thomas, L. L., J. Z. Kronenfeld, and D. B. Kronenfeld
  1976   "Asdiwal Crumbles: A Critique of Lévi-Straussian Myth Analysis." *American Ethnologist* 3:147–73.
Thompson, J. Eric S.
  1966   *The Rise and Fall of Maya Civilization.* 2d ed. enlarged. Norman, Okla.: University of Oklahoma Press.
Thompson, Stith
  1929   *Tales of the North American Indians.* Cambridge: Harvard University Press.
Turner, Harriet
  1973   Personal communication.
Turner, Victor
  1964   "Betwixt and Between: The Liminal Period in *Rites de Passage.*" In *Symposium on New Approaches to the Study of Religion,* edited by June Helm. Proceedings of the Annual Meeting of the American Ethnological Society, 1964. Seattle: University of Washington Press.
Tyler, Stephen A.
  1969   "Introduction." In *Cognitive Anthropology,* edited by Stephen A. Tyler. New York: Holt, Rinehart and Winston.
  1972   "Context and Alternation in Koya Kinship Terminology." In *Directions in Sociolinguistics,* edited by John J. Gumperz and Dell Hymes. New York: Holt, Rinehart and Winston.
Vaughan, James Daniel
  1975a   "Haida Potlatch and Society: Testing a Structural Analysis." Paper presented to the Northwest Coast Studies Conference, Simon Fraser University.
  1975b   "Tlingit Potlatching and Marriage Patterns: A Critique of a Structural Analysis." Paper presented to the Northwest Anthropological Society, Central Washington University.
Vickers, Kathleen Collinson
  1971   Personal communication to John Dunn. Prince Rupert, British Columbia.
Voget, Fred W.
  1956   "The American Indian in Transition." *American Anthropologist* 58 (2):249–60.
Wagner, H.
  1933   *Spanish Explorations in the Strait of Juan de Fuca.* Santa Ana: Fine Arts Press.
Walbran, Capt. John T.
  n.d.   "The Cruise of the Imperial Eagle." Copy of transcript loaned by Judge Howay, 1936, Provincial Archives, Victoria, B.C.
Walens, Stanley G.
  1981   *Feasting with Cannibals. An Essay on Kwakiutl Cosmology.* Princeton: Princeton University Press.

Wallace, A. F. C.
   1956   "Revitalization Movements." *American Anthropologist* 58 (2):264–
            81.
   1970   *Culture and Personality.* 2d ed. New York: Random House.
   1973   *The Death and Rebirth of the Seneca.* New York: Alfred A. Knopf.
Waller, Alvan
   1844–45 Journal of Alvan Waller. Oregon Historical Society.
Waterman, T. T.
   1914   "The Explanatory Element in the Folk Tales of the North Amer-
            ican Indians." *Journal of American Folk-lore* 27:1–54.
   1973   *Notes on the Ethnology of the Indians of Puget Sound.* Indian Notes
            and Monographs, Misc. Series 59. New York: Museum of the
            American Indian, Heye Foundation.
Watson, James L.
   1976   "Chattel Slavery in Chinese Peasant Society: A Comparative
            Analysis." *Ethnology* 15:361–75.
Weir, Allen
   1900   "Roughing It on Puget Sound in the Early Sixties." *Washington
            Historian* 1 (2):70–75; 1 (3):120–24.
Welsch, Robert
   1975   "Haida Pronouns-Hydaburg Dialect." In *Lektos,* edited by Rob-
            ert St. Clair. (Special issue: Papers from the Tenth International
            Conference on Salishan Languages.)
Wike, Joyce
   1947   "The Effect of the Maritime Fur Trade on Northwest Coast In-
            dian Society." Ph.D. dissertation, Columbia University.
   1952   "The Role of the Dead in Northwest Coast Culture." In *Pro-
            ceedings of the 29th International Congress of Americanists 3,* edited
            by Sol Tax. Chicago: University of Chicago Press.
   1958   "Social Stratification Among the Nootka." *Ethnohistory* 5 (3):219–
            41.
   1962   "Some Nuances of Nootka-Kwakiutl Cannibalism." Paper pre-
            sented at the 66th annual meeting of the American Anthropol-
            ogical Association.
Williams, Johnson
   1916   "Black Tamanous: The Secret Society of the Clallam Indians."
            Washington Historical Quarterly 7 (4):296–300.
Woldt, Adrian
   1884   *Capitain Jacobsen's Reise an der Nordwestkuste Amerikas, 1881–83.*
            Leipzig: M. Spohr.
Work, John
   1944   "The Journal of John Work, 1835." Edited by Henry Drummond
            Dee. *British Columbia Historical Quarterly* 2:127–46; 3:227–44; 4:307–
            18.
Zimmerman, Heinrich
   1930   *Zimmerman's Captain Cook.* Edited by F. W. Howay. Toronto: Ca-
            nadian Historical Studies.

Index

Adams, John: on Gitksan crests, 37, 38
Adoption, 84
Alaska Steamship Company, 159
Alexcee, Fred: Tsimshian artist at Port Simpson, 110
Ambilaterality: of Wakashans and Salishans, xvi
Angels: winning woman from shamanism, 144, 145
Angoon: Tlingit village, 308–9
Animals: chief of, xvii, 14, 35; in legend, 3–15; talking, 5, 145; multiple births, 6; relationship to human forms, 7, 13; revenge of Mountain Goats, 7; as skin shifters, 7–8; Beaver, 10; Wolf, 10; Bear, 11; altered perceptions of, 11–13; Prince of (Tsimshian crest), 31; conjured up by the Devil, 146. *See also* Dog
Asdiwal: mythic character among Sea Lions, 11
Avunculocality: Tsimshian, 40, 60; Haida, 193

Balch, James: chief at Jamestown, 264, 273n; killed by white, 268
Barbeau, Marius, 16n, 17, 26, 64, 120
Baronovitch, Charles Vincent (Austrian Marquis): ran saltery and trade at Karta Bay, 159. *See* Skowal
Baxbaxwalanuxiwae: Kwakiutl patron of cannibal ritual, 250, 304
Bella Coola: house front, 121
Benedict, Ruth, 311
Beynon, William: Tsimshian scholar, xvi, xix, 6, 16n, 17; on crests, 20, 26; on moieties, 37; works with Viola Garfield, 138, 313
Bible: as cure for shamanism, 145
Bini: as Carrier prophet, 137, 142–43; as Beaver chief (Kwiis), 138; five commandments of, 142; lost everything gambling, 142; vision of Chief of the Skies, 143; special language and ritual of, 143. *See also* Haleyt
Birds: beaks, 11, 120, 134; monster crest composites, 34
Boas, Franz, xi, 1, 3; relied on texts, xvi, 118; on Tsimshian verbs, 80; on Hamatsa ritual, 250

Body-House-Cosmos model, 111
Bölscher, Marianne: on succession to chiefship, 213
Boston: ship seized by Nootka in 1803, 240; vessel of John Jewett, 249
Bullhead design, 118

Candlefish: importance of, xiii; in legend, 129; run predicted by shaman, 140
Cane: used in ritual, 140
Cannibalism: epicurean, and famine, 239, 244; ritual, 240; among Haisla and Tlingit, 244; Bella Coola dog and raw salmon eaters, 244, 298; as covert insult to whites, 245; compared to Windigo complex, 253; and European ethnocentrism, 253; natives denied Eucharist, 254; related to dogs and incest, 297. *See also* Hamatsa
Canoe. *See* Copper canoe
Carpenter, Edmund: puns in Northwest art, 35
Catholic: missionary, 142; Tsimshian convert, 145; as bread, 145
Cedar: importance of, xiii
Change: linguistic, xxi; motivation for, 272; cosmic, 289
Charter: function of Haida myth, 193
Chemakum: defeated by Klallam, 256
Chief of Wealth, 111
Chiefship: Tsimshian, 21, 190; crests, 30; Haida rules for succession to, 191, 195, 213; requirements, 194, 198; structural inconsistencies of, 194, 202n; appointment, 197; waging war, 198; popularity, 212; Klallam, 259
Chilcat blanket: designs, 21, 128, 132–33, 136; as symbol, 130–31. *See also* Pentagon design
Chinese: kinship compared to Tsimshian, 83
Class. *See* Social class
Cod, 157
Collison, William: missionary to Haida, 200
Cook, James: Mexican influence, 240n4, 247n4; skulls and roasted hands offered for sale at Resolution Cove, 246
Copper canoe: in legend, 116

337

Contributors

PAMELA AMOSS, *PM Consulting, Seattle, Washington*

MARGARET B. BLACKMAN, *Department of Anthropology, State University of New York, College at Brockport, Brockport, New York*

JOHN ASHER DUNN, *Department of Anthropology, University of Oklahoma, Norman, Oklahoma*

WILLIAM W. ELMENDORF, *Department of Anthropology (Emeritus), University of Wisconsin, Madison, Wisconsin*

CAROL M. EASTMAN, *Department of Anthropology, University of Washington, Seattle, Washington*

MARJORIE HALPIN, *Museum of Anthropology, University of British Columbia, Vancouver, British Columbia*

ALICE BEE KASAKOFF, *Department of Anthropology, University of South Carolina, Columbia, South Carolina*

FREDERICA DE LAGUNA, *Department of Anthropology (Emeritus), Bryn Mawr College, Bryn Mawr, Pennsylvania*

L. L. LANGNESS, *Department of Anthropology, University of California, Los Angeles, California*

GEORGE F. MACDONALD, *National Museums of Canada, Ottawa, Canada*

STEPHEN A. MCNEARY, *University of Pennsylvania, Philadelphia, Pennsylvania*

JAY MILLER, *Cultrix Research, Seattle, Washington*

MARY LEE STEARNS, *Department of Anthropology, Simon Fraser University, Burnaby, British Columbia*

WAYNE SUTTLES, *Department of Anthropology, Portland State University, Portland, Oregon*

J. DANIEL VAUGHAN, *Department of Anthropology, University of Washington, Seattle, Washington*

JOYCE WIKE, *Department of Anthropology, Nebraska Wesleyan University, Lincoln, Nebraska*